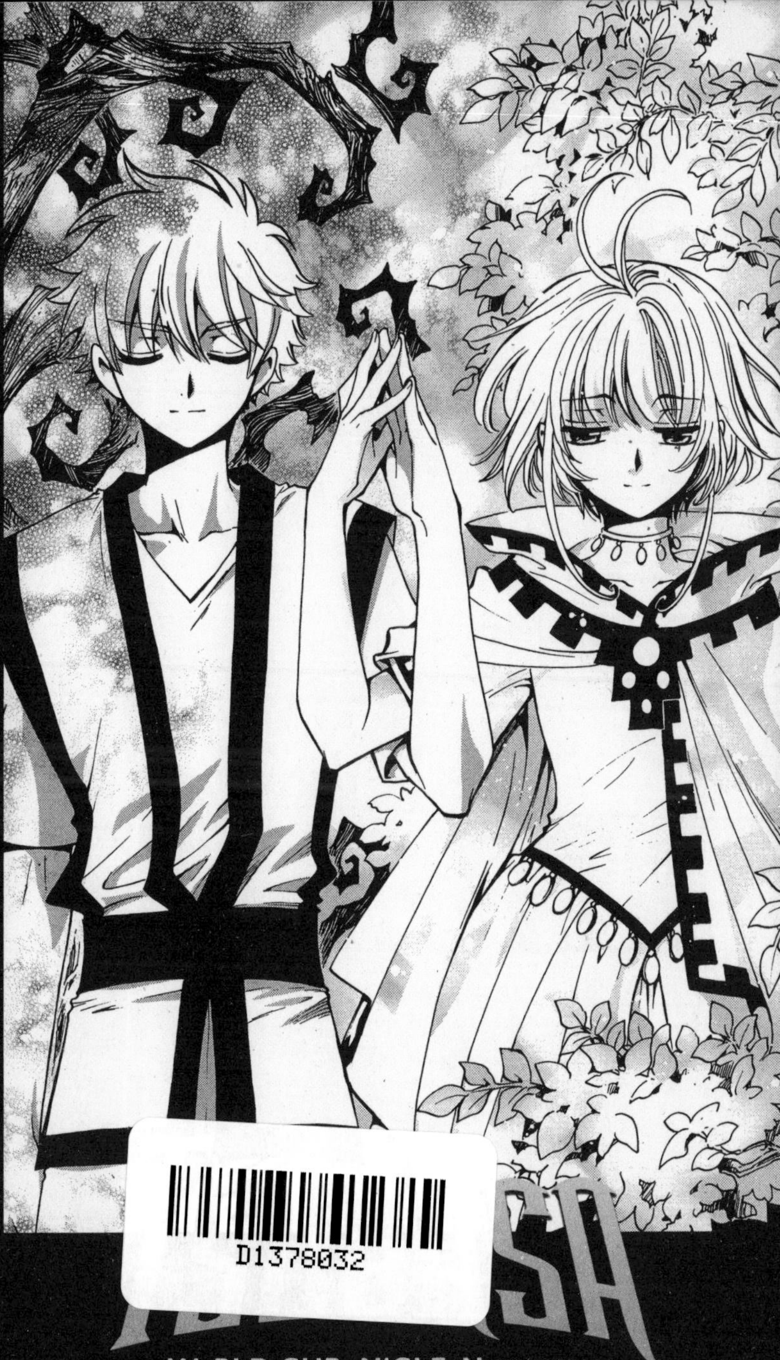

WoRLD CHRoNiCLE: NIRAIKANAI

TSUBASA

WoRLD CHRoNiCLE: NIRAIKANAI

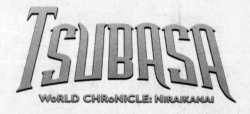

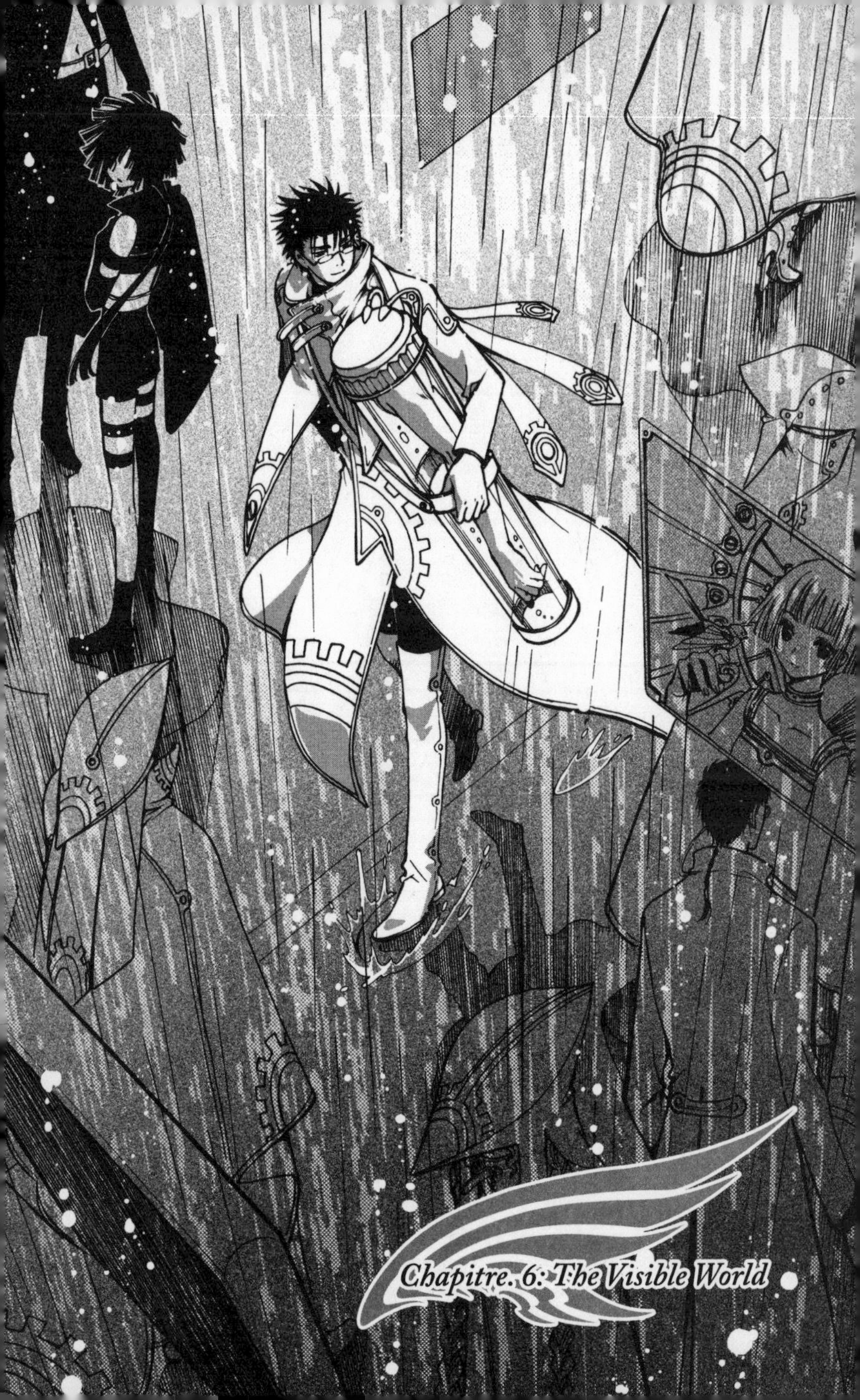
Chapitre. 6: The Visible World

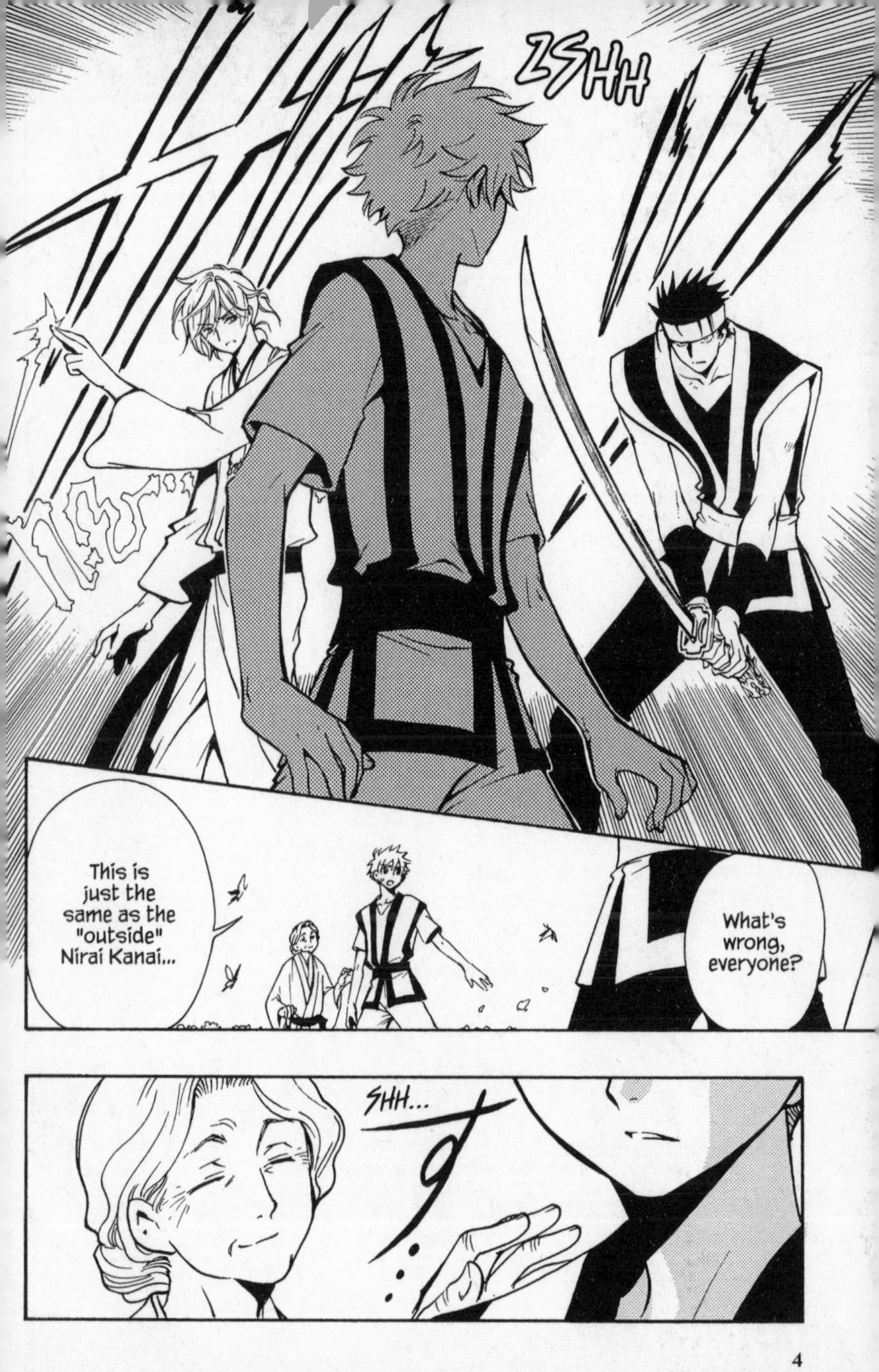
ZSHH
What's wrong, everyone?
This is just the same as the "outside" Nirai Kanai...
SHH...

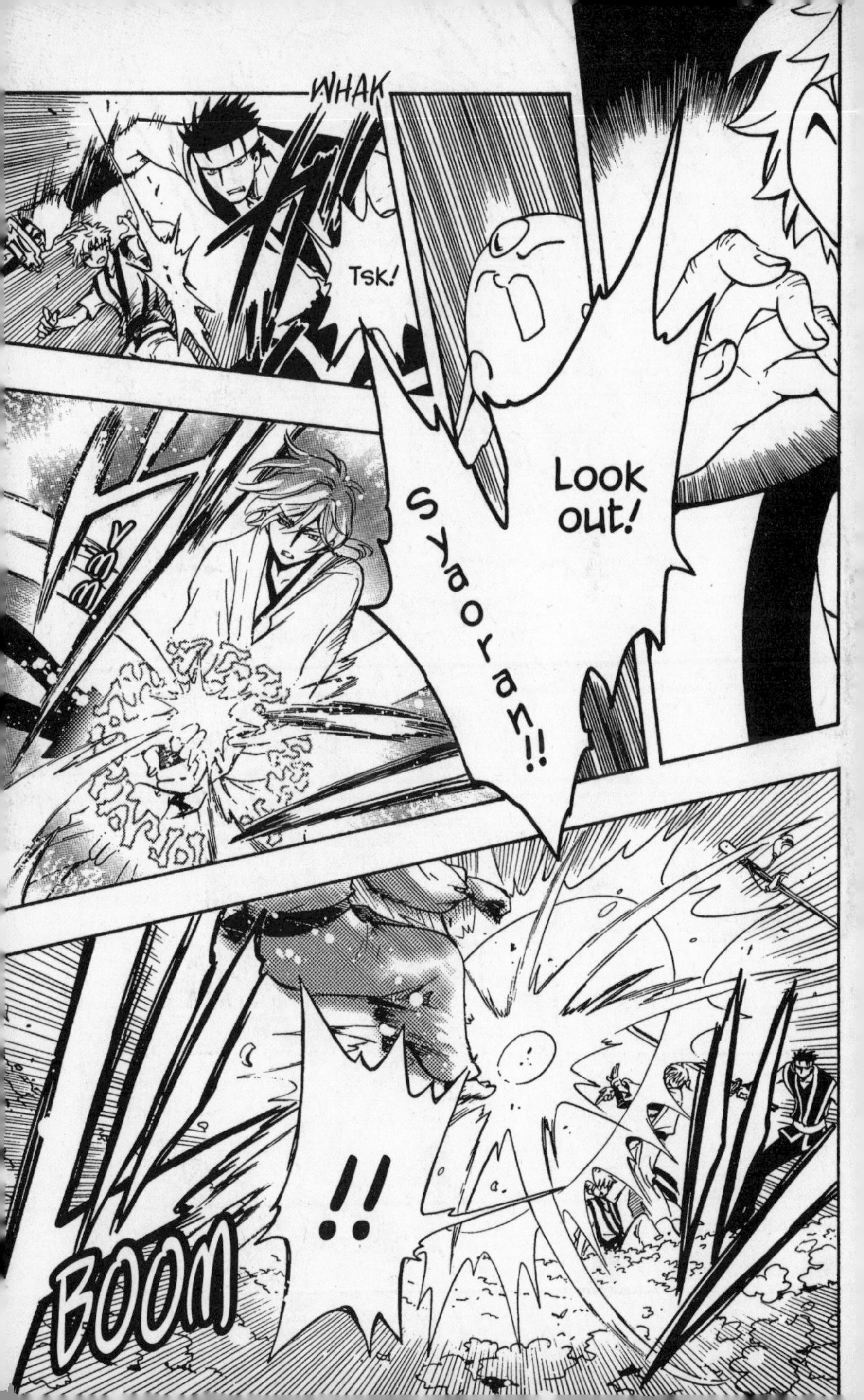
Look out!
Syaoran!!
WHAK
TSK!
!!
BOOM

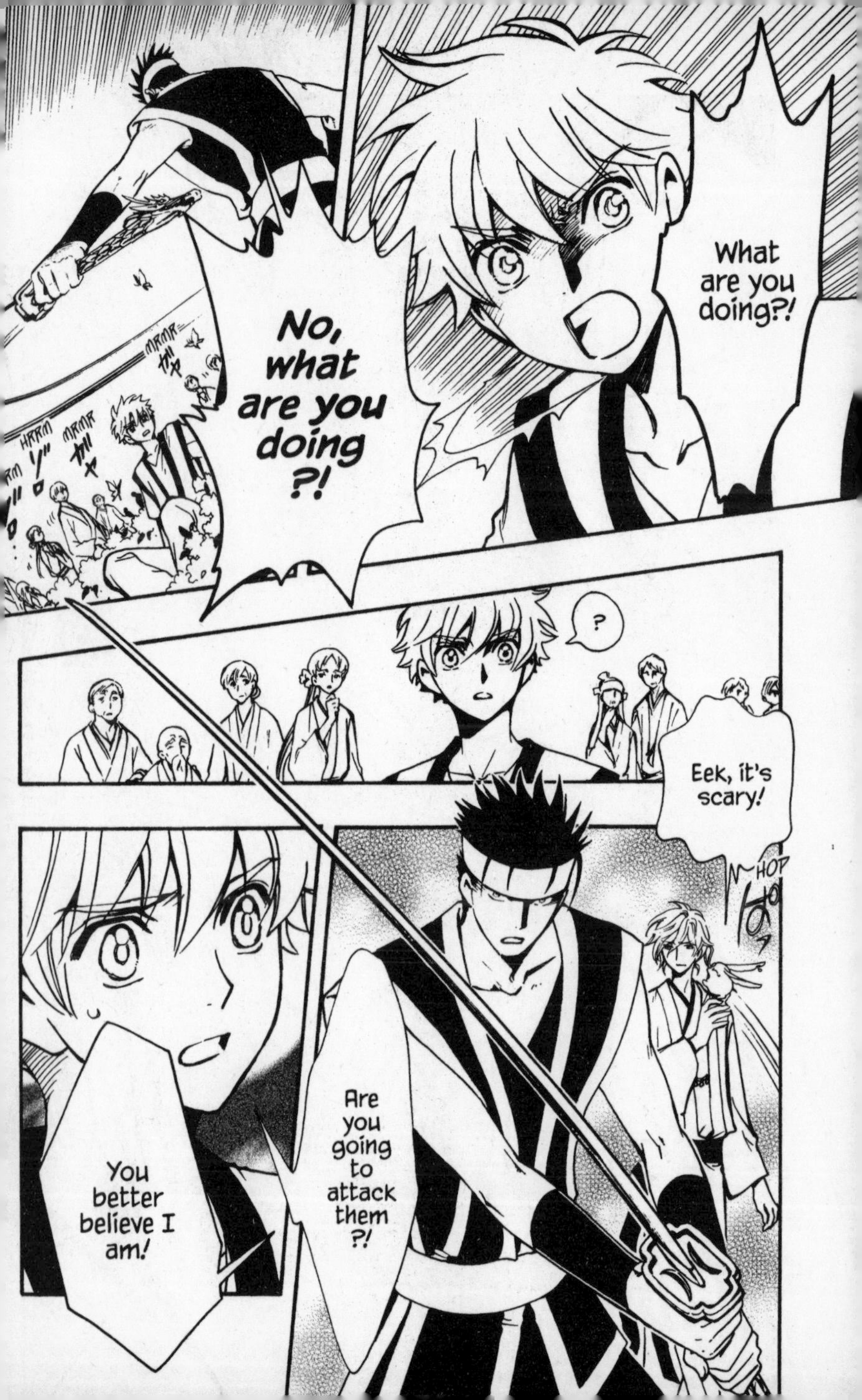
What are you doing?!
No, what are you doing?!
MRMR
HRRM
MRMR
?
Eek, it's scary!
HOP
Are you going to attack them?!
You better believe I am!

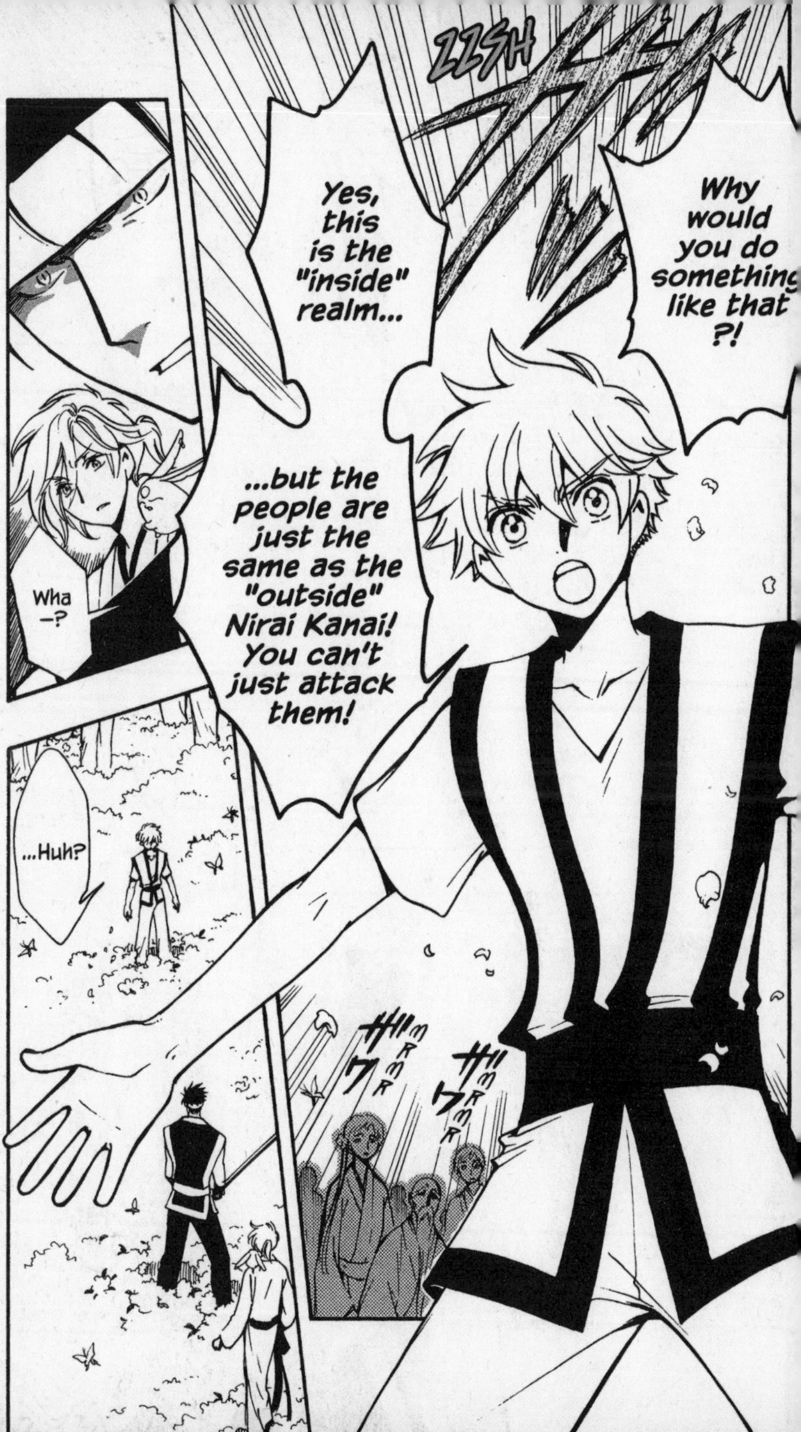
ZZSH
Why would you do something like that?!
Yes, this is the "inside" realm...
...but the people are just the same as the "outside" Nirai Kanai! You can't just attack them!
Wha—?
...Huh?

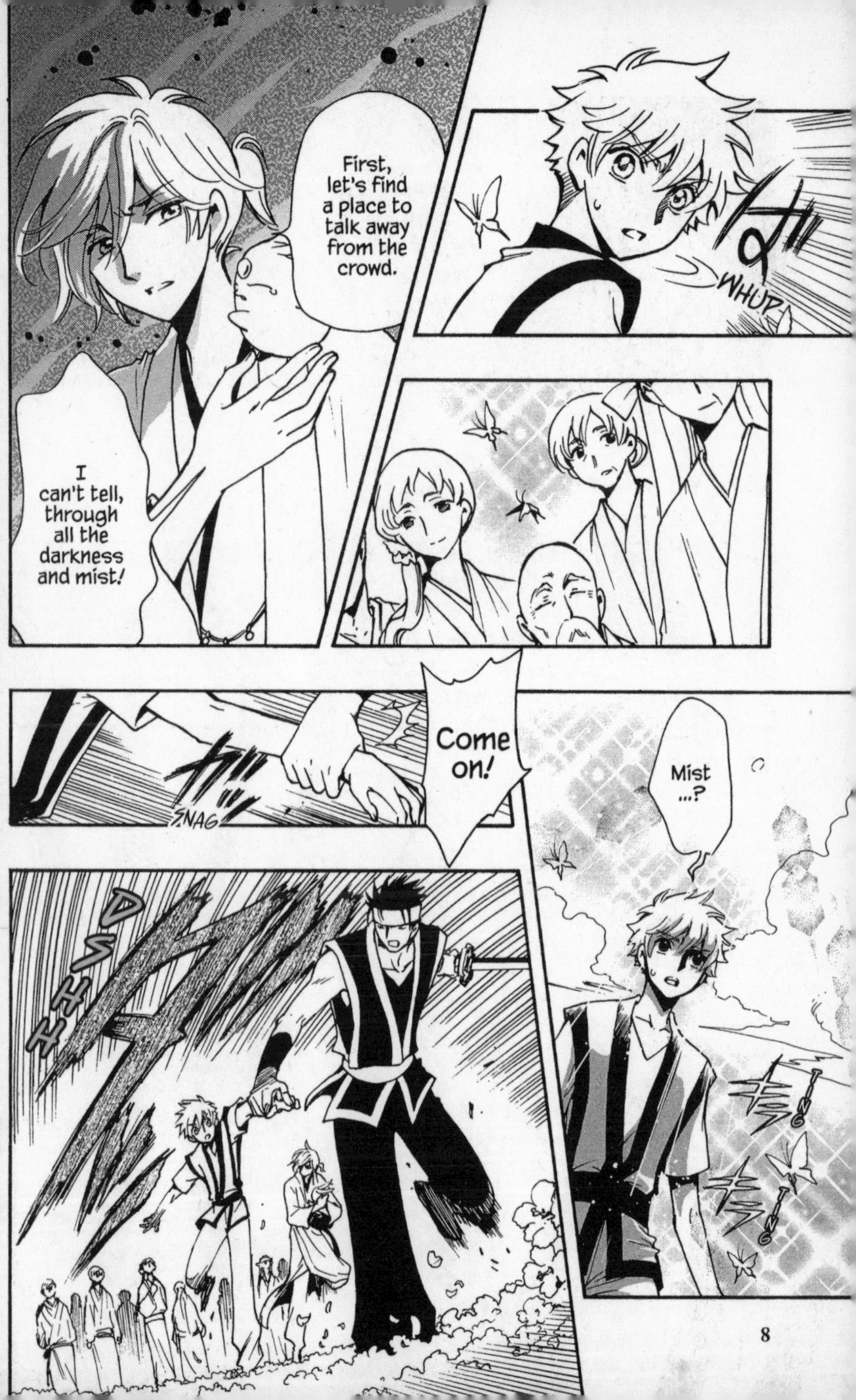
WHUP
First, let's find a place to talk away from the crowd.
I can't tell, through all the darkness and mist!
Mist ...?
TING
TING
Come on!
SNAG
DSHH

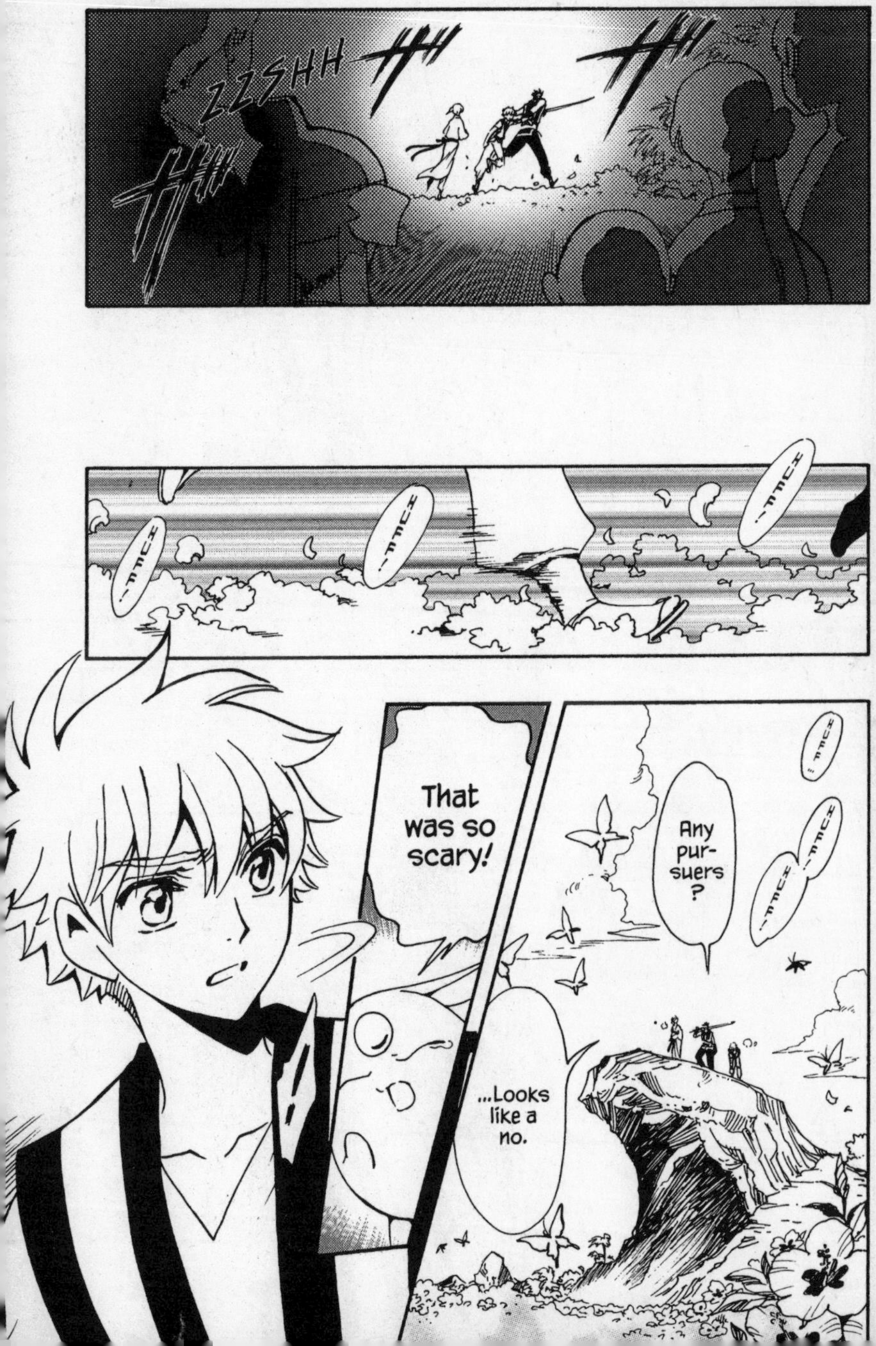
ZZSHH
HUFF!
HUFF!
HUFF!
HUFF...
HUFF!
HUFF!
Any pursuers?
...Looks like a no.
That was so scary!

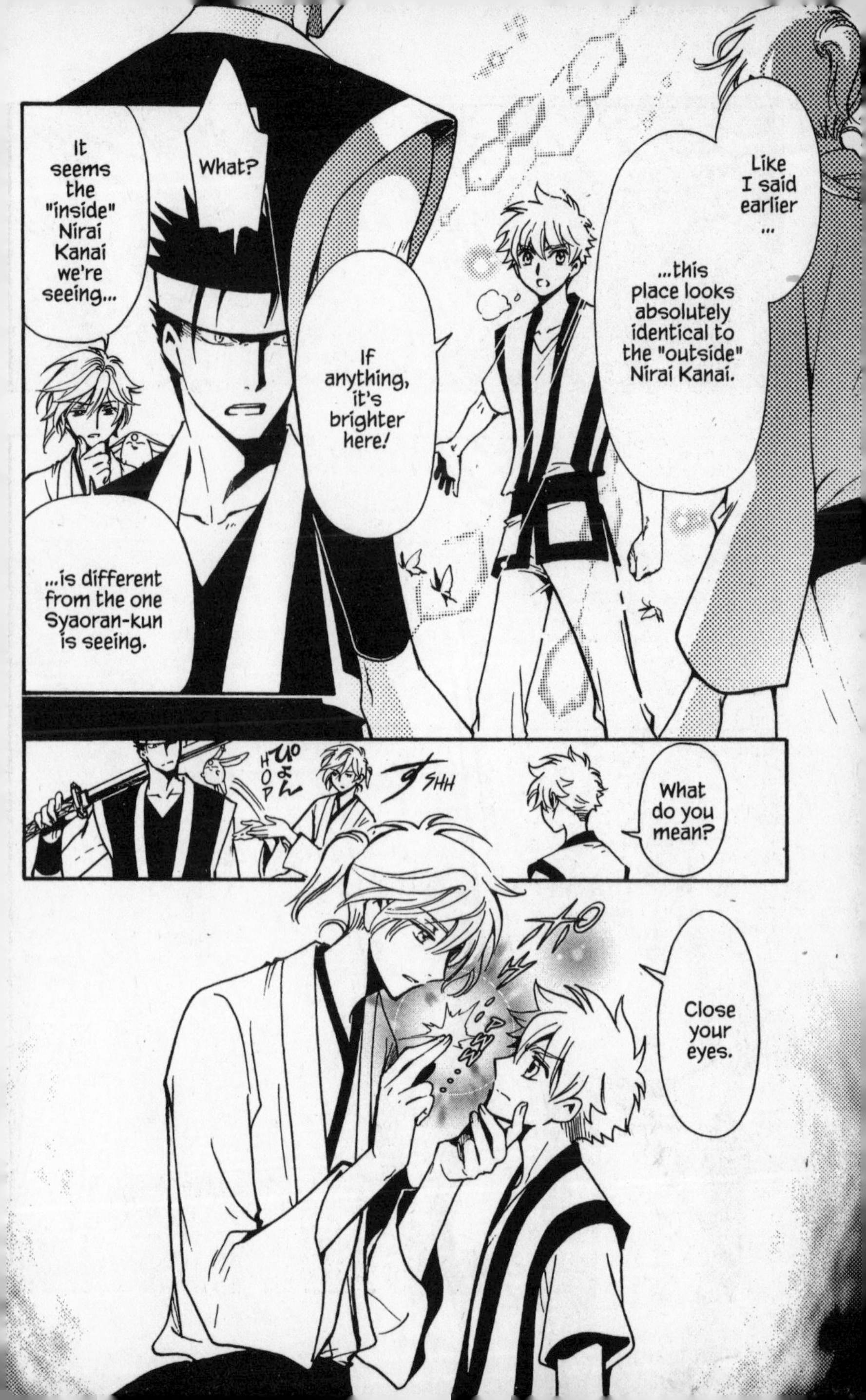
Like I said earlier ...
...this place looks absolutely identical to the "outside" Nirai Kanai.
If anything, it's brighter here!
What?
It seems the "inside" Nirai Kanai we're seeing...
...is different from the one Syaoran-kun is seeing.
What do you mean?
す SHH
ぴょん HOP
Close your eyes.

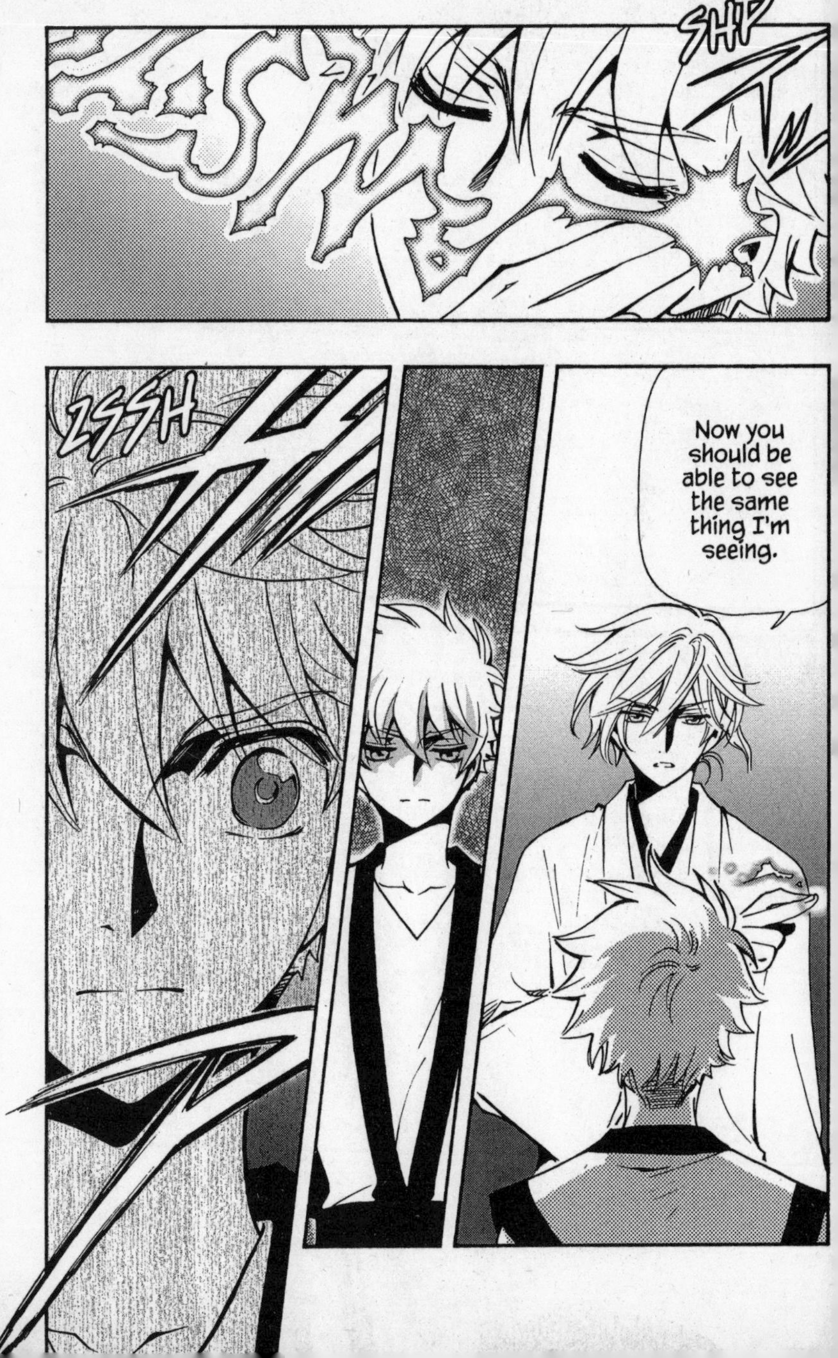
SHP
Now you should be able to see the same thing I'm seeing.
ZSSH

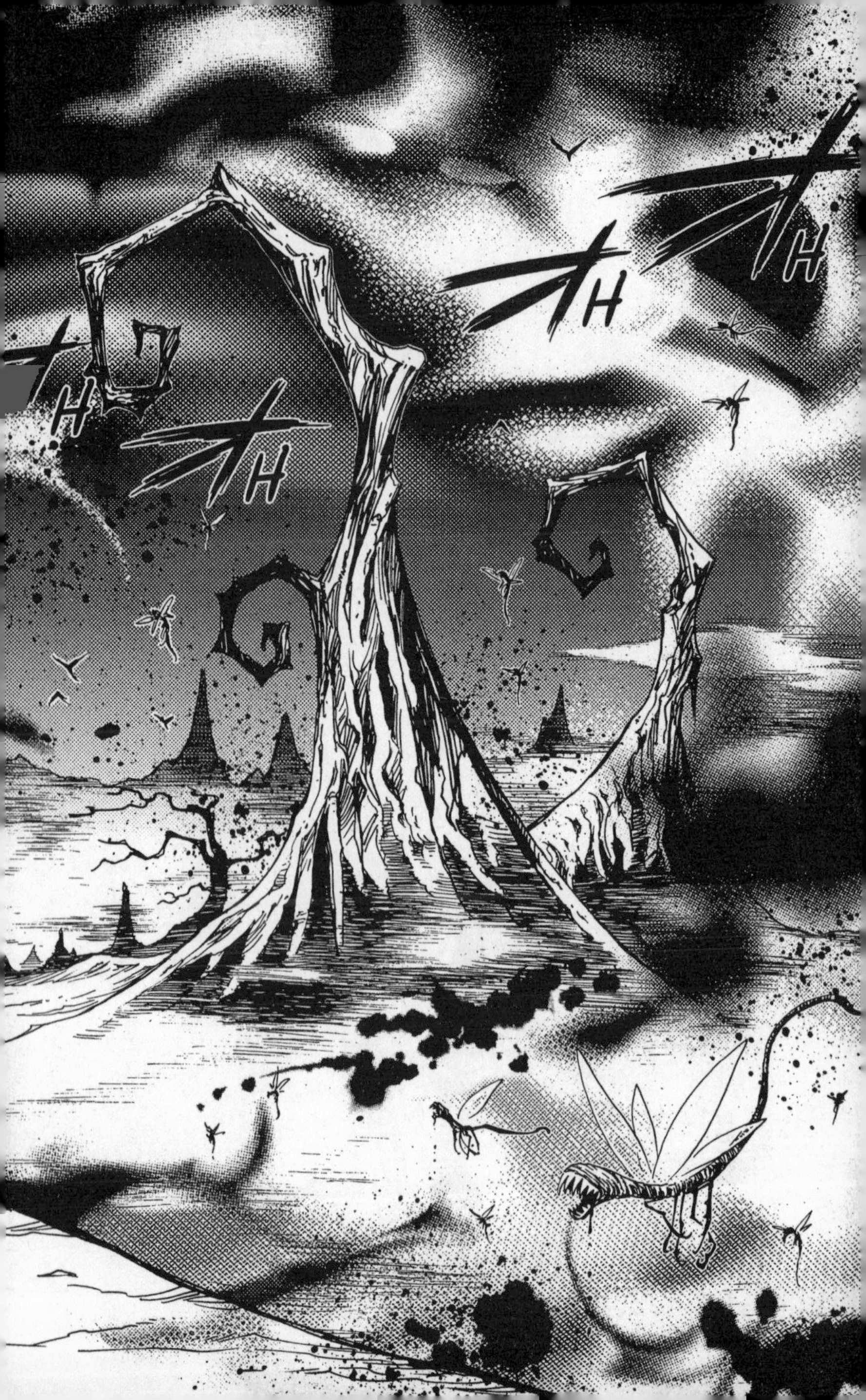
FH
FH
FH
FH

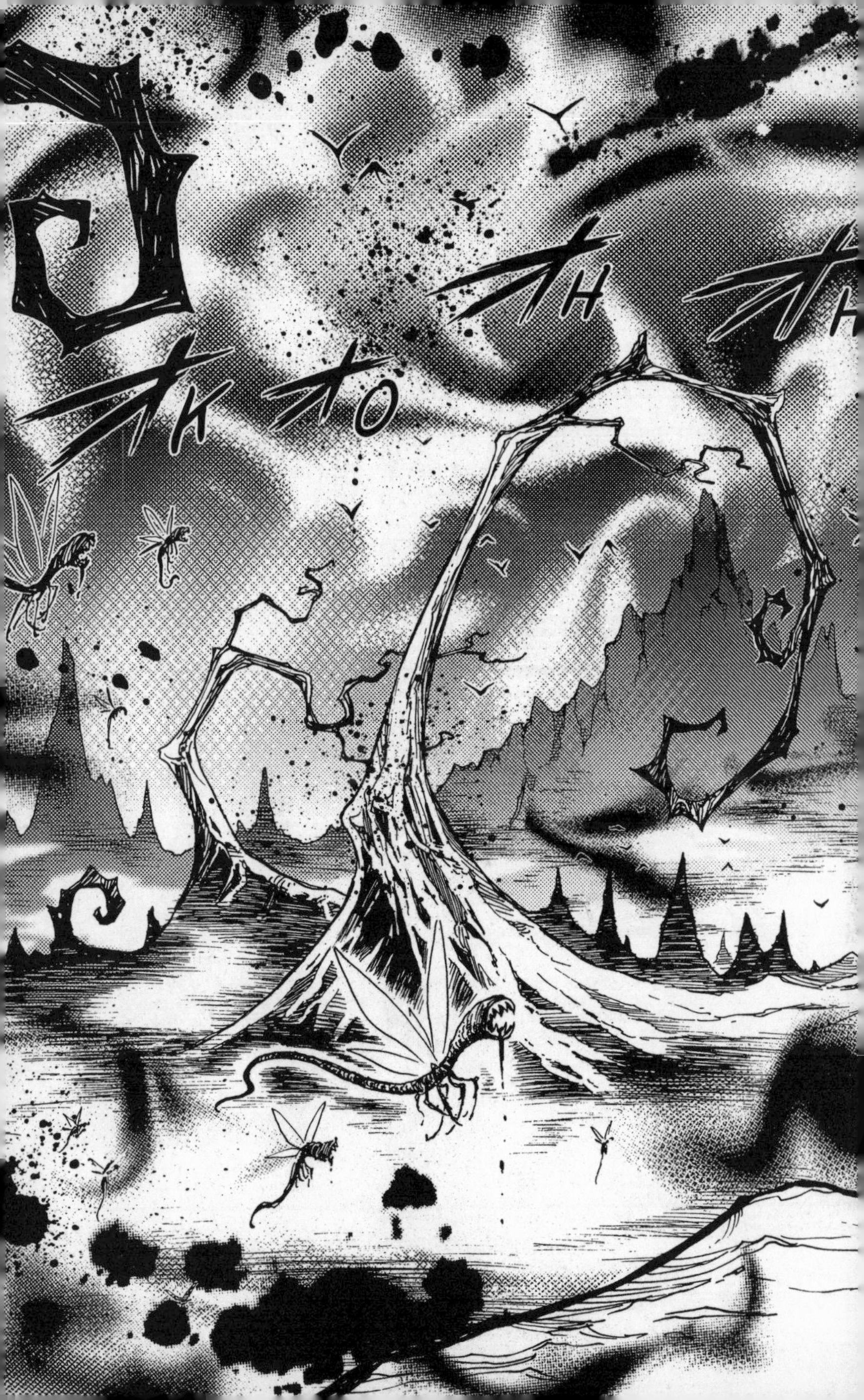
KOHH

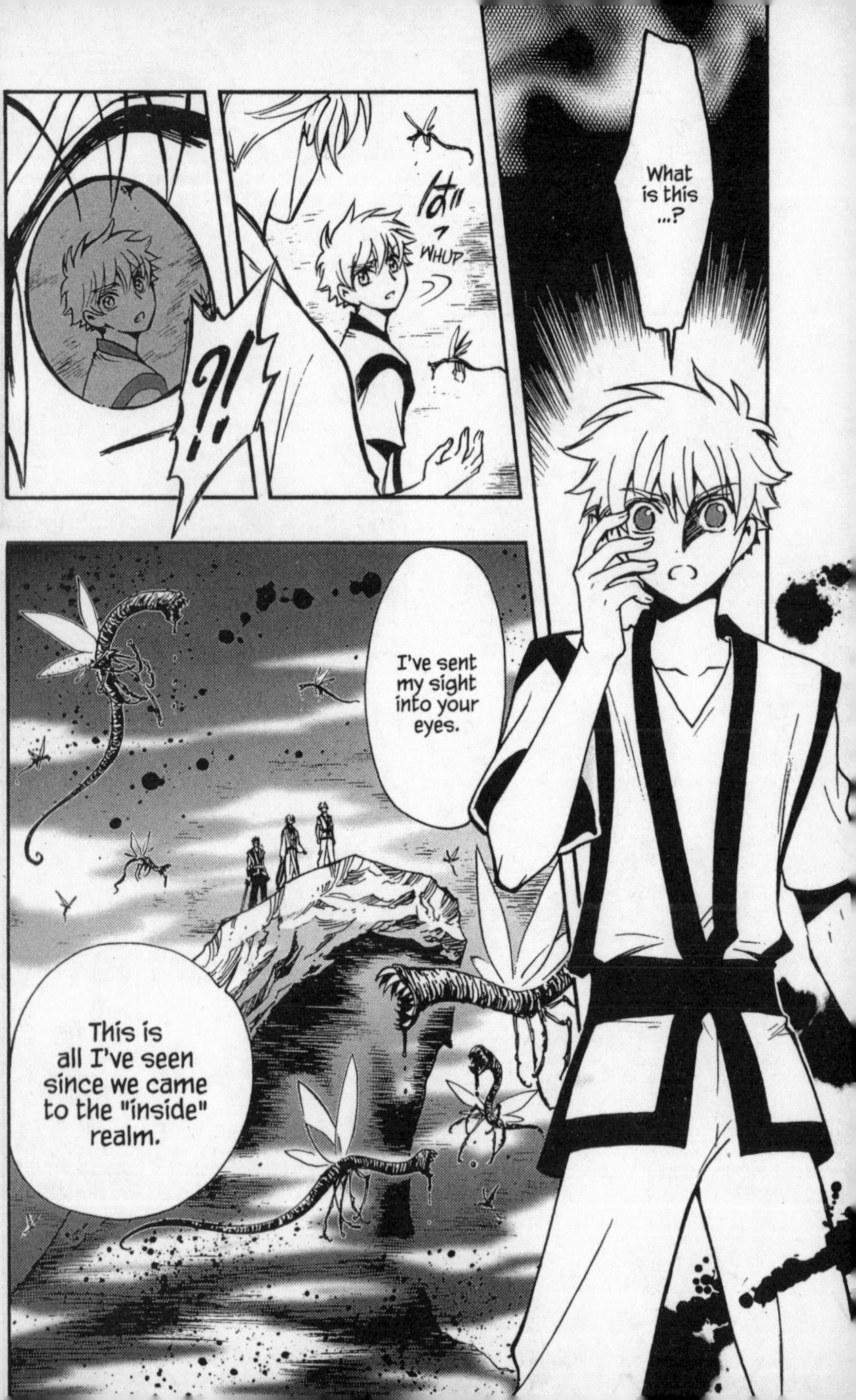
What is this ...?
WHUP
?!
I've sent my sight into your eyes.
This is all I've seen since we came to the "inside" realm.

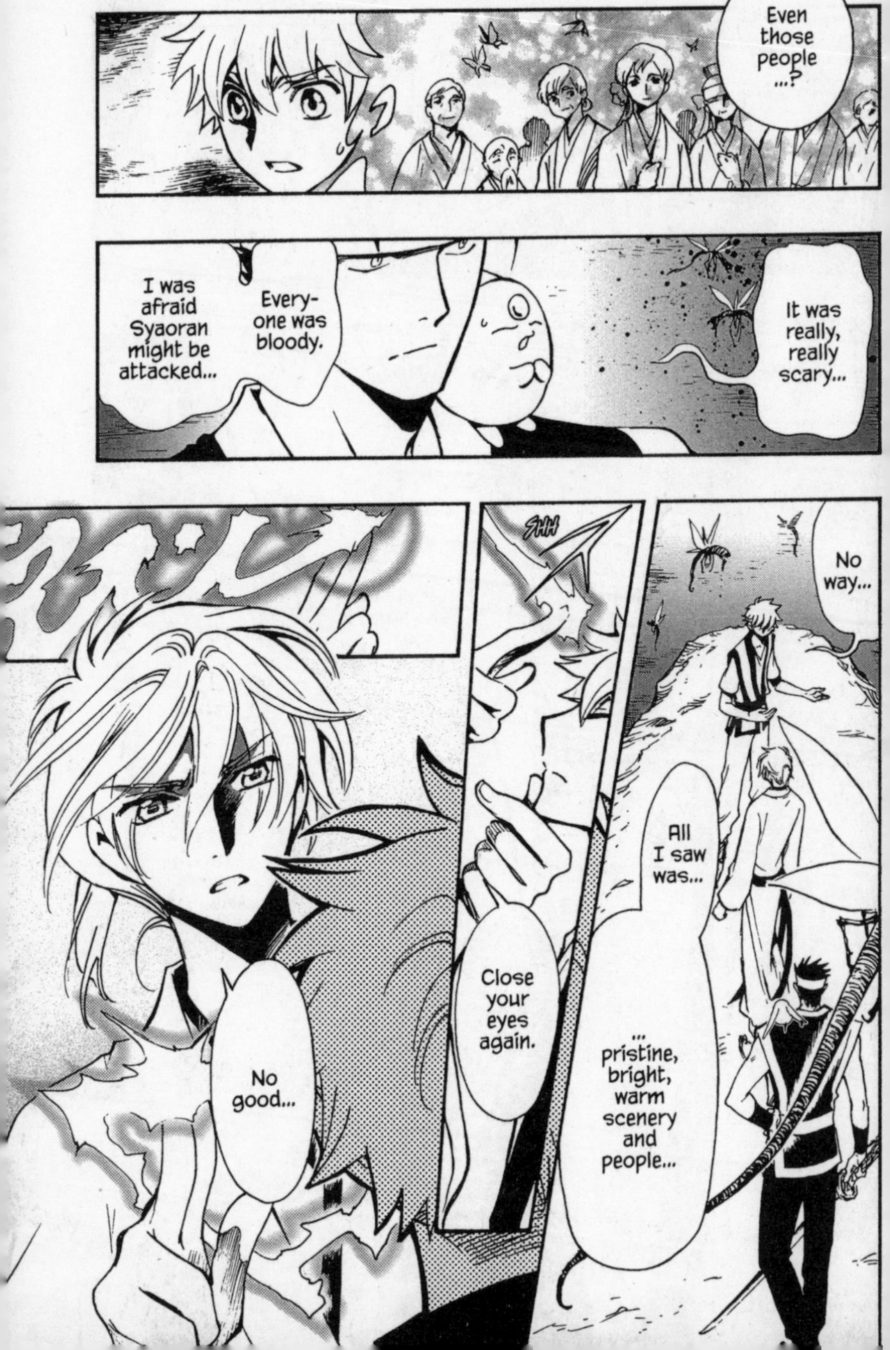
Even those people ...?
It was really, really scary...
Every-one was bloody.
I was afraid Syaoran might be attacked...
No way...
All I saw was...
... pristine, bright, warm scenery and people...
SHH
Close your eyes again.
No good...

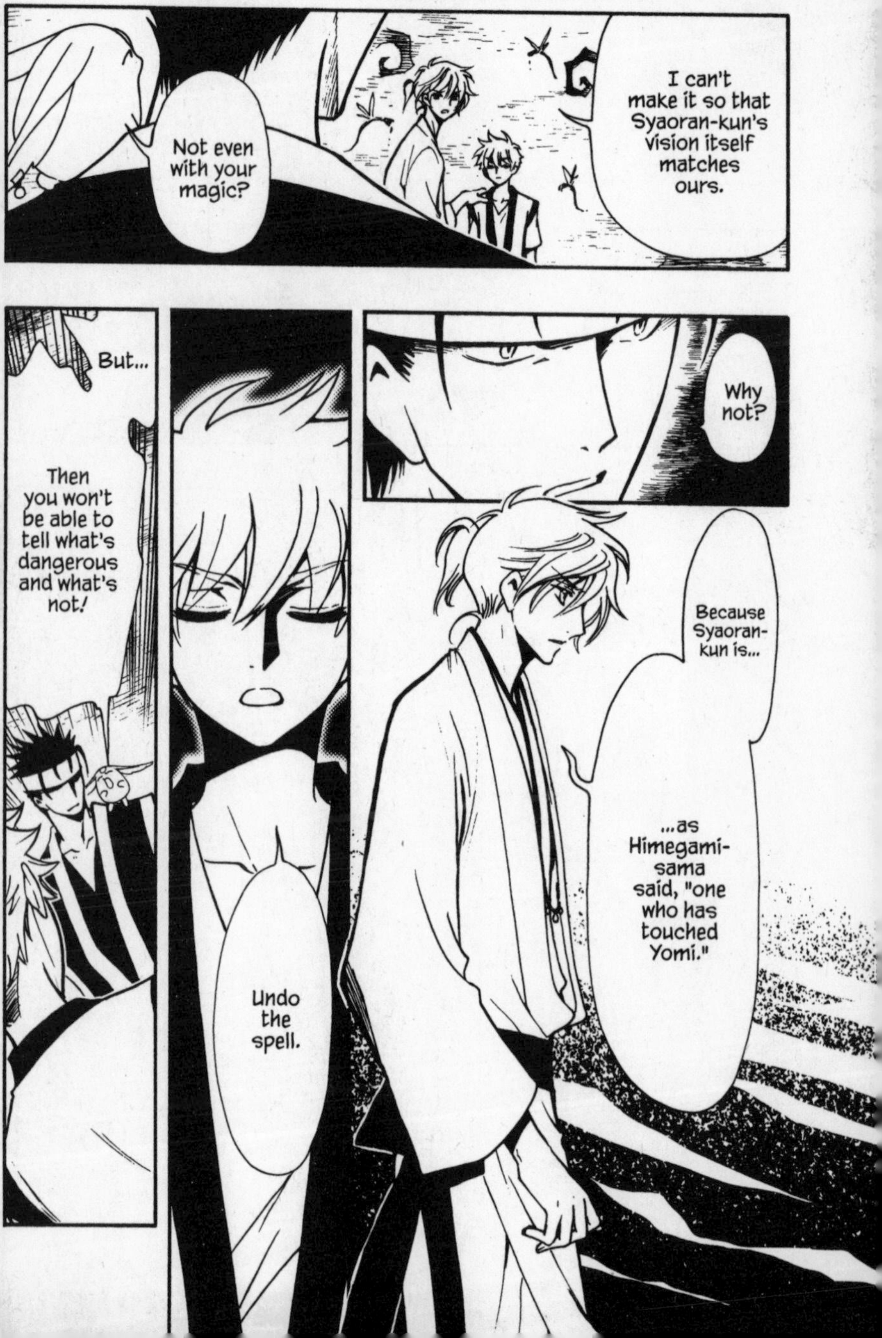
I can't make it so that Syaoran-kun's vision itself matches ours.
Not even with your magic?
Why not?
Because Syaoran-kun is...
...as Himegami-sama said, "one who has touched Yomi."
Undo the spell.
But...
Then you won't be able to tell what's dangerous and what's not!

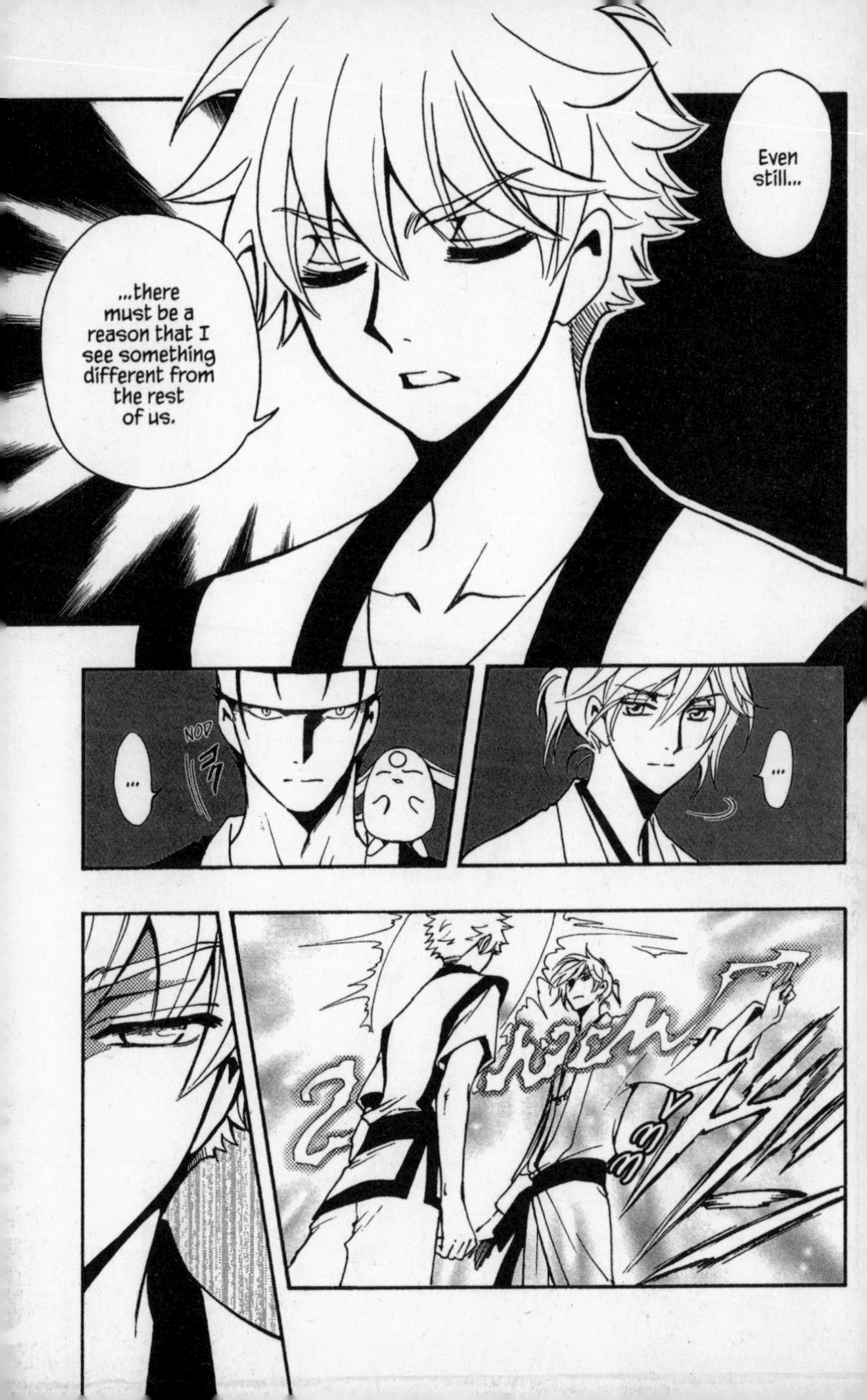
Even still...
...there must be a reason that I see something different from the rest of us.
...
NOD
...

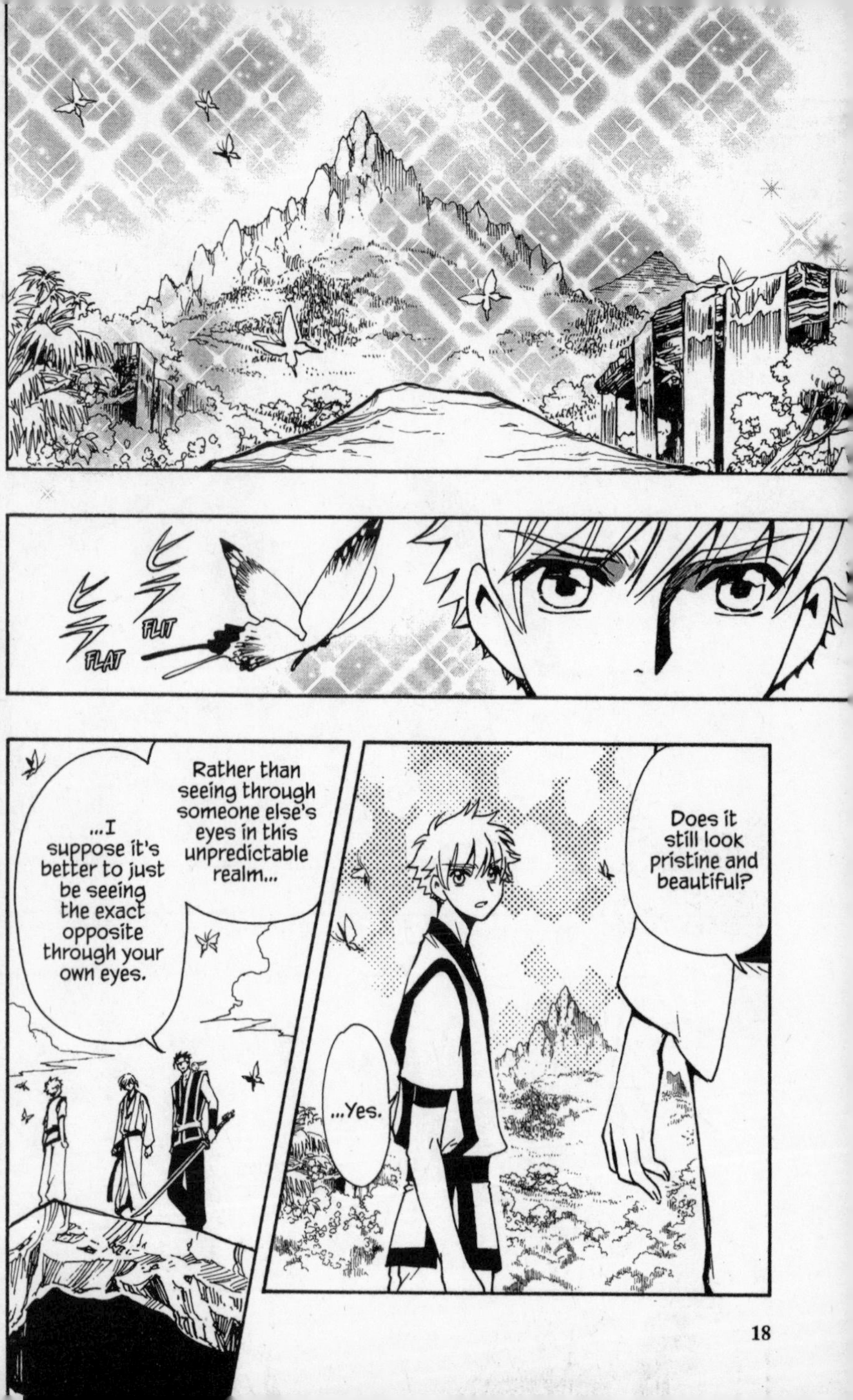
ヒラ
FLIT
ヒラ
FLAT
Does it still look pristine and beautiful?
...Yes.
Rather than seeing through someone else's eyes in this unpredictable realm...
...I suppose it's better to just be seeing the exact opposite through your own eyes.

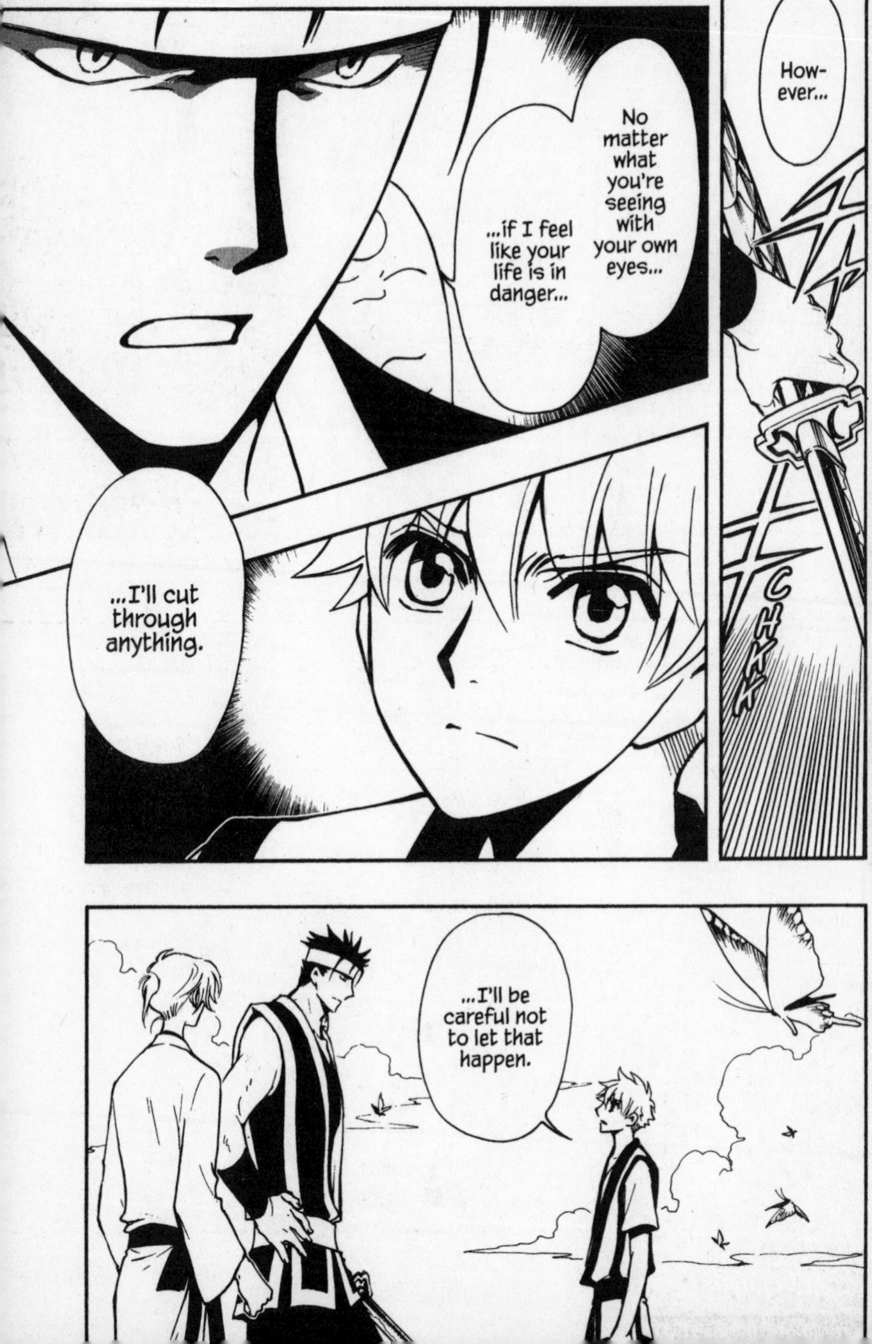
How-ever...
CHKK
No matter what you're seeing with your own eyes...
...if I feel like your life is in danger...
...I'll cut through anything.
...I'll be careful not to let that happen.

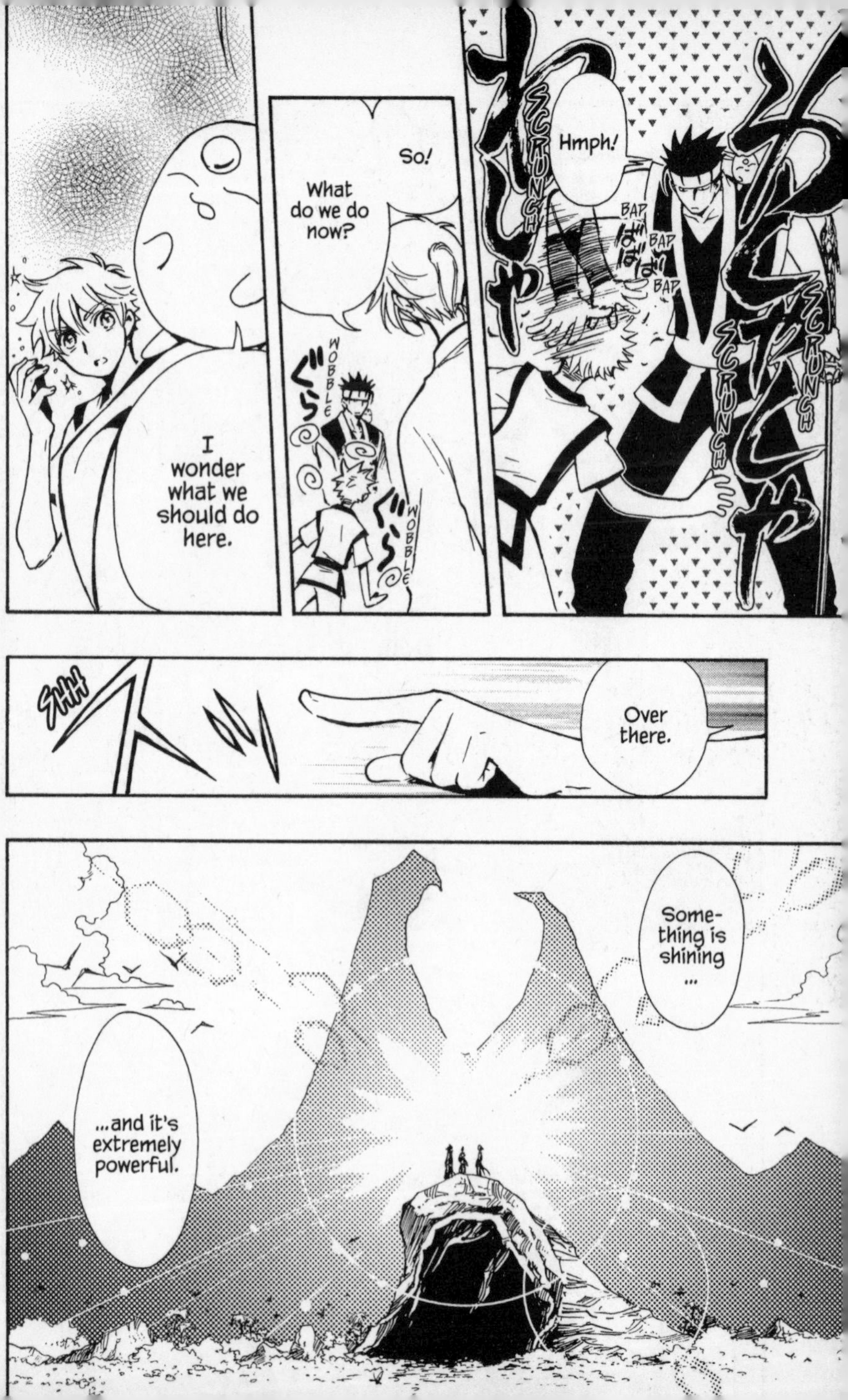
Hmph!
SCRUNCH
BAP BAP BAP
SCRUNCH
SCRUNCH
So!
What do we do now?
WOBBLE
WOBBLE
I wonder what we should do here.
Over there.
SHHH
Some-thing is shining...
...and it's extremely powerful.

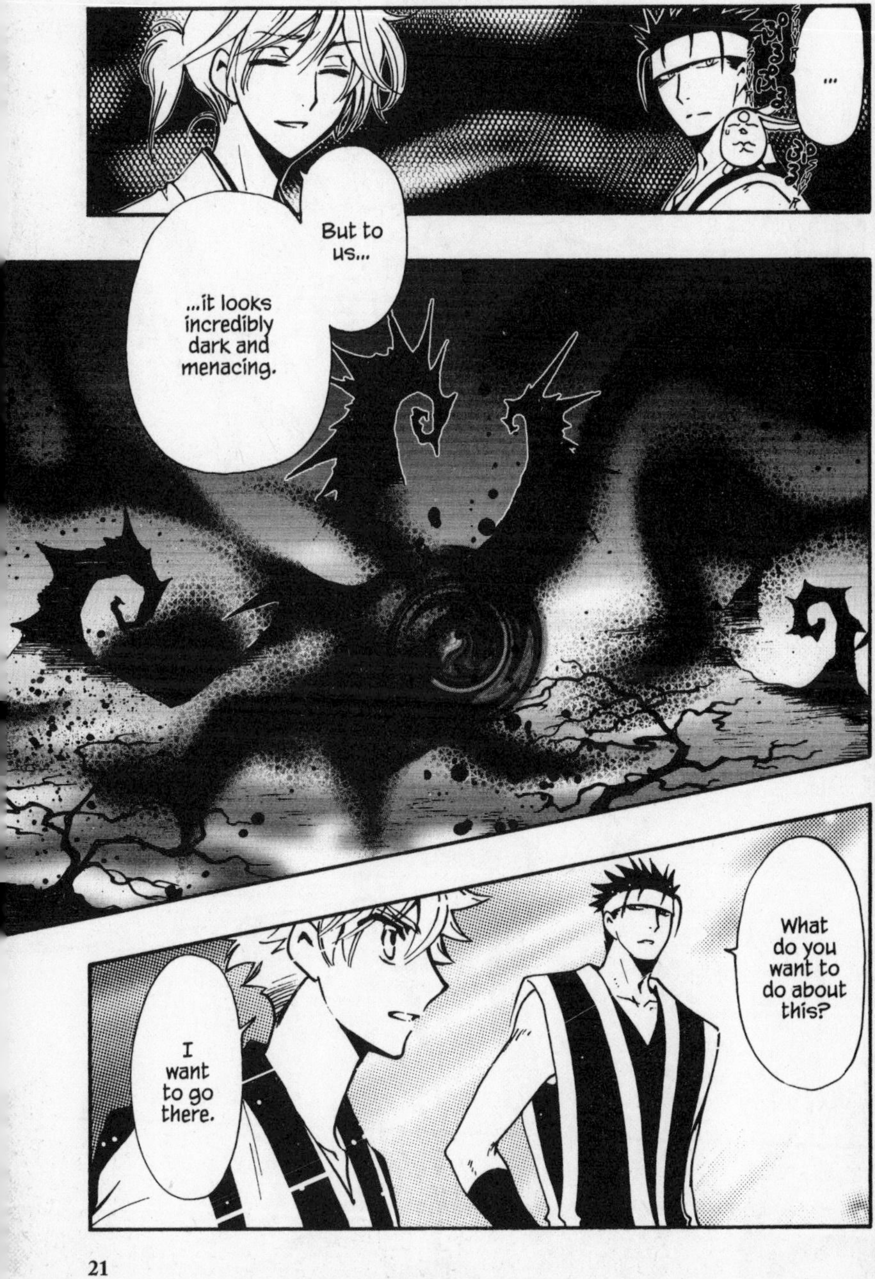
...
SHIVR
SHIVR
SHIVR
But to us...
...it looks incredibly dark and menacing.
What do you want to do about this?
I want to go there.

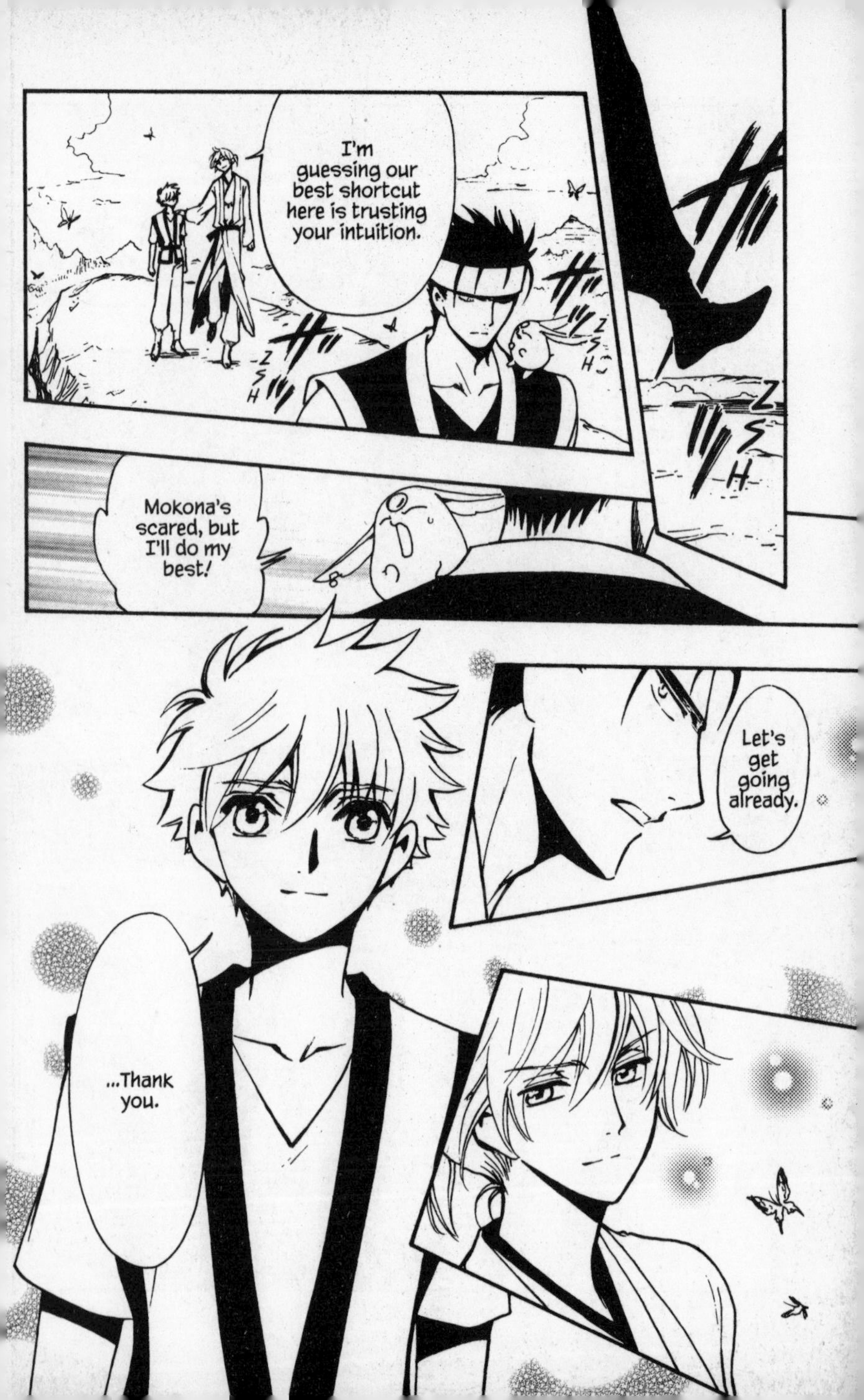
ZSH
I'm guessing our best shortcut here is trusting your intuition.
ZSH
ZSH
Mokona's scared, but I'll do my best!
Let's get going already.
...Thank you.

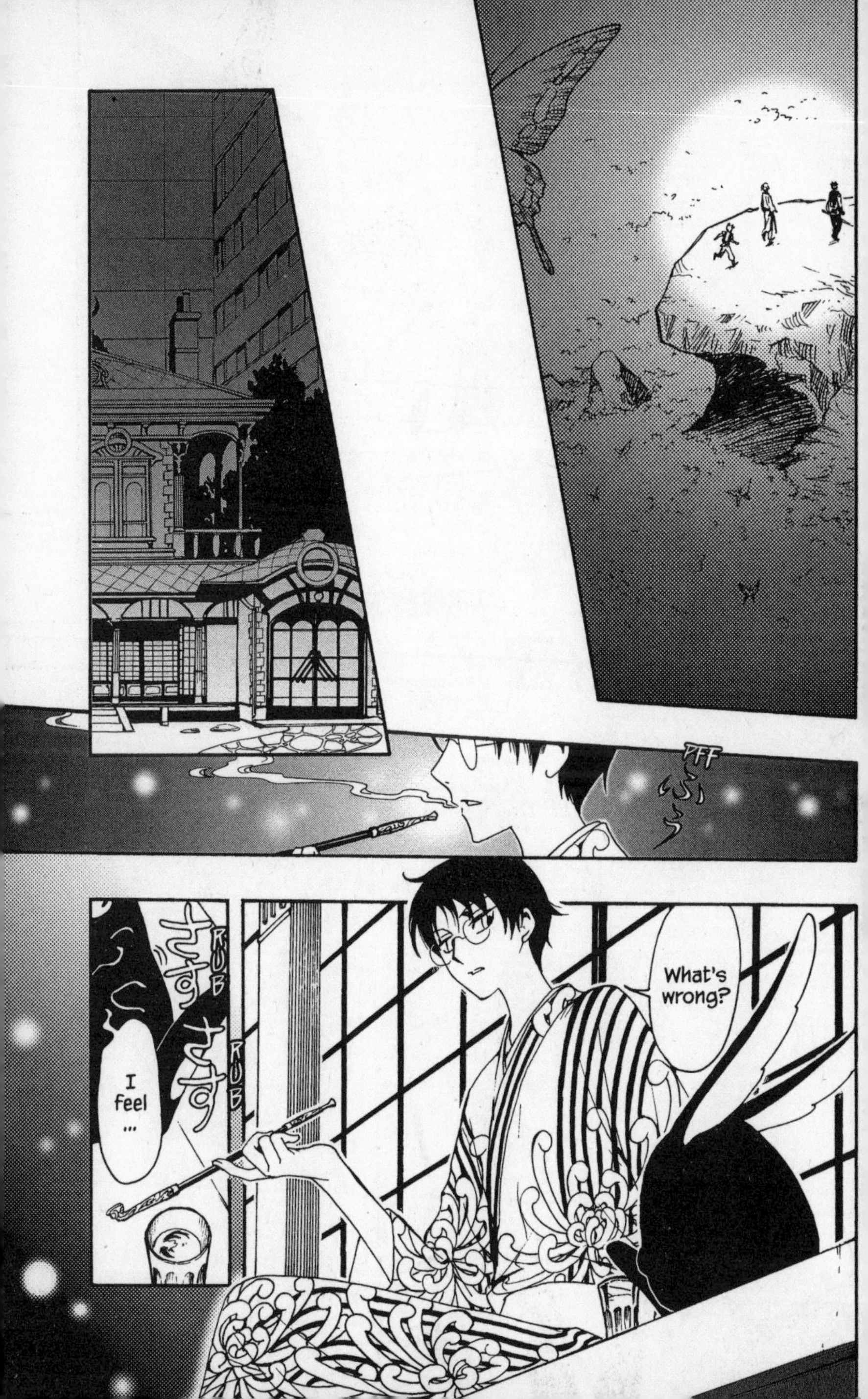
PFF
ふぅ
What's wrong?
RUB
さす
RUB
さす
I feel ...

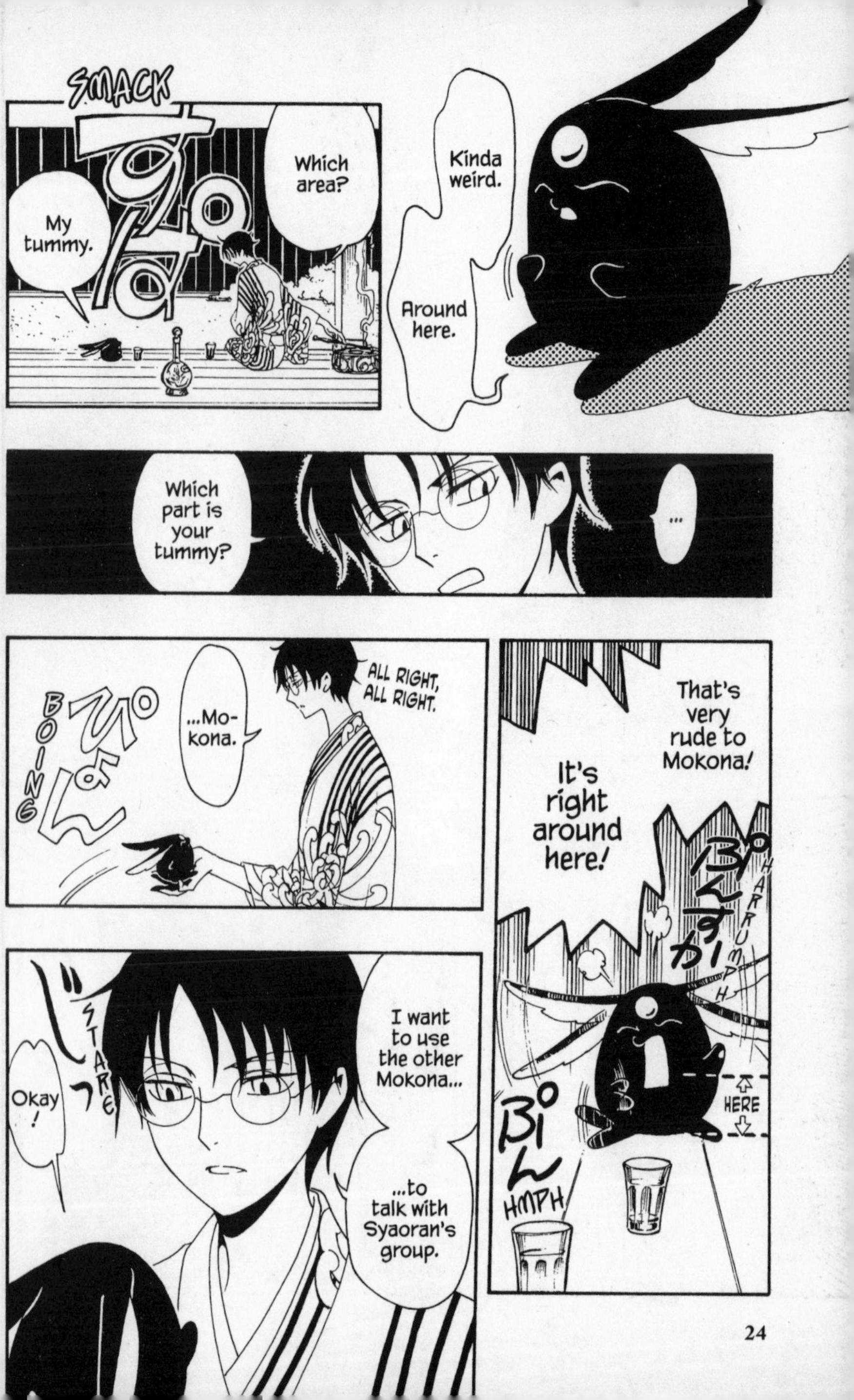
Kinda weird.
Around here.
Which area?
My tummy.
SMACK
...
Which part is your tummy?
That's very rude to Mokona!
It's right around here!
HARRUMPH
HERE
HMPH
...Mo-kona.
ALL RIGHT, ALL RIGHT.
BOING
I want to use the other Mokona...
...to talk with Syaoran's group.
STARE
Okay!

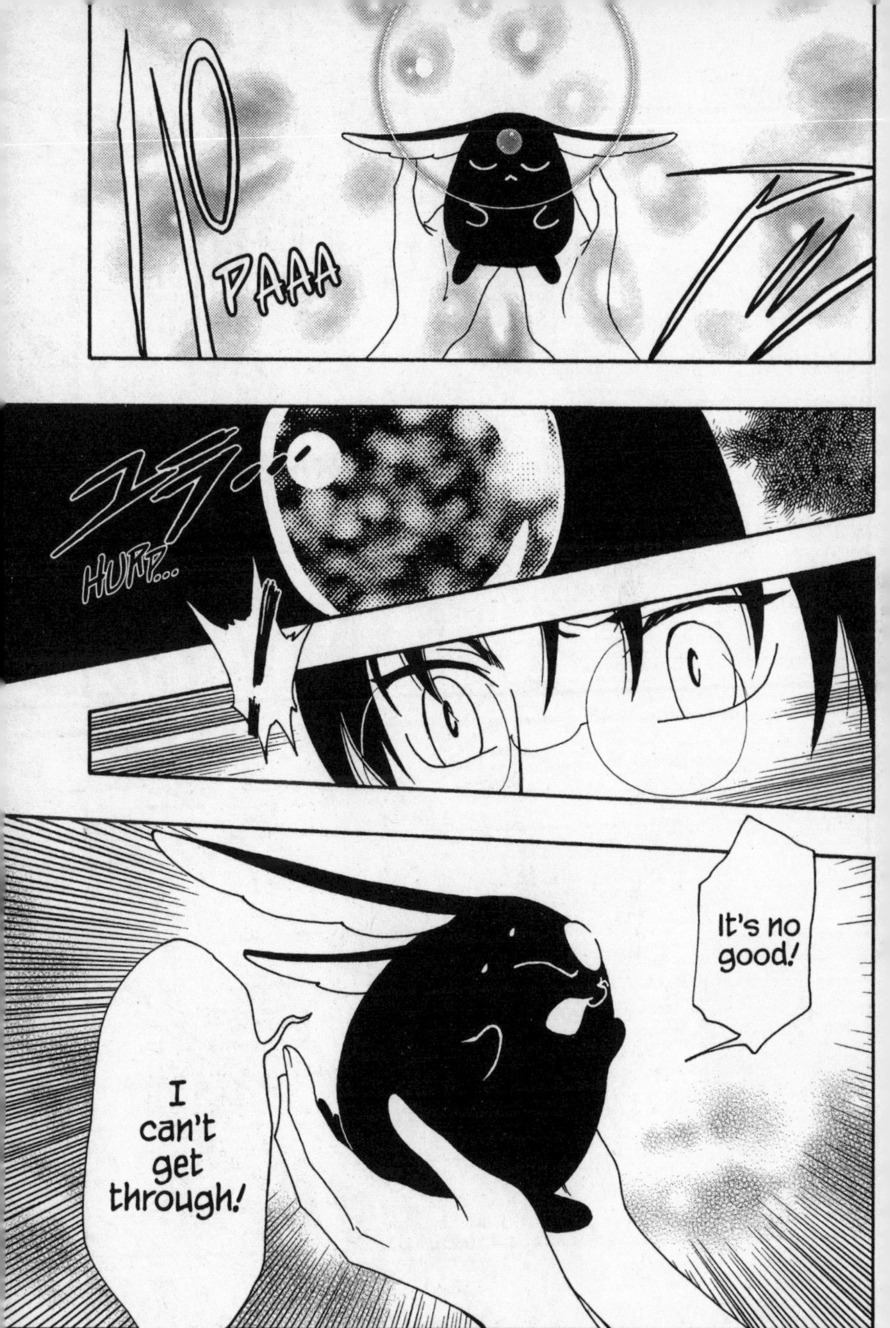
PAAA
HURP...
It's no good!
I can't get through!

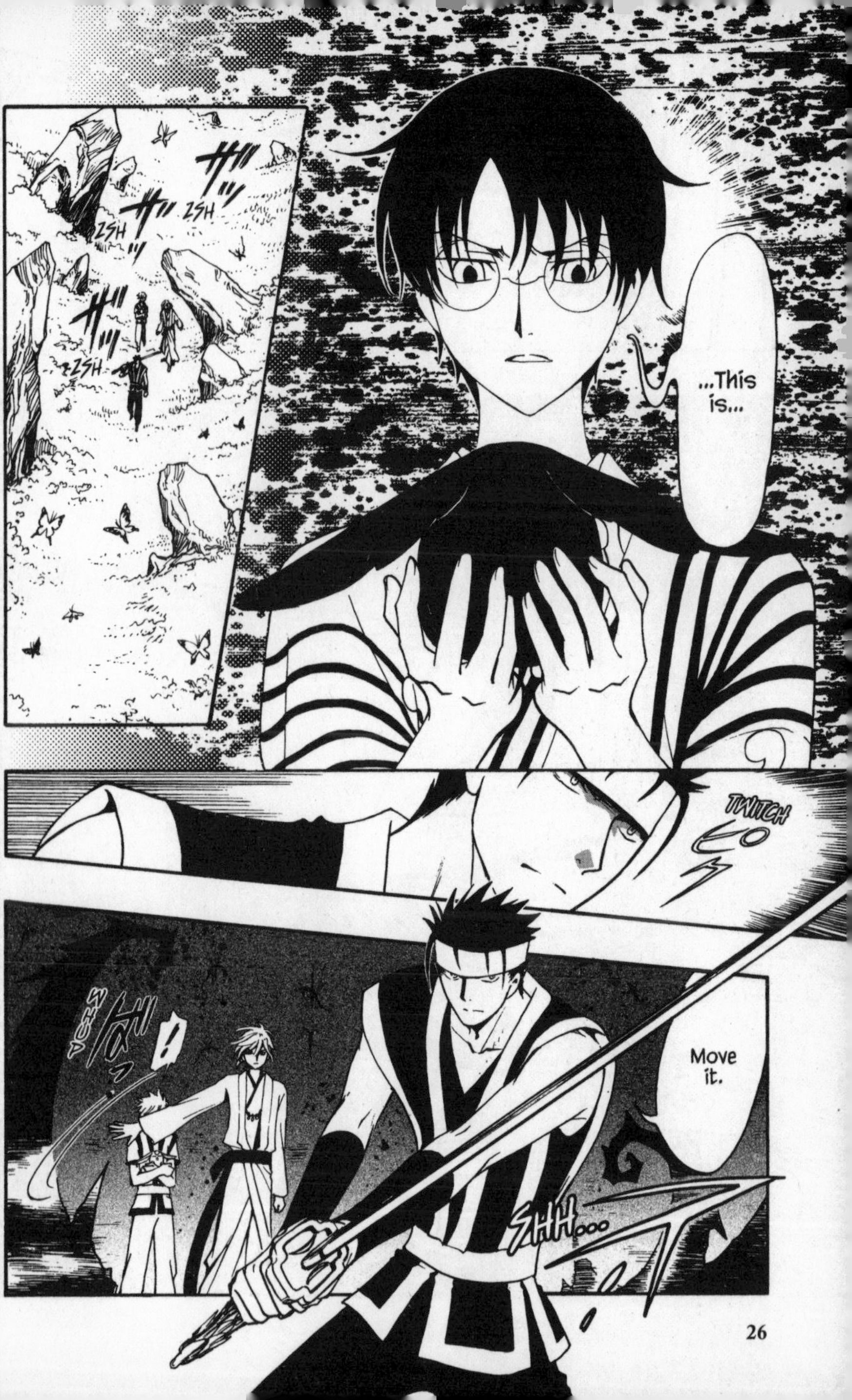
...This is...
ZSH
ZSH
ZSH
TWITCH
Move it.
!
SHH...

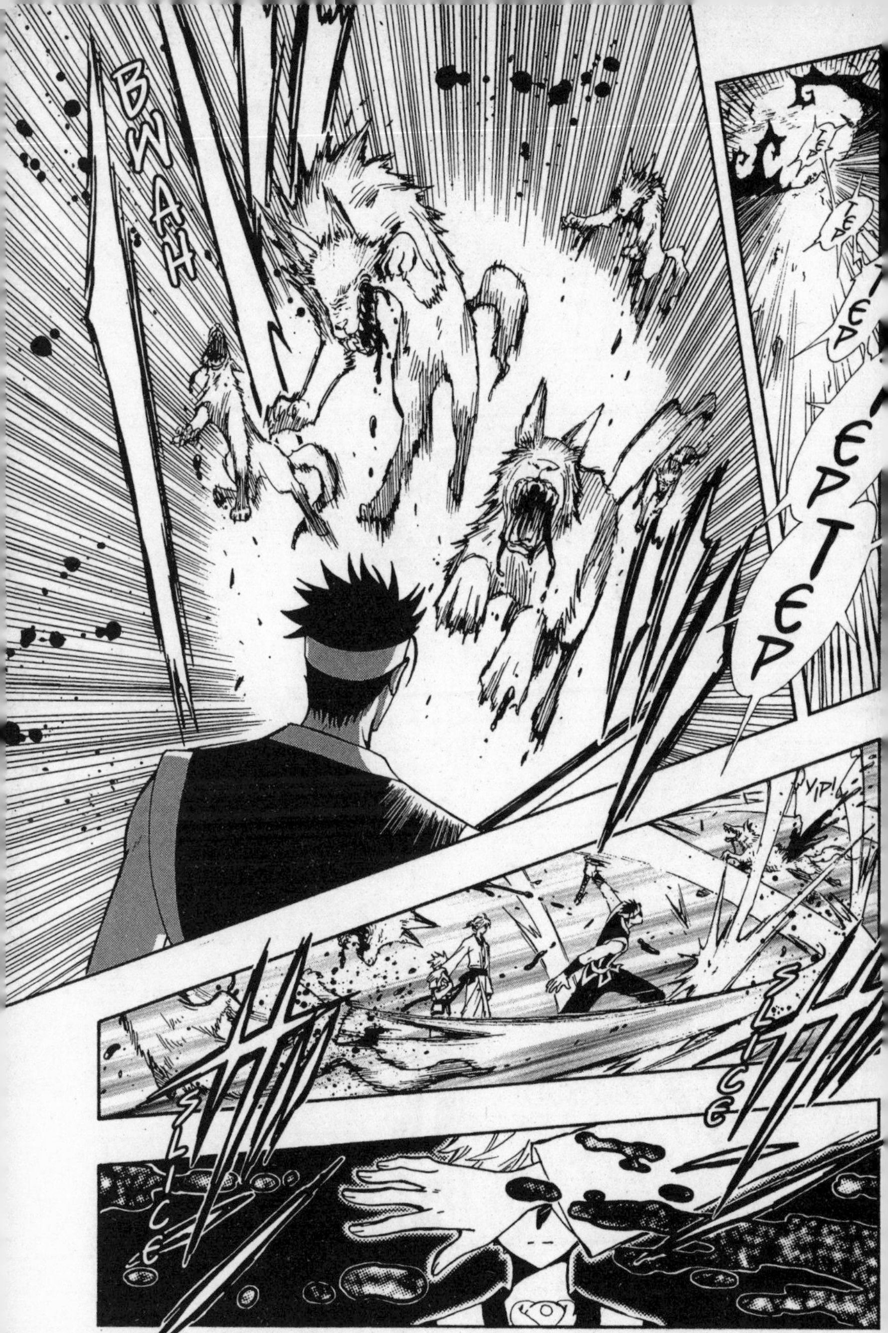
TEP
TEP
TEP
BWAH
TEP TEP TEP
YIP!
SLICE
SLICE

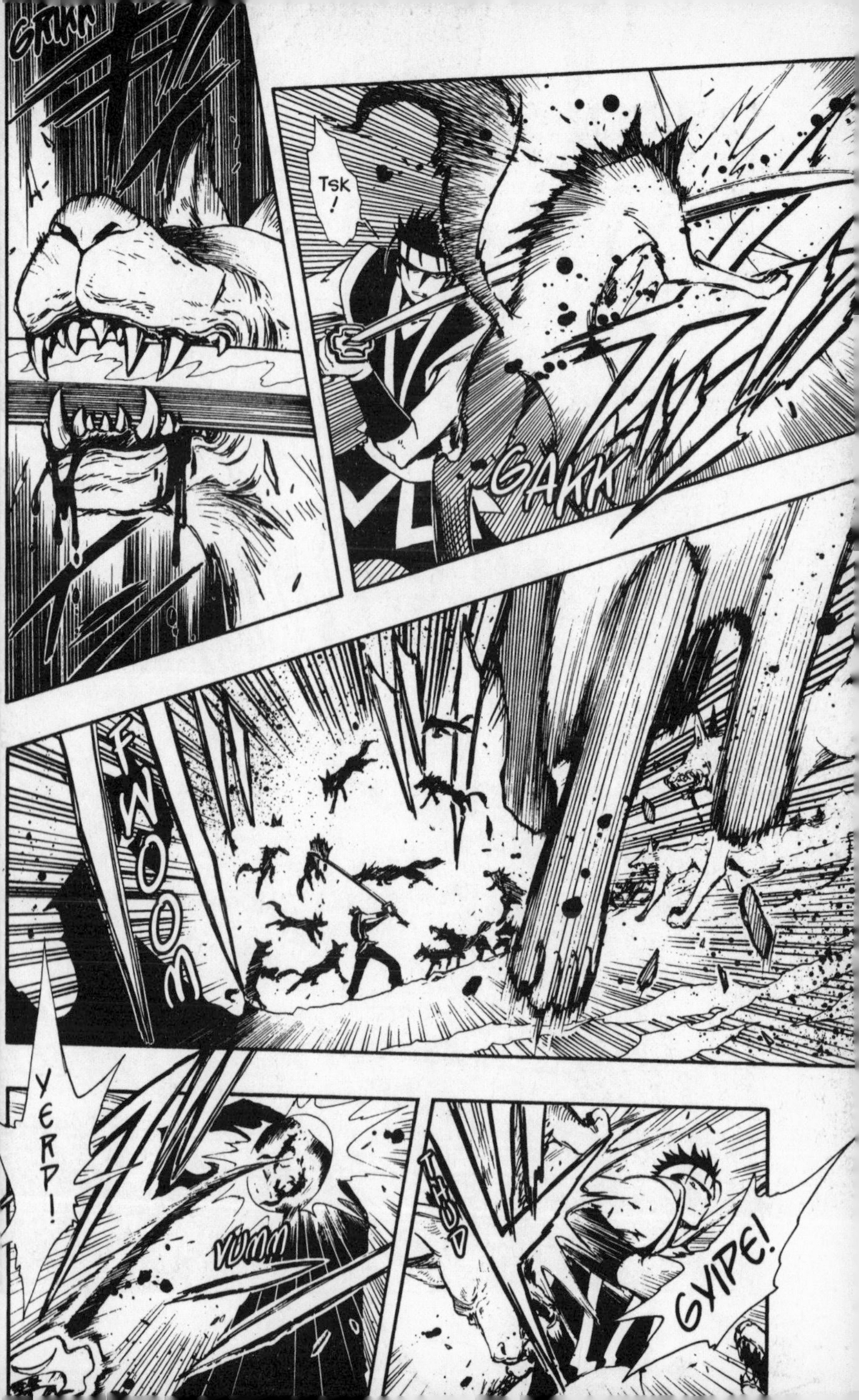
TSK!
GAKK
FWOOOM
THOD
GYIPE!
YERP!
VUMM

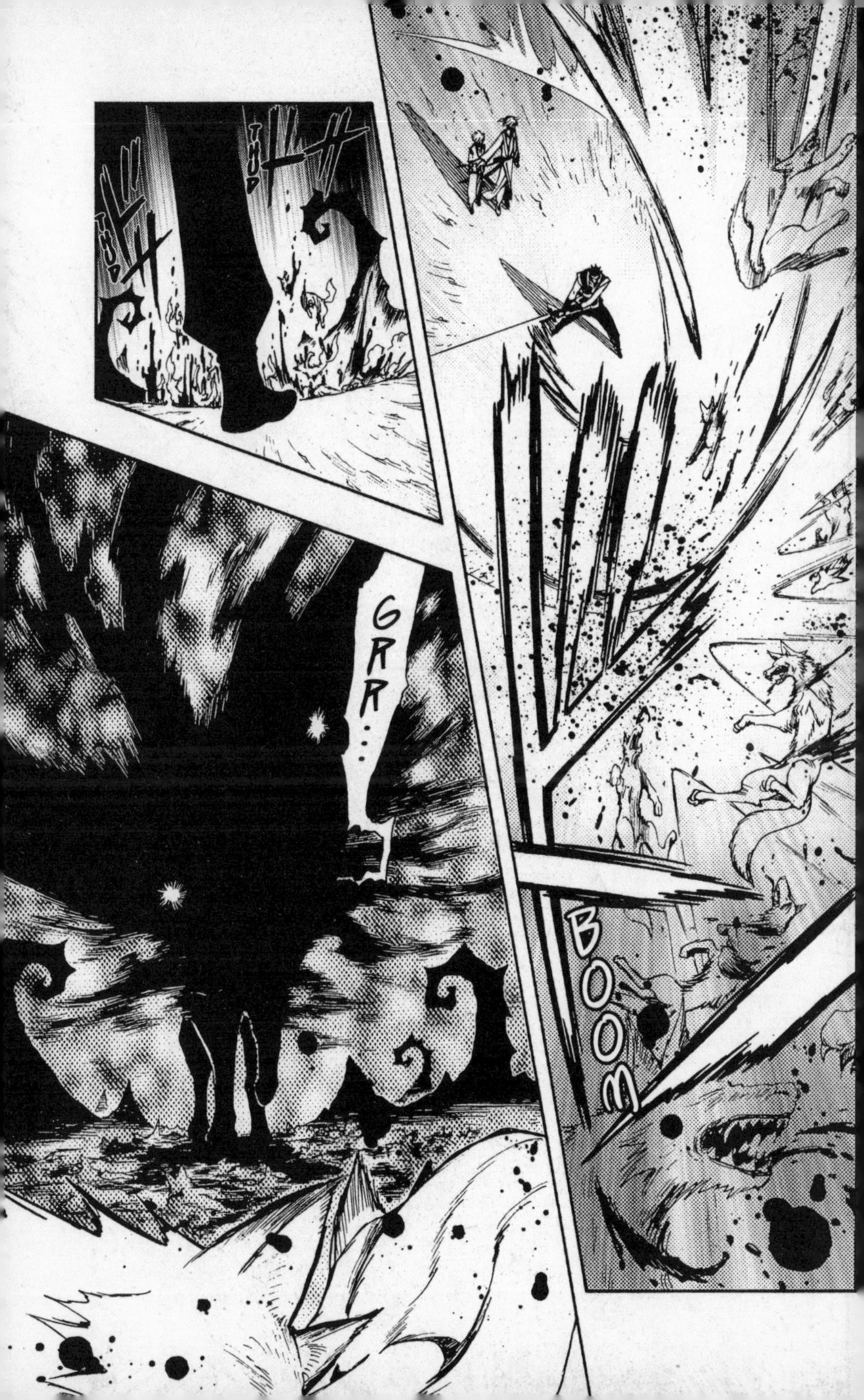
BOOM
THUD
THUD
GRR...

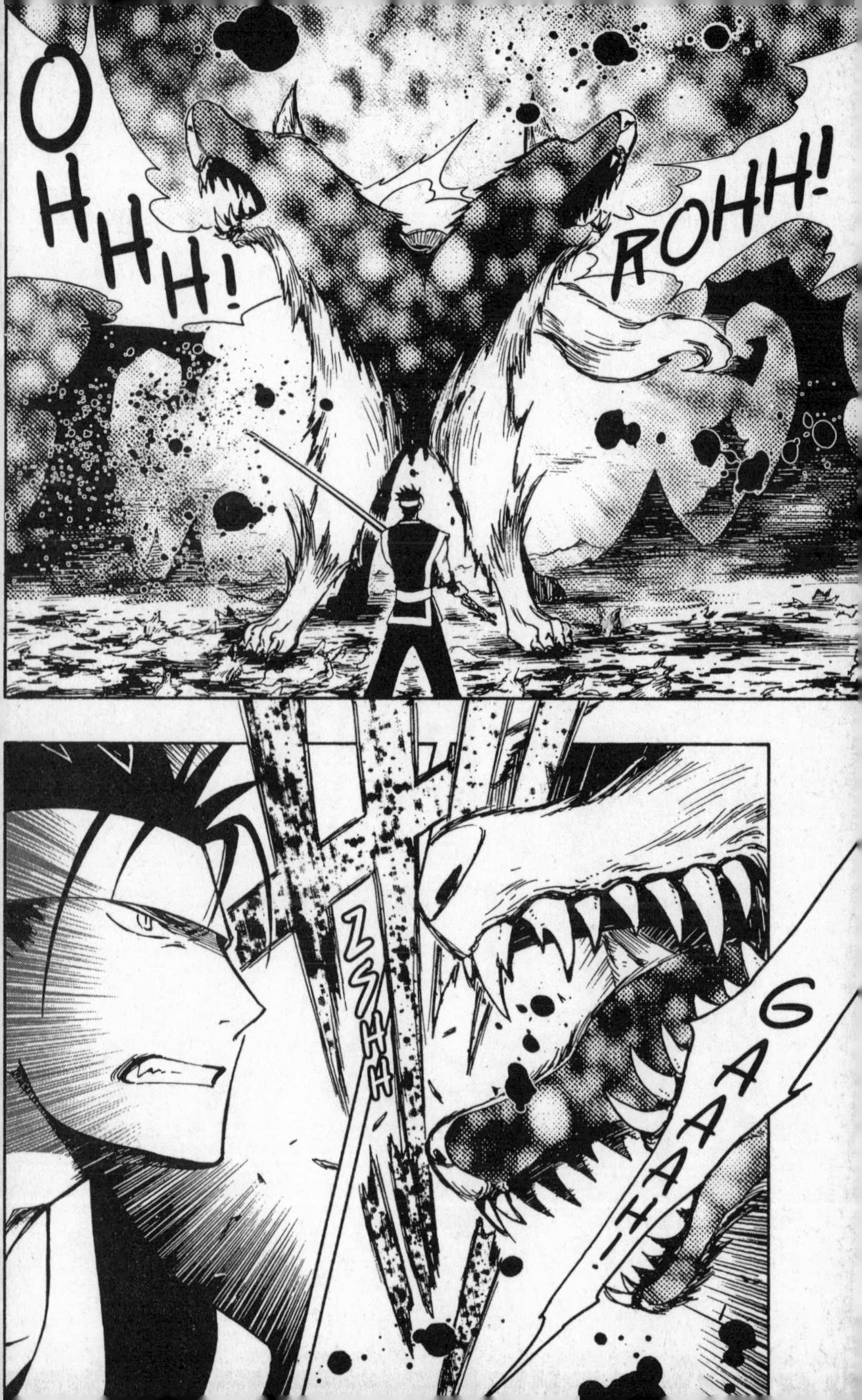
ROHH!
OHHH!
GAAAH!
ZSHH

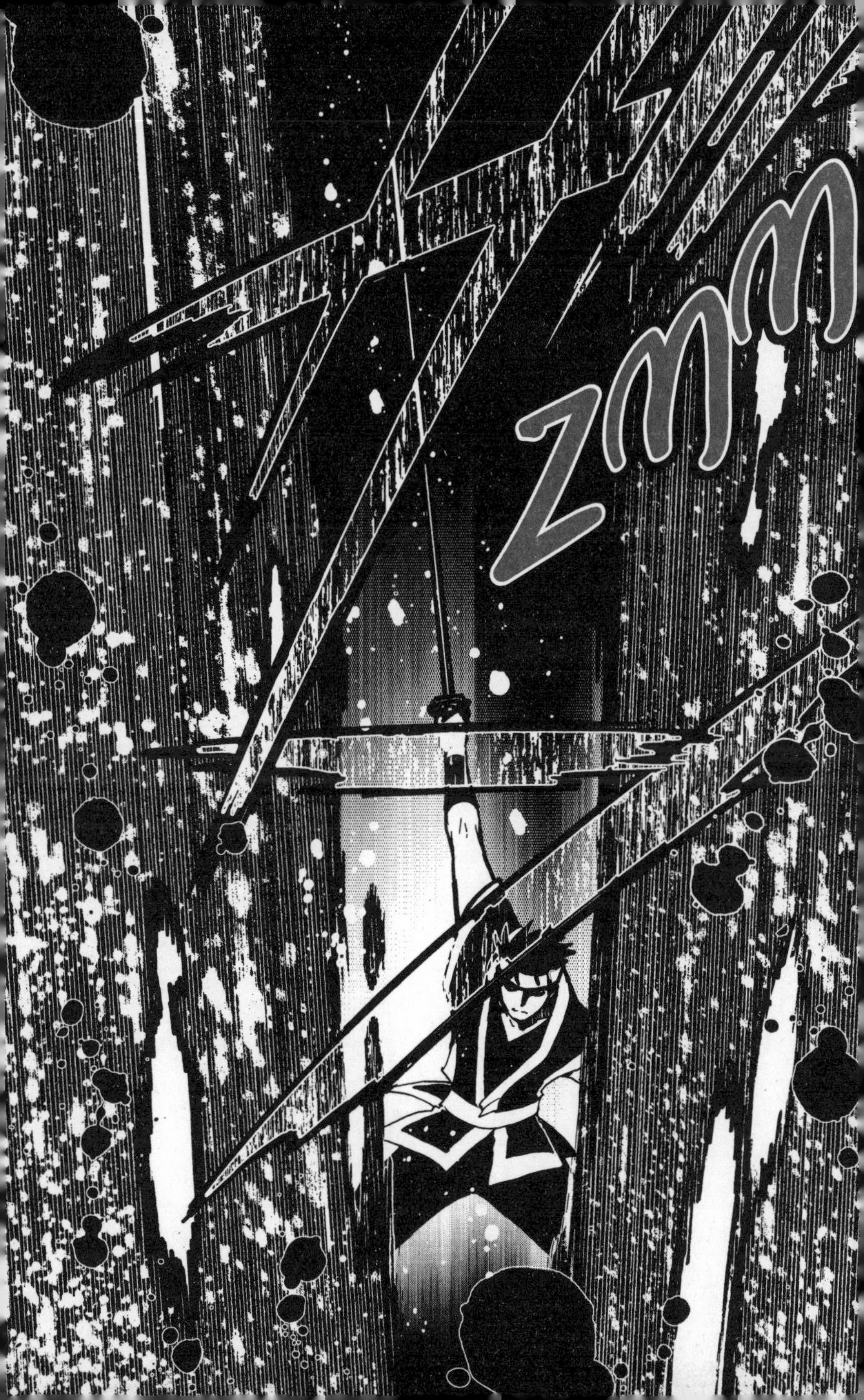
ZMM

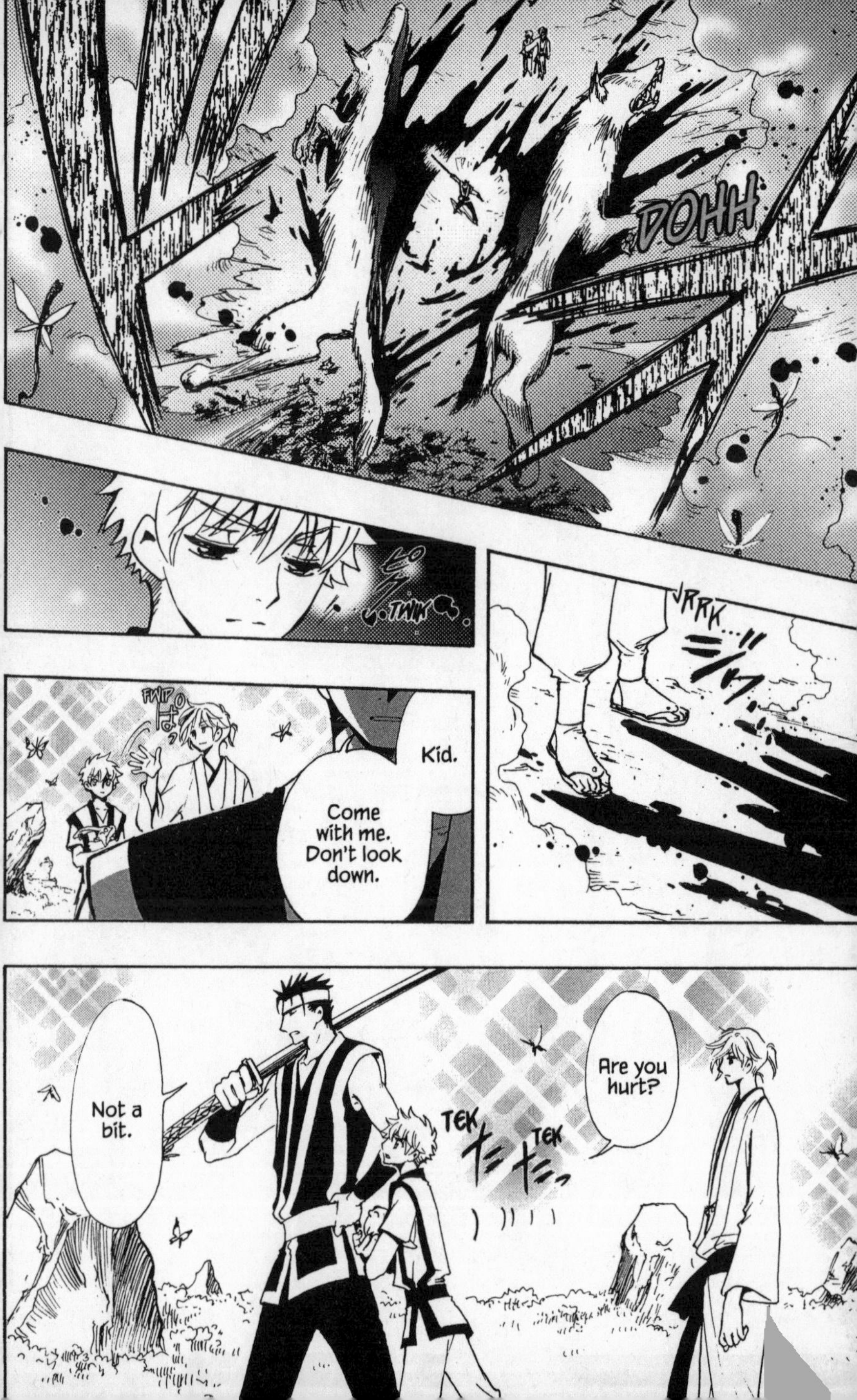
DOHH
JRRK...
TWIK
FWIP
Kid.
Come with me. Don't look down.
Are you hurt?
TEK
TEK
Not a bit.

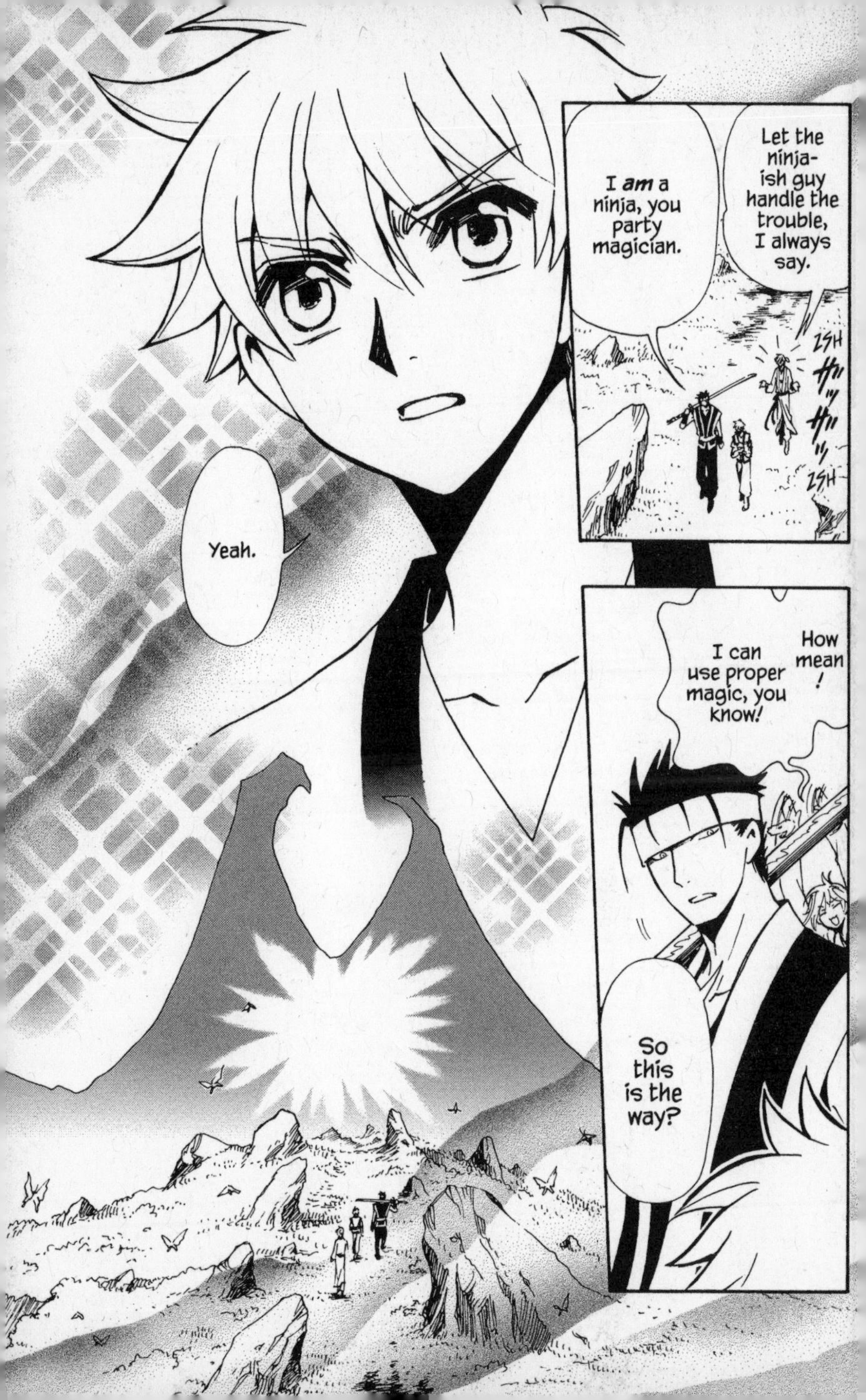
Let the ninja-ish guy handle the trouble, I always say.
I *am* a ninja, you party magician.
ZSH
ZSH
How mean!
I can use proper magic, you know!
So this is the way?
Yeah.

TSUBASA

WoRLD CHRoNiCLE: NIRAIKANAI

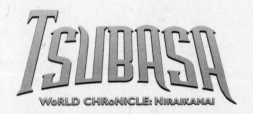

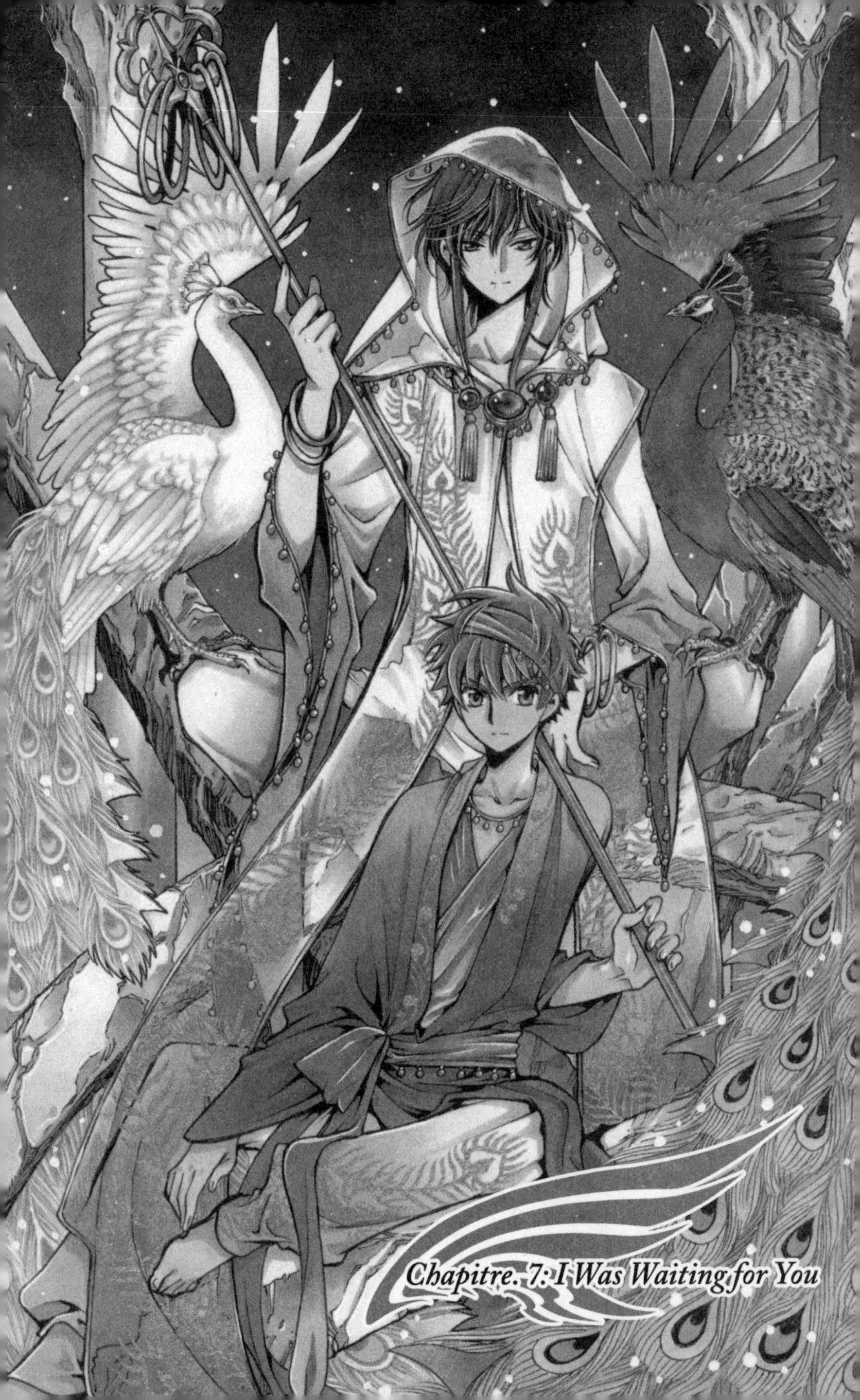
Chapitre. 7: I Was Waiting for You

TSUBASA

WoRLD CHRoNiCLE: NIRAIKANAI

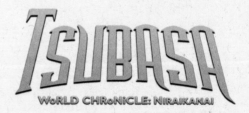

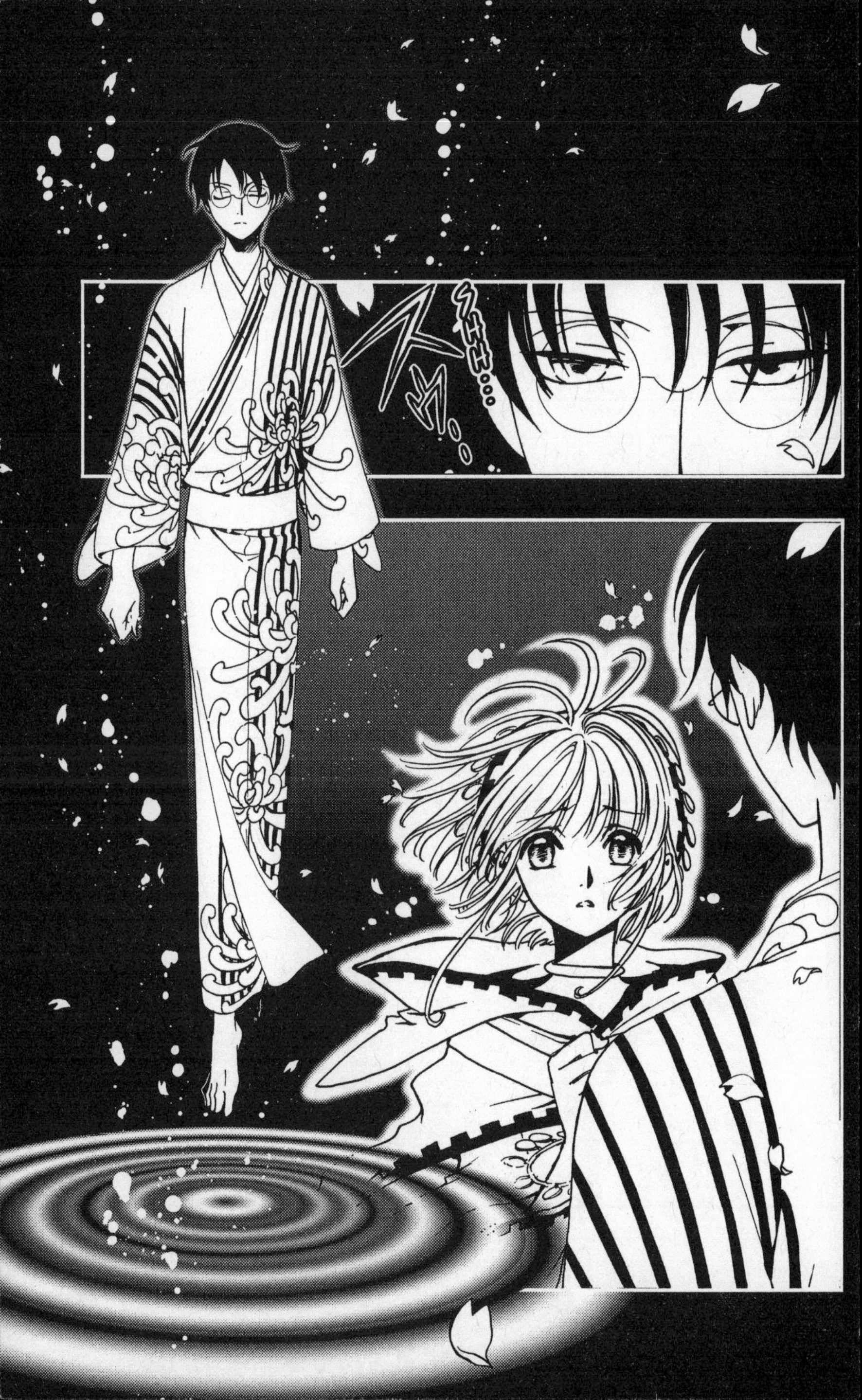
SHHH...

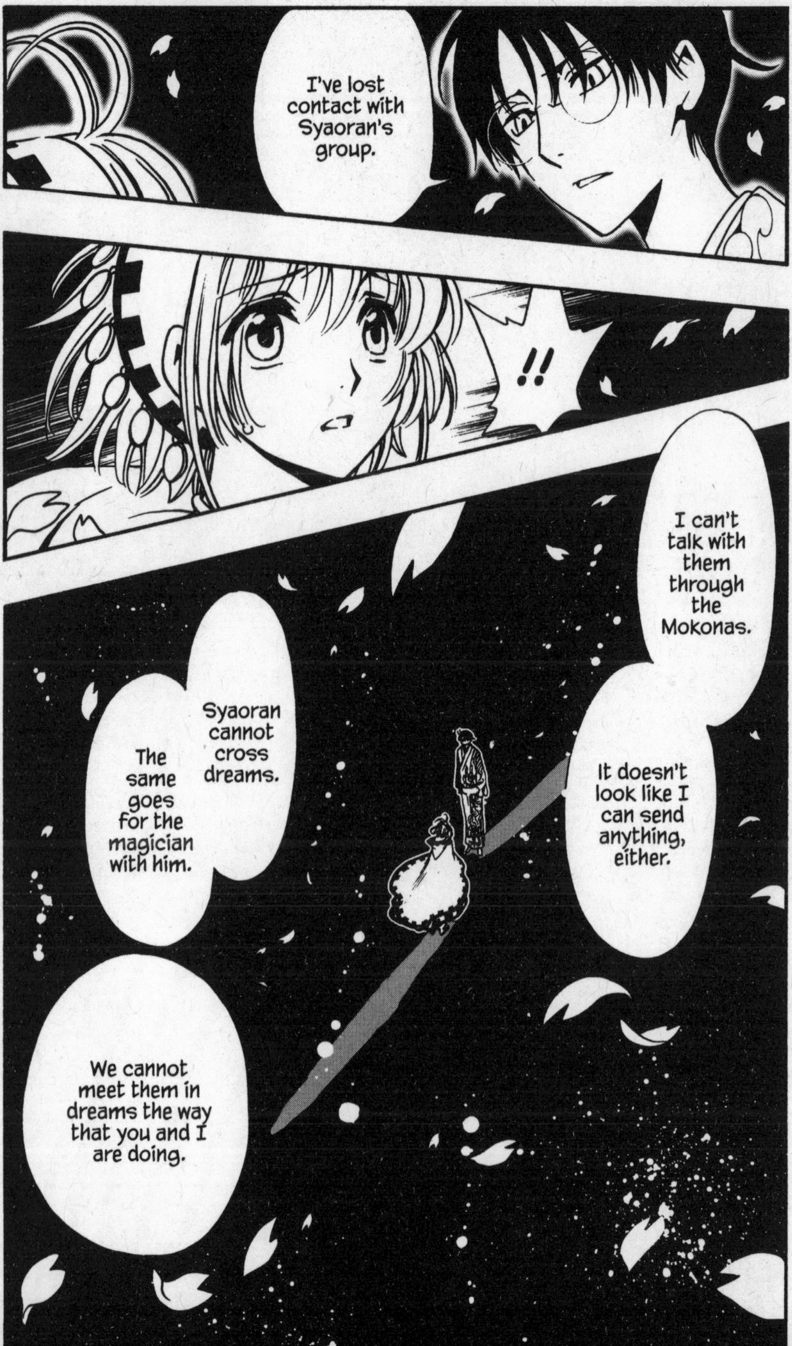
I've lost contact with Syaoran's group.
!!
I can't talk with them through the Mokonas.
It doesn't look like I can send anything, either.
Syaoran cannot cross dreams.
The same goes for the magician with him.
We cannot meet them in dreams the way that you and I are doing.

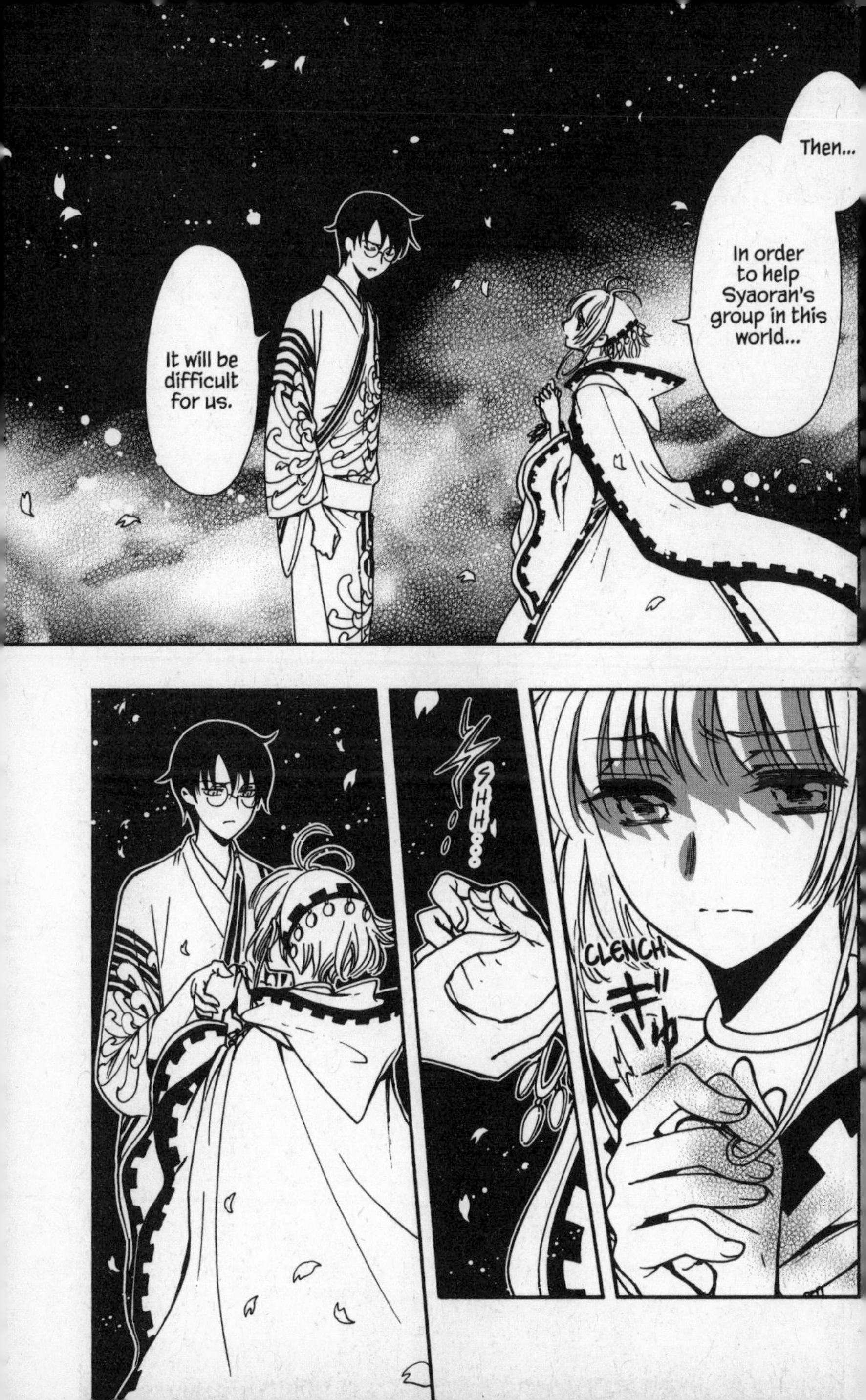
Then...
In order to help Syaoran's group in this world...
It will be difficult for us.

CLENCH
SHH...

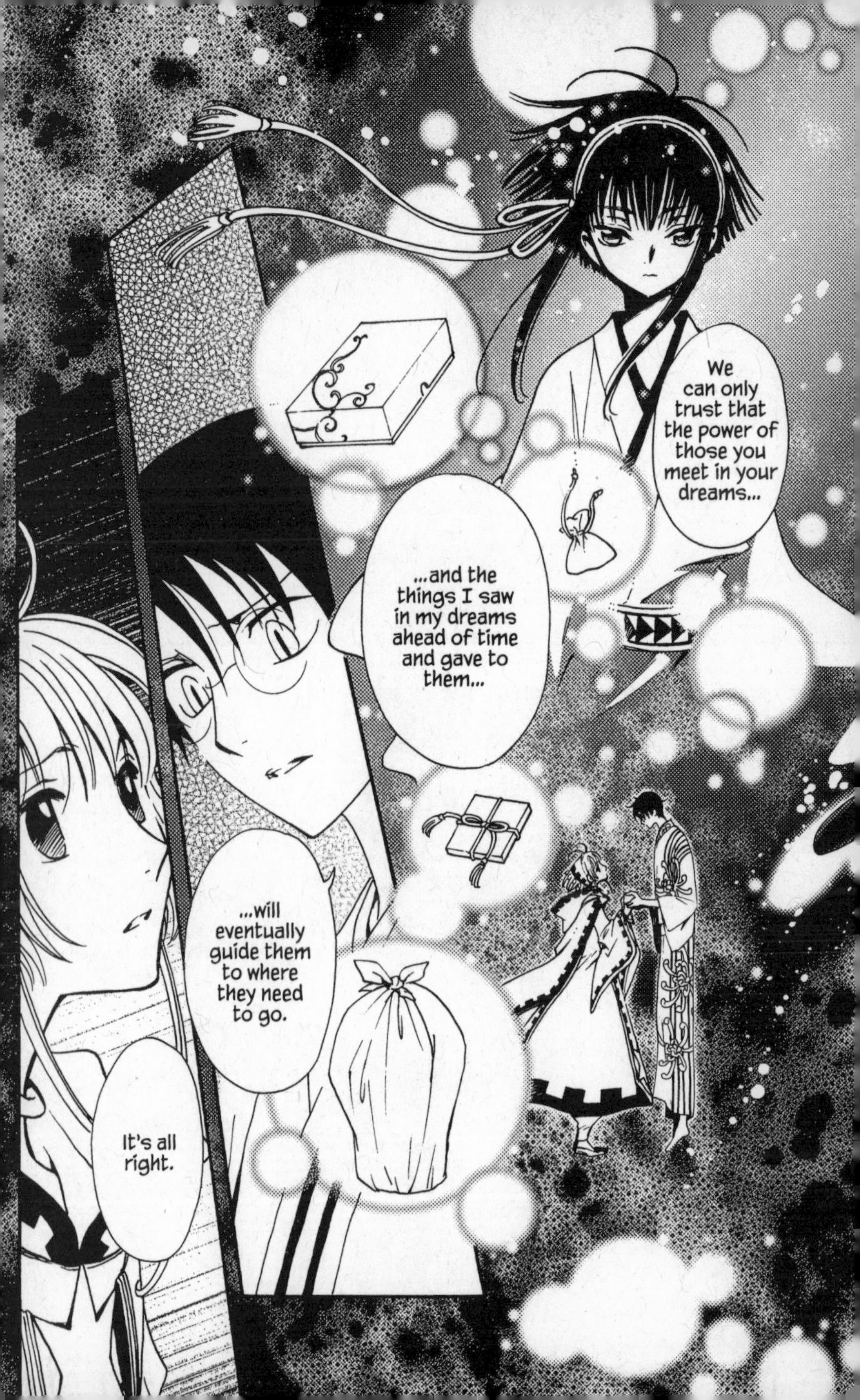
We can only trust that the power of those you meet in your dreams...
...and the things I saw in my dreams ahead of time and gave to them...
...will eventually guide them to where they need to go.
It's all right.

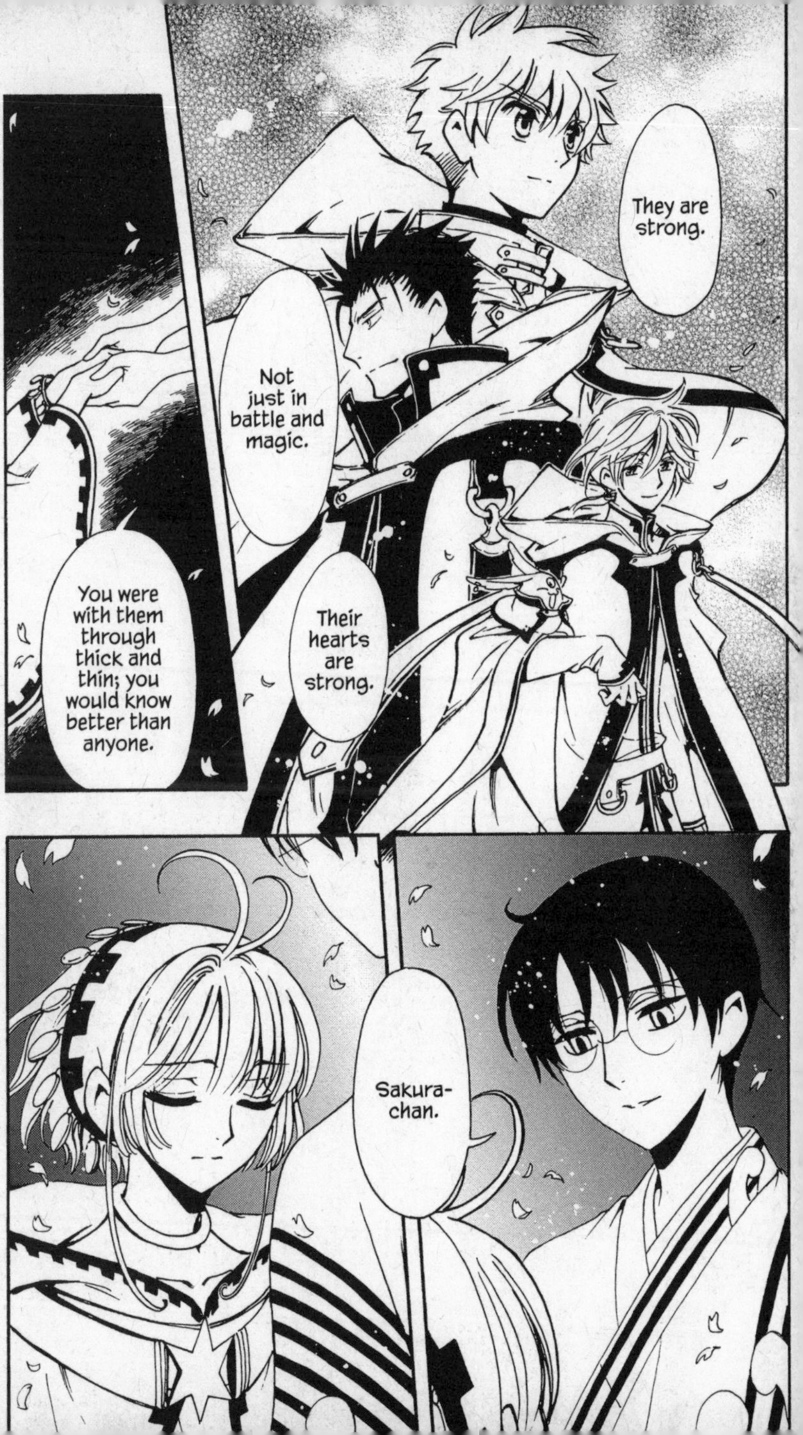
They are strong.
Not just in battle and magic.
Their hearts are strong.
You were with them through thick and thin; you would know better than anyone.
Sakura-chan.

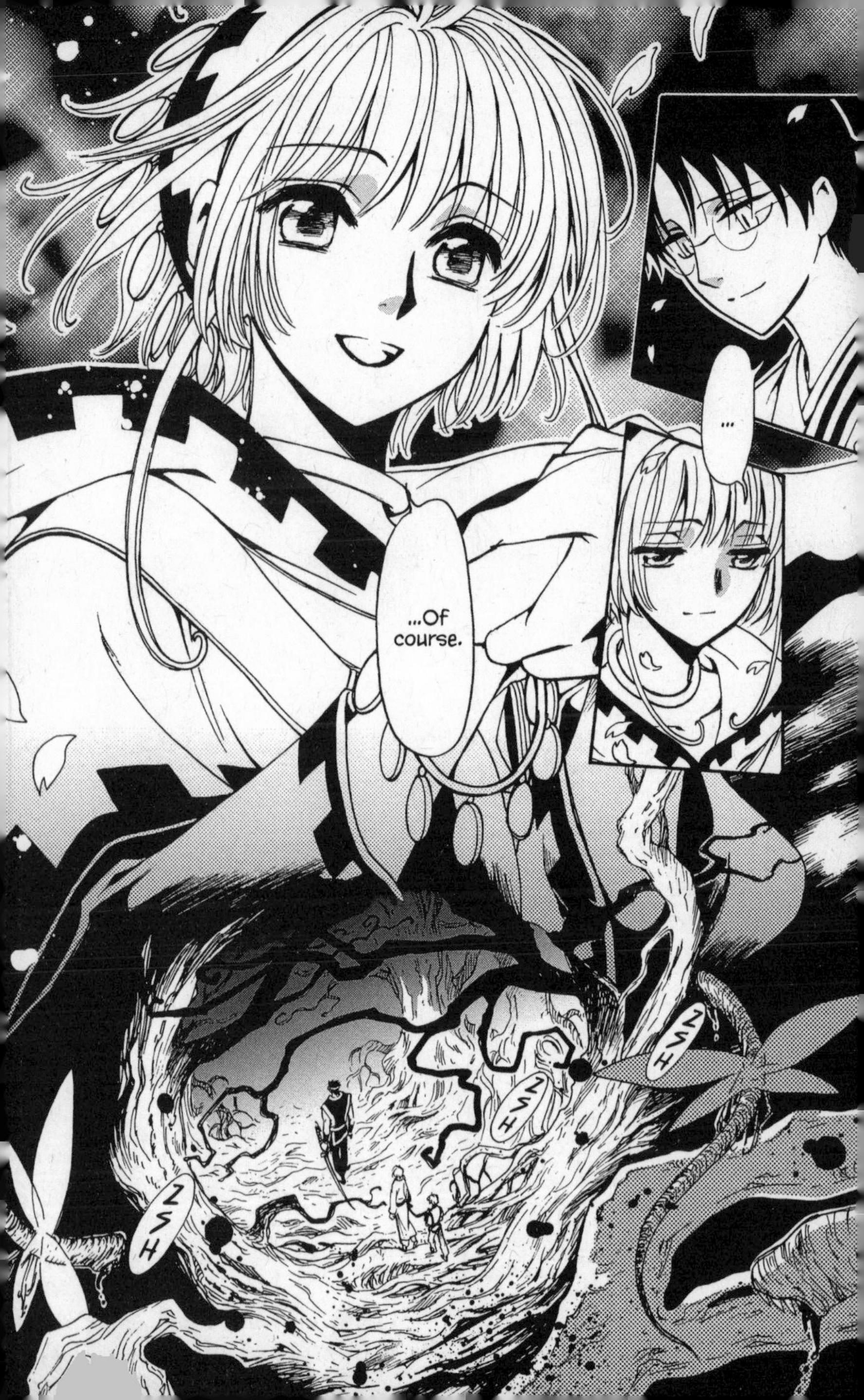
...
...Of course.
ZSSH
ZSSH
ZSSH

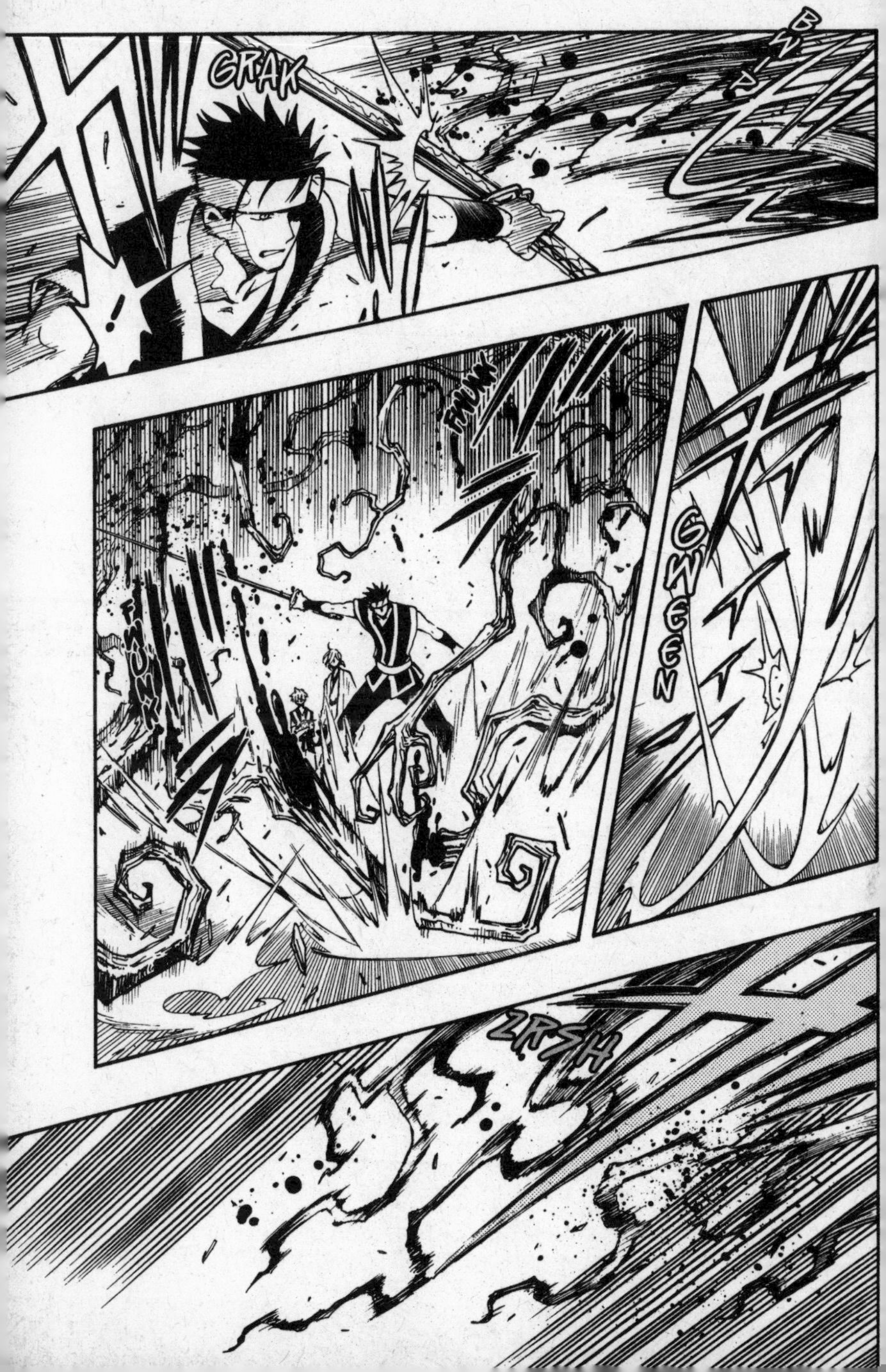
BWIP
GRAK
GWEEN
FWUNK
FWUNK
ZRSH

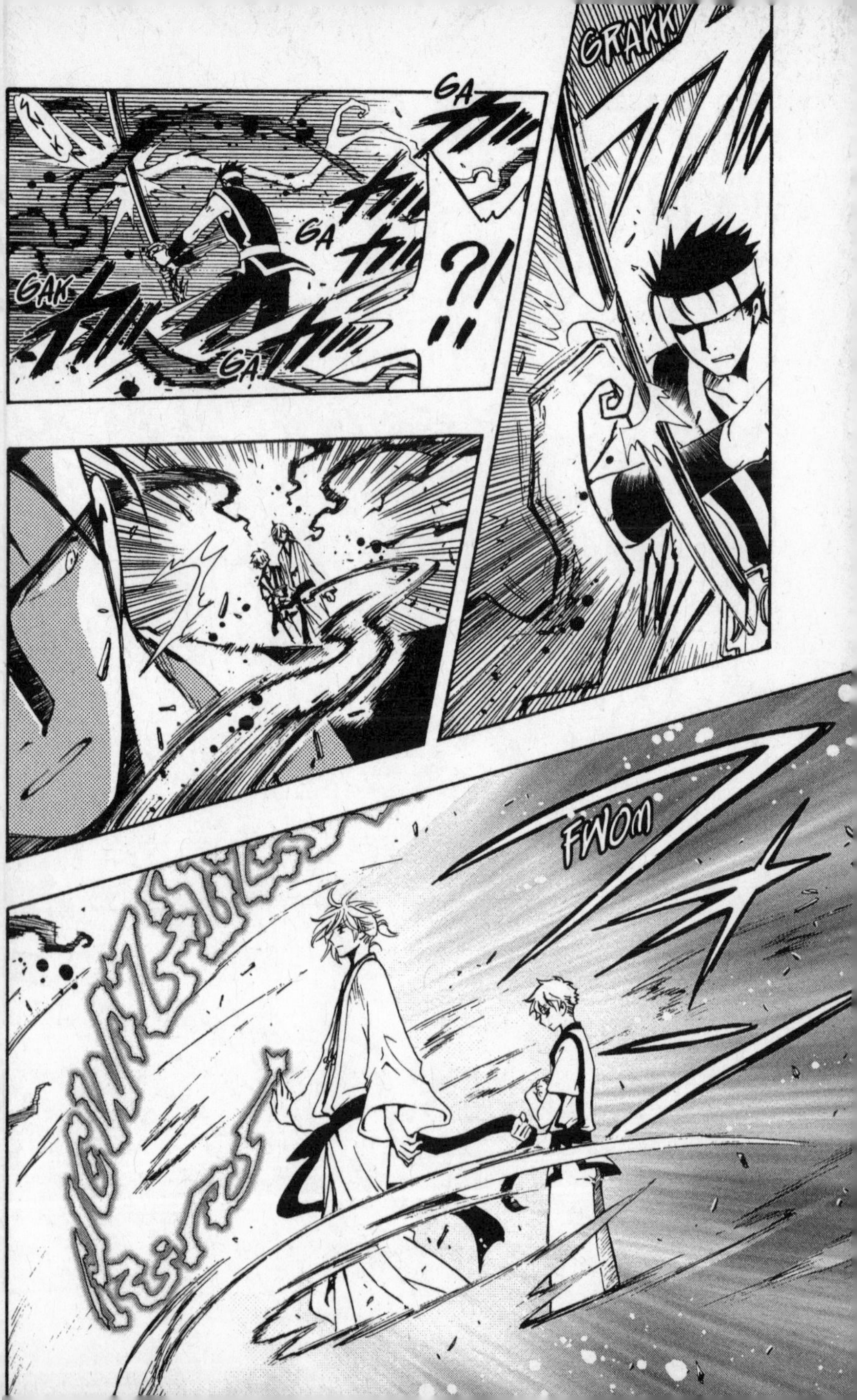
GRAKK
GA
GA
GAK
GA
?!!
FWOM

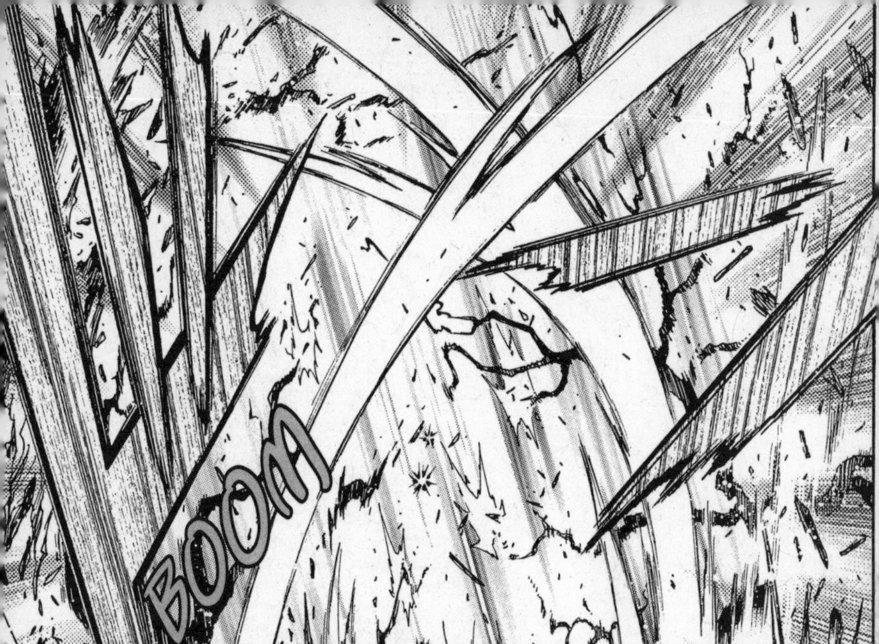
BOOM

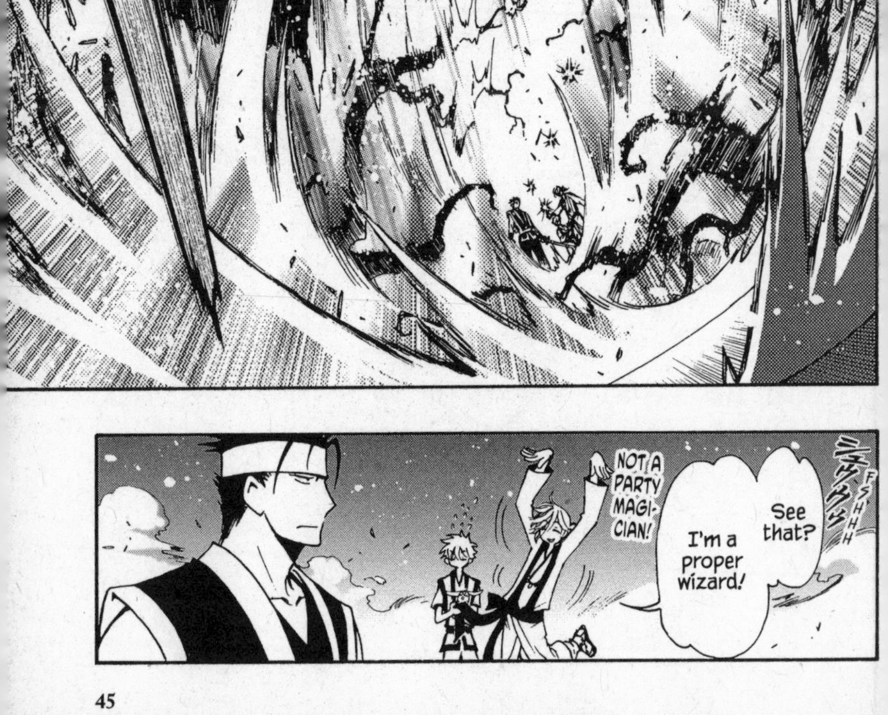
FSHHH
See that?
I'm a proper wizard!
NOT A PARTY MAGI-CIAN!

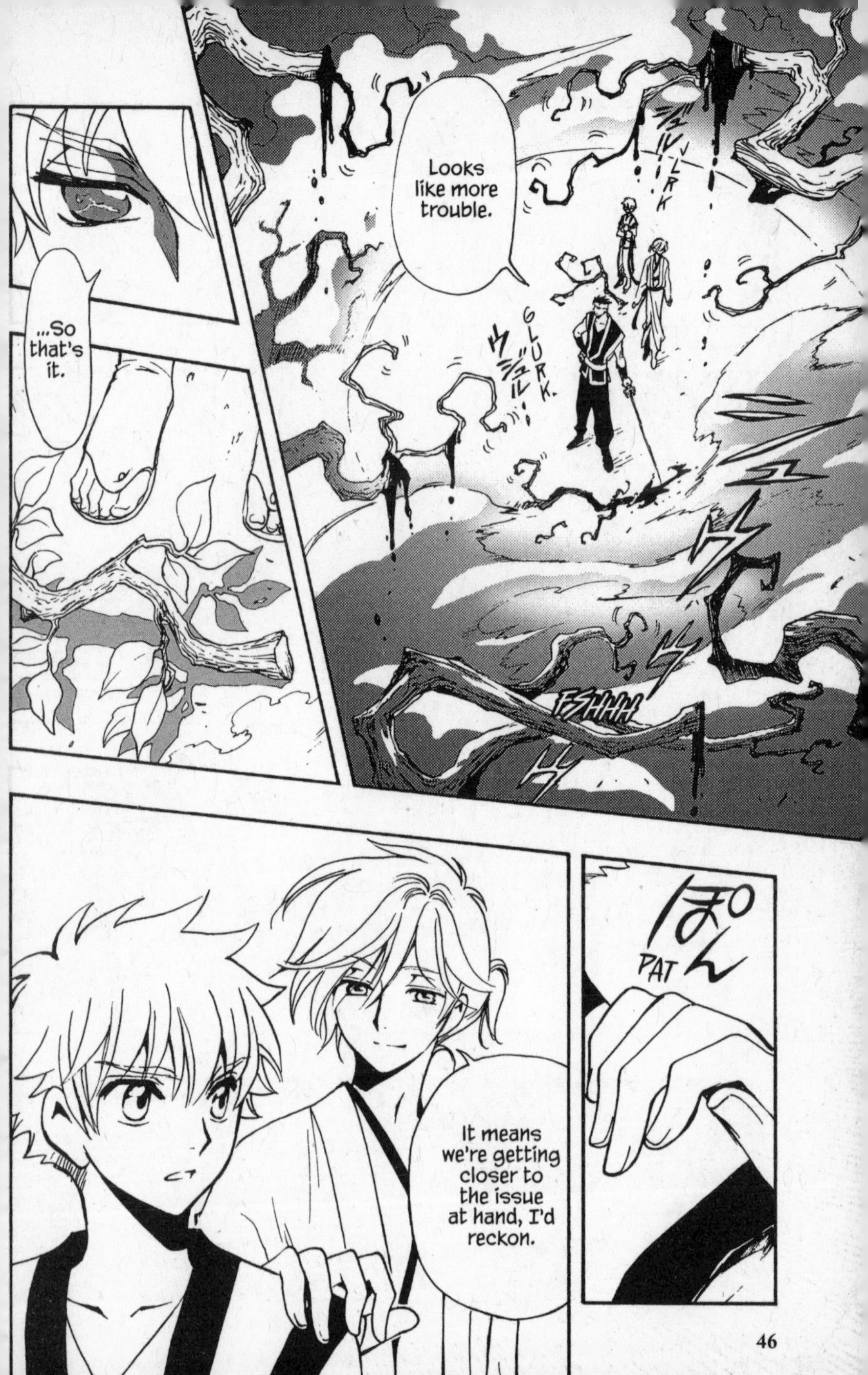
Looks like more trouble.
JLRK
GLURK.
FSHHH
...So that's it.
ぽん
PAT
It means we're getting closer to the issue at hand, I'd reckon.

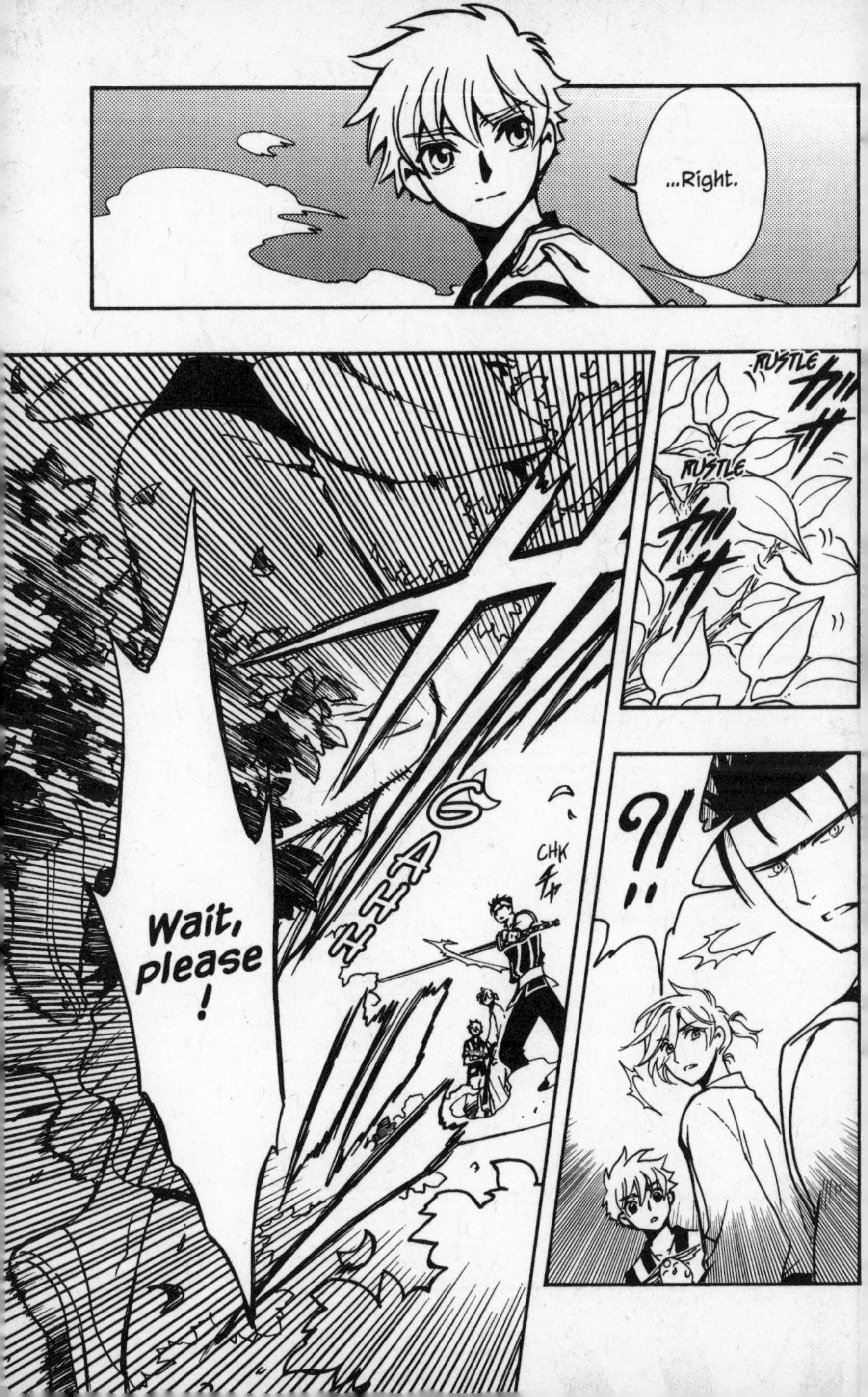
...Right.
RUSTLE
RUSTLE
?!!
GAHH
CHK
Wait, please!

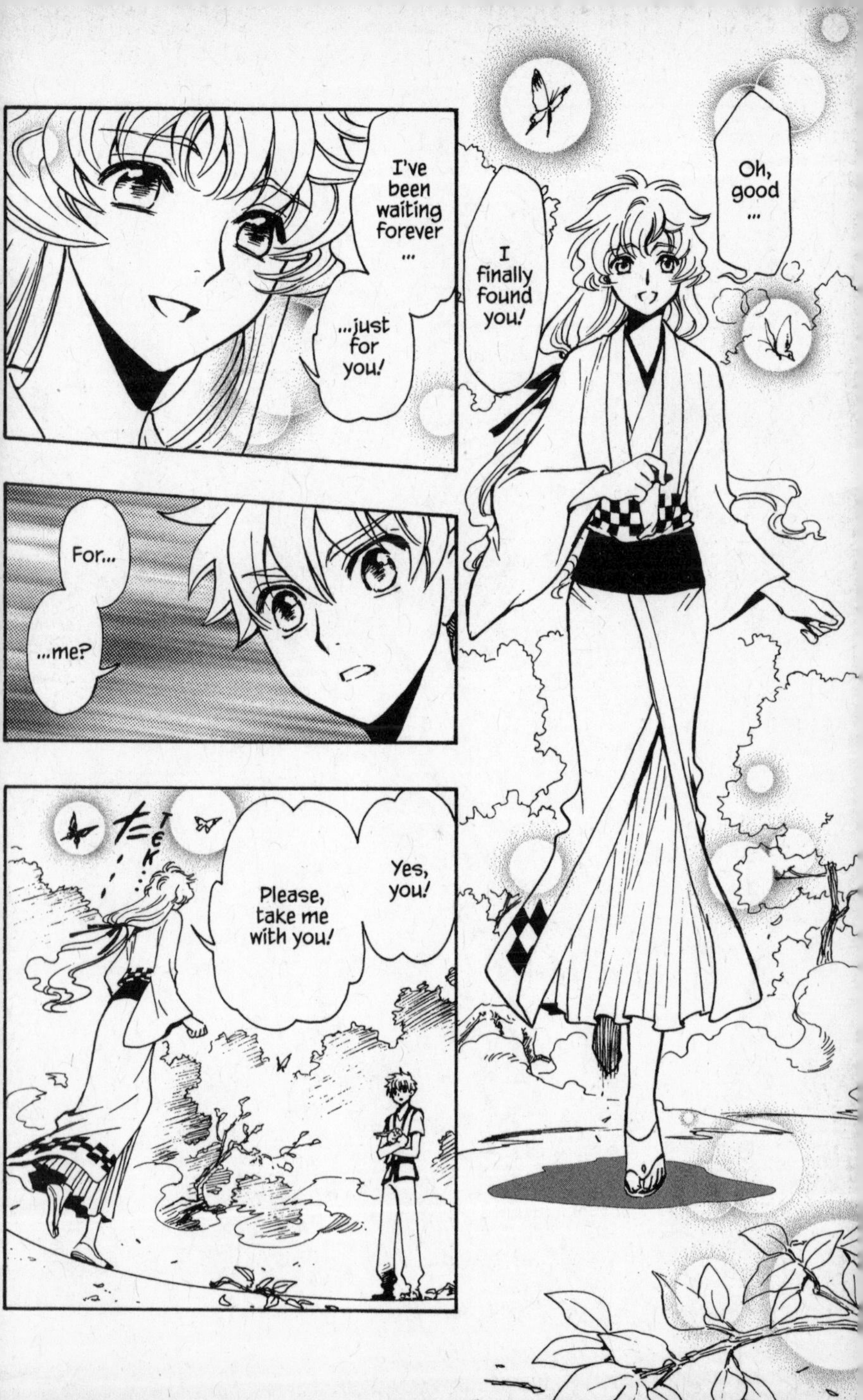
Oh, good ...
I finally found you!
I've been waiting forever ...
...just for you!
For...
...me?
TEK
Yes, you!
Please, take me with you!

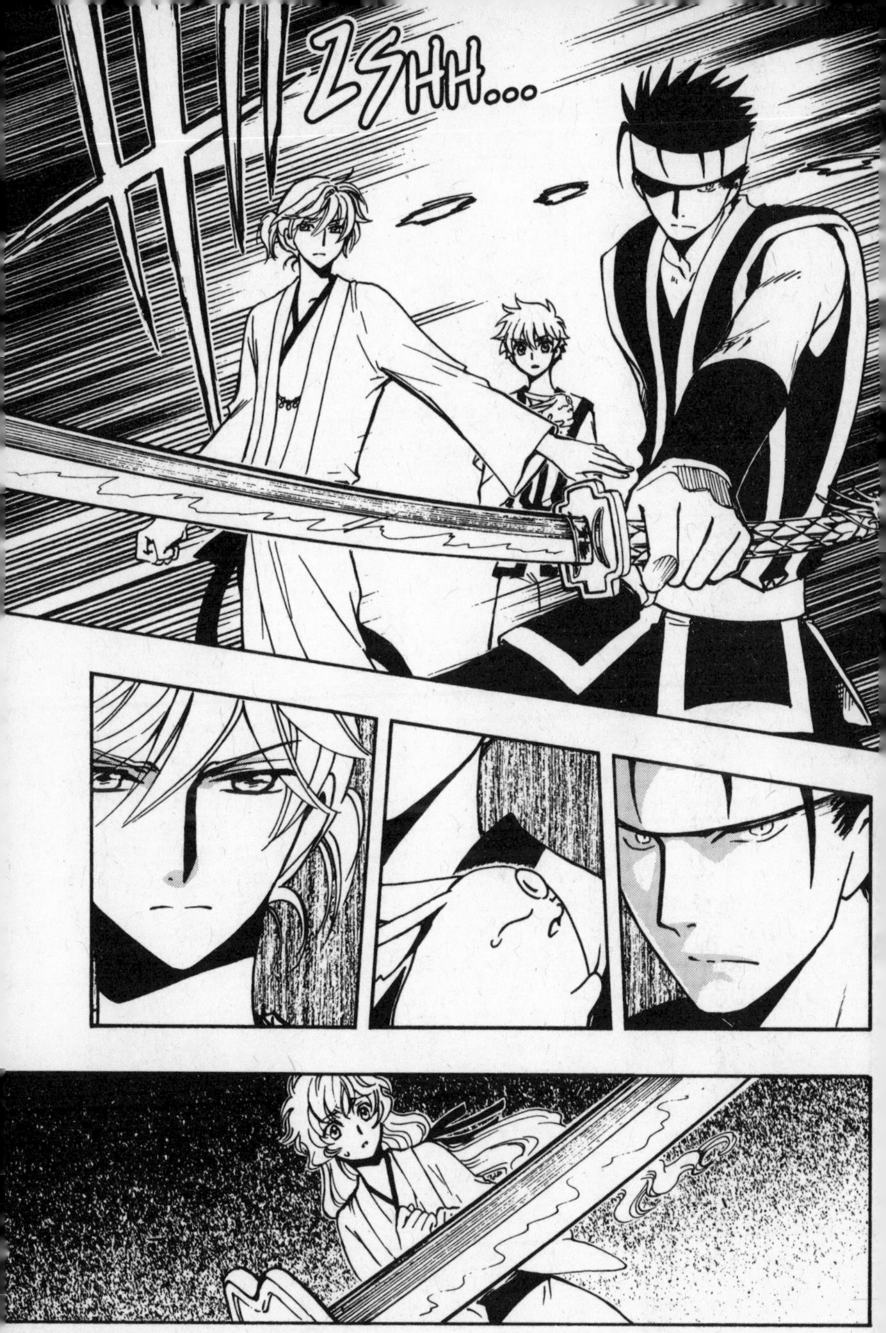
ZSHH...

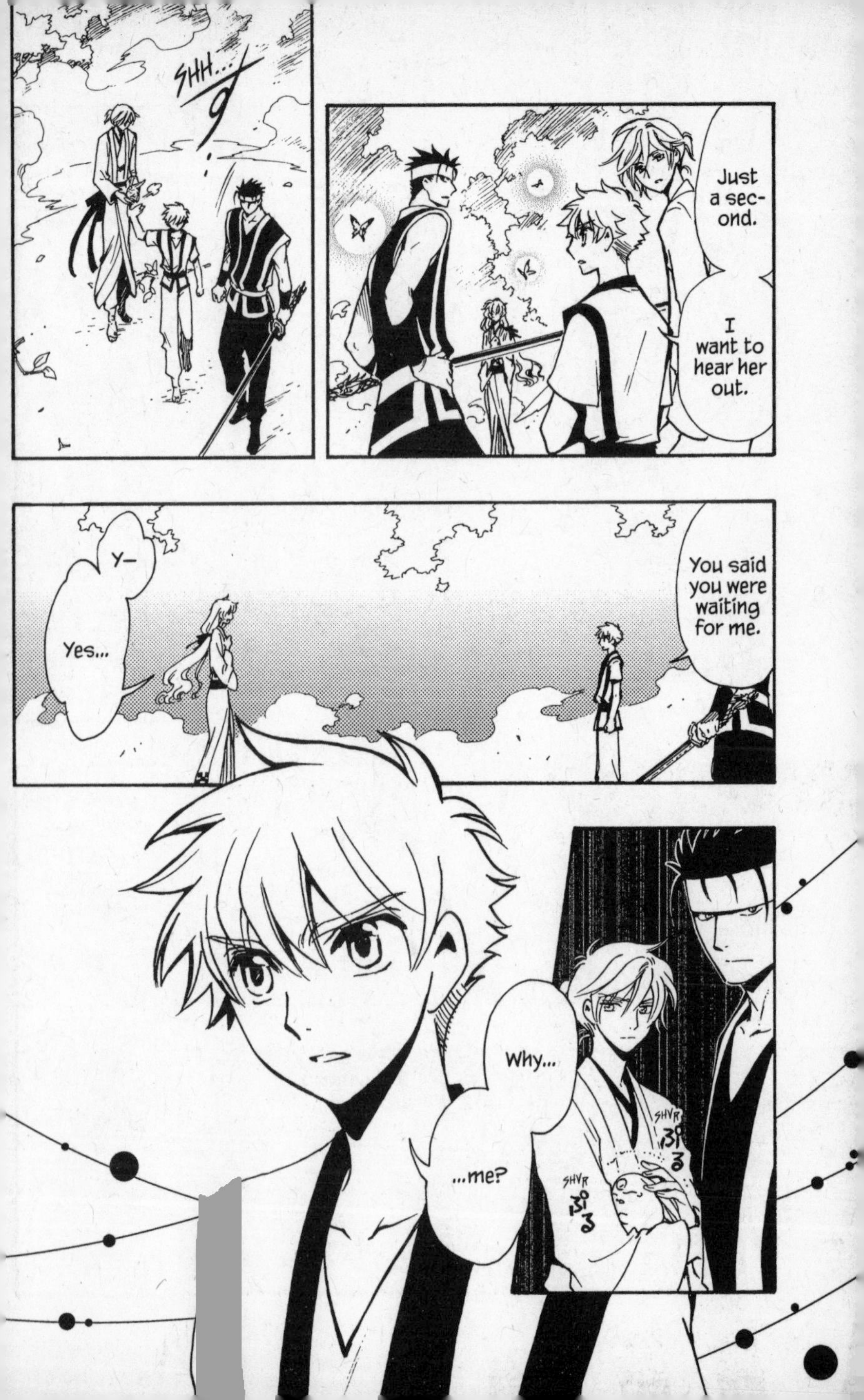
Just a second.
I want to hear her out.
SHH...
You said you were waiting for me.
Y—
Yes...
Why...
...me?
SHVR ぷる
SHVR ぷる

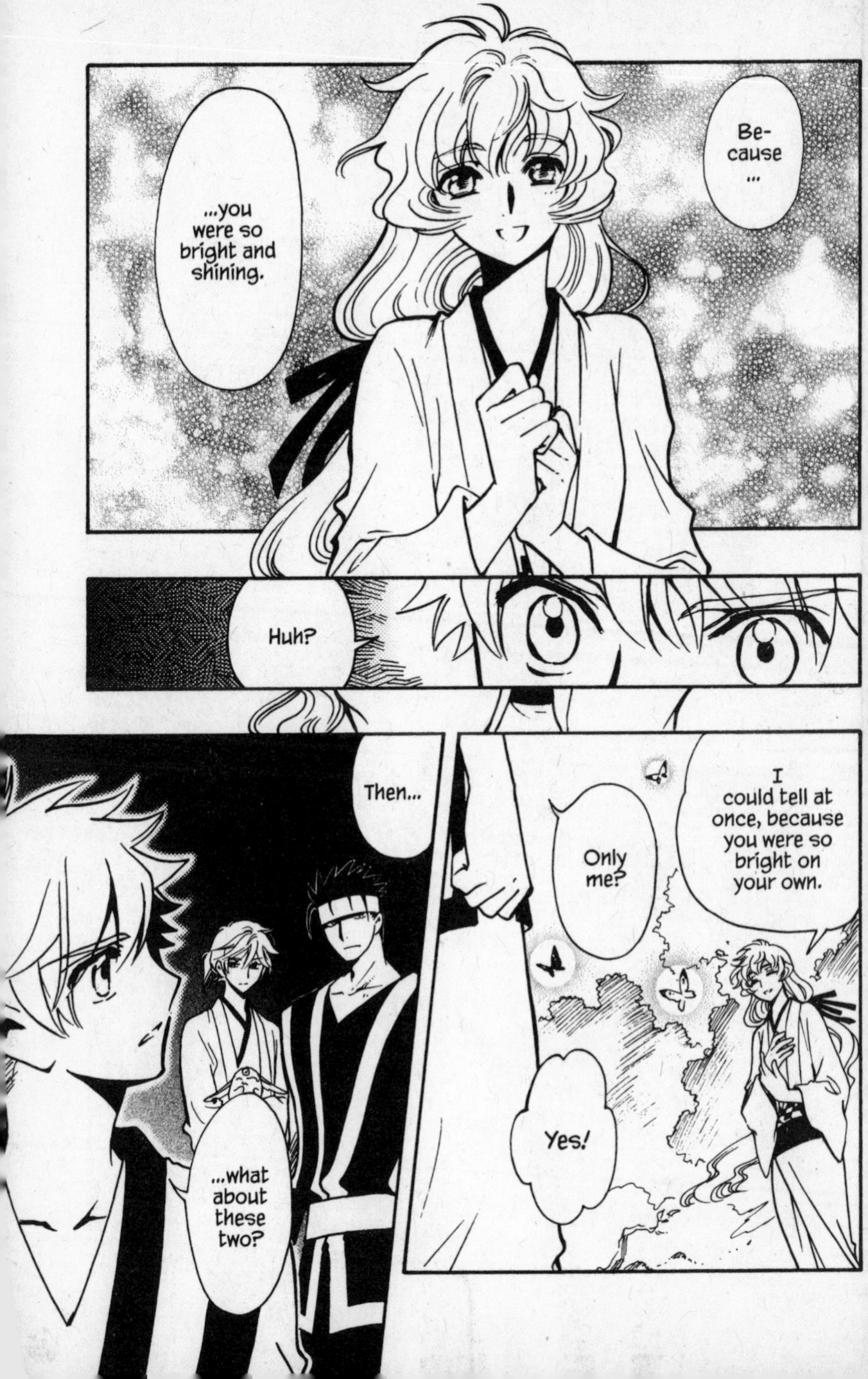
Be-cause...
...you were so bright and shining.
Huh?
I could tell at once, because you were so bright on your own.
Only me?
Yes!
Then...
...what about these two?

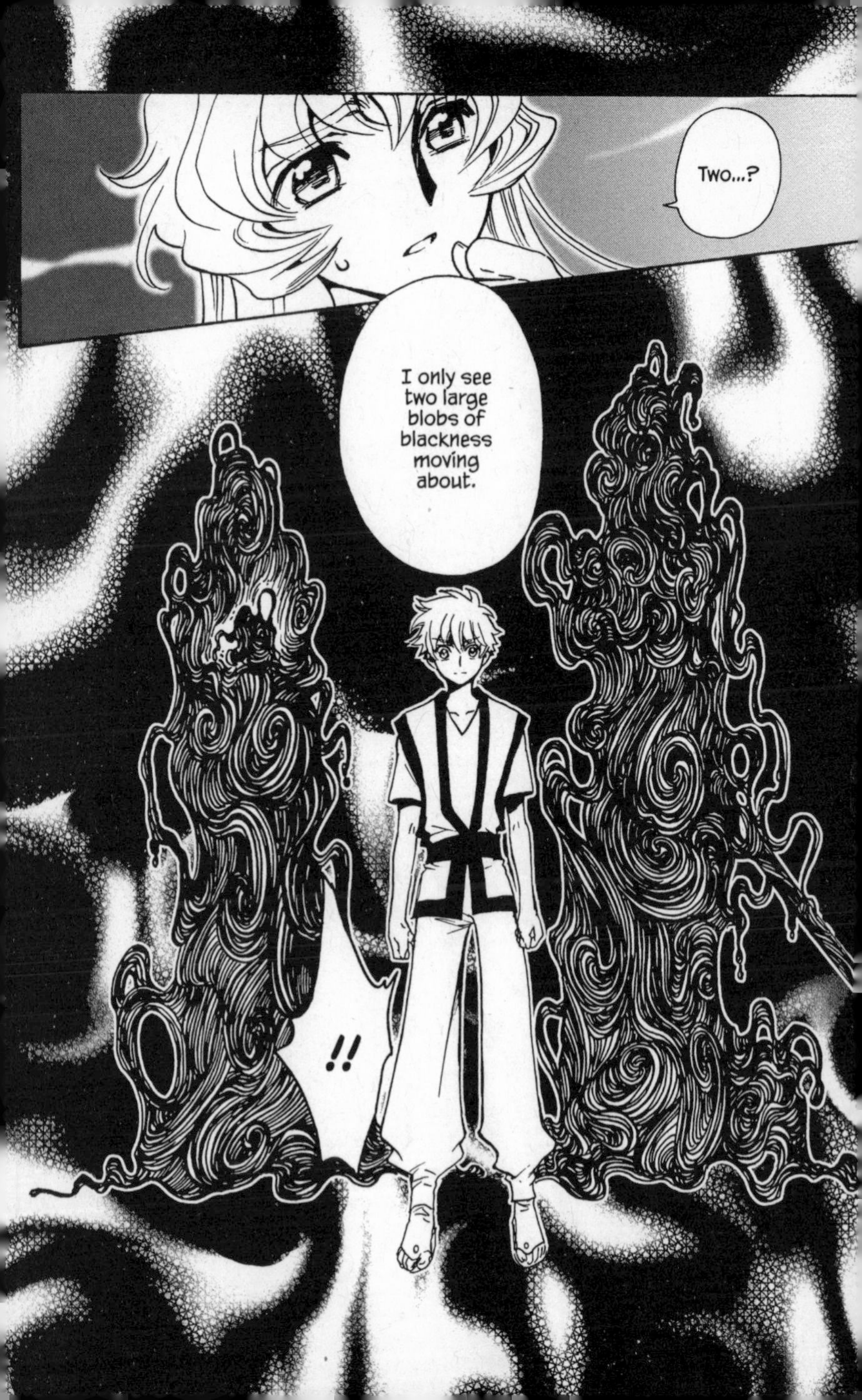
Two...?
I only see two large blobs of blackness moving about.
!!

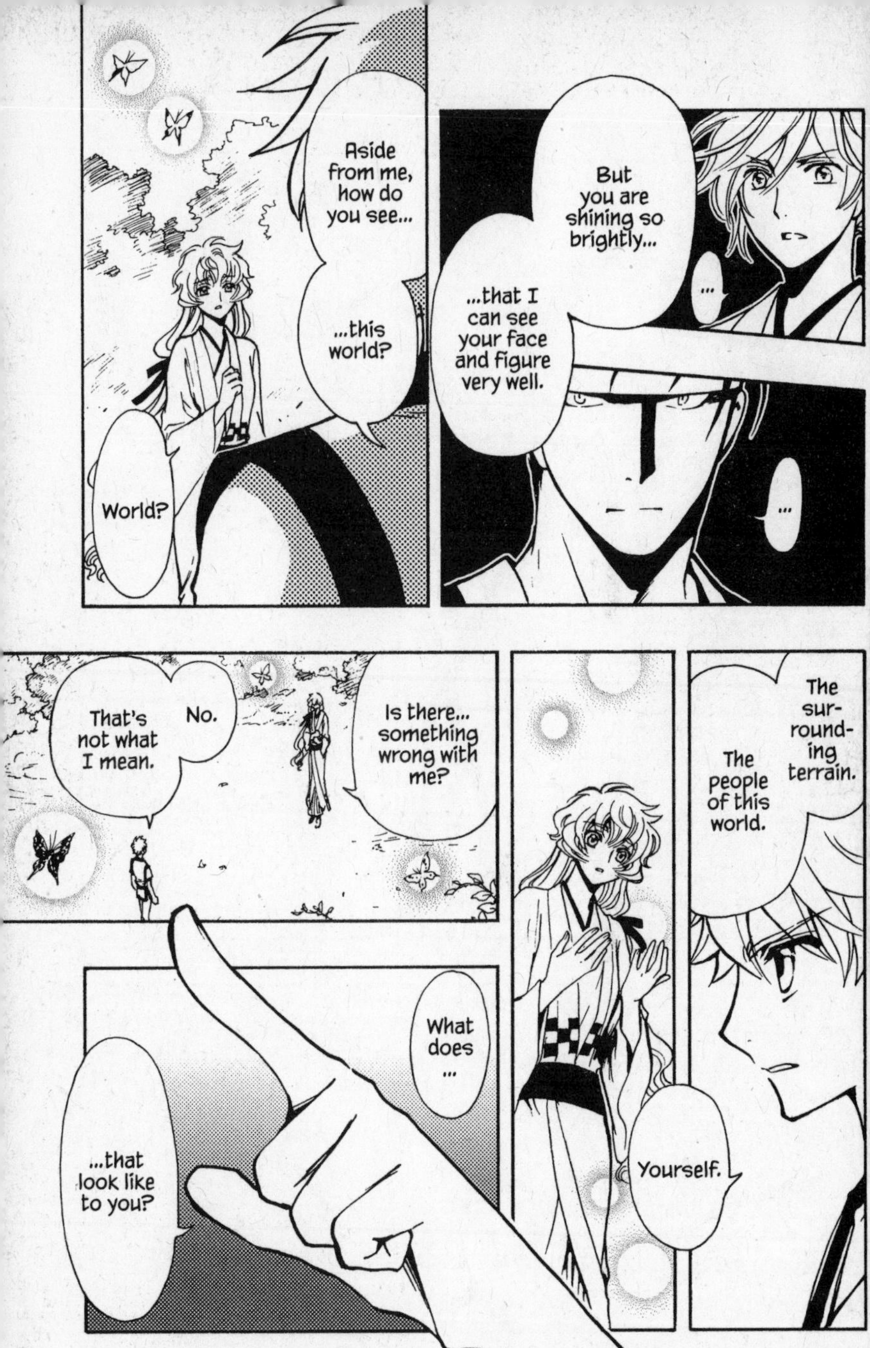

But you are shining so brightly...
...that I can see your face and figure very well.
...
...
Aside from me, how do you see...
...this world?
World?
The sur-rounding terrain.
The people of this world.
Yourself.
Is there... something wrong with me?
No.
That's not what I mean.
What does ...
...that look like to you?

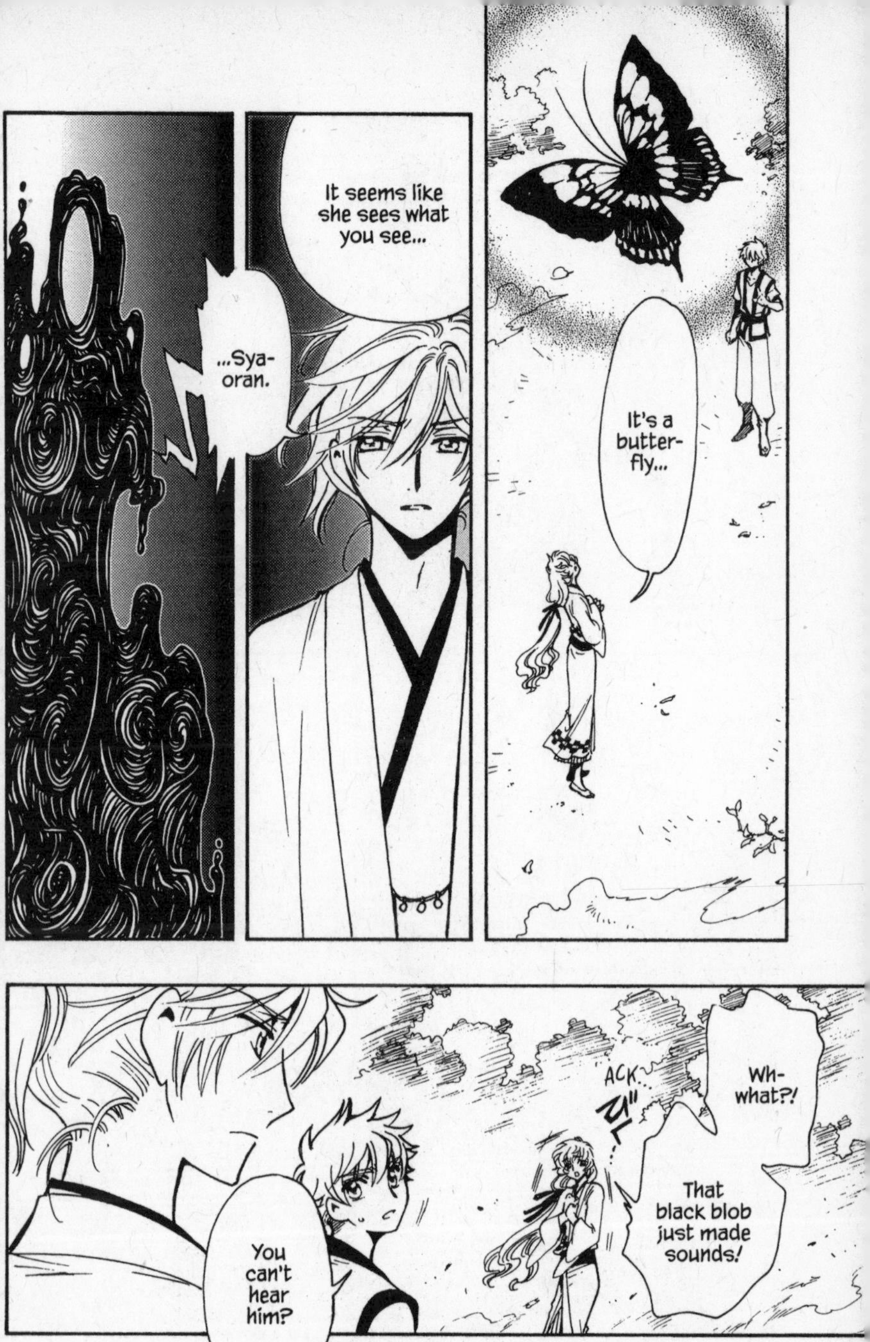
It's a butterfly...
It seems like she sees what you see...
...Sya-oran.
Wh-what?!
ACK...
That black blob just made sounds!
You can't hear him?

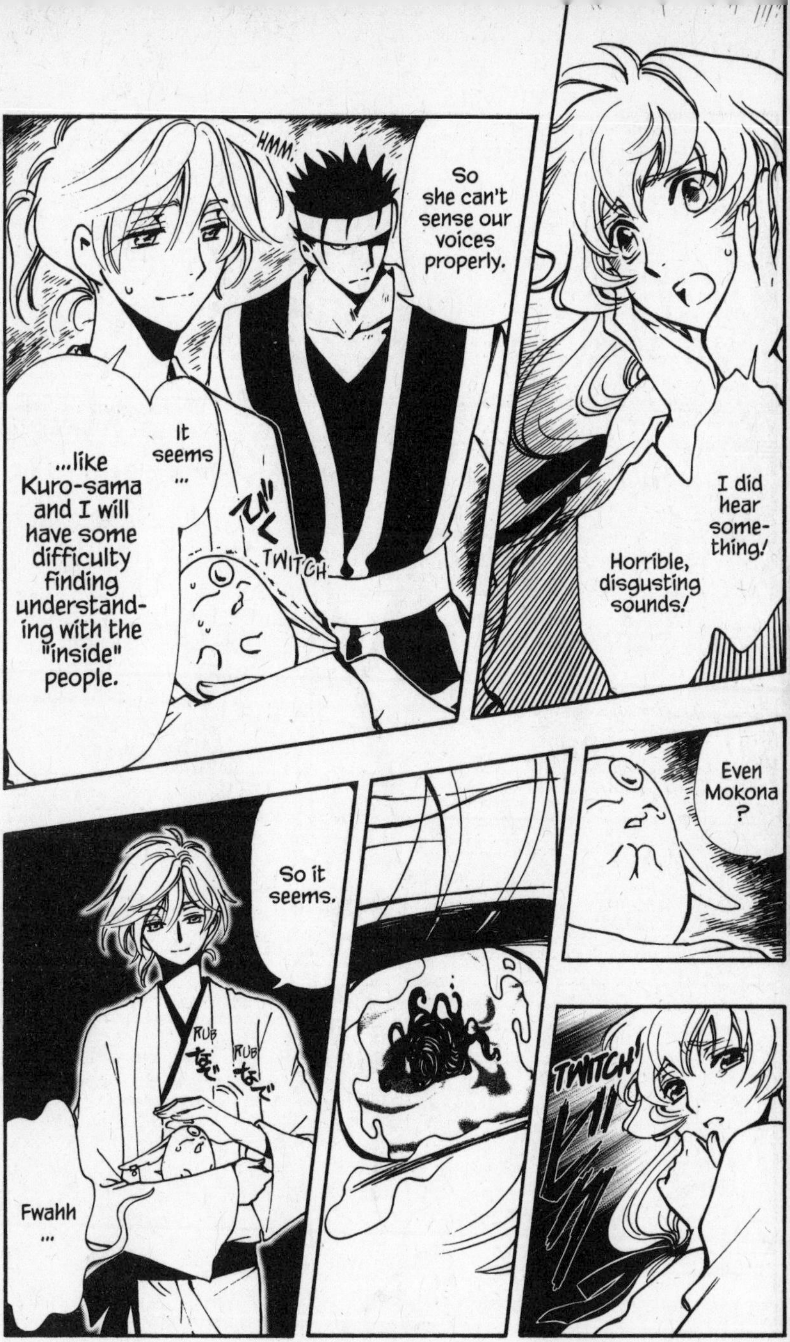
I did hear some-thing!
Horrible, disgusting sounds!
So she can't sense our voices properly.
HMM.
It seems ...
...like Kuro-sama and I will have some difficulty finding understand-ing with the "inside" people.
びく
TWITCH
Even Mokona ?
TWITCH
So it seems.
RUB
なで
RUB
なで
Fwahh ...

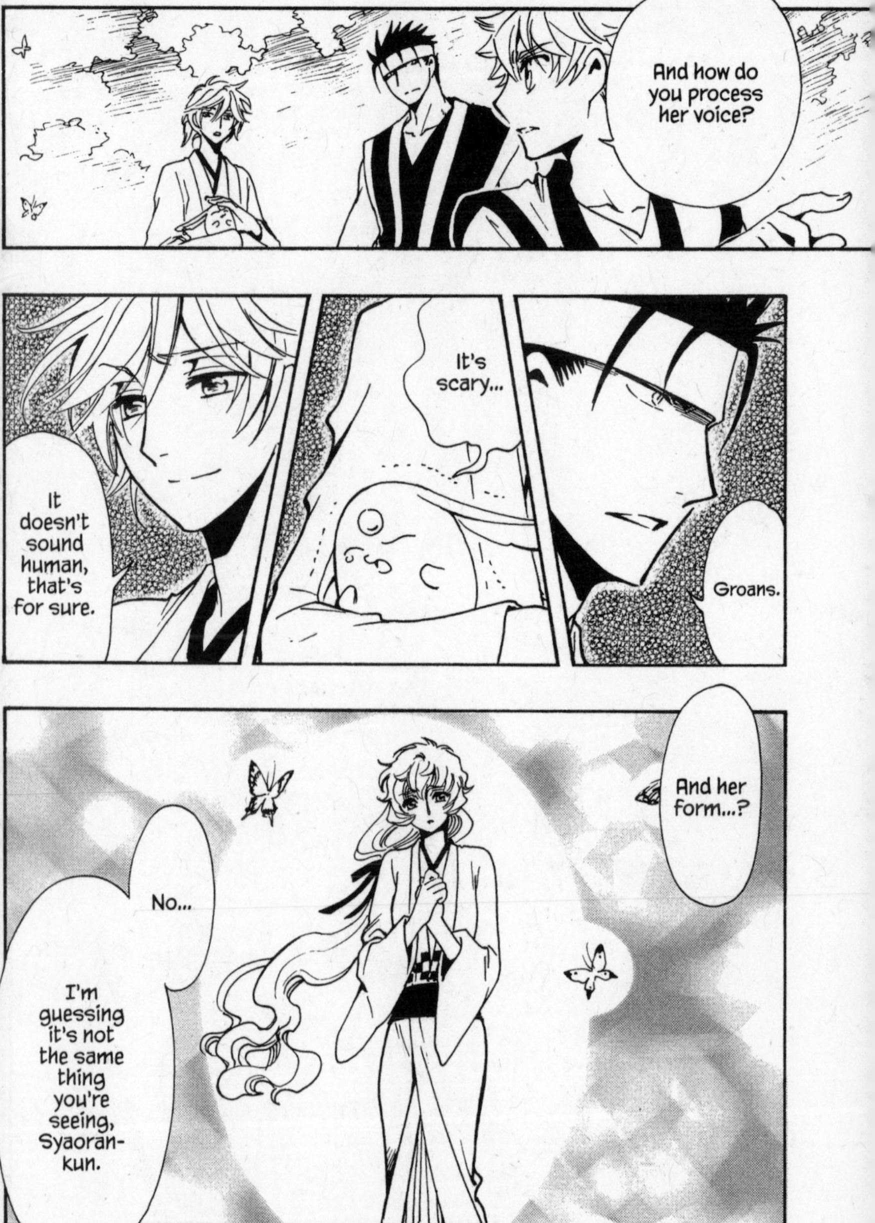
And how do you process her voice?
Groans.
It's scary...
It doesn't sound human, that's for sure.
And her form...?
No...
I'm guessing it's not the same thing you're seeing, Syaoran-kun.

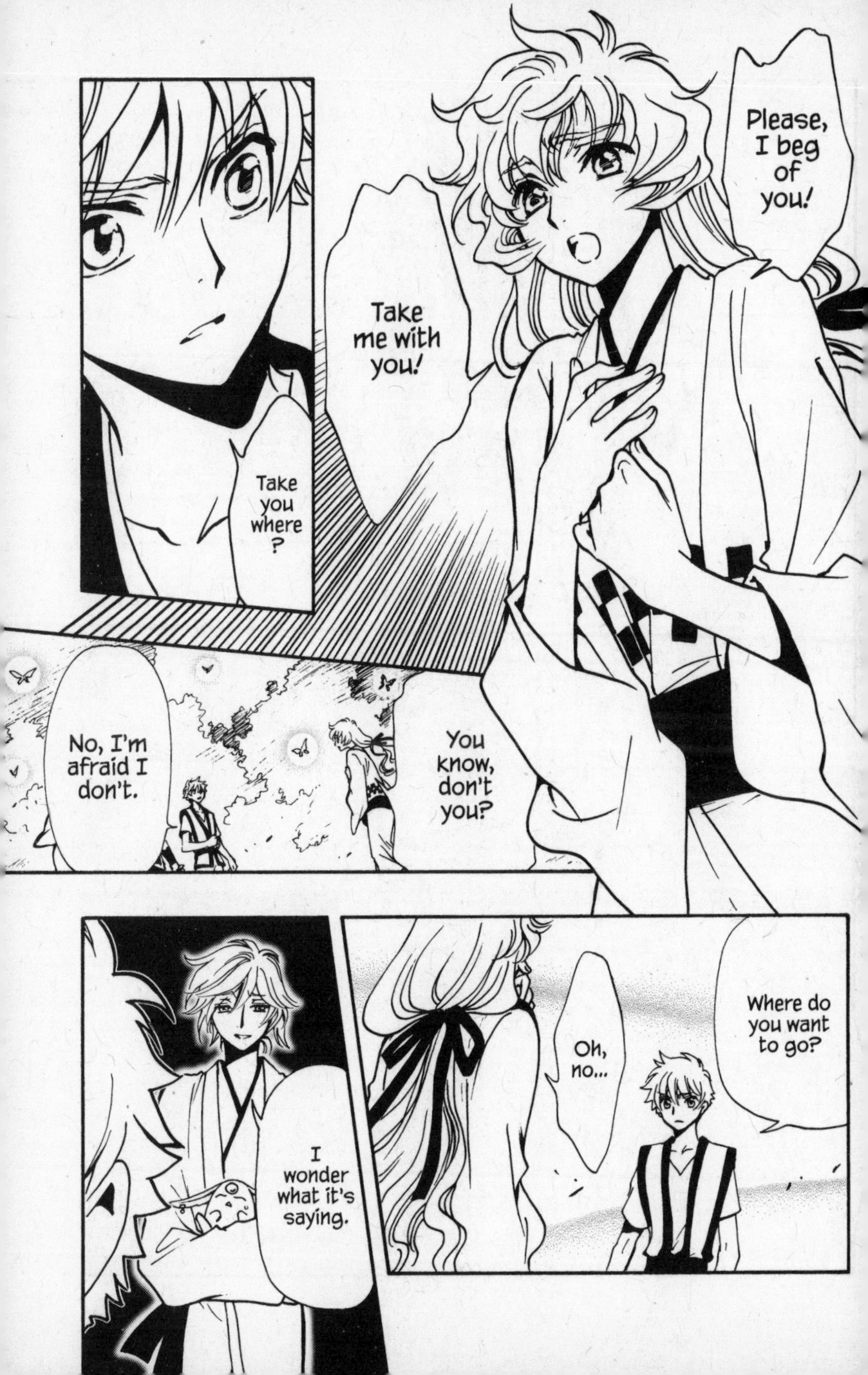
Please, I beg of you!
Take me with you!
Take you where?
You know, don't you?
No, I'm afraid I don't.
Where do you want to go?
Oh, no...
I wonder what it's saying.

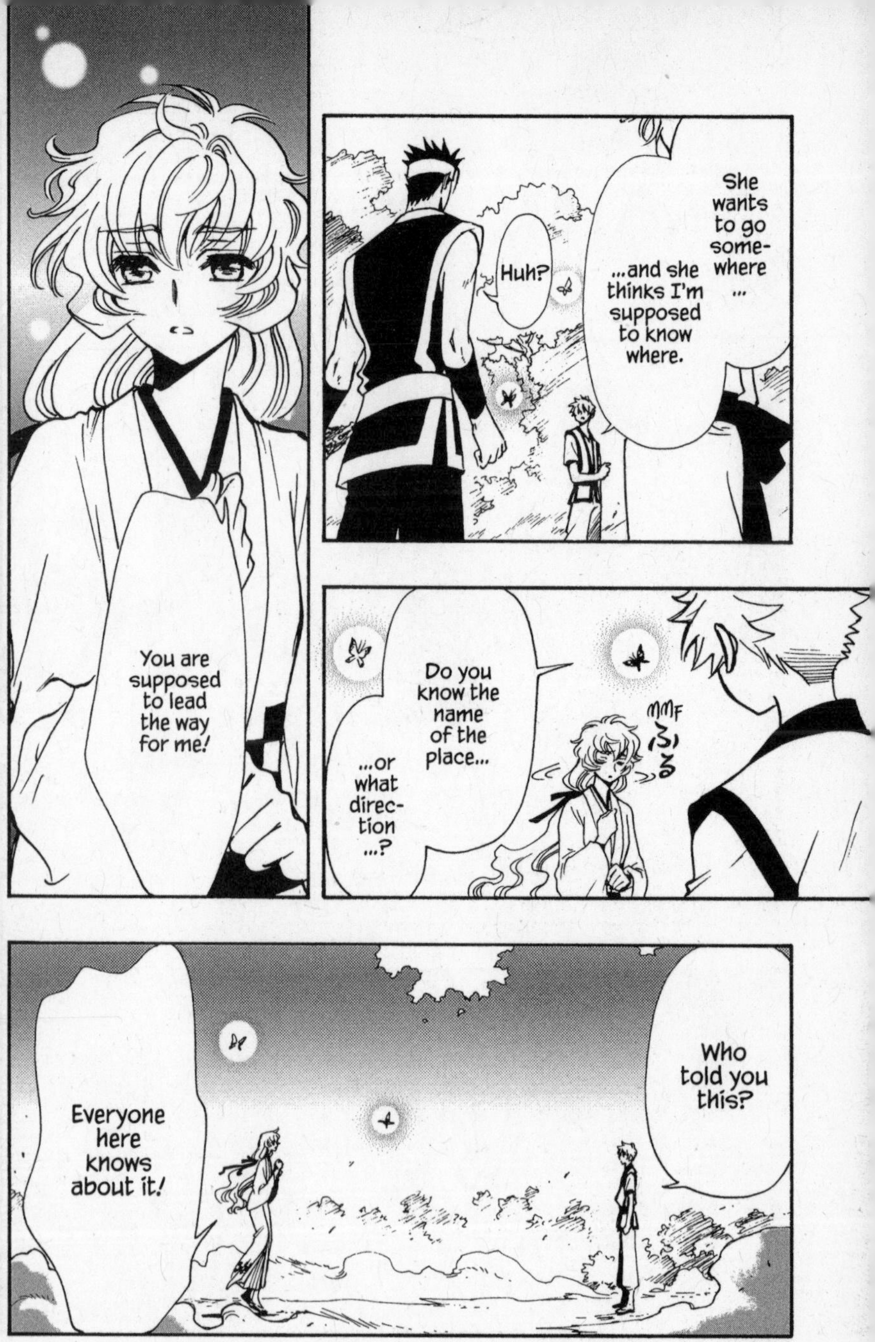
She wants to go some-where ...
...and she thinks I'm supposed to know where.
Huh?
Do you know the name of the place...
...or what direc-tion ...?
MMF
ふる
You are supposed to lead the way for me!
Who told you this?
Everyone here knows about it!

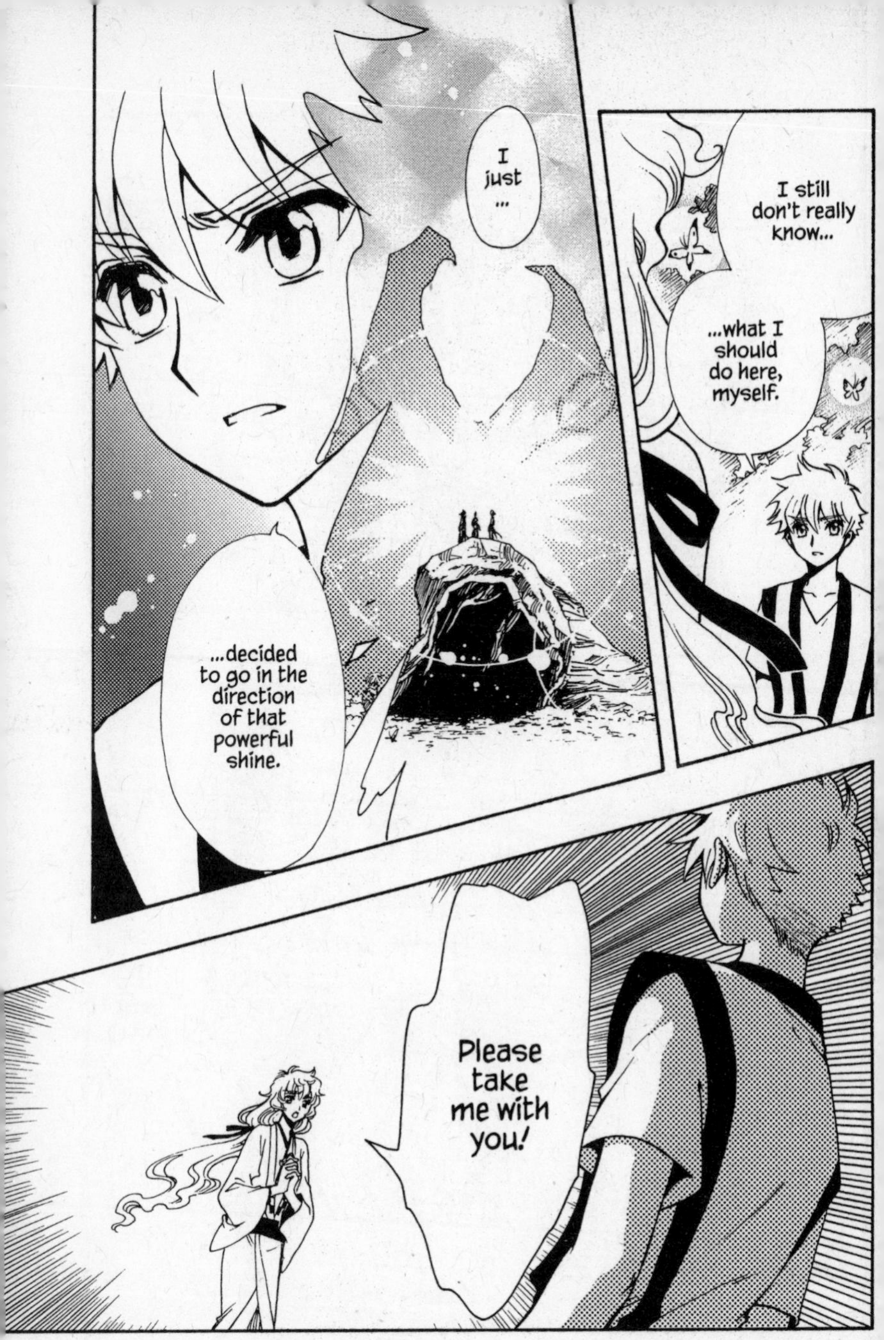
I still don't really know...
...what I should do here, myself.
I just ...
...decided to go in the direction of that powerful shine.
Please take me with you!

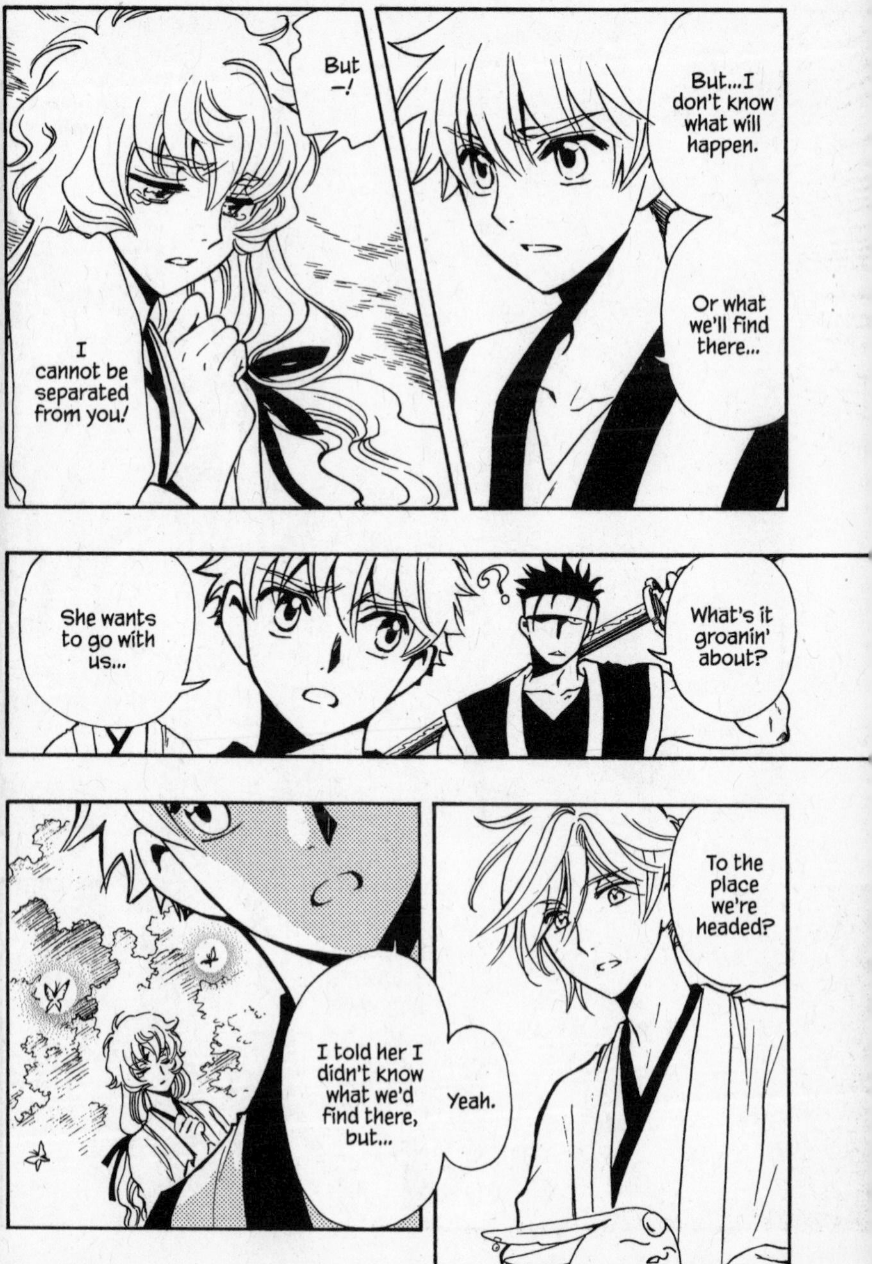
But...I don't know what will happen.
Or what we'll find there...
But —!
I cannot be separated from you!
What's it groanin' about?
She wants to go with us...
To the place we're headed?
Yeah.
I told her I didn't know what we'd find there, but...

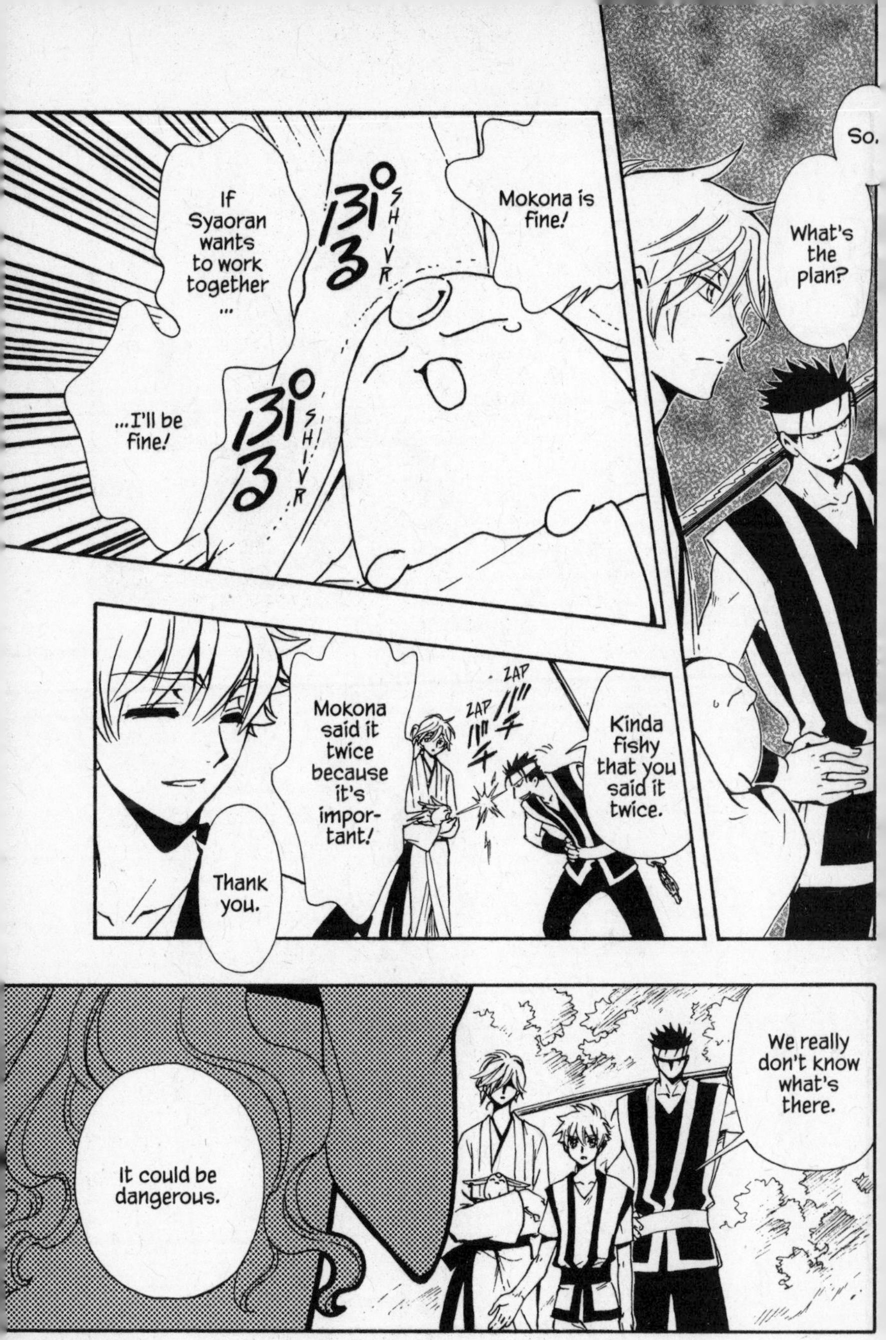
So.
What's the plan?
Mokona is fine!
SHIVR
SHIVR
If Syaoran wants to work together ...
...I'll be fine!
Kinda fishy that you said it twice.
ZAP
ZAP
Mokona said it twice because it's important!
Thank you.
We really don't know what's there.
It could be dangerous.

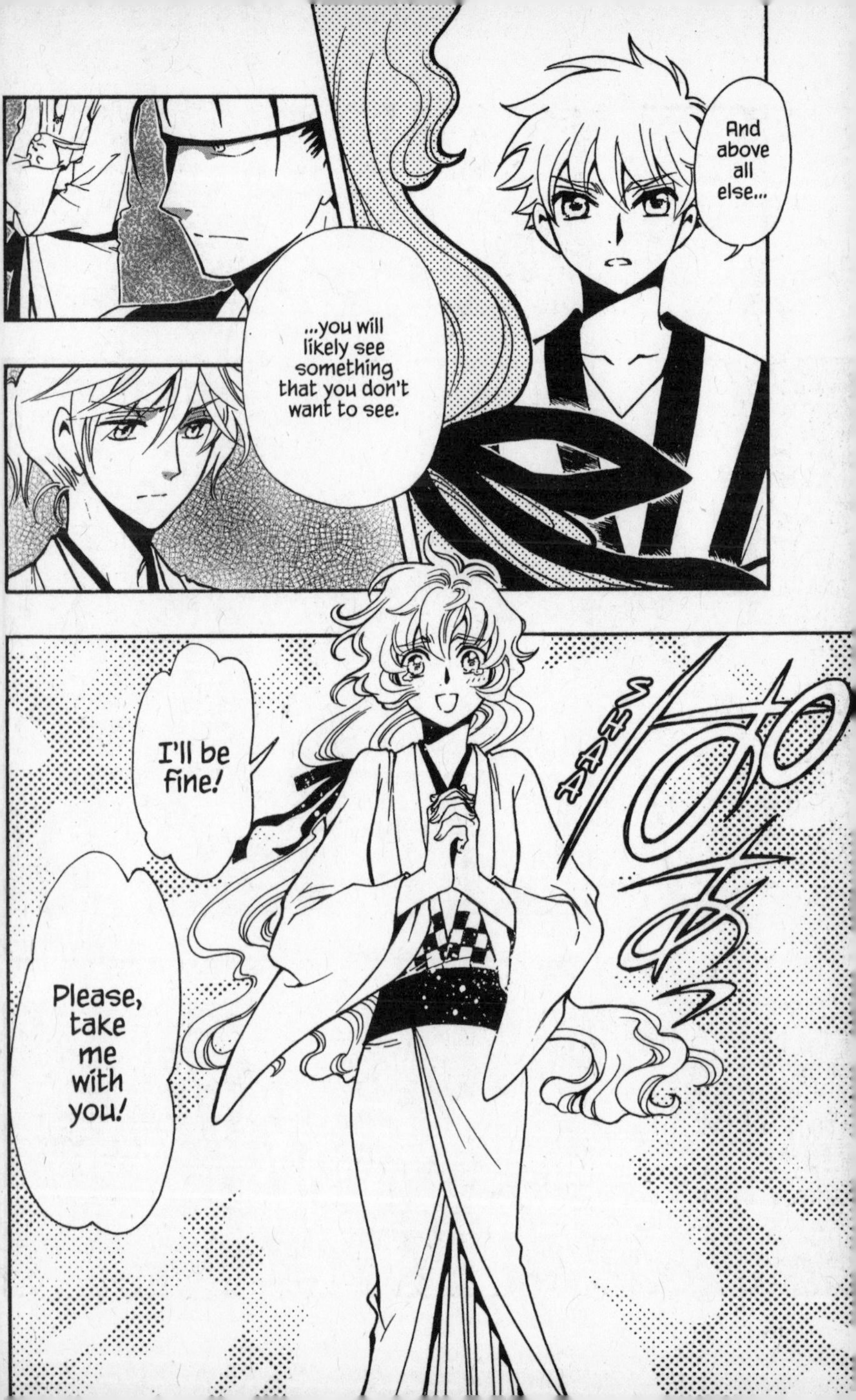
And above all else...
...you will likely see something that you don't want to see.
SHAA
I'll be fine!
Please, take me with you!

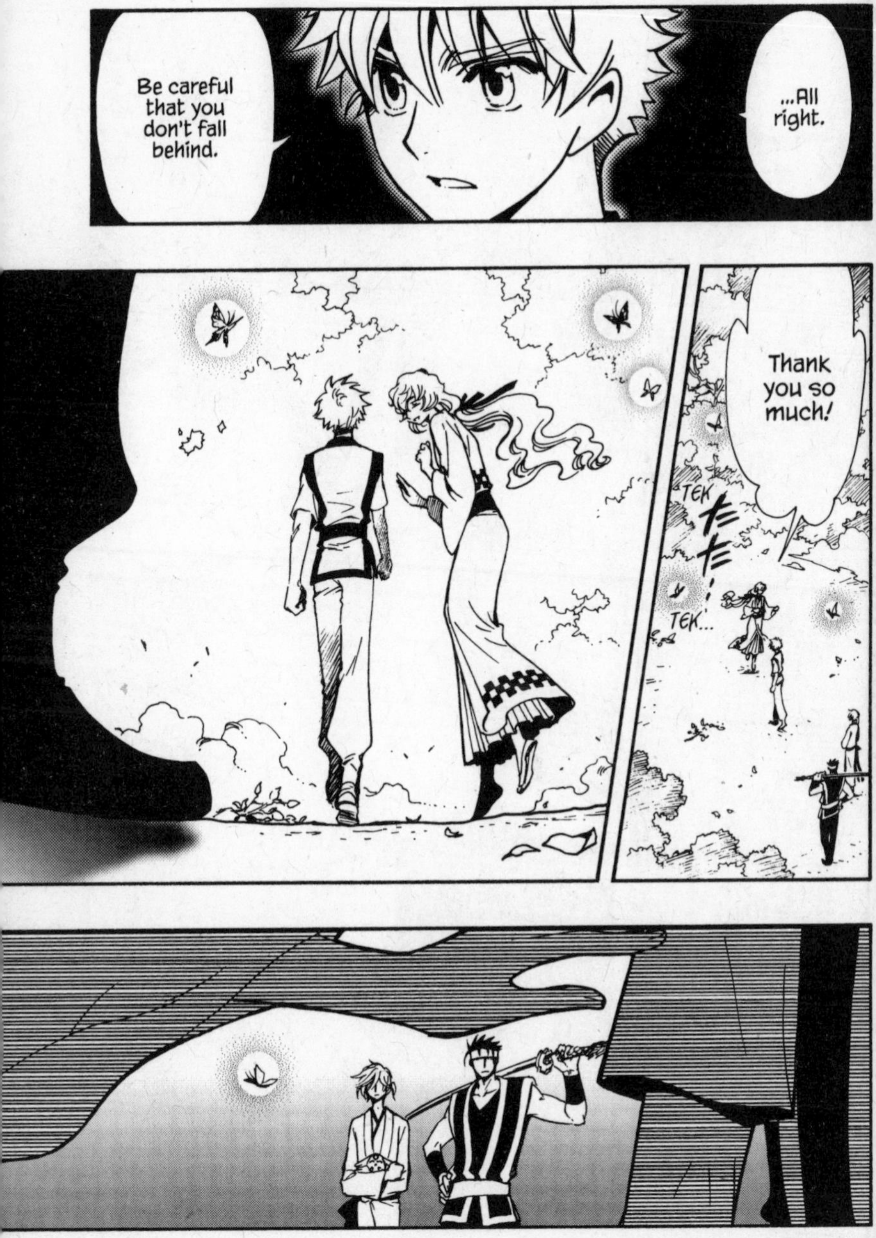
Be careful that you don't fall behind.
...All right.
Thank you so much!
TEK
TEK...

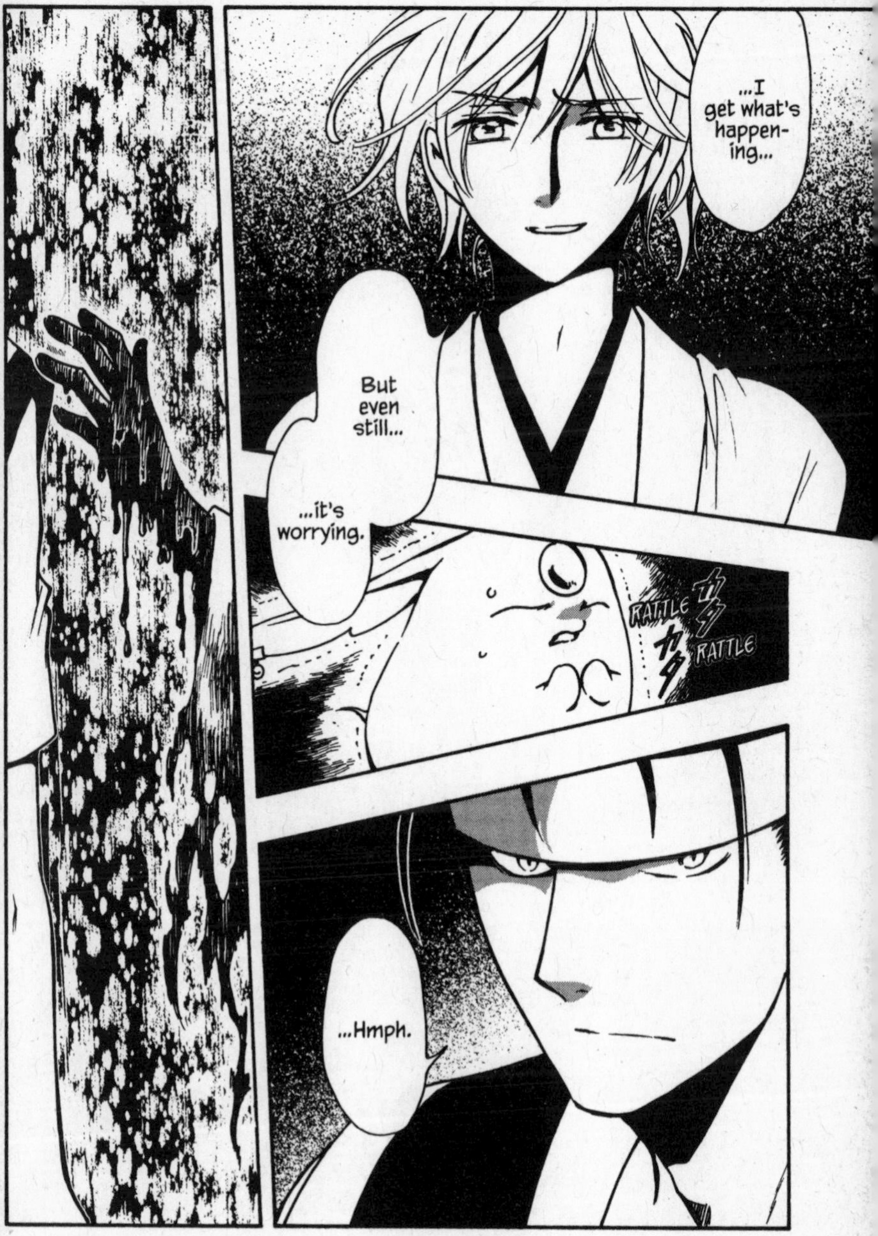
...I get what's happen-ing...
But even still...
...it's worrying.
RATTLE カタ
カタ RATTLE
...Hmph.

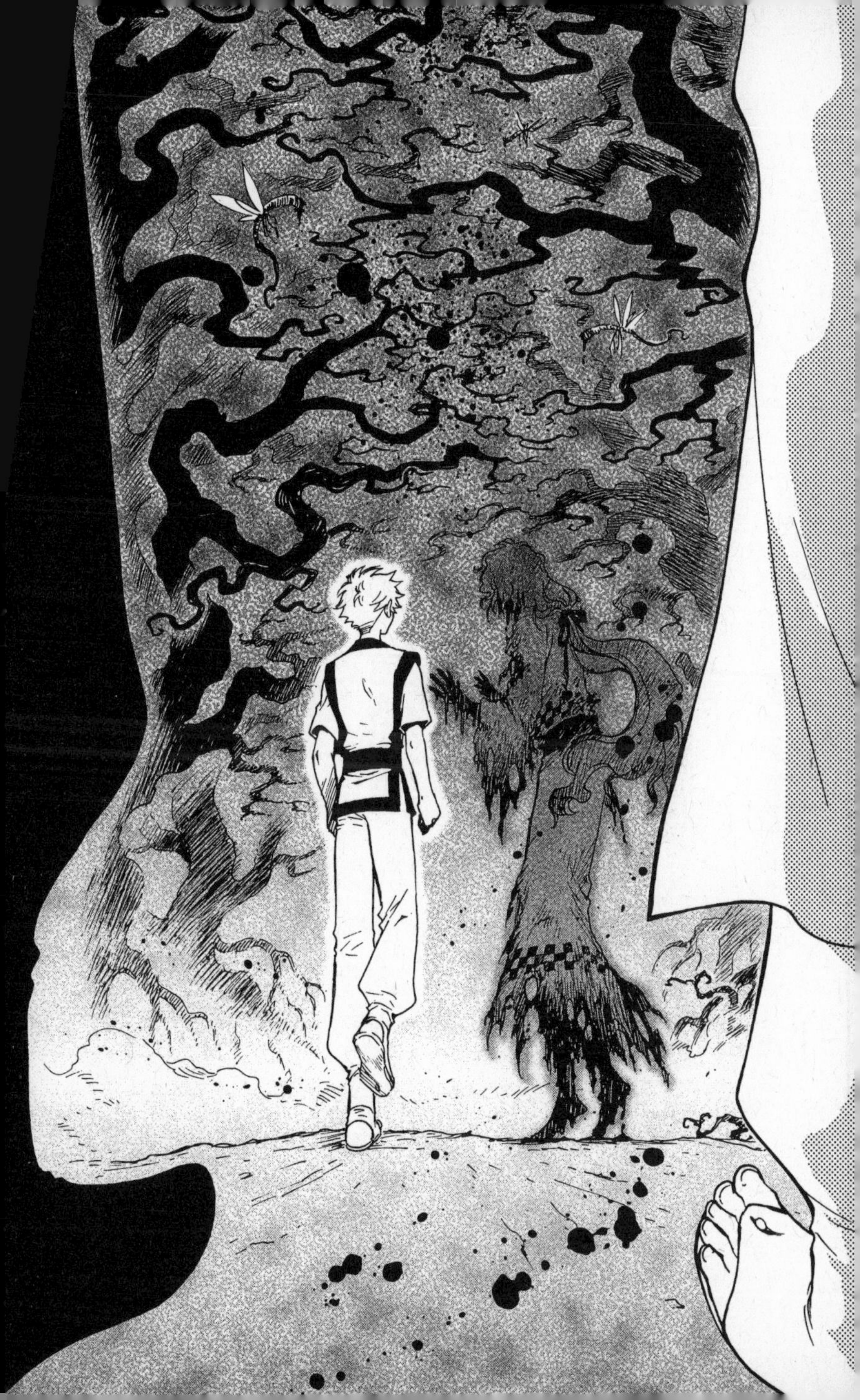

TSUBASA

WoRLD CHRoNiCLE: NIRAIKANAI

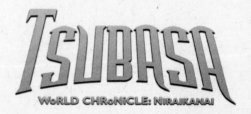

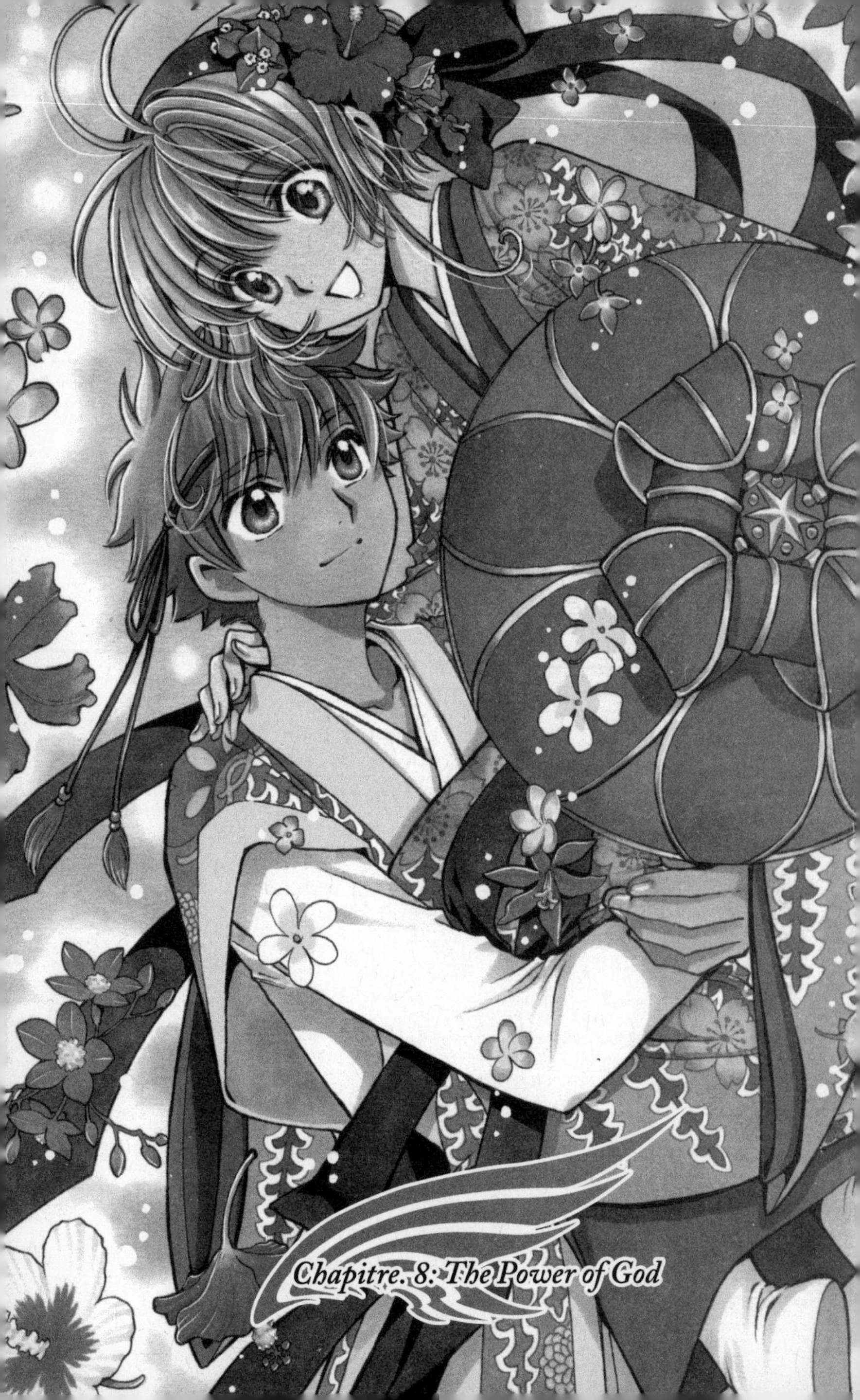
Chapitre. 8: The Power of God

TSUBASA

WoRLD CHRoNiCLE: NIRAIKANAI

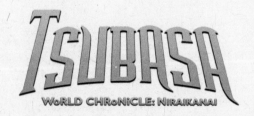

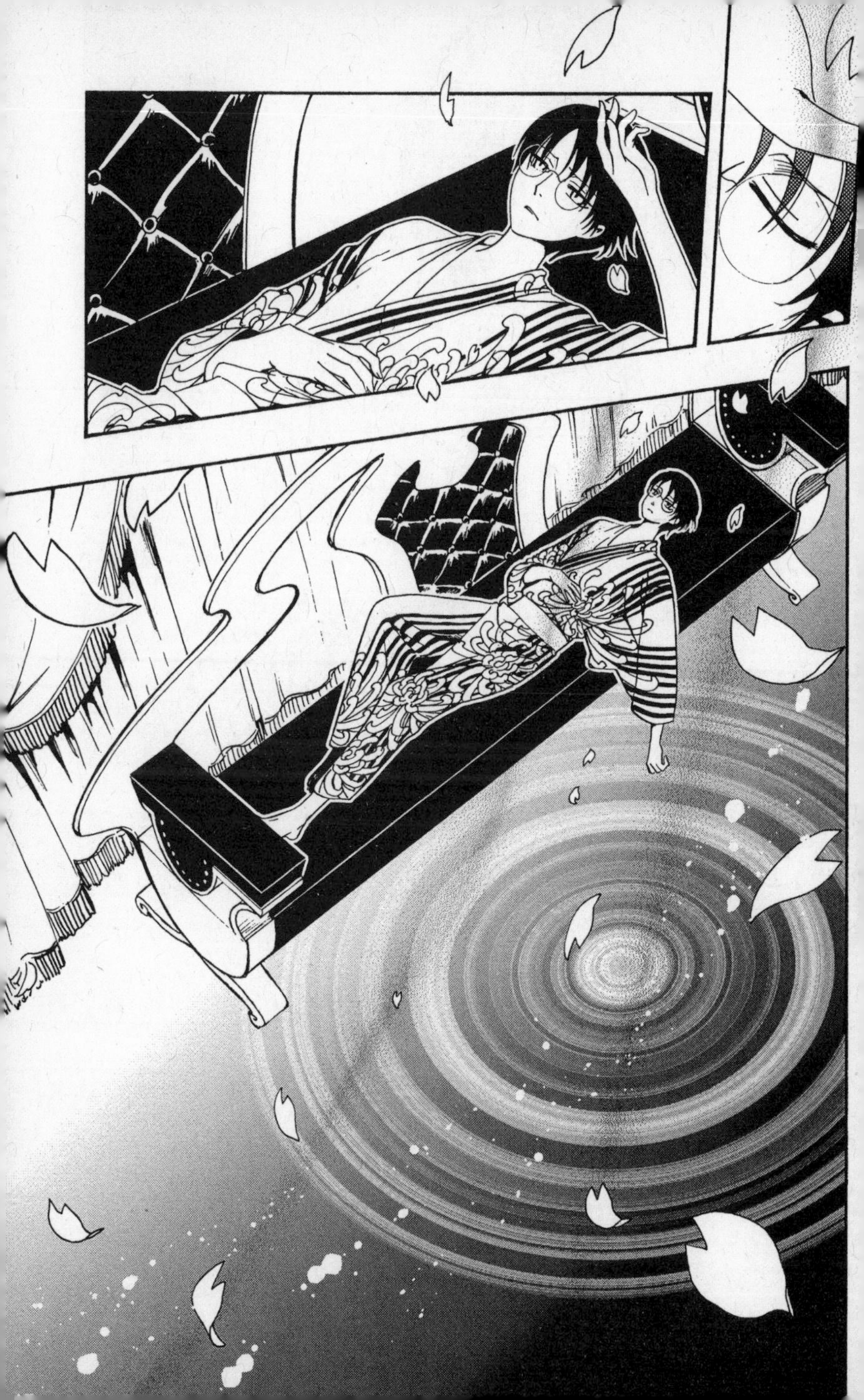

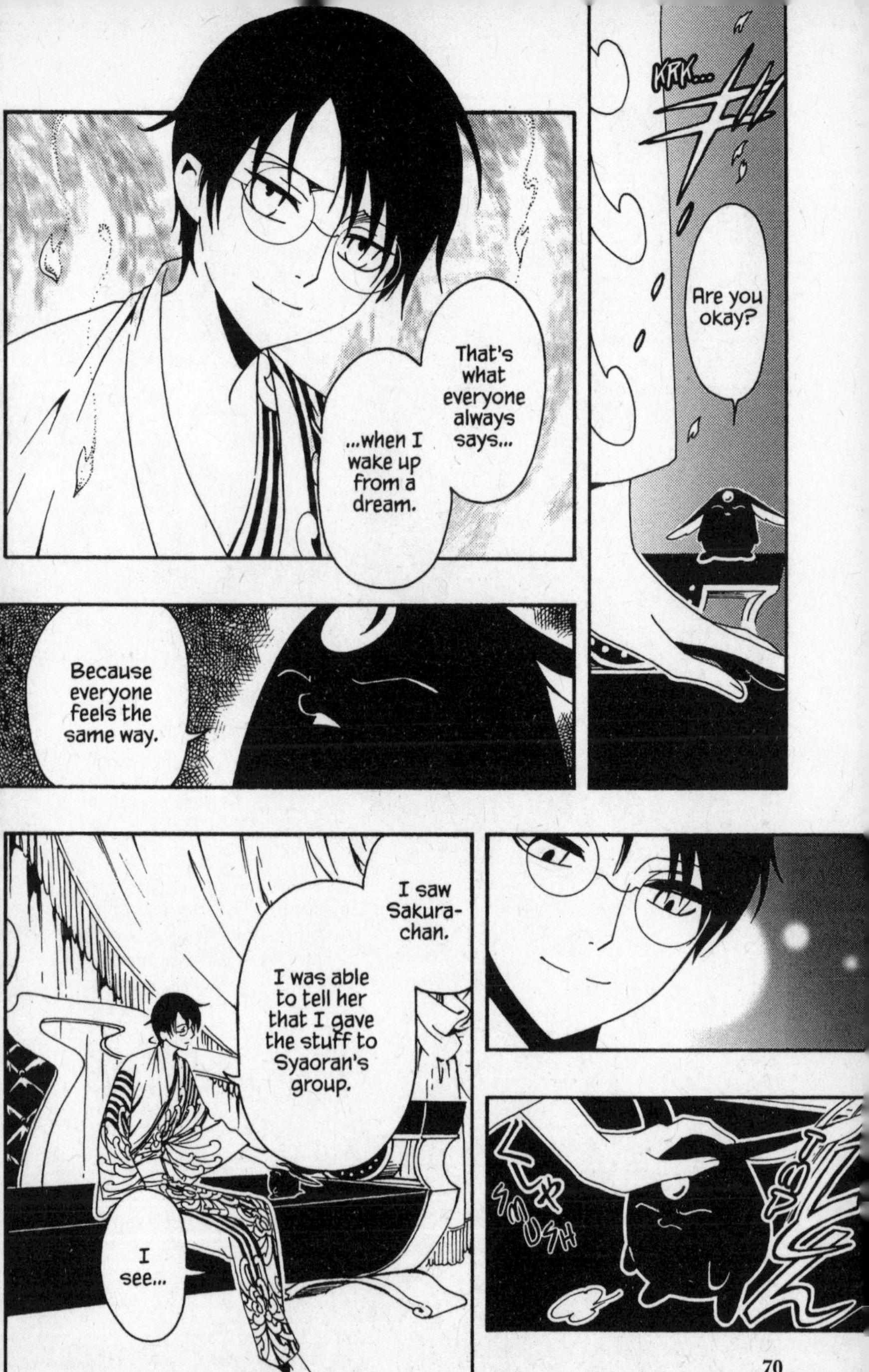
KRK...
Are you okay?
That's what everyone always says...
...when I wake up from a dream.
Because everyone feels the same way.
SMUSH
I saw Sakura-chan.
I was able to tell her that I gave the stuff to Syaoran's group.
I see...

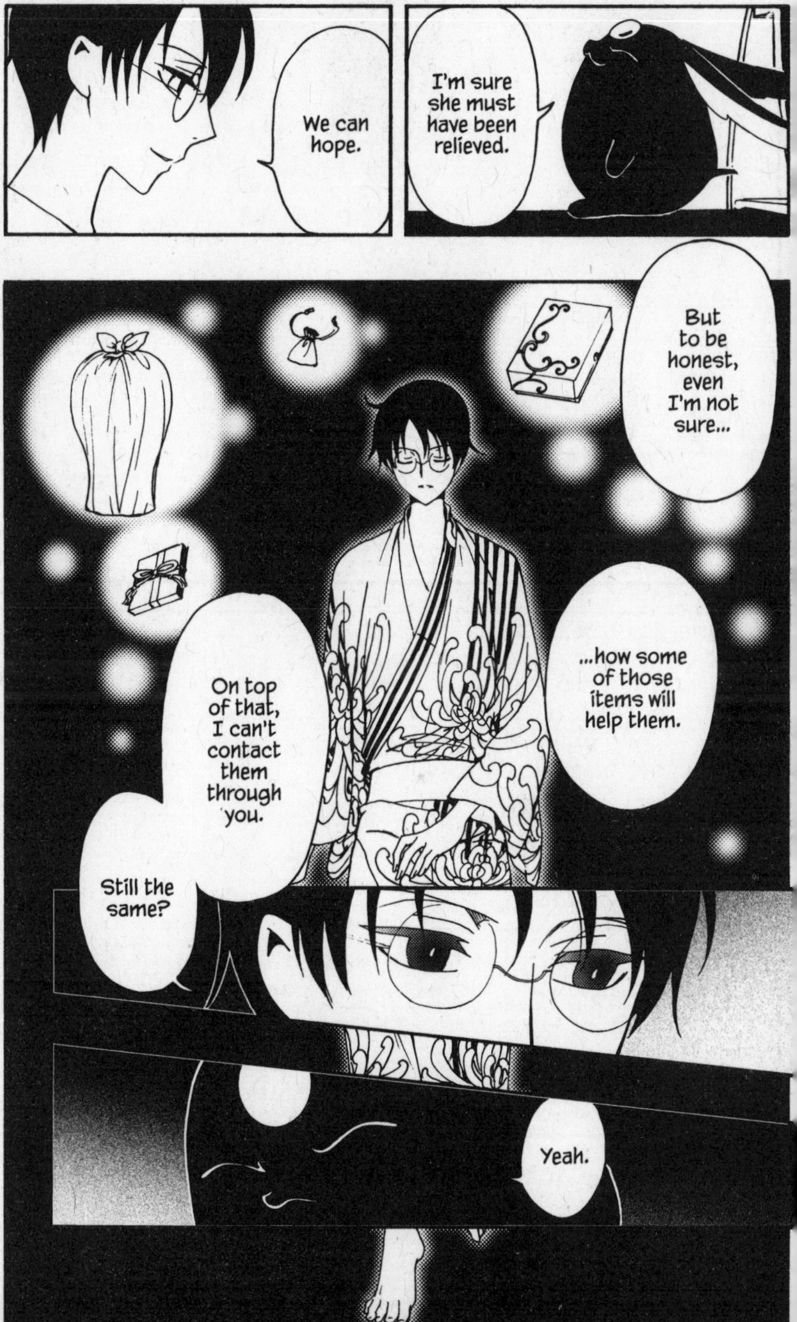
I'm sure she must have been relieved.
We can hope.
But to be honest, even I'm not sure...
...how some of those items will help them.
On top of that, I can't contact them through you.
Still the same?
Yeah.

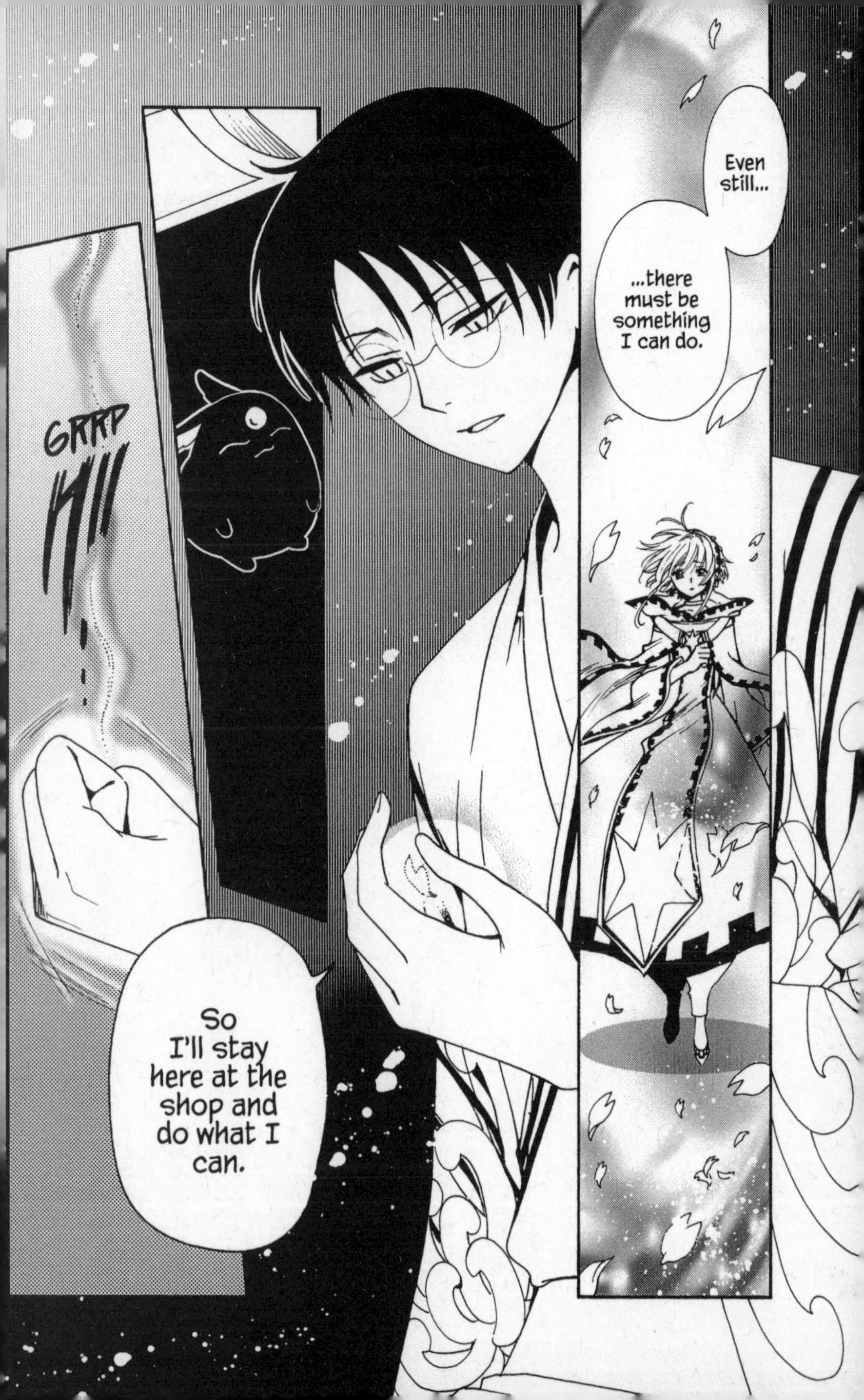
Even still...
...there must be something I can do.
So I'll stay here at the shop and do what I can.
GRRP

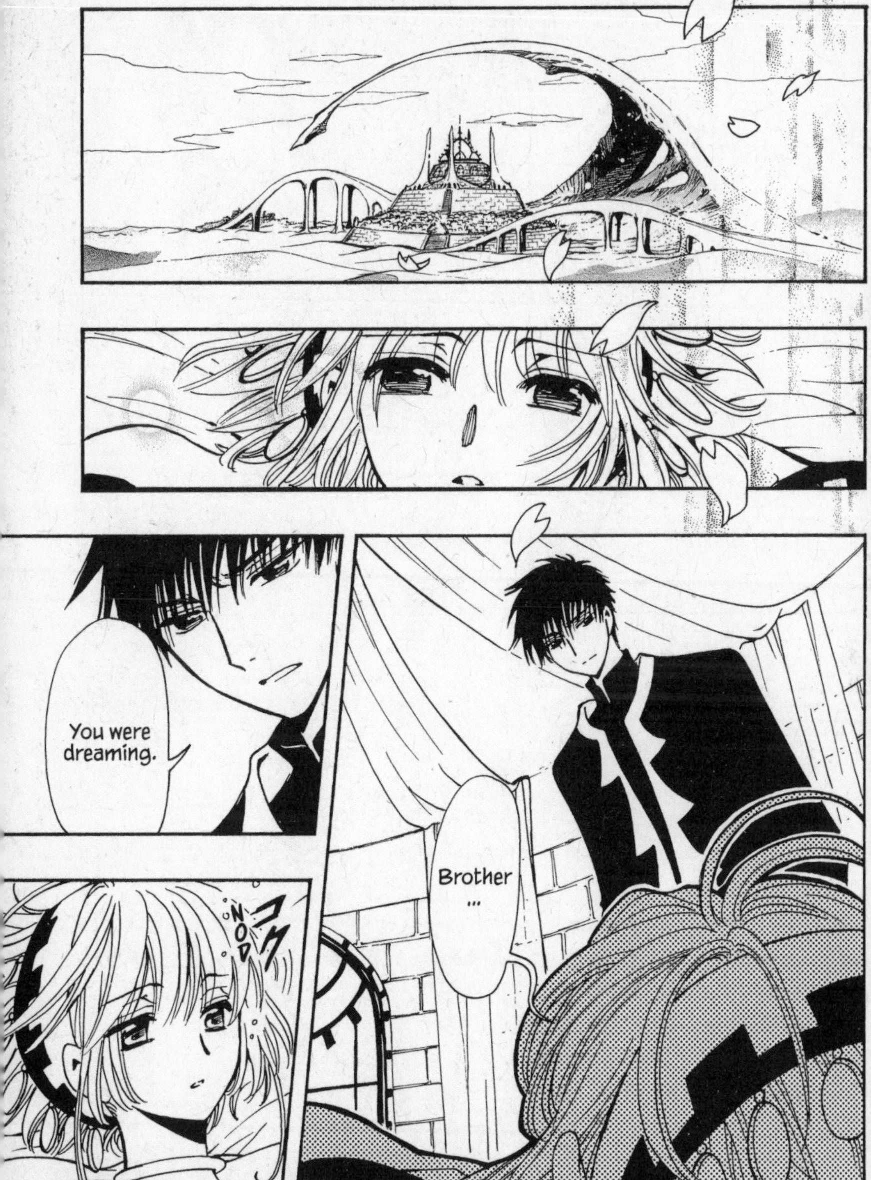
Brother
...
You were dreaming.
NOD

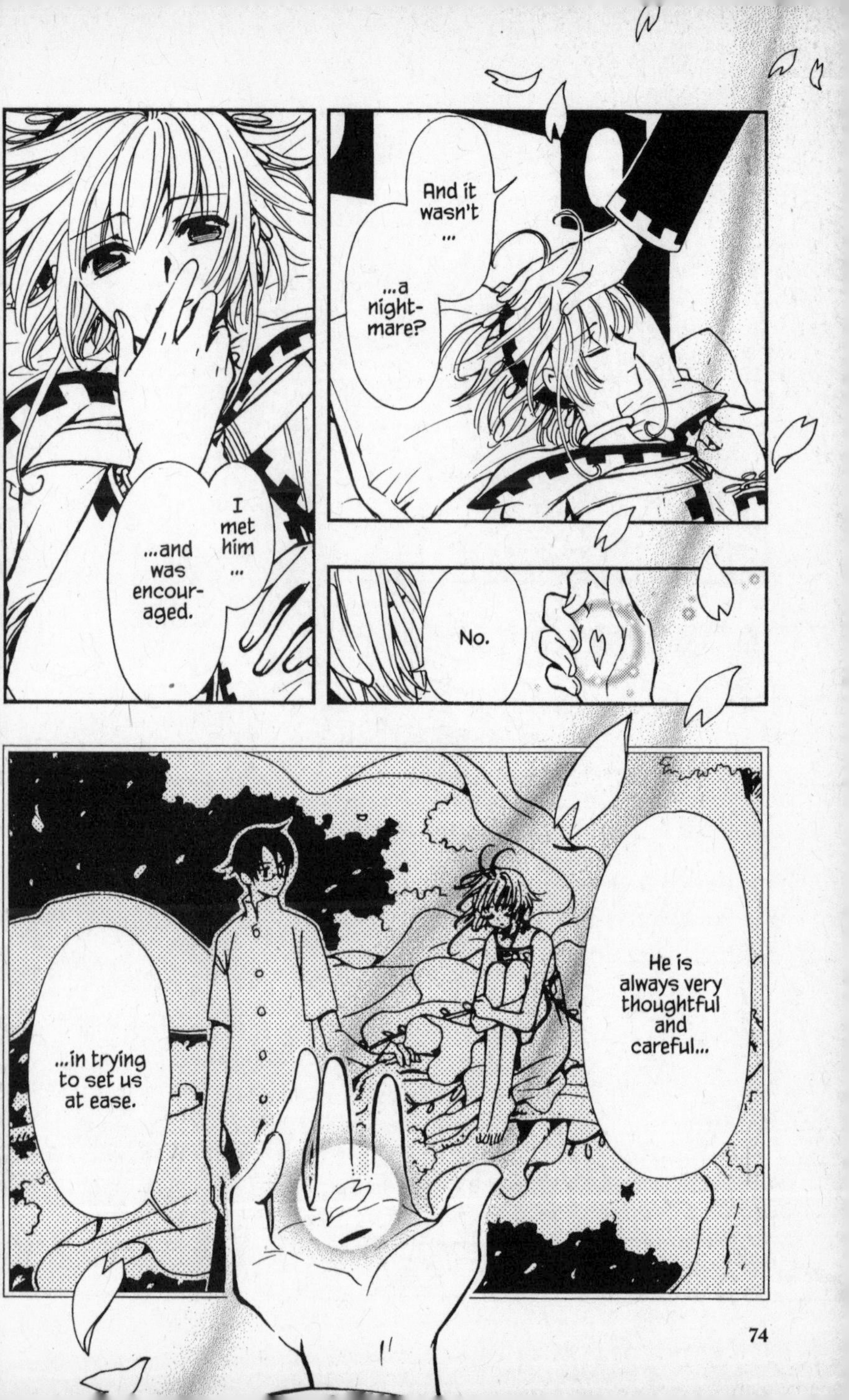
And it wasn't ...
...a night-mare?
No.
I met him ...
...and was encour-aged.
He is always very thoughtful and careful...
...in trying to set us at ease.

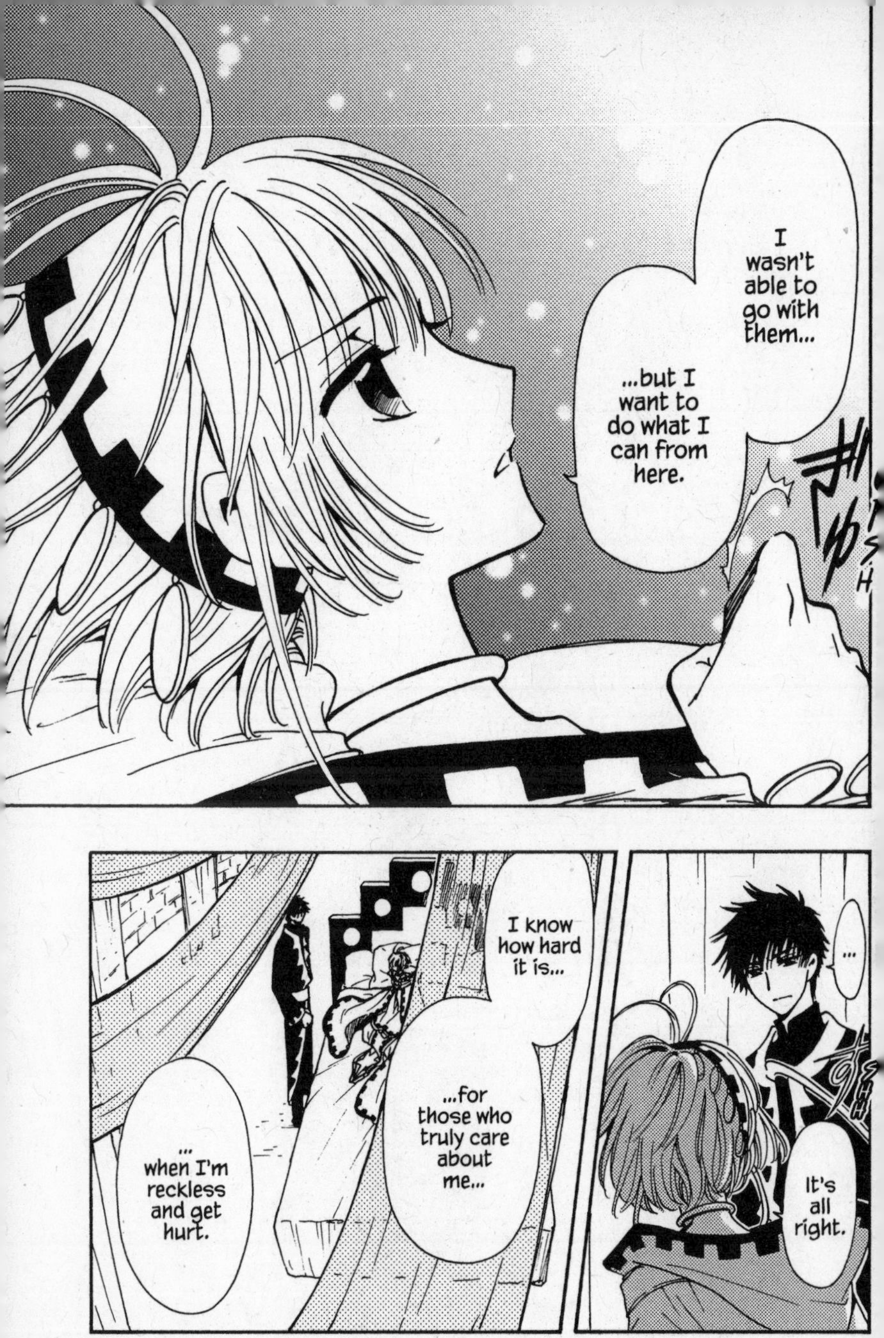
I wasn't able to go with them...
...but I want to do what I can from here.
...
It's all right.
I know how hard it is...
...for those who truly care about me...
...when I'm reckless and get hurt.

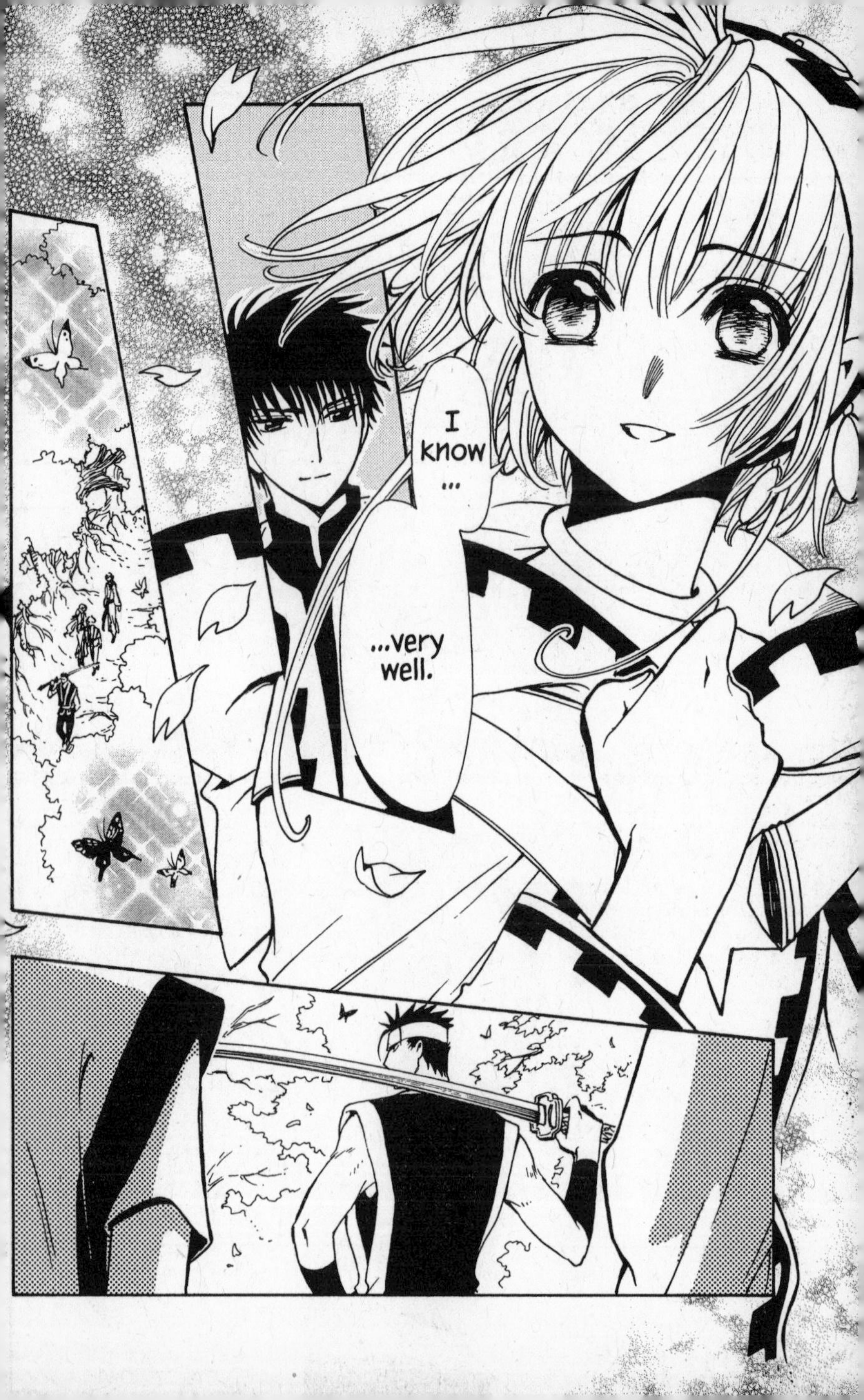
I know...
...very well.

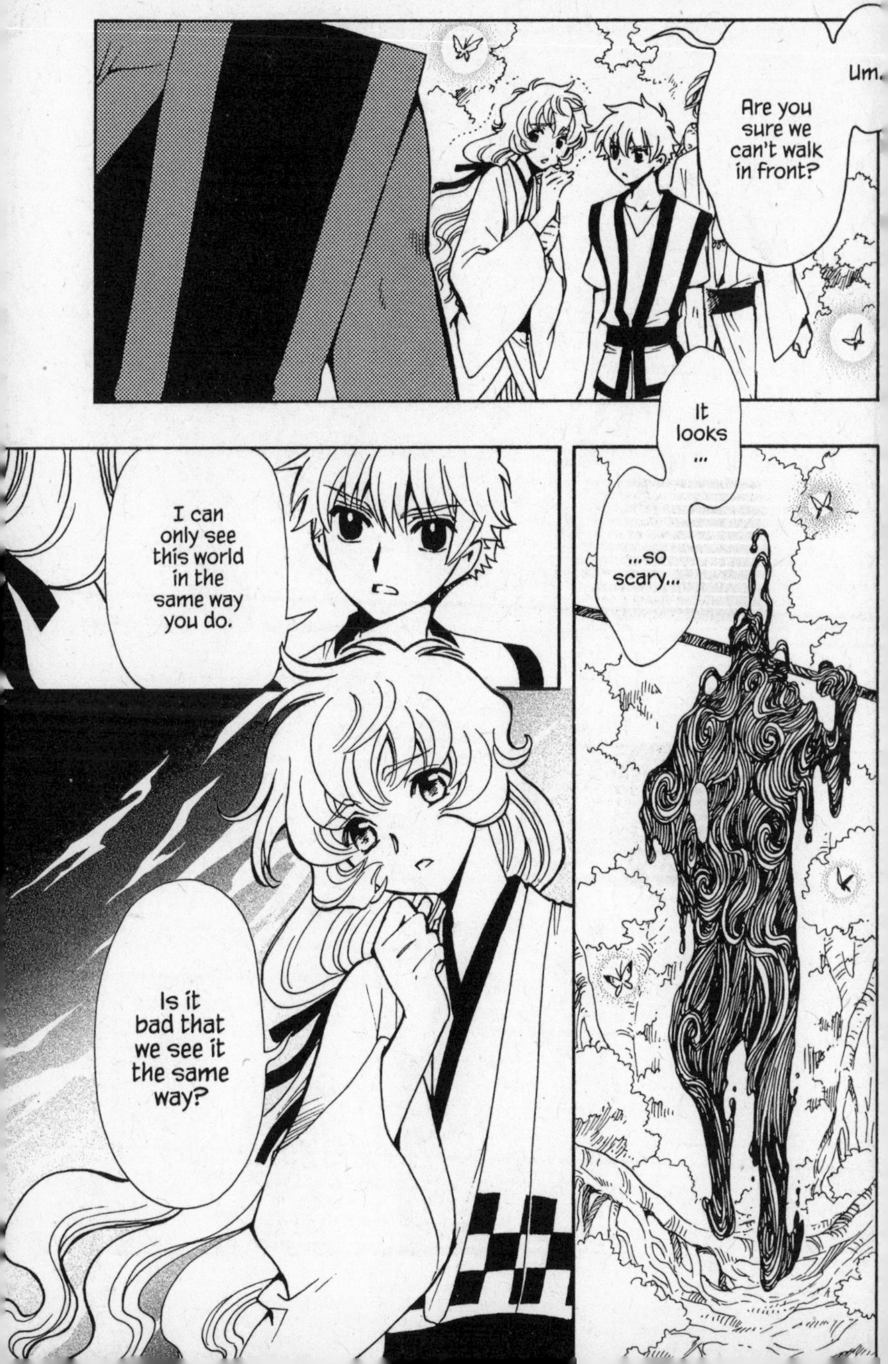
Um.
Are you sure we can't walk in front?
It looks ...
...so scary...
I can only see this world in the same way you do.
Is it bad that we see it the same way?

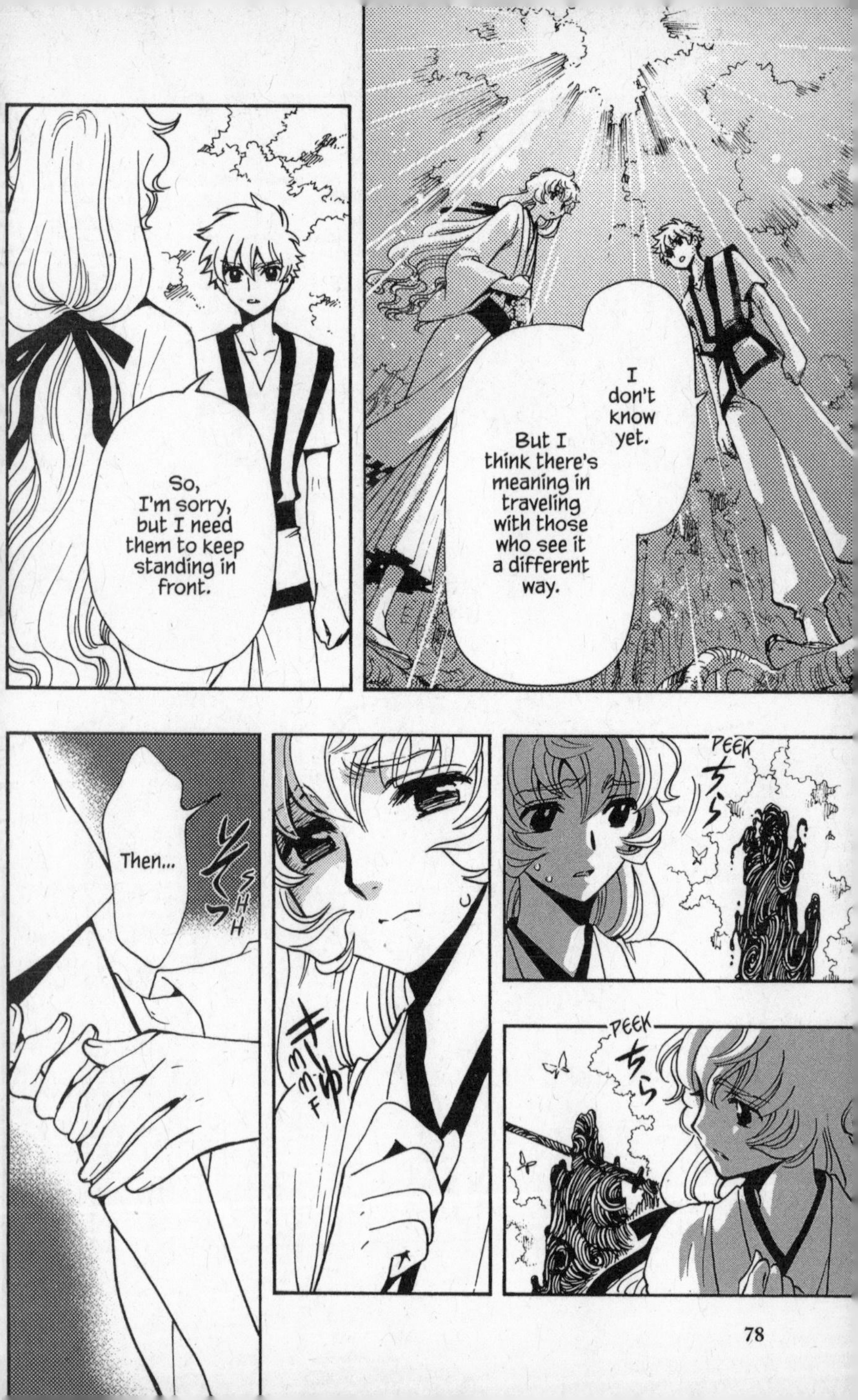
I don't know yet.
But I think there's meaning in traveling with those who see it a different way.
So, I'm sorry, but I need them to keep standing in front.
PEEK
ちら
PEEK
ちら
MMF
キュ
SHH
そっ
Then...

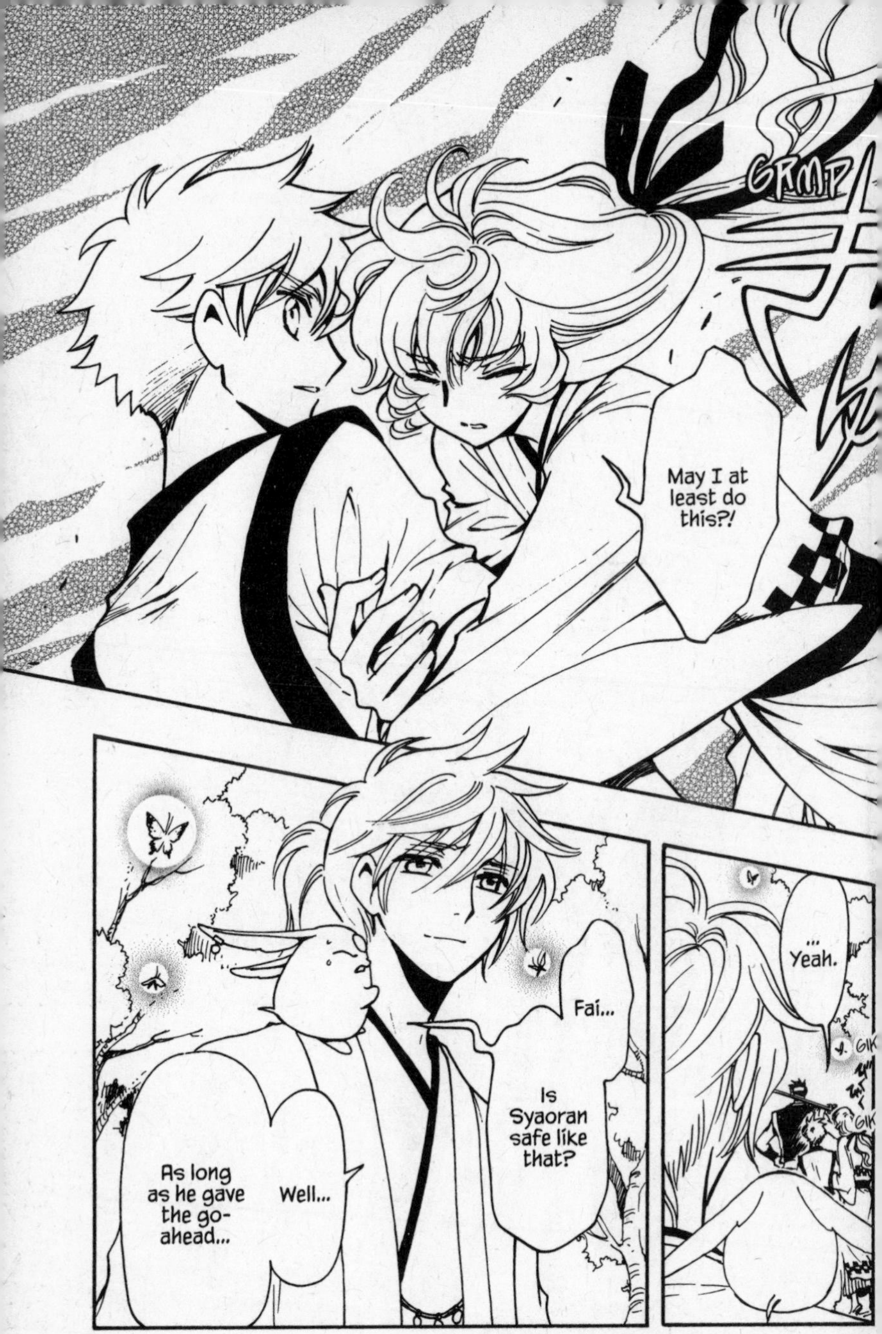
GRMP
May I at least do this?!
... Yeah.
GIK
GIK
Fai...
Is Syaoran safe like that?
Well...
As long as he gave the go-ahead...

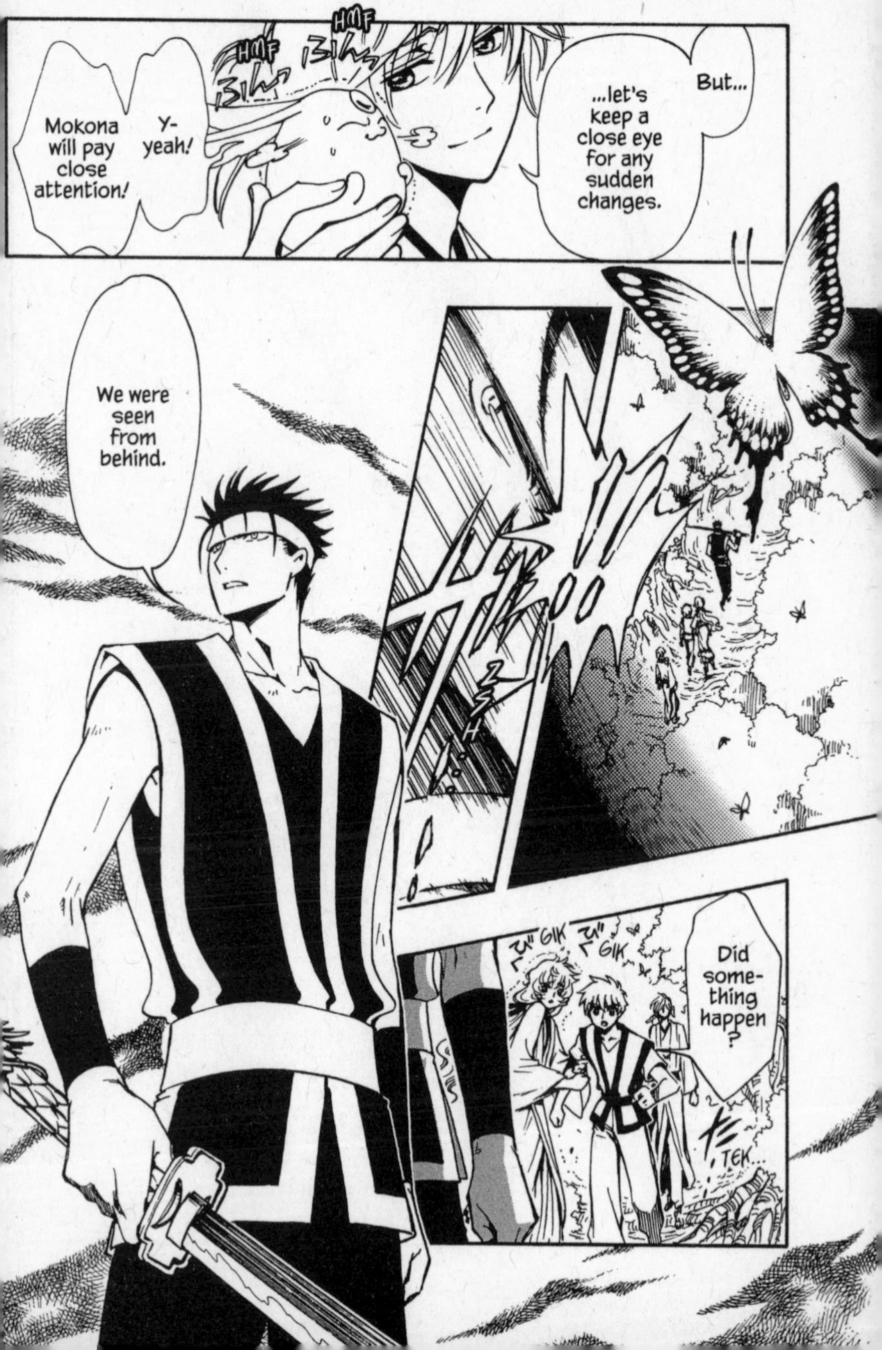
But...
...let's keep a close eye for any sudden changes.
HMF
HMF
Y-yeah!
Mokona will pay close attention!
ZSH
GIK
GIK
Did something happen?
TEK...
We were seen from behind.

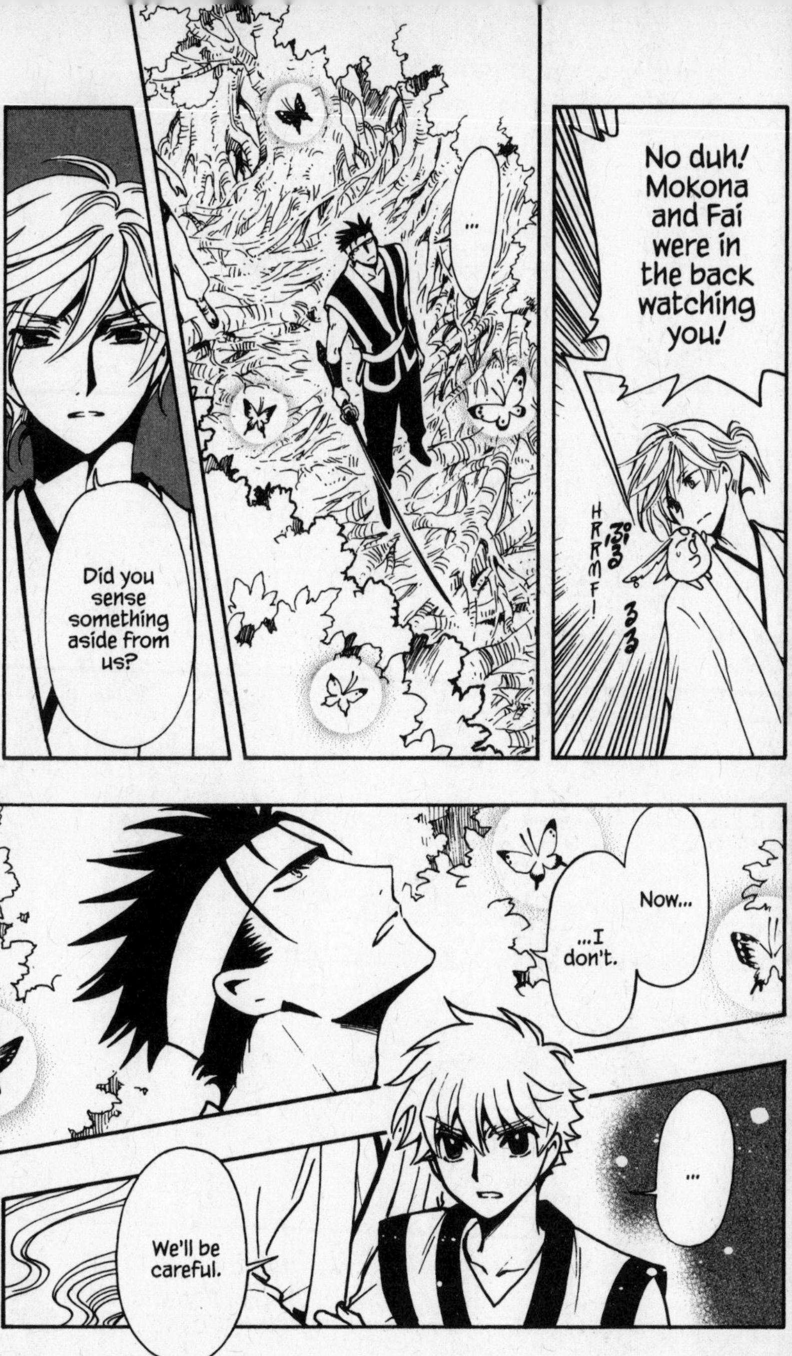
No duh! Mokona and Fai were in the back watching you!
HRRMF!
...
Did you sense something aside from us?
Now...
...I don't.
...
We'll be careful.

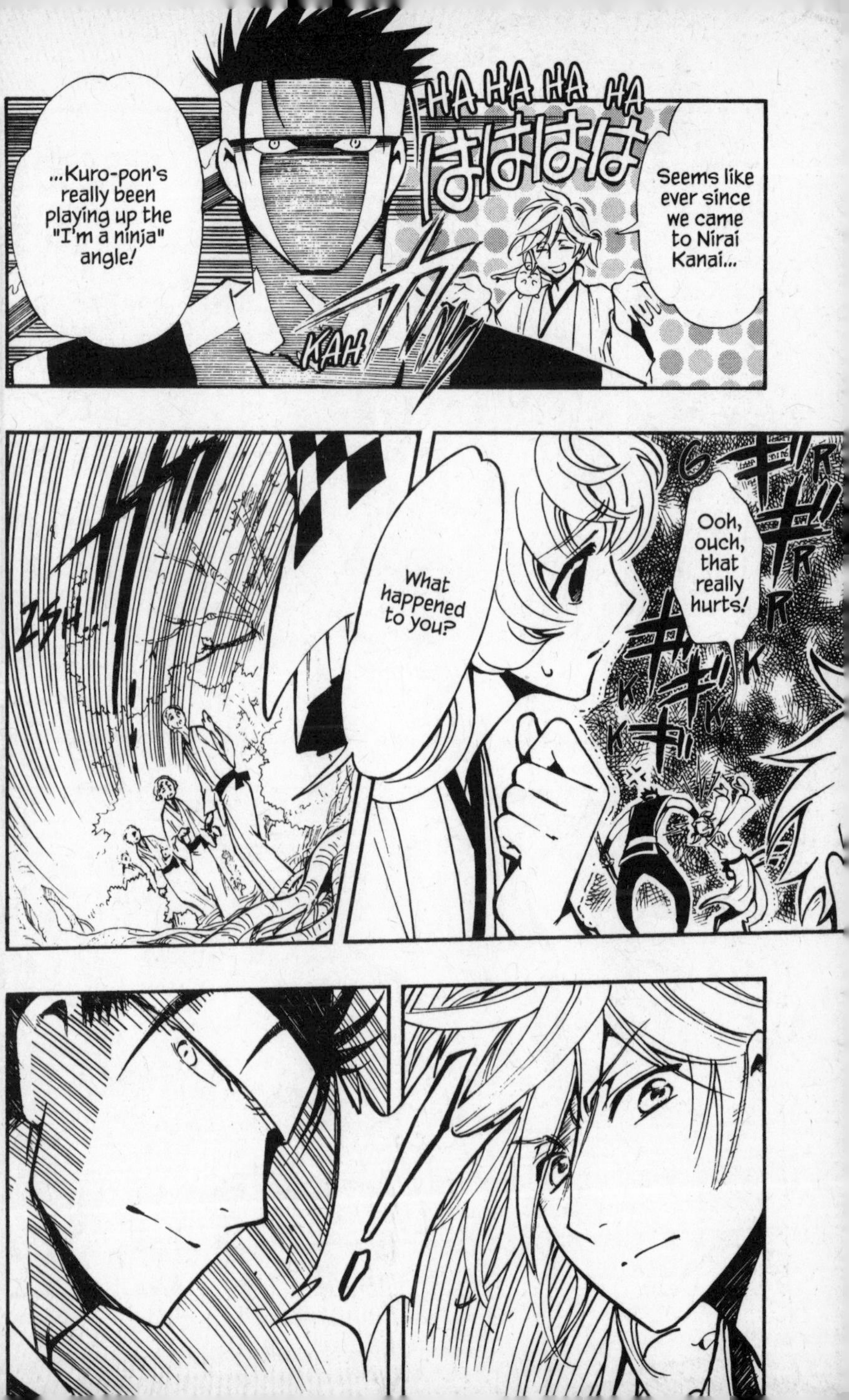
HA HA HA HA HA
はははは
Seems like ever since we came to Nirai Kanai...
...Kuro-pon's really been playing up the "I'm a ninja" angle!
KAH
Ooh, ouch, that really hurts!
What happened to you?
ZSH...

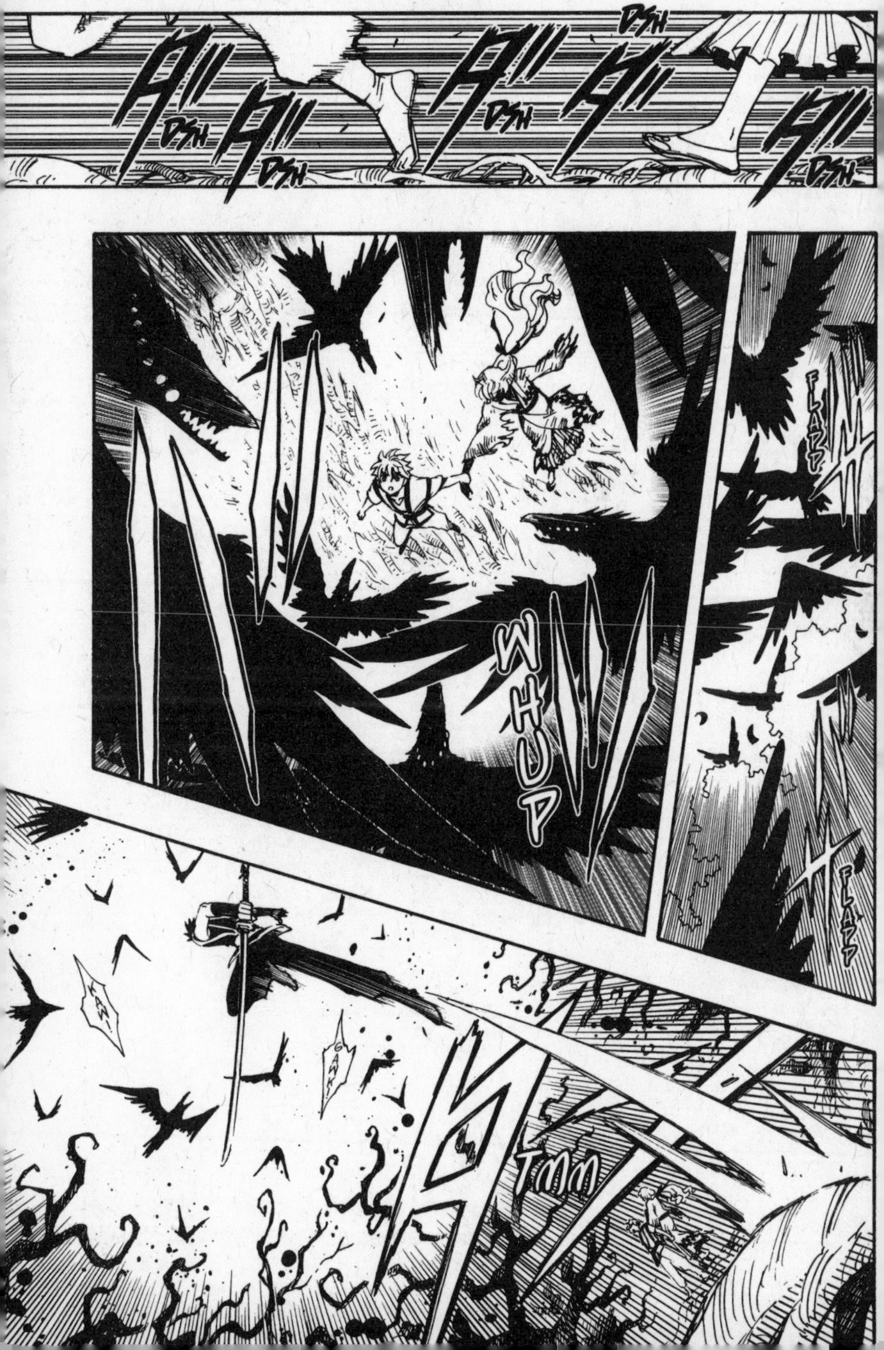
ダ" DSH
ダ" DSH
ダ" DSH
ダ" DSH
ダ" DSH
FLAPP
FLAPP
WHUP
KAW!
GAWK
TMM

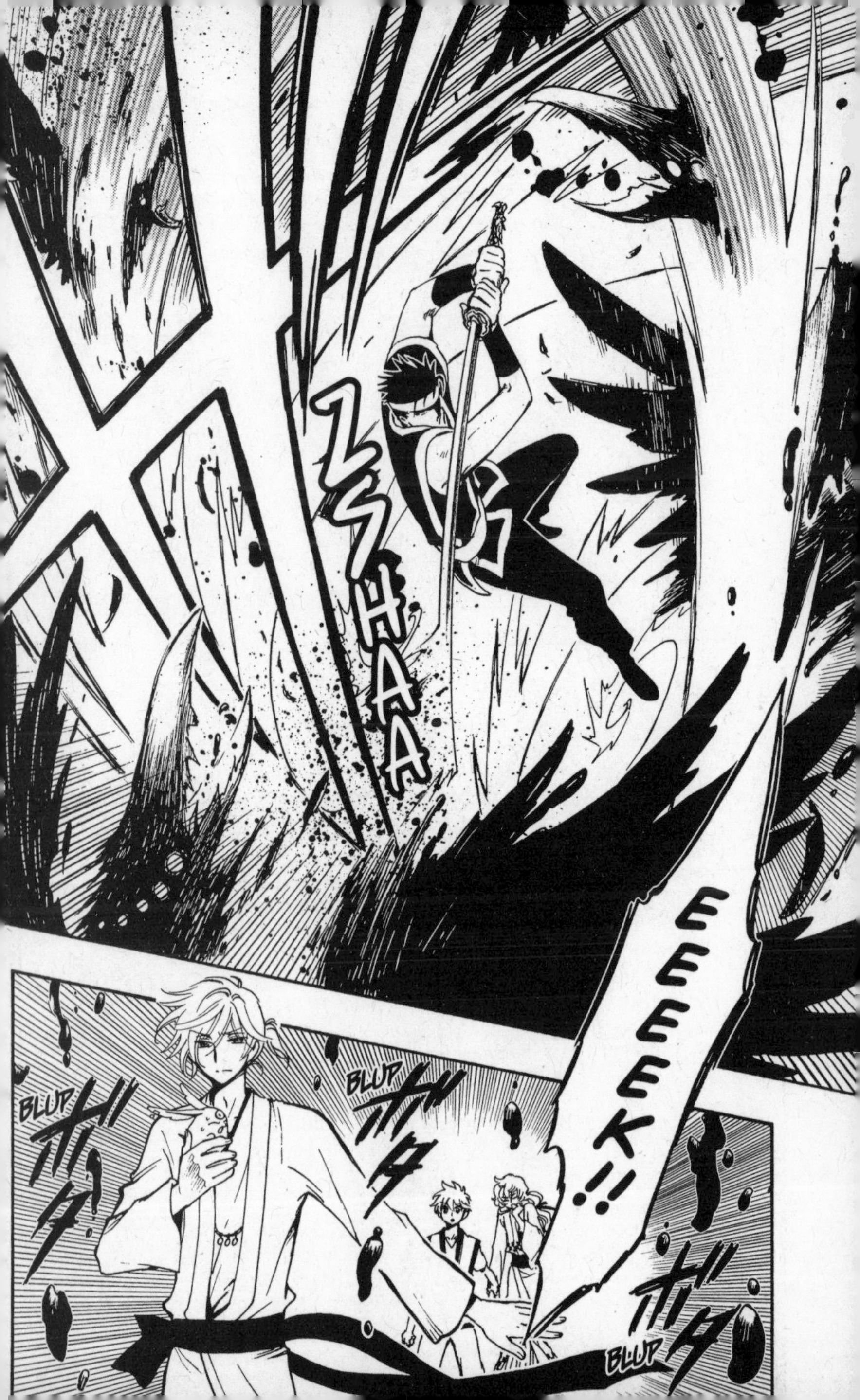
ZSHAA
EEEEEK!!
BLUP
BLUP
BLUP

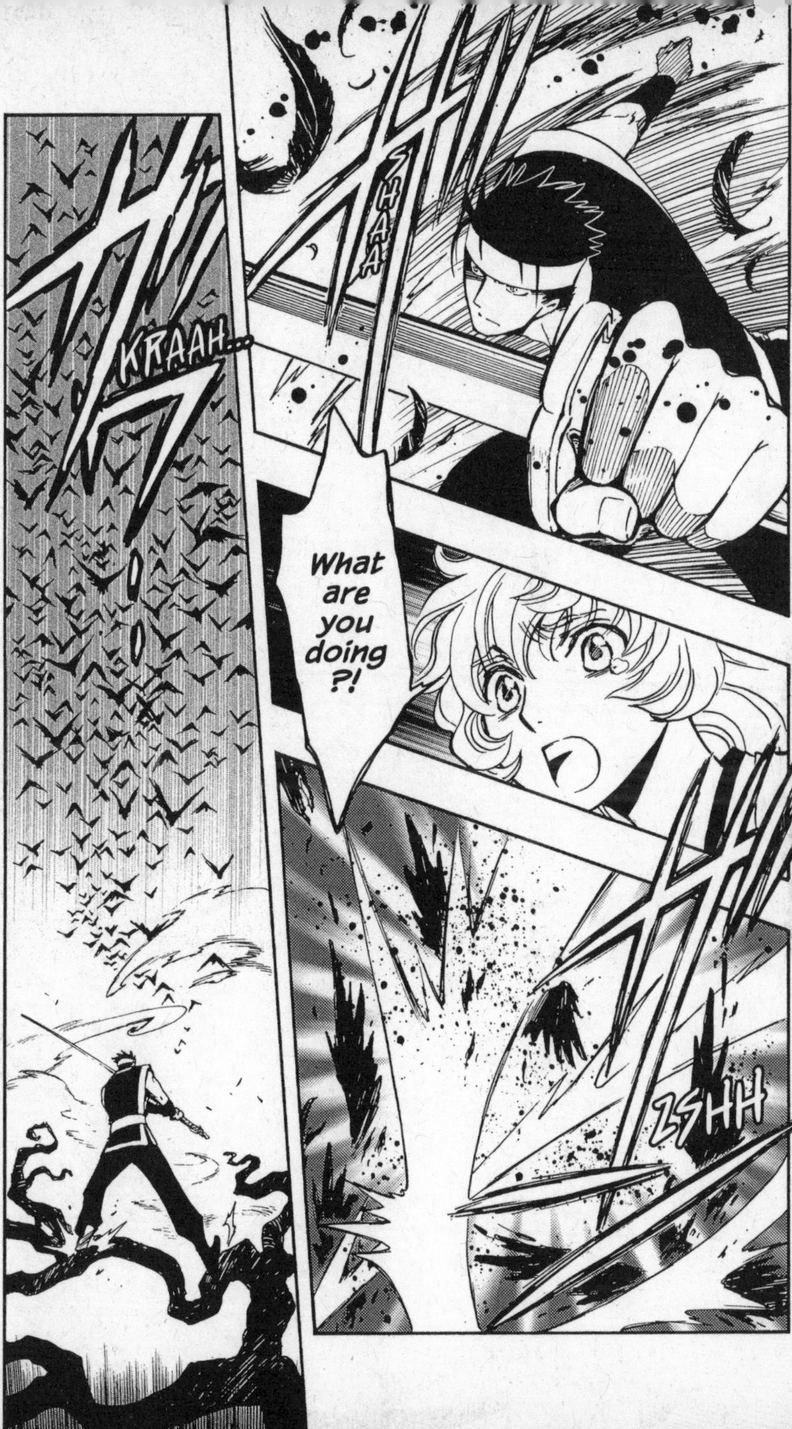
SHAAA
What are you doing?!
ZSHH
KRAAH...

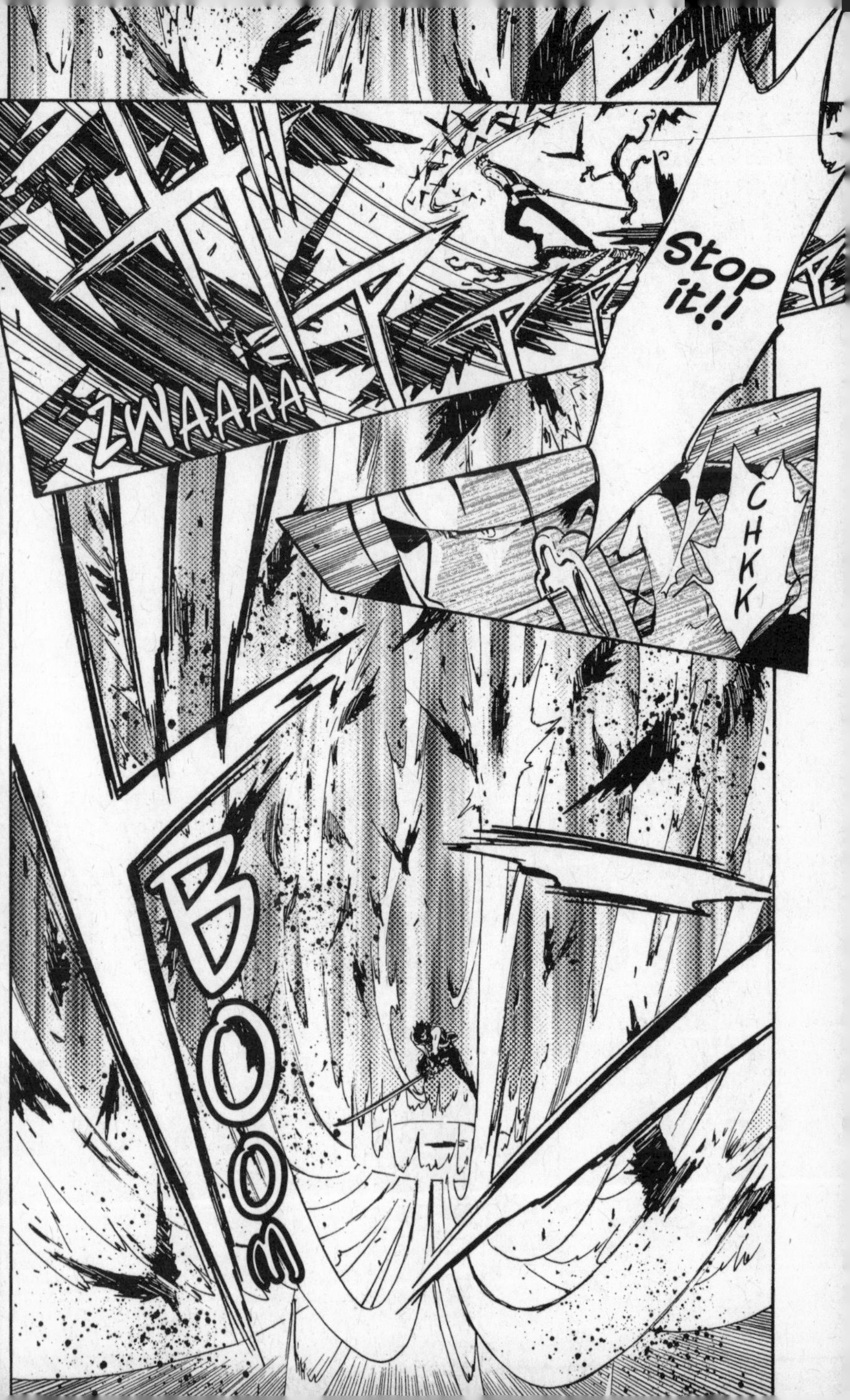
Stop it!!
ZWAAAA
CHKK
BOOoo

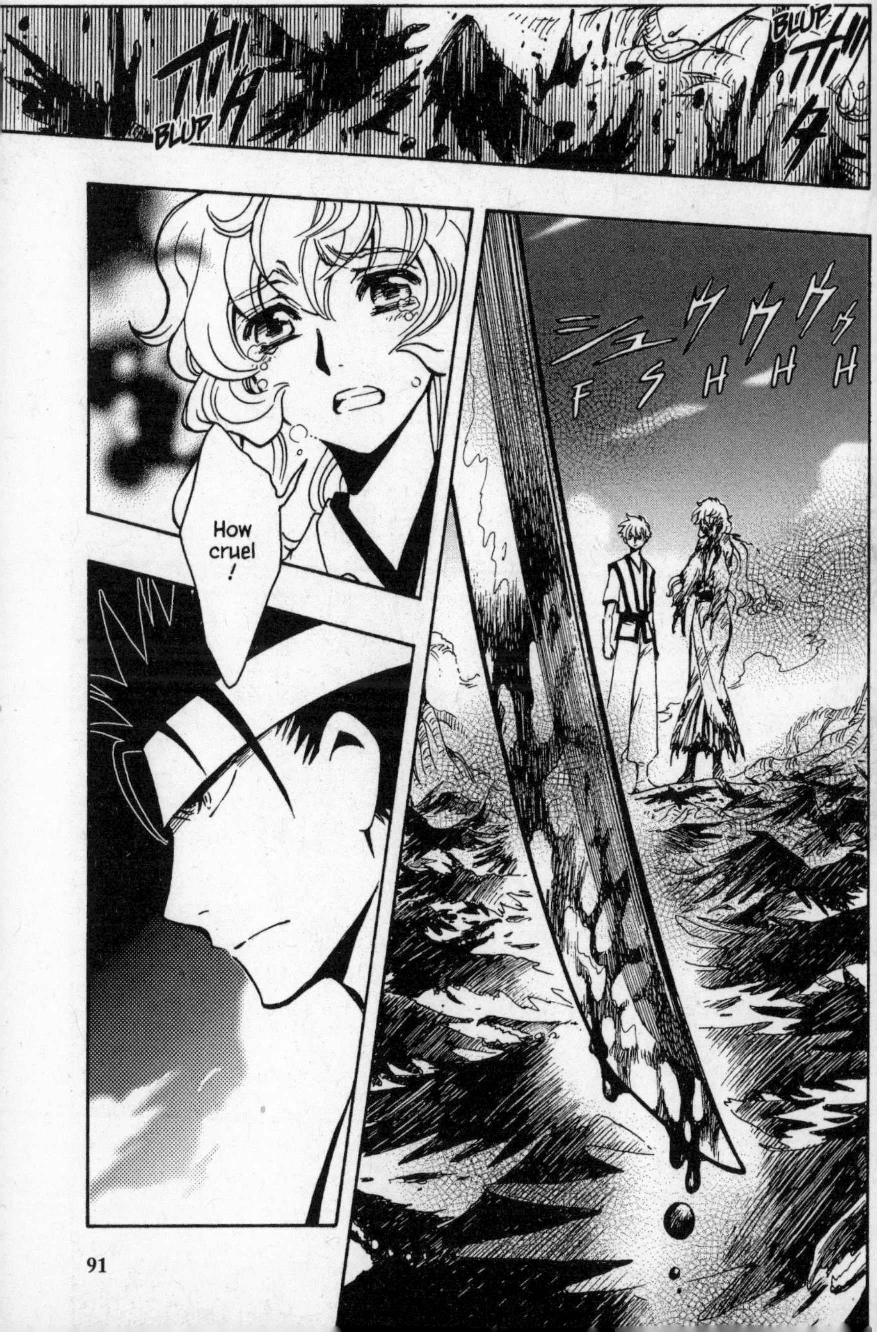
BLUP
BLUP
FSHHH
How cruel!

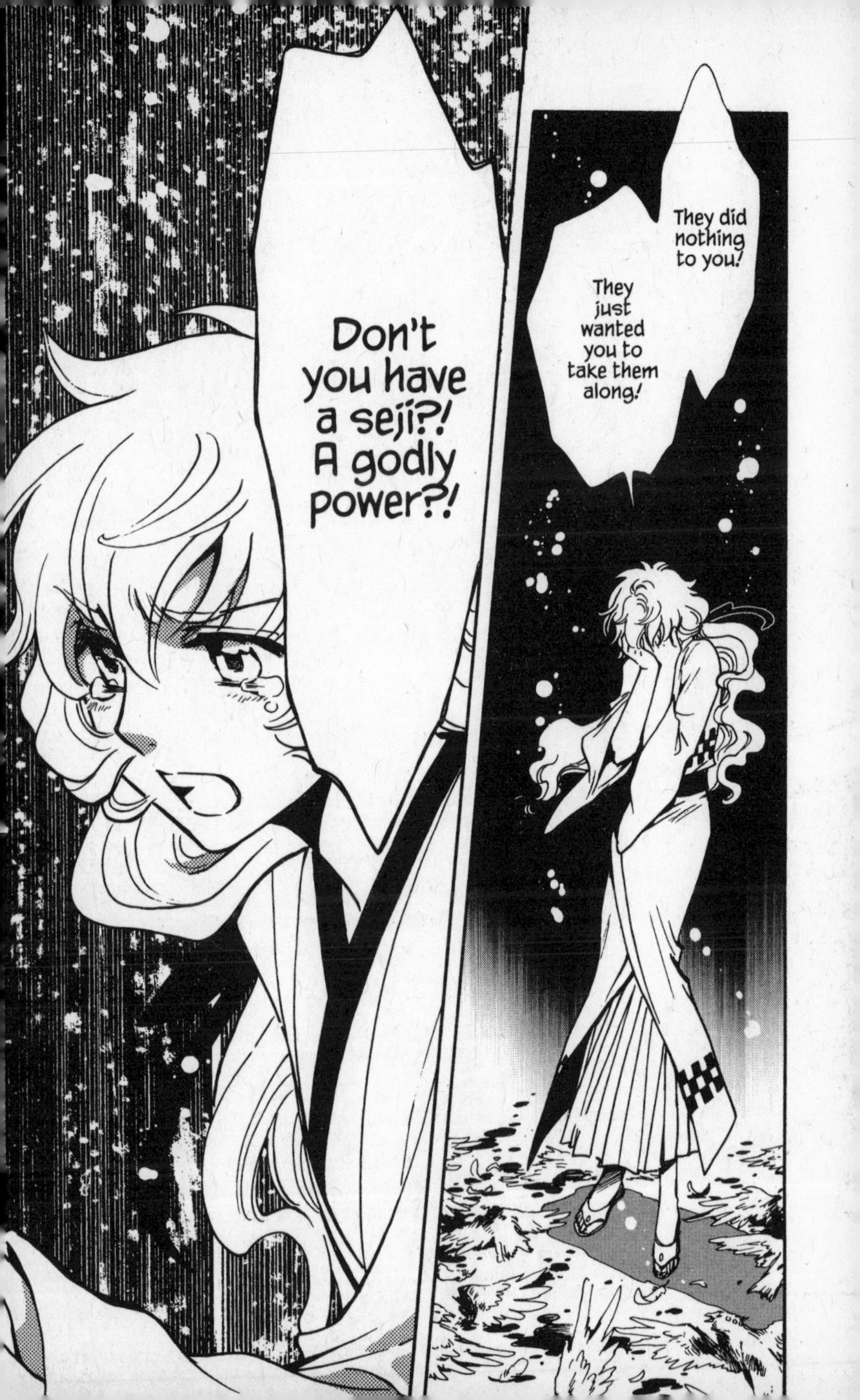
They did nothing to you!
They just wanted you to take them along!
Don't you have a seji?! A godly power?!

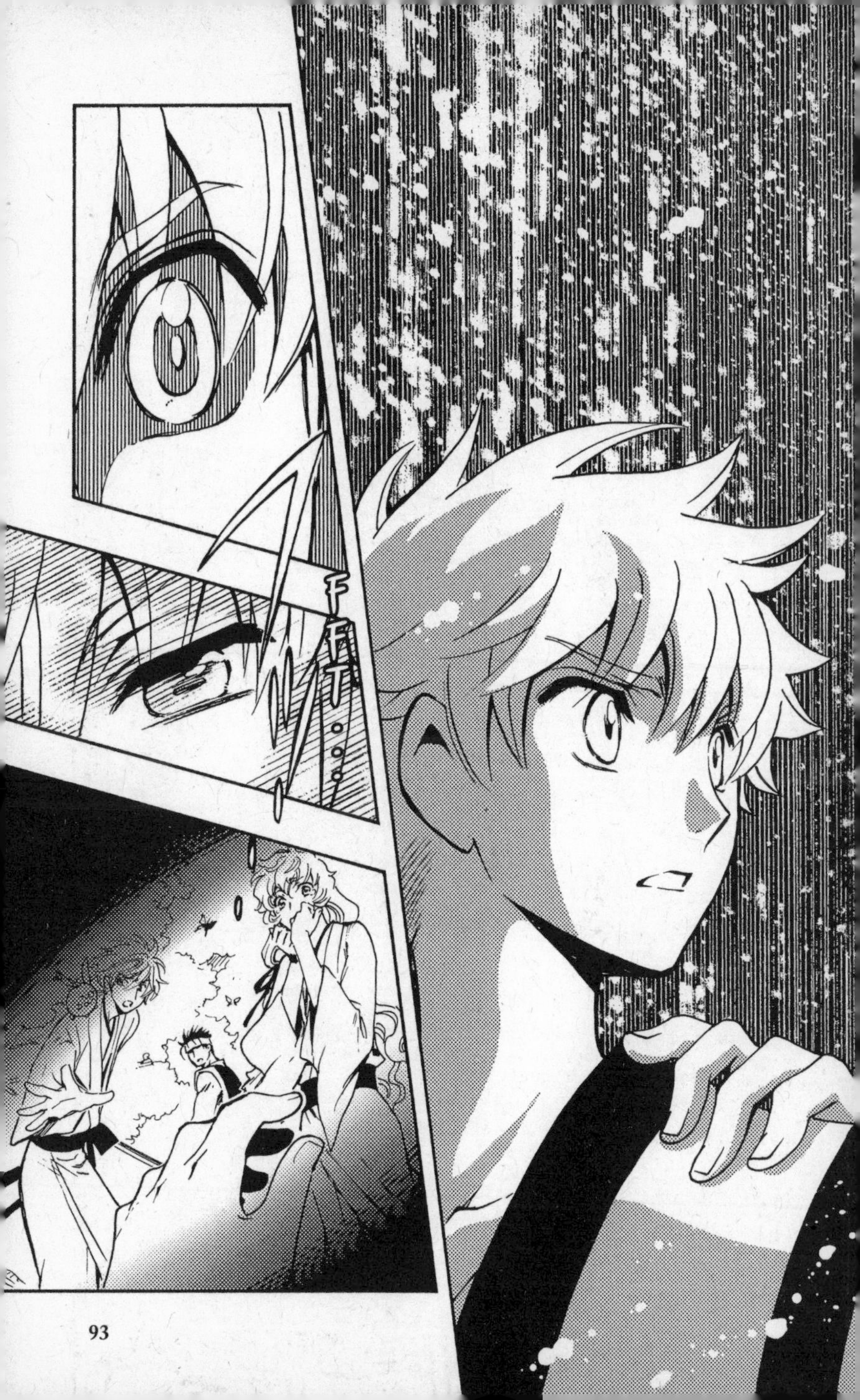
FFFT...

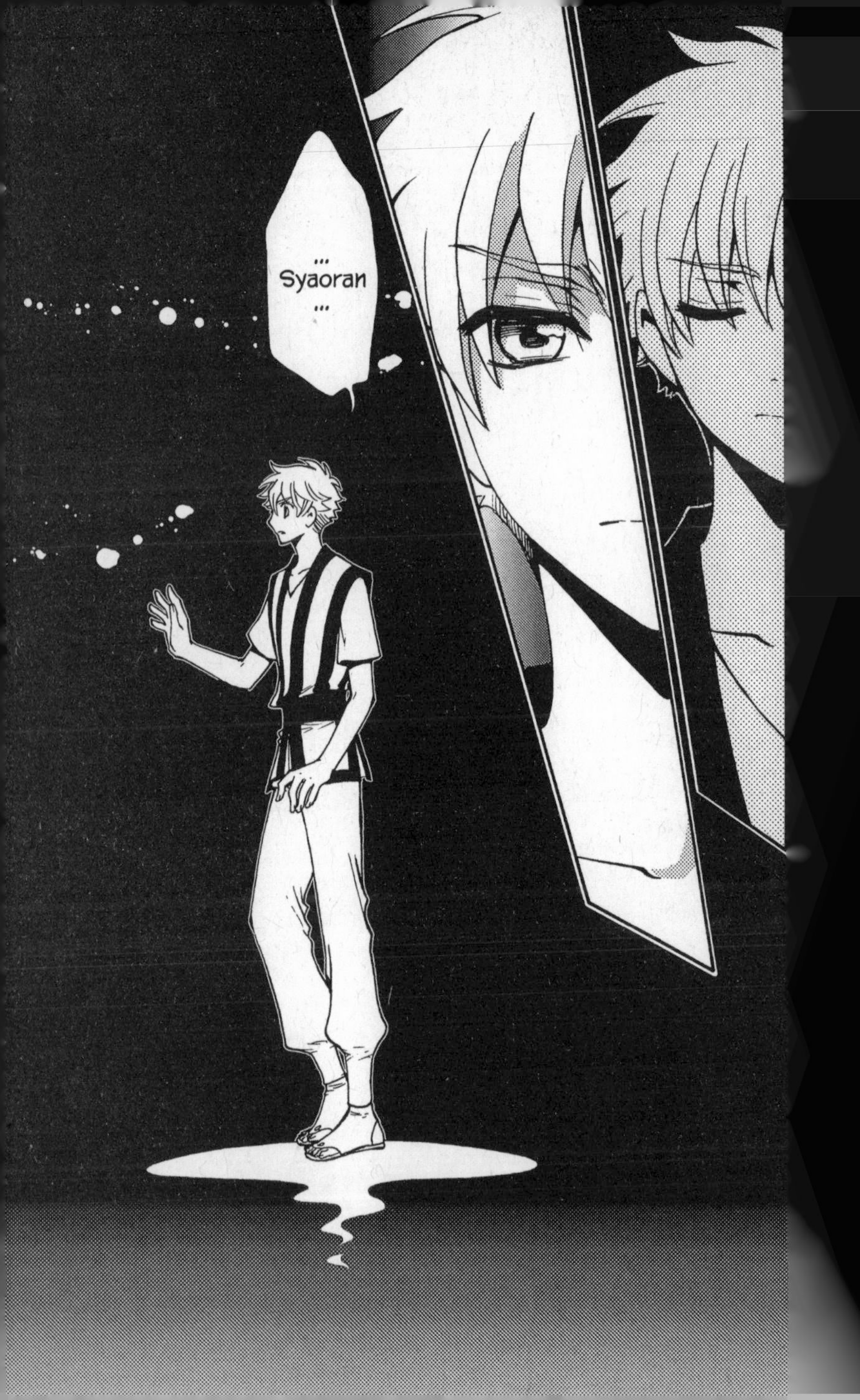
...
Syaoran
...

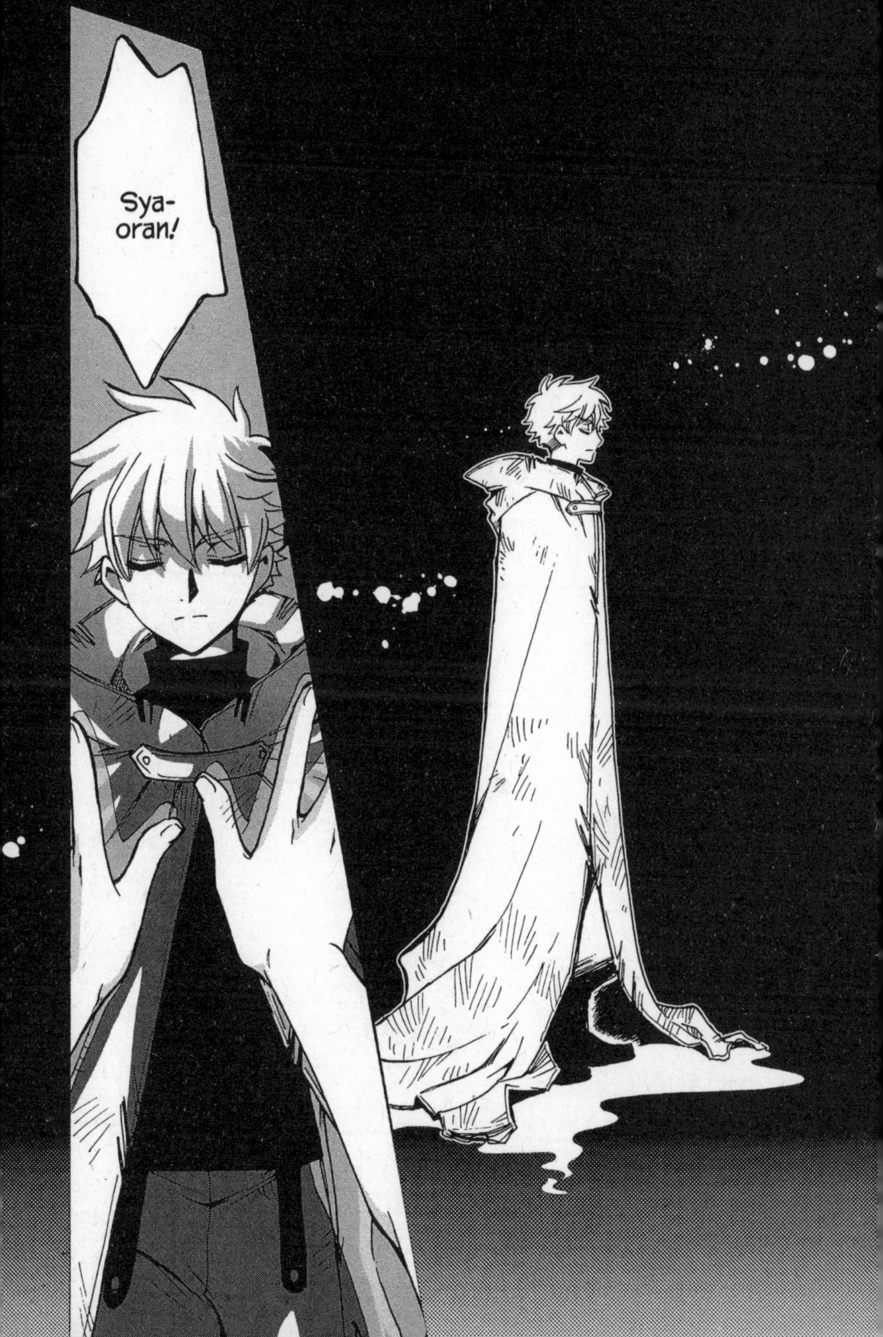
Sya-oran!

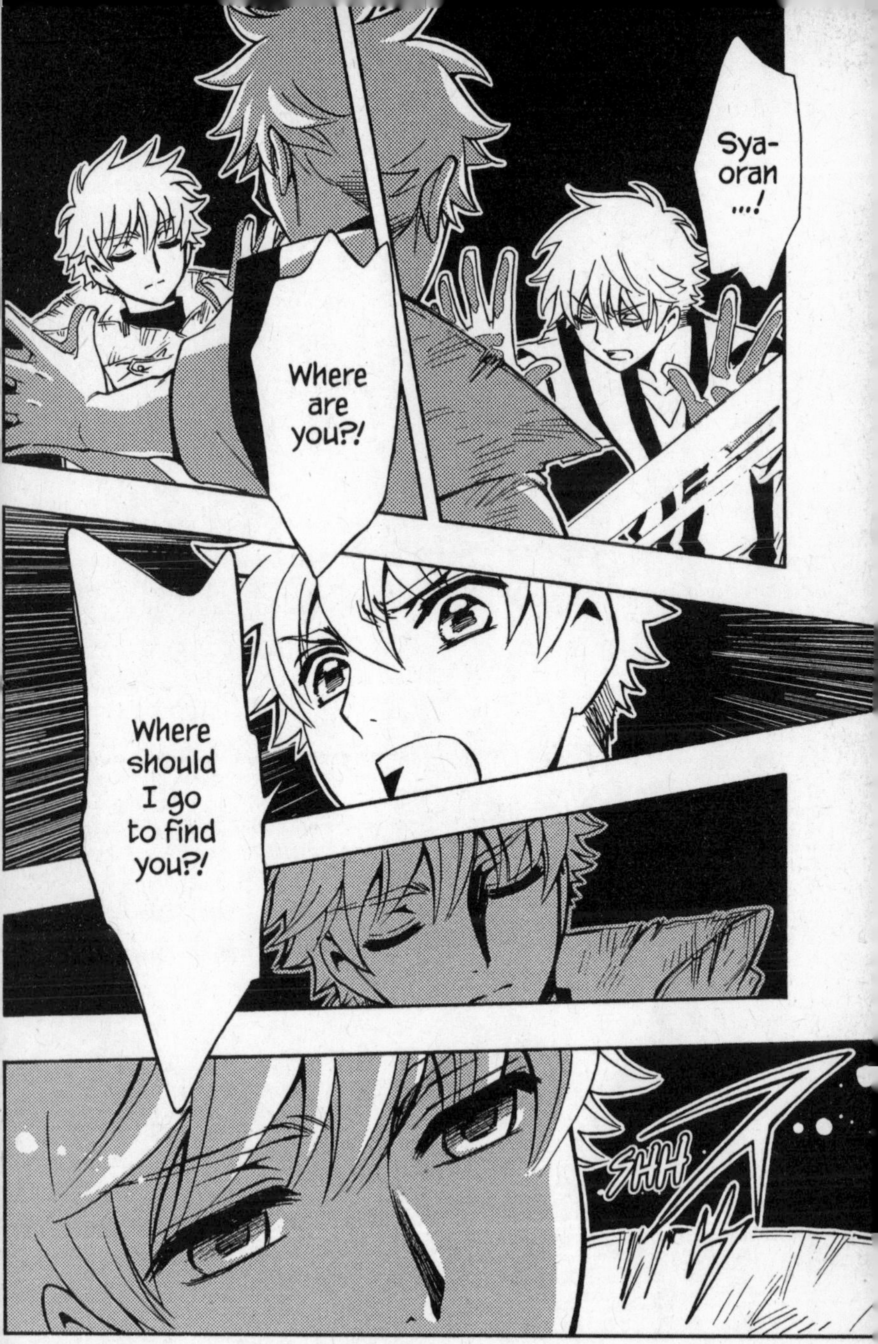
Sya-oran ...!
Where are you?!
Where should I go to find you?!
SHH

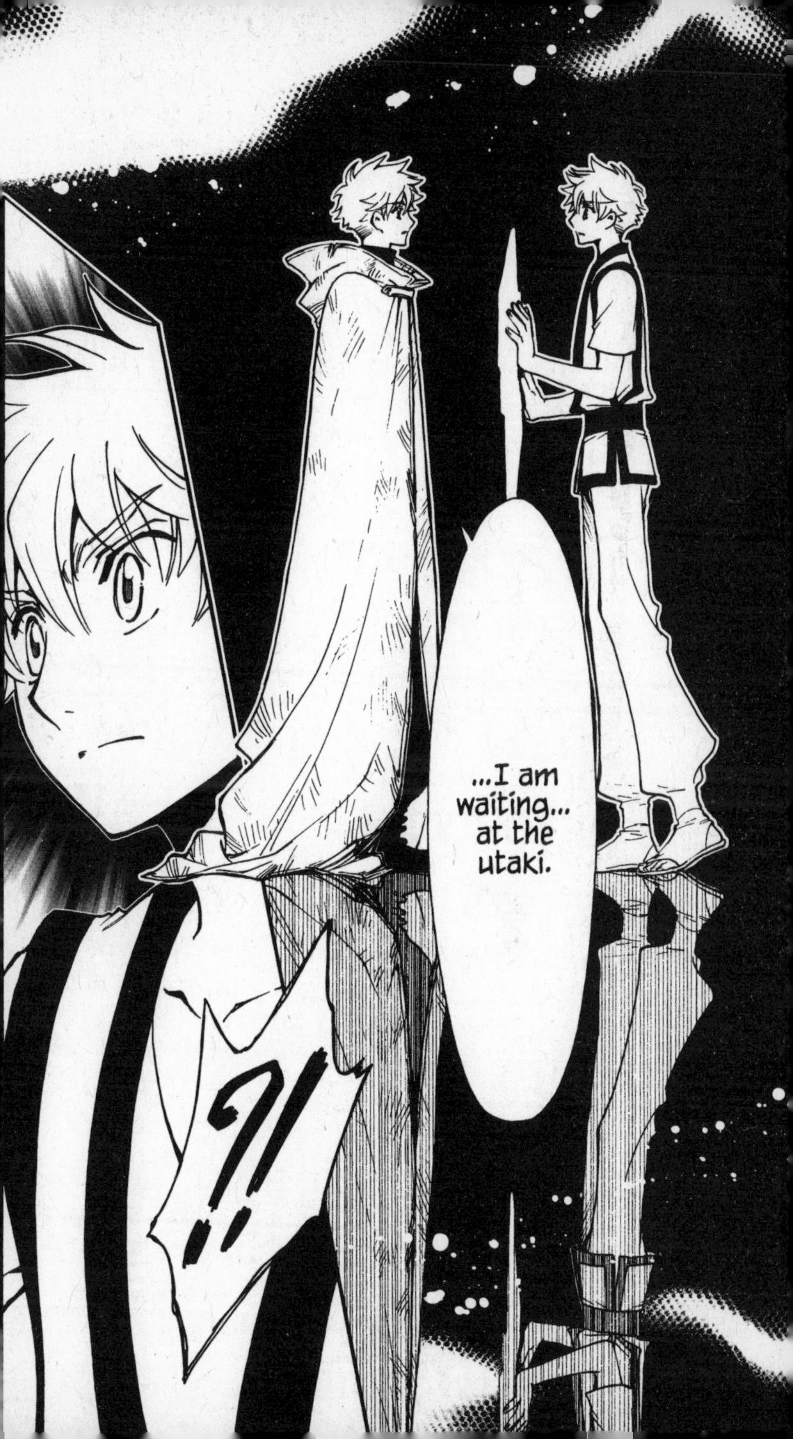
...I am waiting... at the utaki.
?!

TSUBASA
WoRLD CHRoNiCLE: NIRAIKANAI

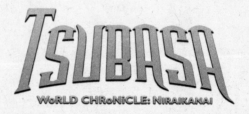

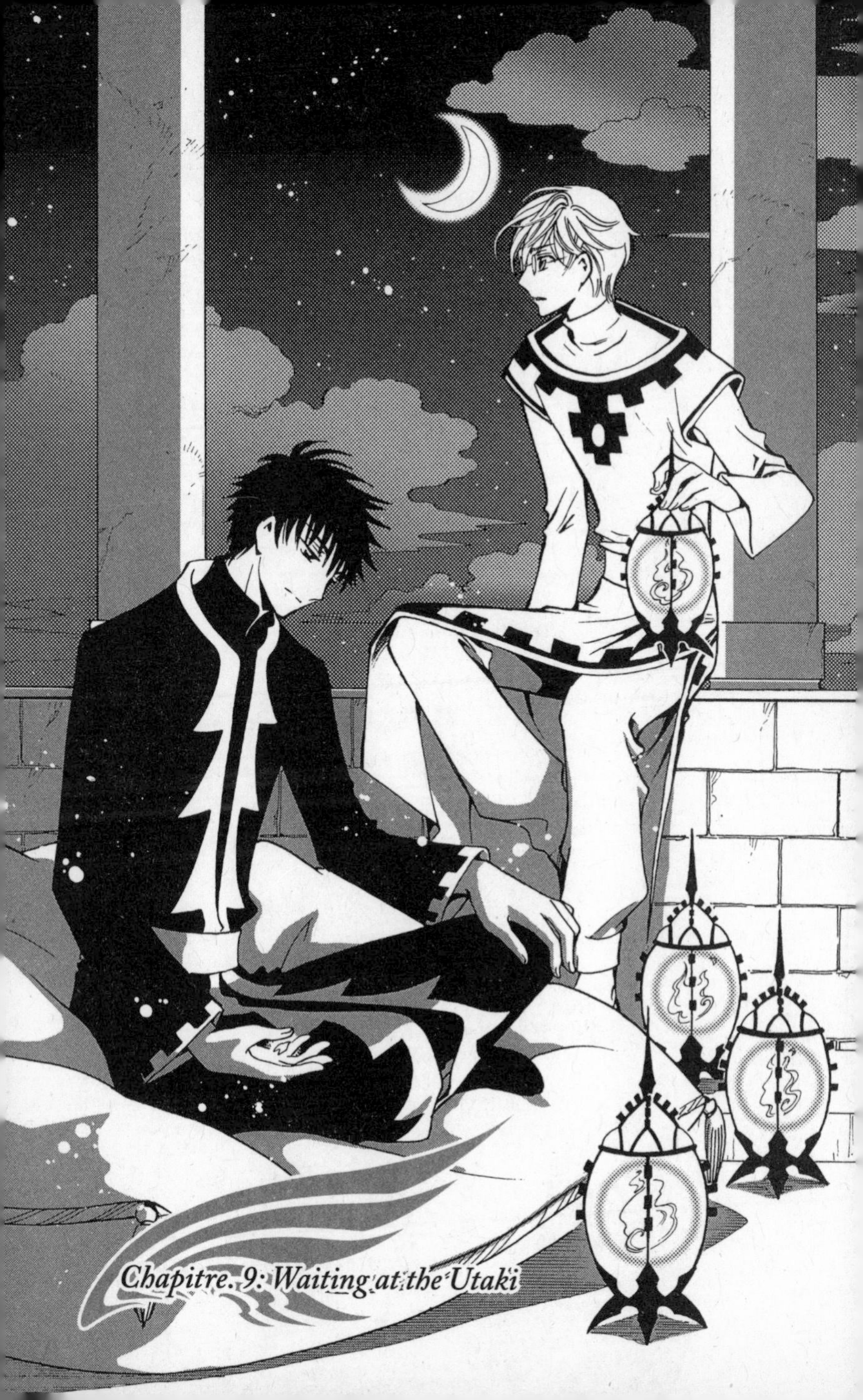
Chapitre. 9: Waiting at the Utaki

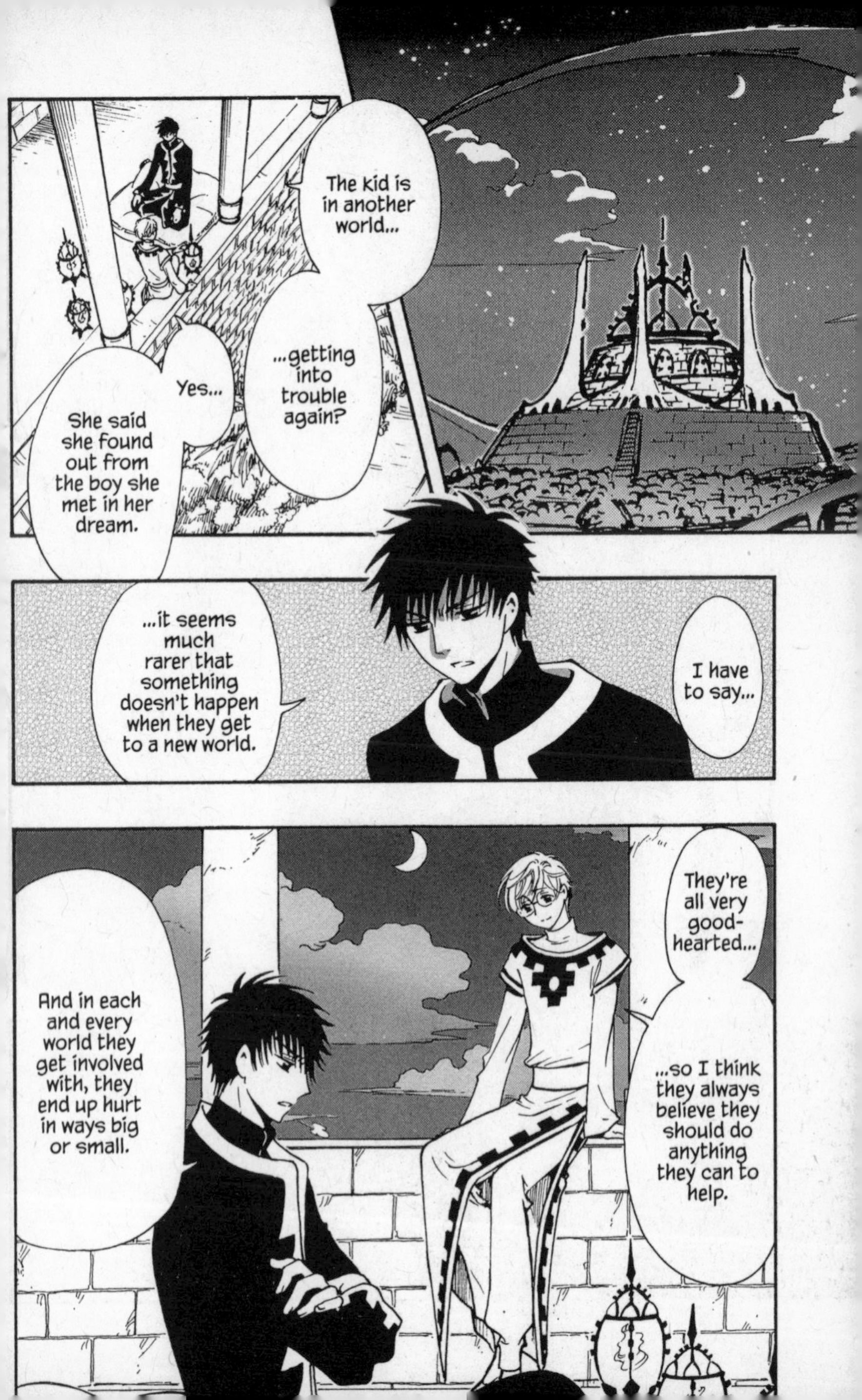
The kid is in another world...
...getting into trouble again?
Yes...
She said she found out from the boy she met in her dream.
I have to say...
...it seems much rarer that something doesn't happen when they get to a new world.
They're all very good-hearted...
...so I think they always believe they should do anything they can to help.
And in each and every world they get involved with, they end up hurt in ways big or small.

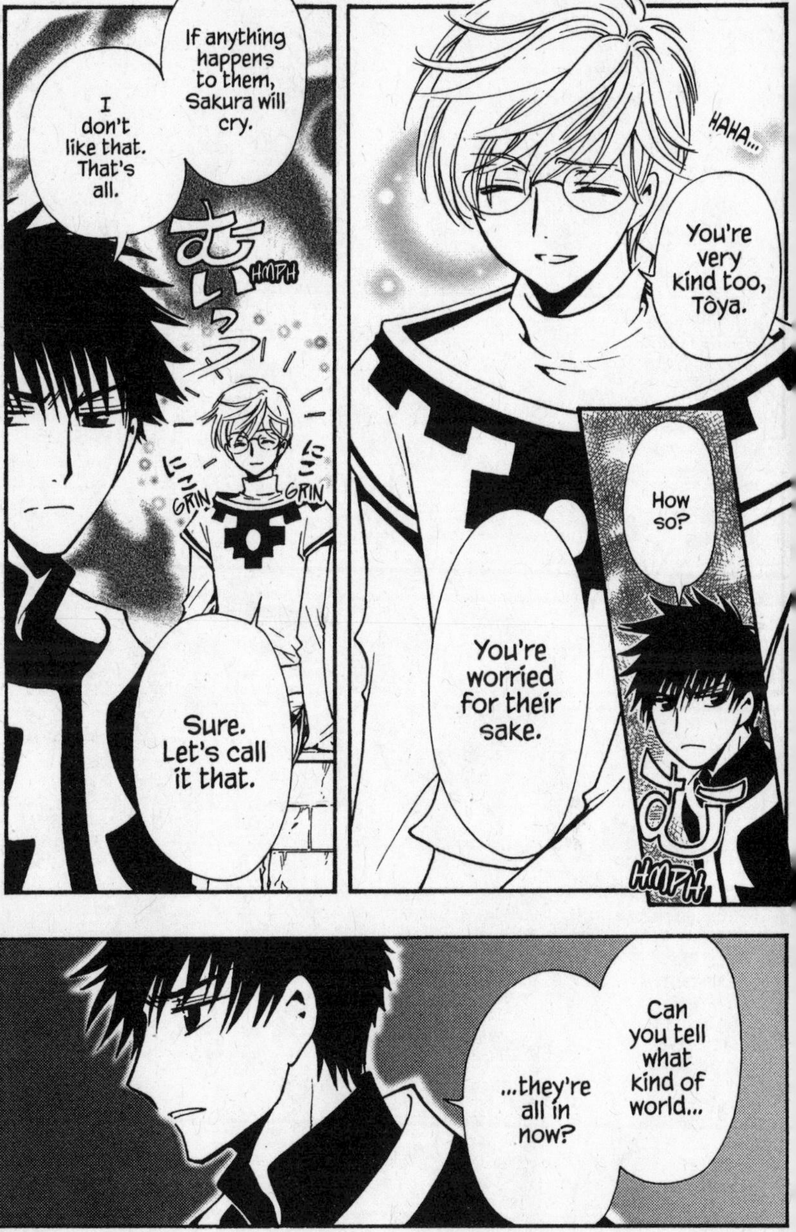
HAHA...
You're very kind too, Tôya.
How so?
You're worried for their sake.
HMPH
If anything happens to them, Sakura will cry.
I don't like that. That's all.
HMPH
GRIN
GRIN
Sure. Let's call it that.
Can you tell what kind of world...
...they're all in now?

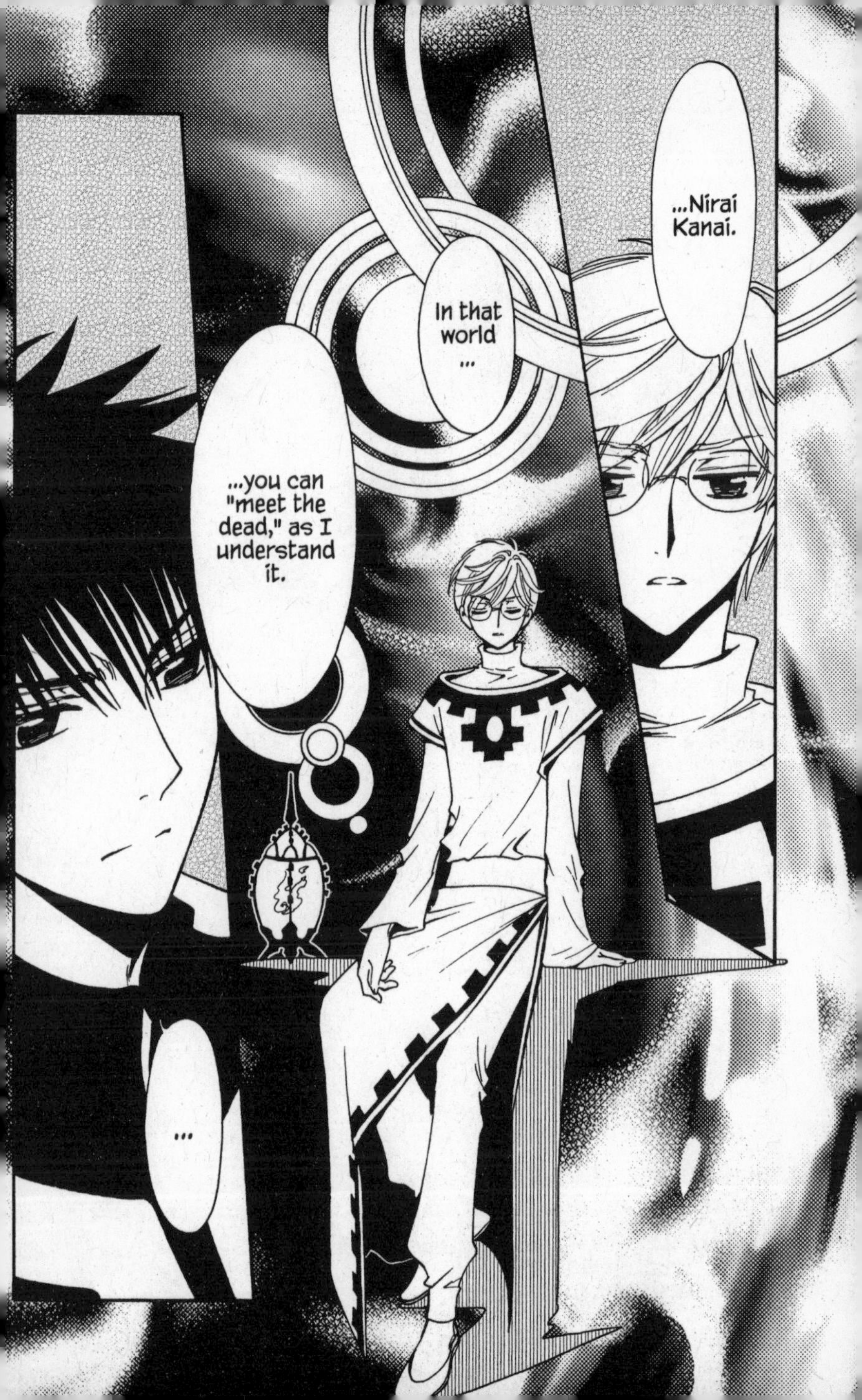
...Nirai Kanai.
In that world ...
...you can "meet the dead," as I understand it.
...

Or... And will meeting the dead be a fortunate thing for them?

I don't know.

But...

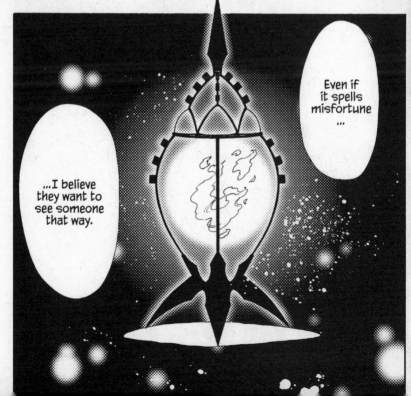

Even if it spells misfortune...

...I believe they want to see someone that way.

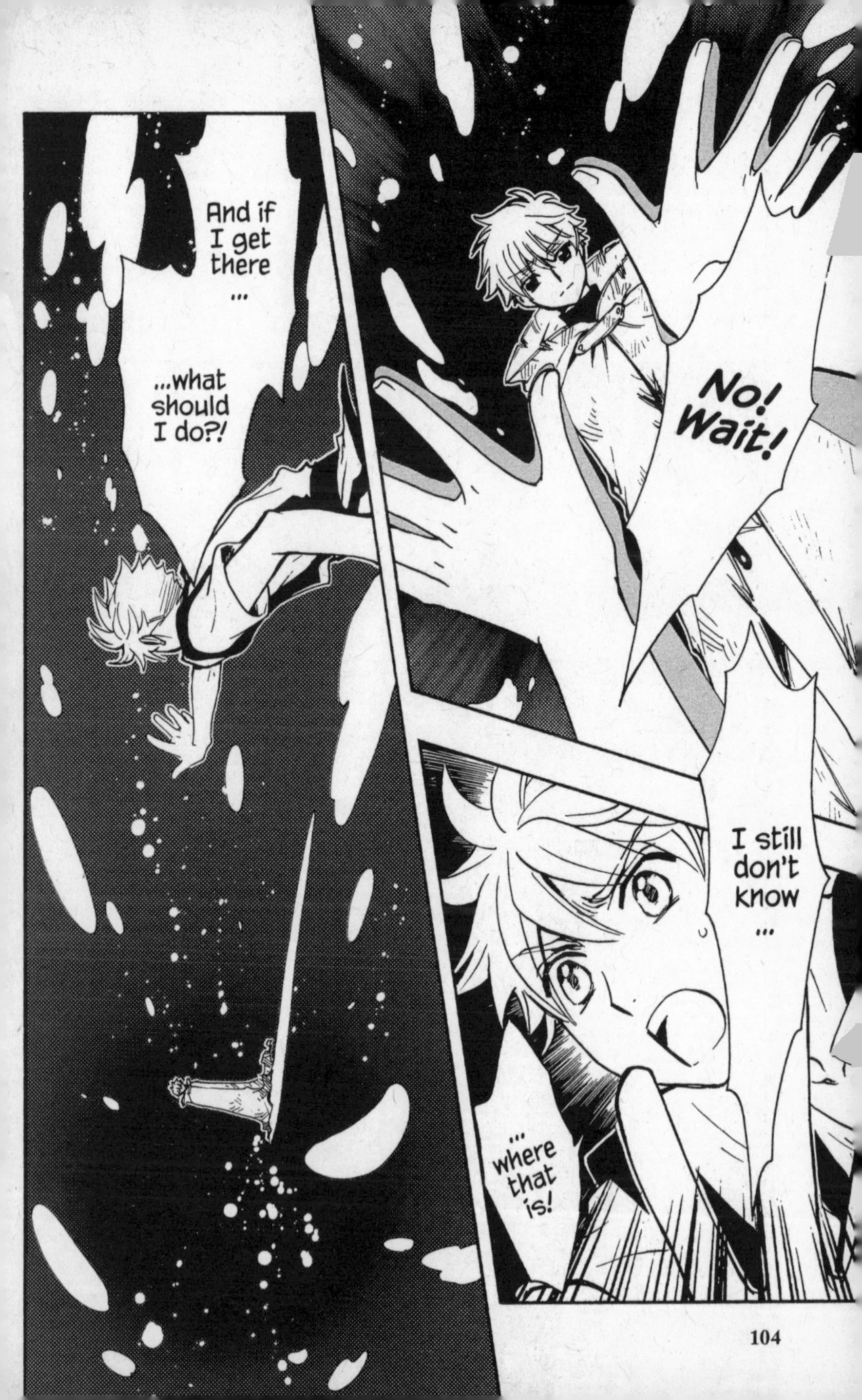
No! Wait!
I still don't know ...
... where that is!
And if I get there ...
...what should I do?!

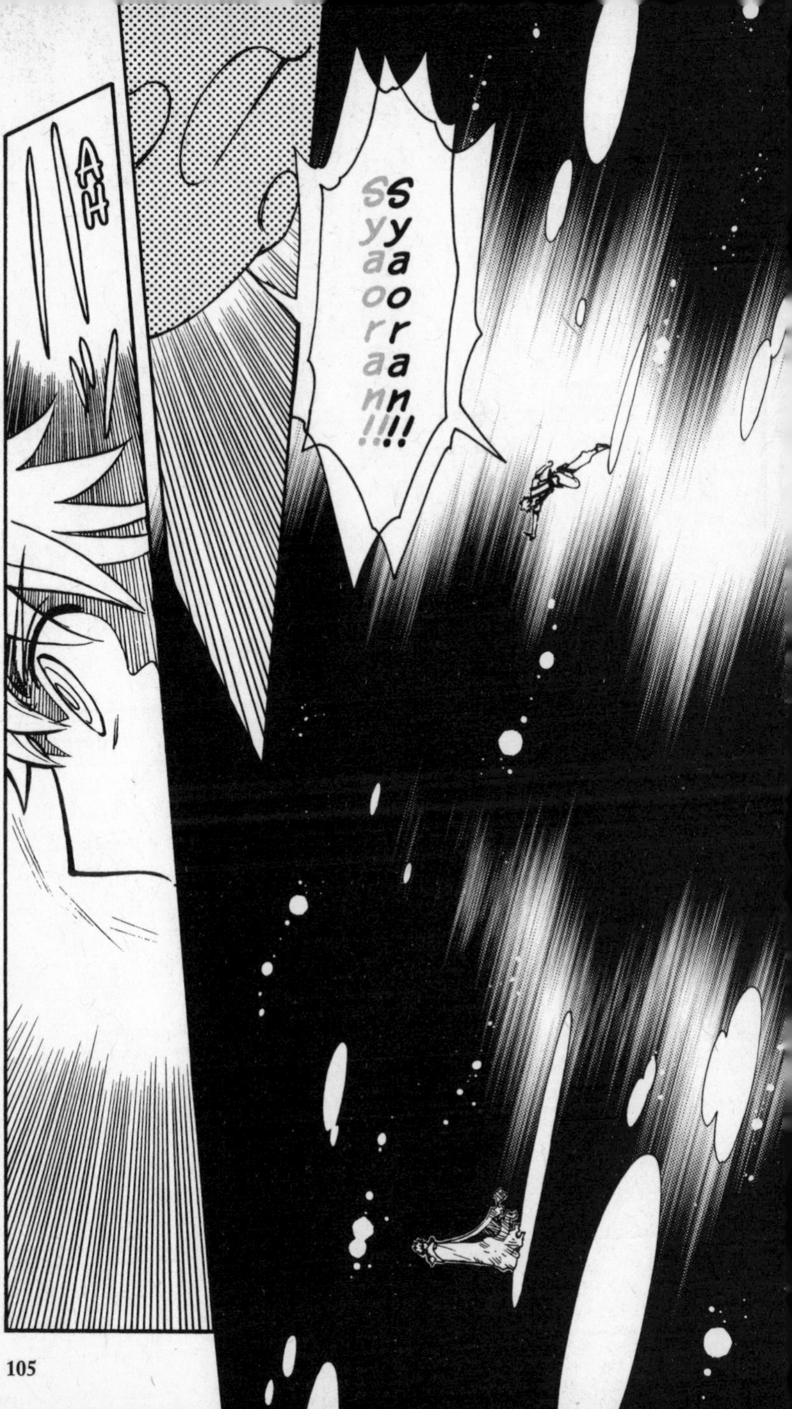
Syaoran!!
AH

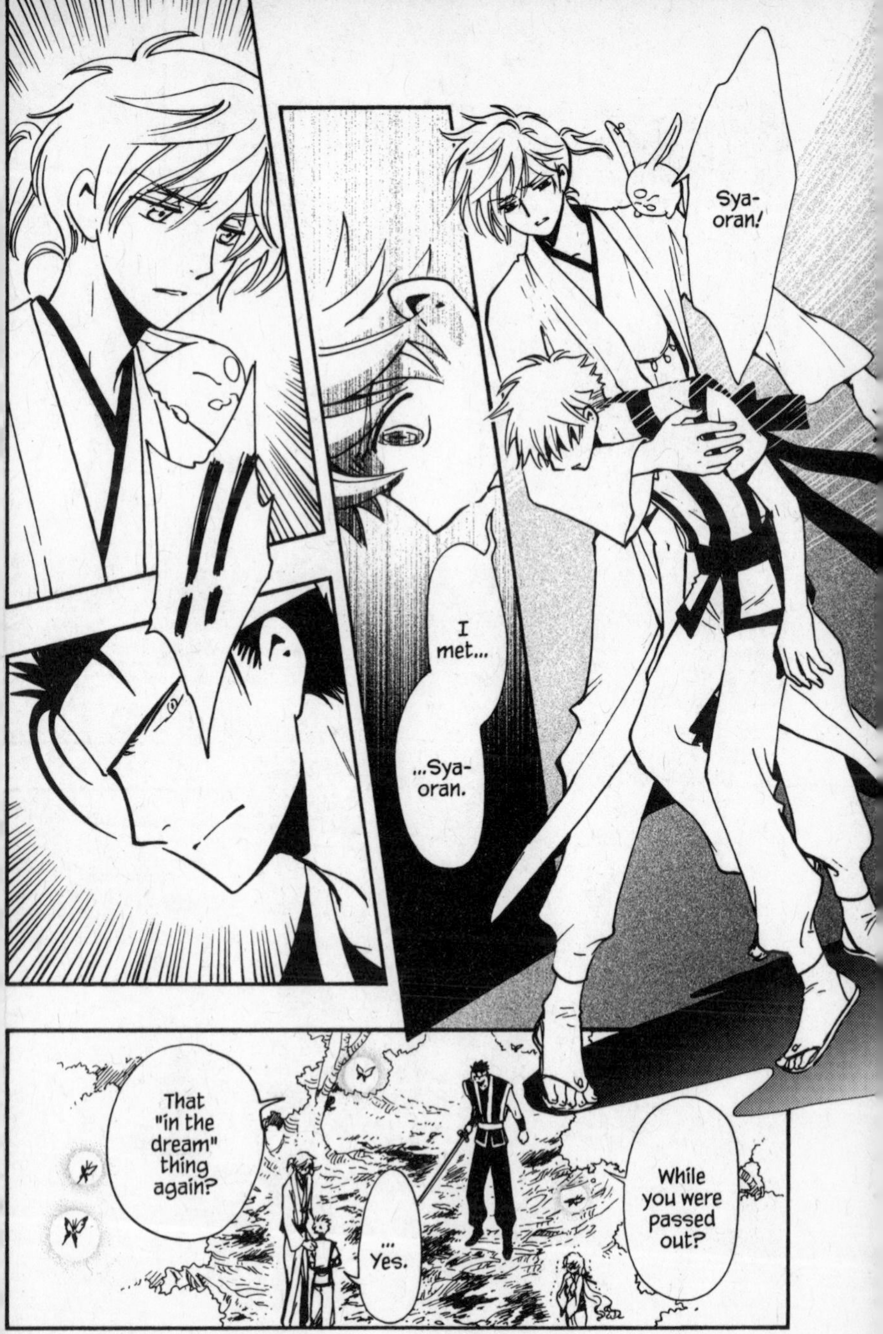
Sya-
oran!
I
met...
...Sya-
oran.
While
you were
passed
out?
...
Yes.
That
"in the
dream"
thing
again?

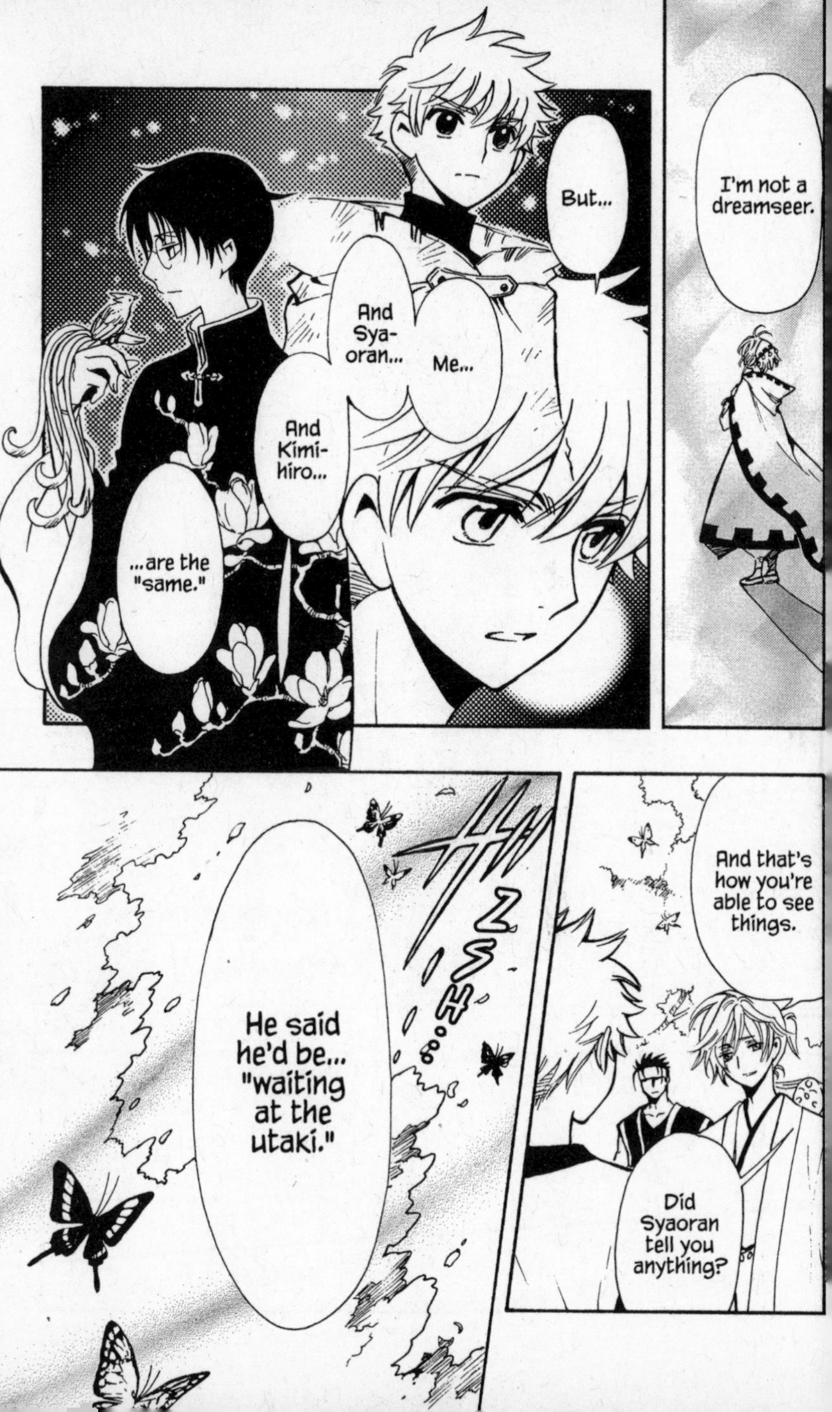
I'm not a dreamseer.
But...
Me...
And Syaoran...
And Kimihiro...
...are the "same."
And that's how you're able to see things.
Did Syaoran tell you anything?
ZSH...
He said he'd be... "waiting at the utaki."

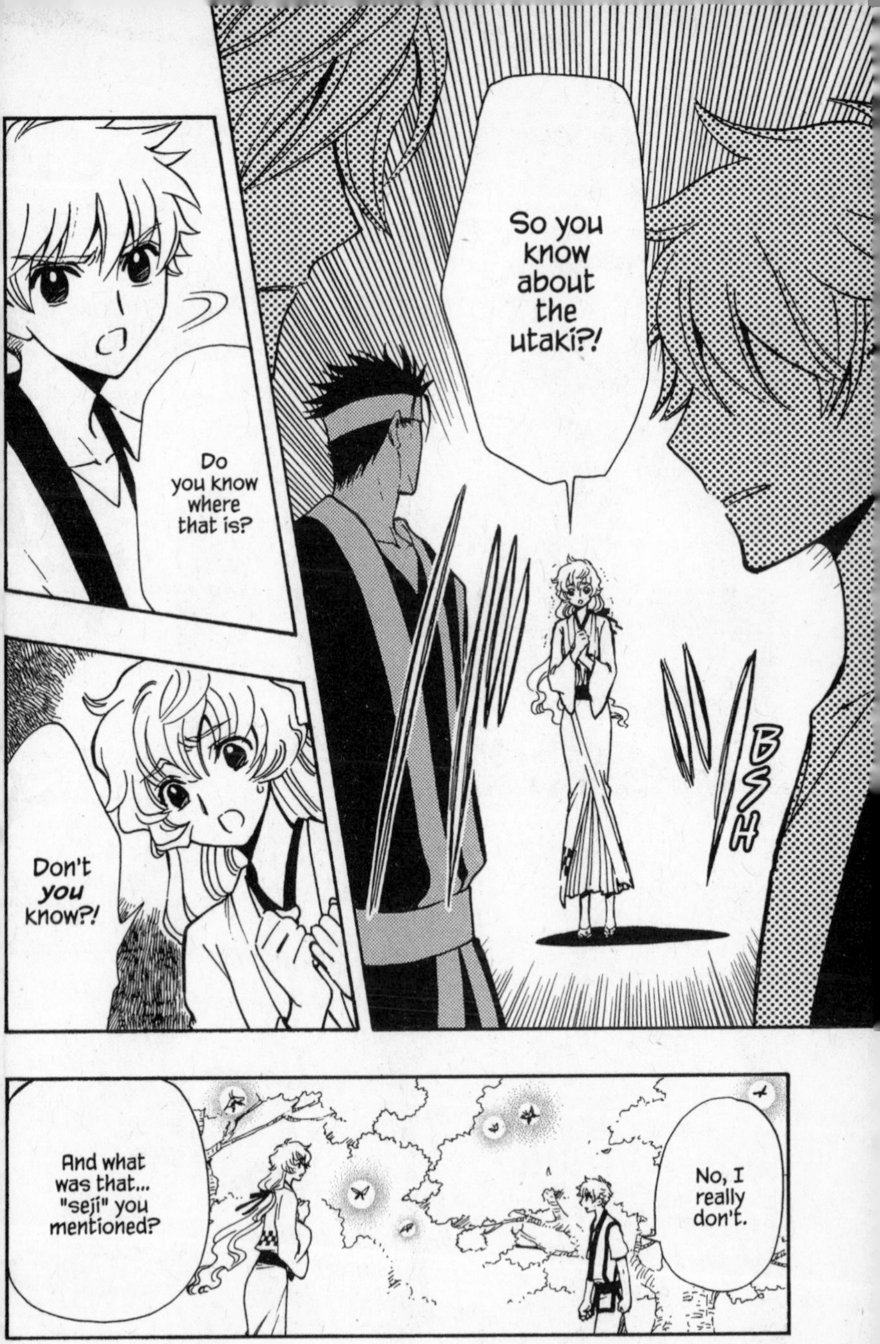
So you know about the utaki?!
BSH
Do you know where that is?
Don't *you* know?!
No, I really don't.
And what was that... "seji" you mentioned?

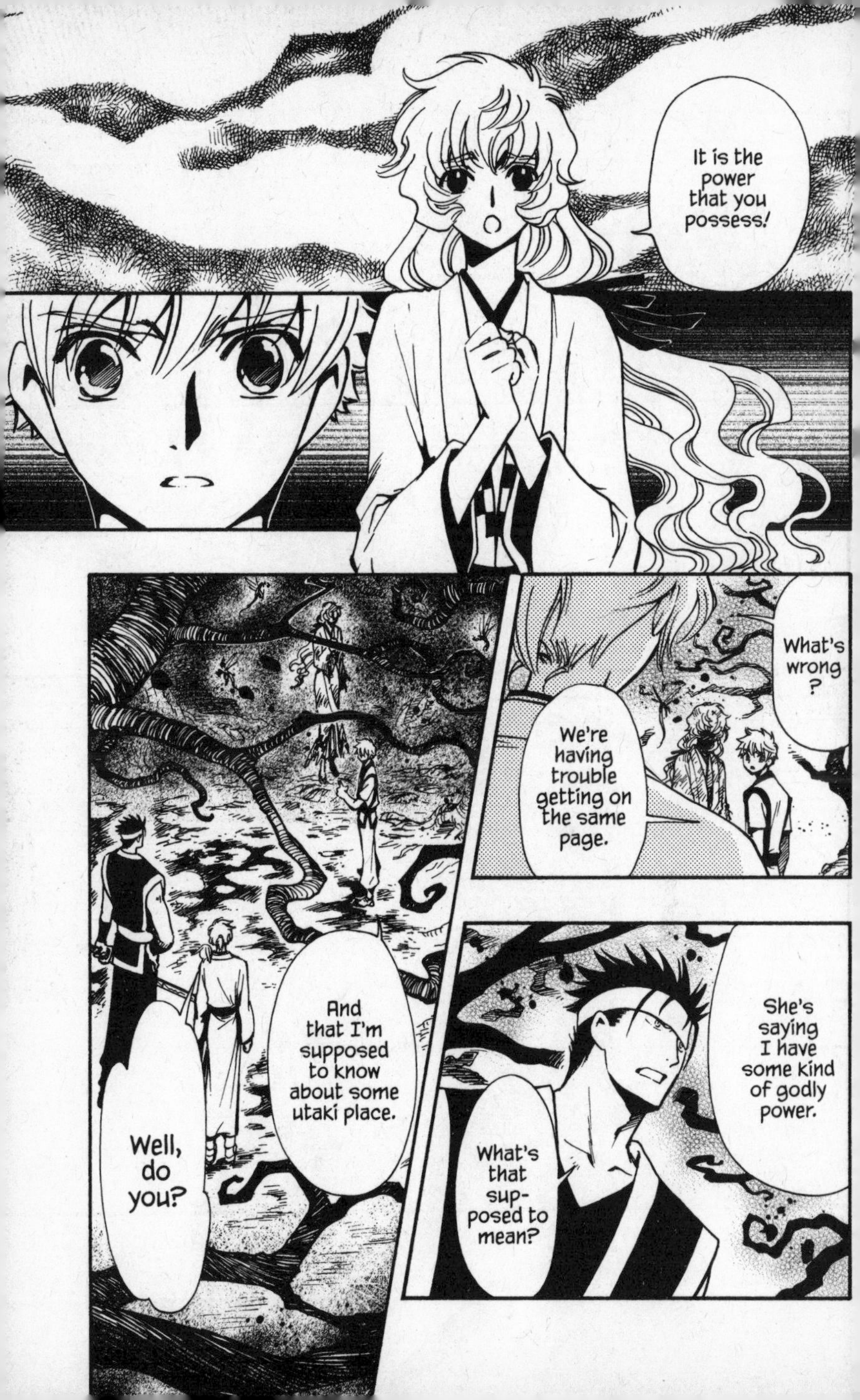
It is the power that you possess!
What's wrong?
We're having trouble getting on the same page.
She's saying I have some kind of godly power.
What's that sup-posed to mean?
And that I'm supposed to know about some utaki place.
Well, do you?

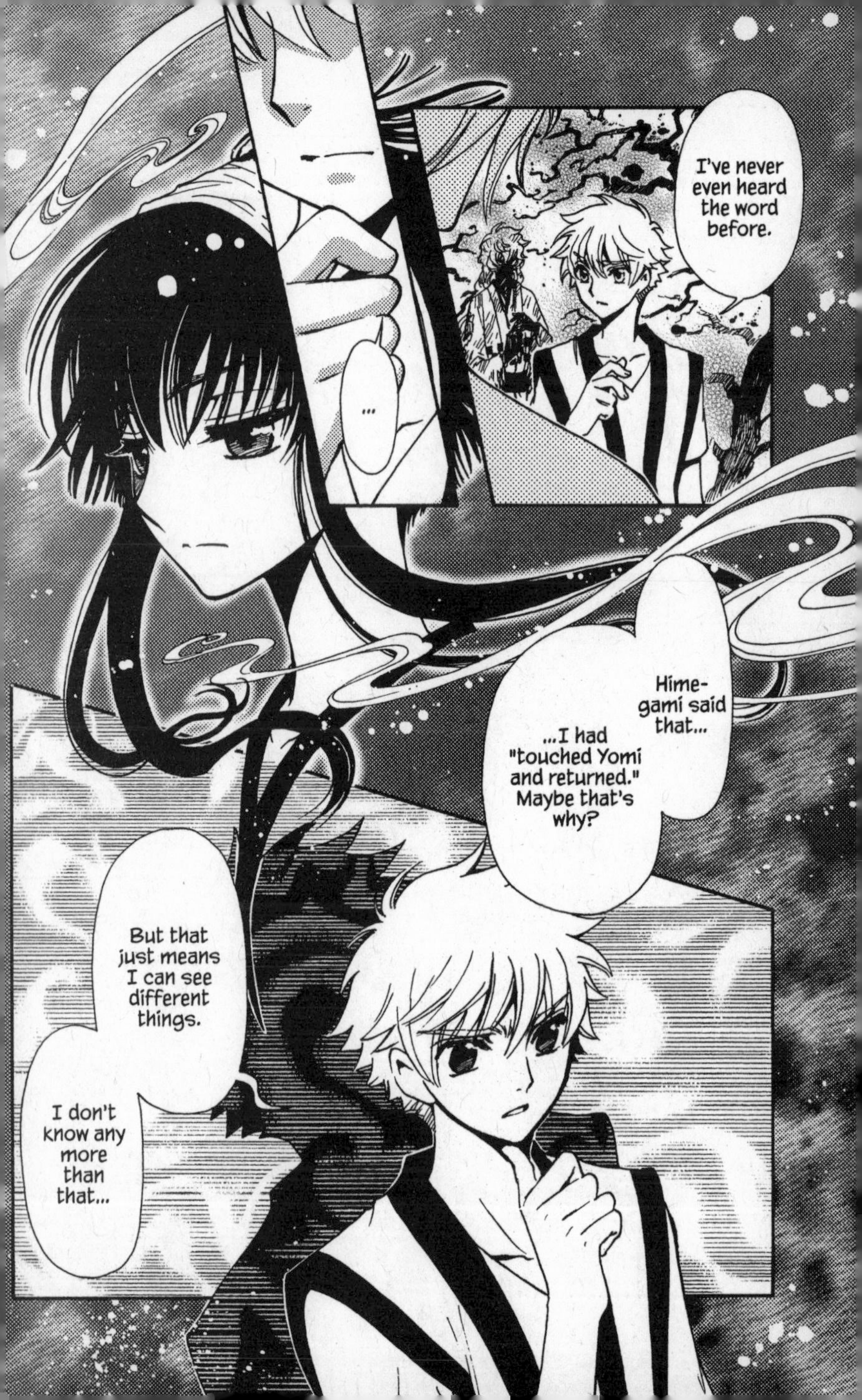
I've never even heard the word before.
...
Hime-gami said that...
...I had "touched Yomi and returned." Maybe that's why?
But that just means I can see different things.
I don't know any more than that...

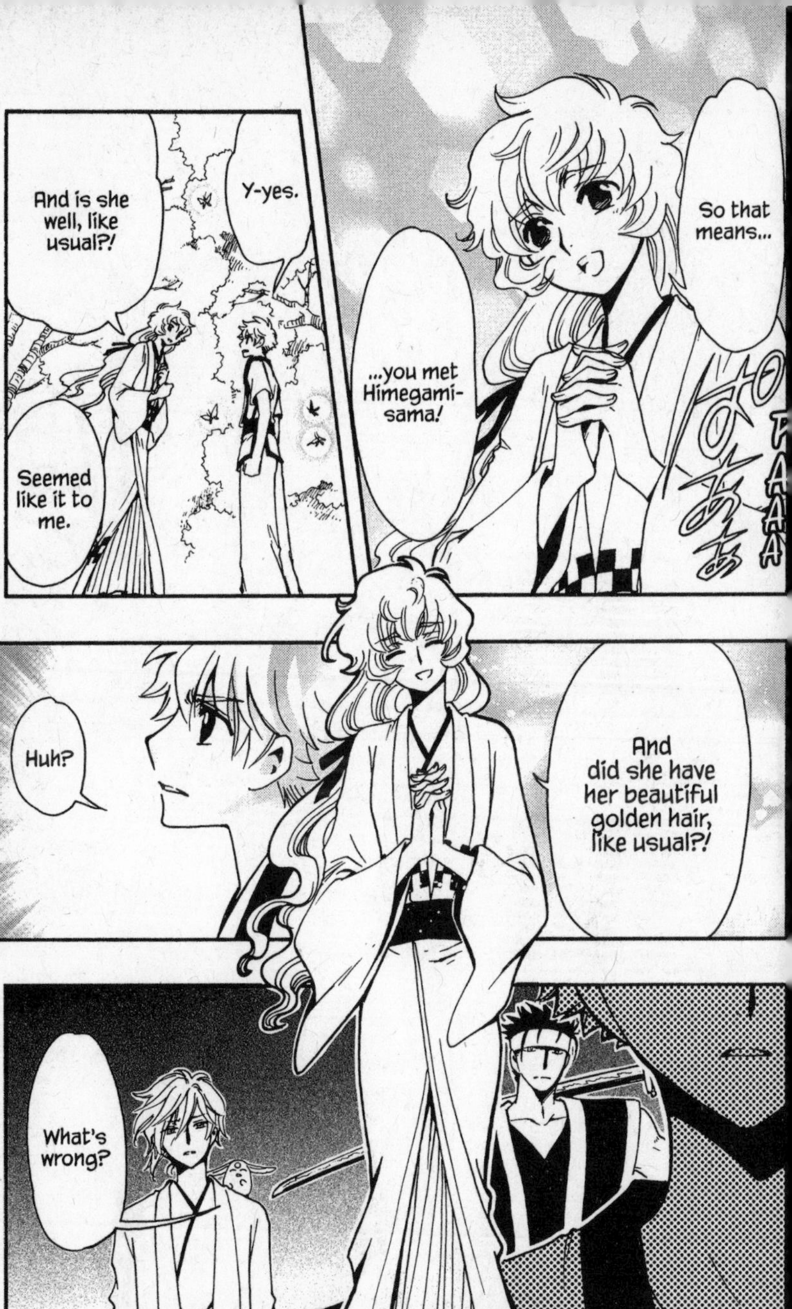
So that means...
...you met Himegami-sama!
ぱあぁ
PAAA
Y-yes.
And is she well, like usual?!
Seemed like it to me.
And did she have her beautiful golden hair, like usual?!
Huh?
What's wrong?

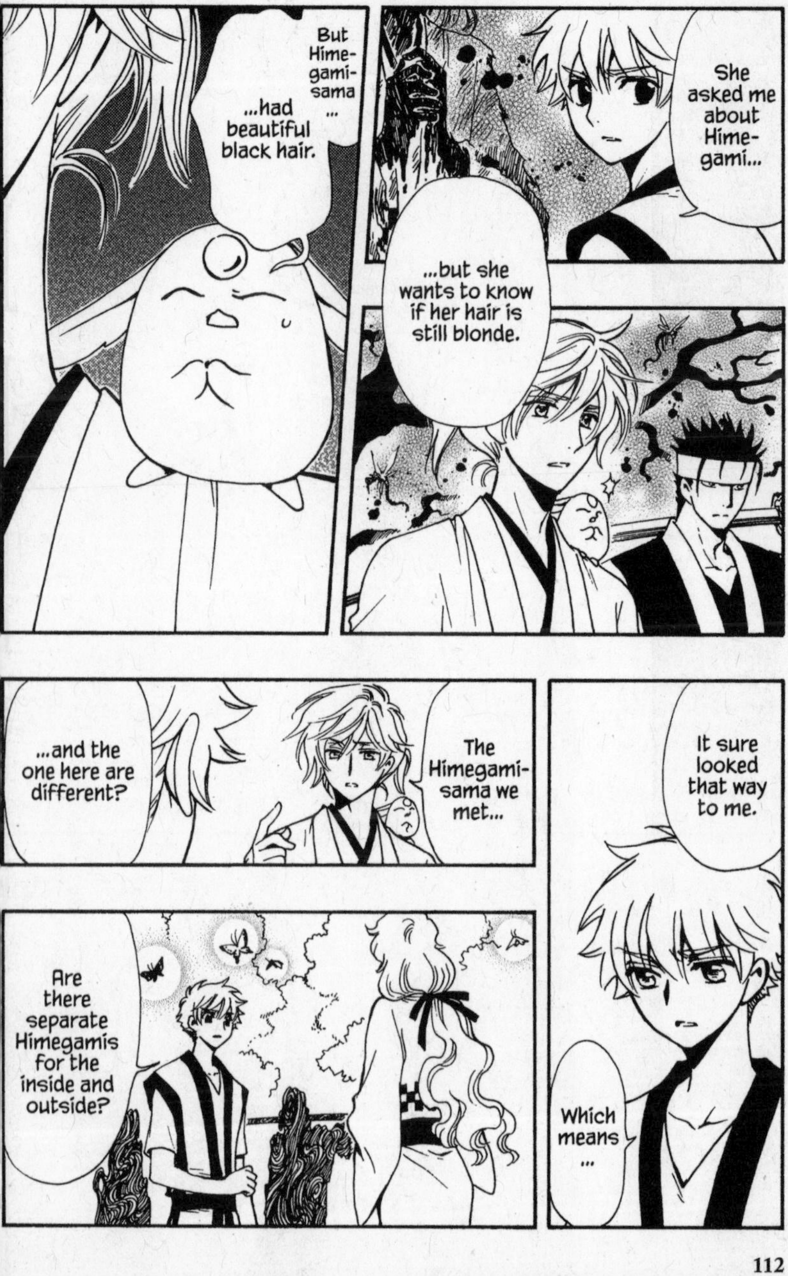
She asked me about Hime-gami...
...but she wants to know if her hair is still blonde.
But Hime-gami-sama ...
...had beautiful black hair.
It sure looked that way to me.
Which means ...
The Himegami-sama we met...
...and the one here are different?
Are there separate Himegamis for the inside and outside?

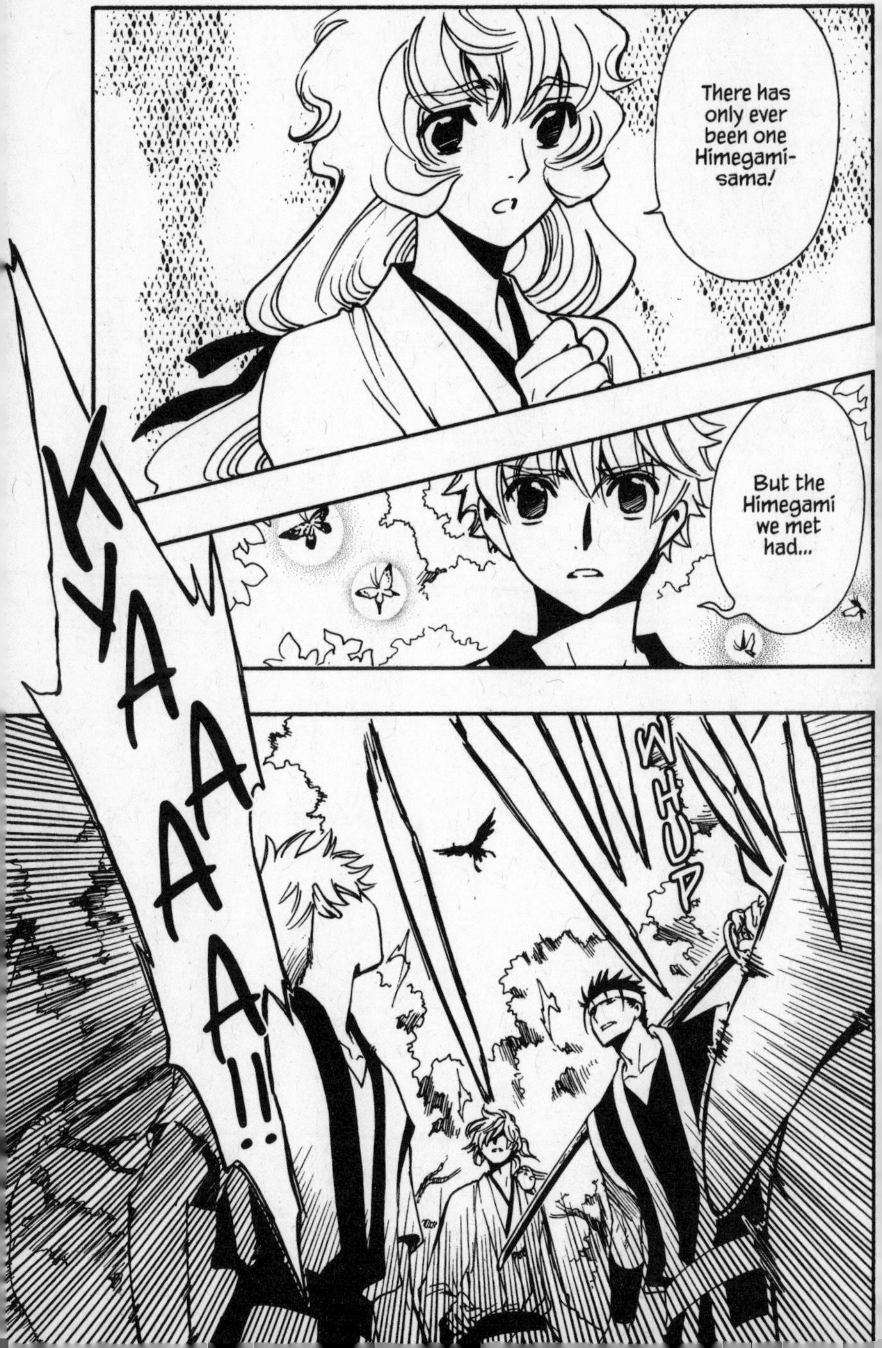
There has only ever been one Himegami-sama!
But the Himegami we met had...
KYAAAAA!!
WHUD

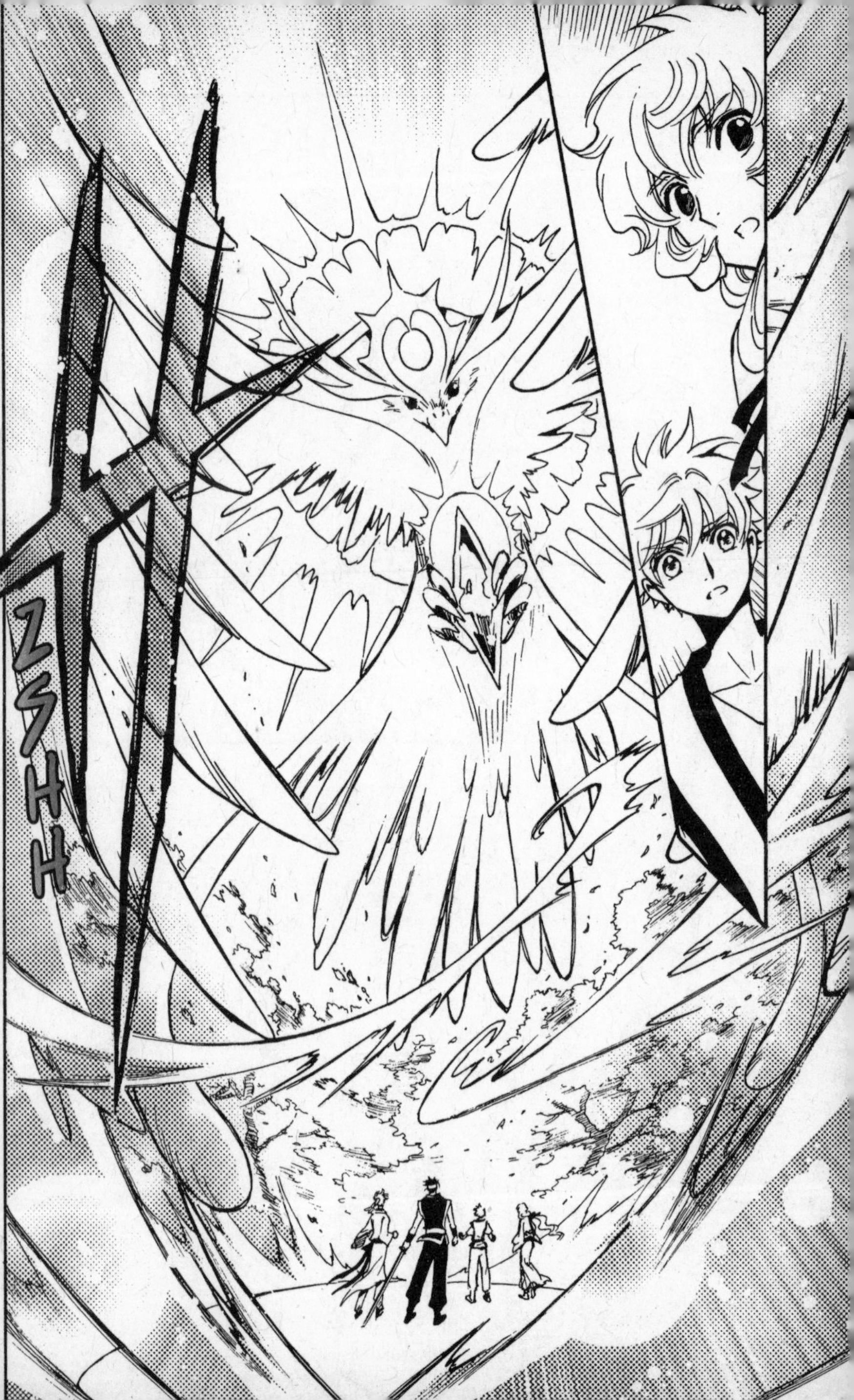
ZSHH

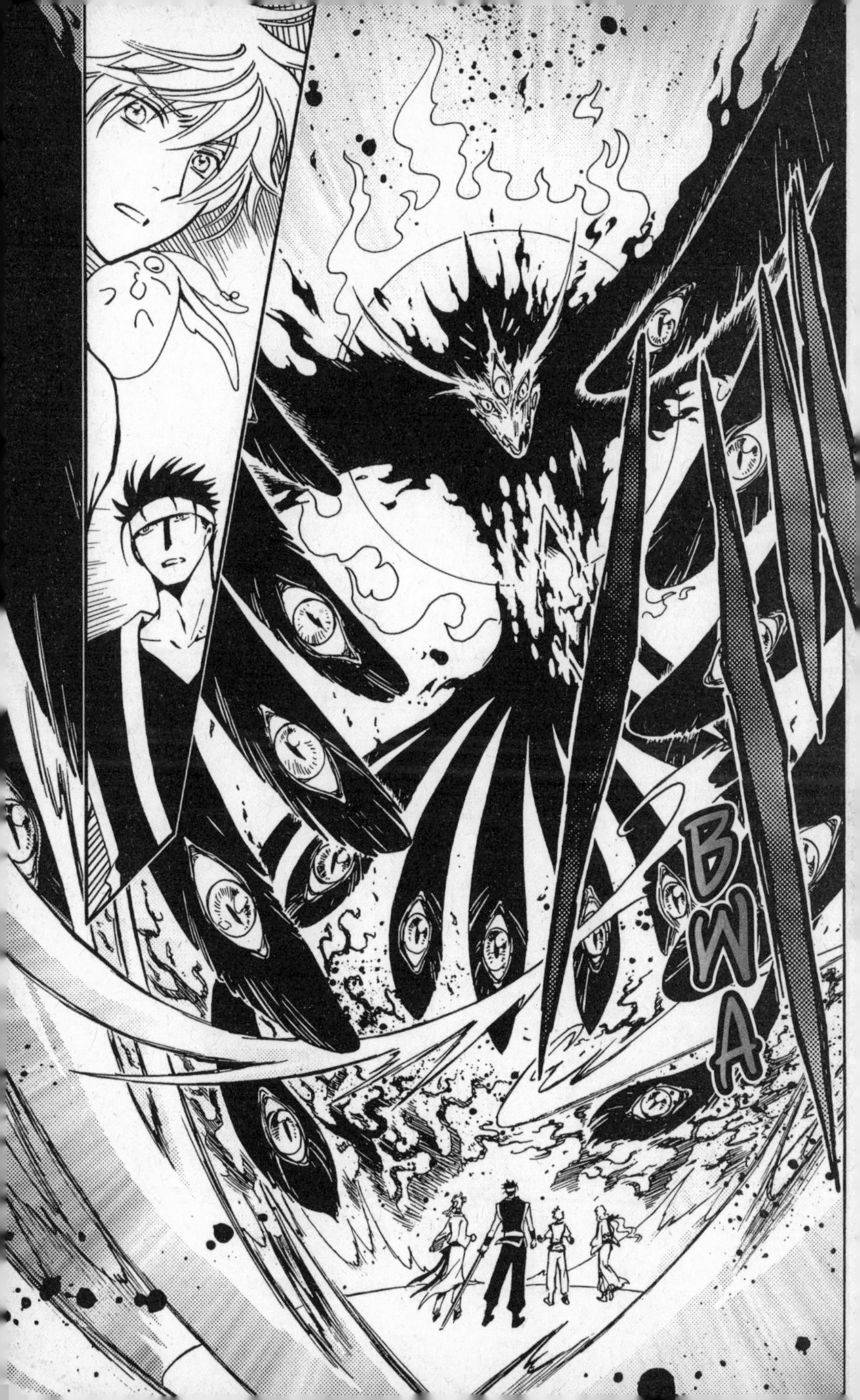
BWA

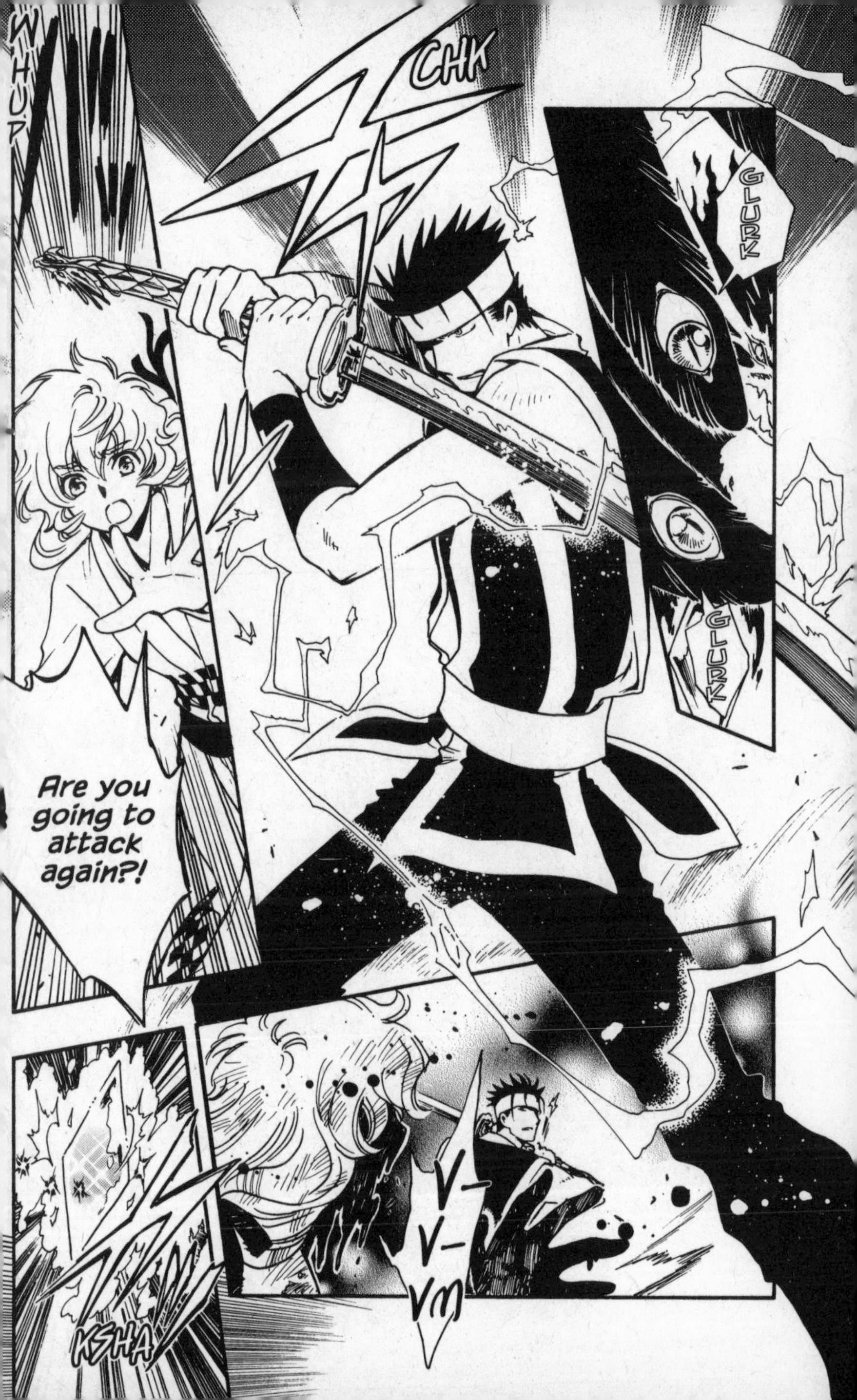
CHK
GLURK
GLURK
WHUP
Are you going to attack again?!
V-V-VM
KSHA

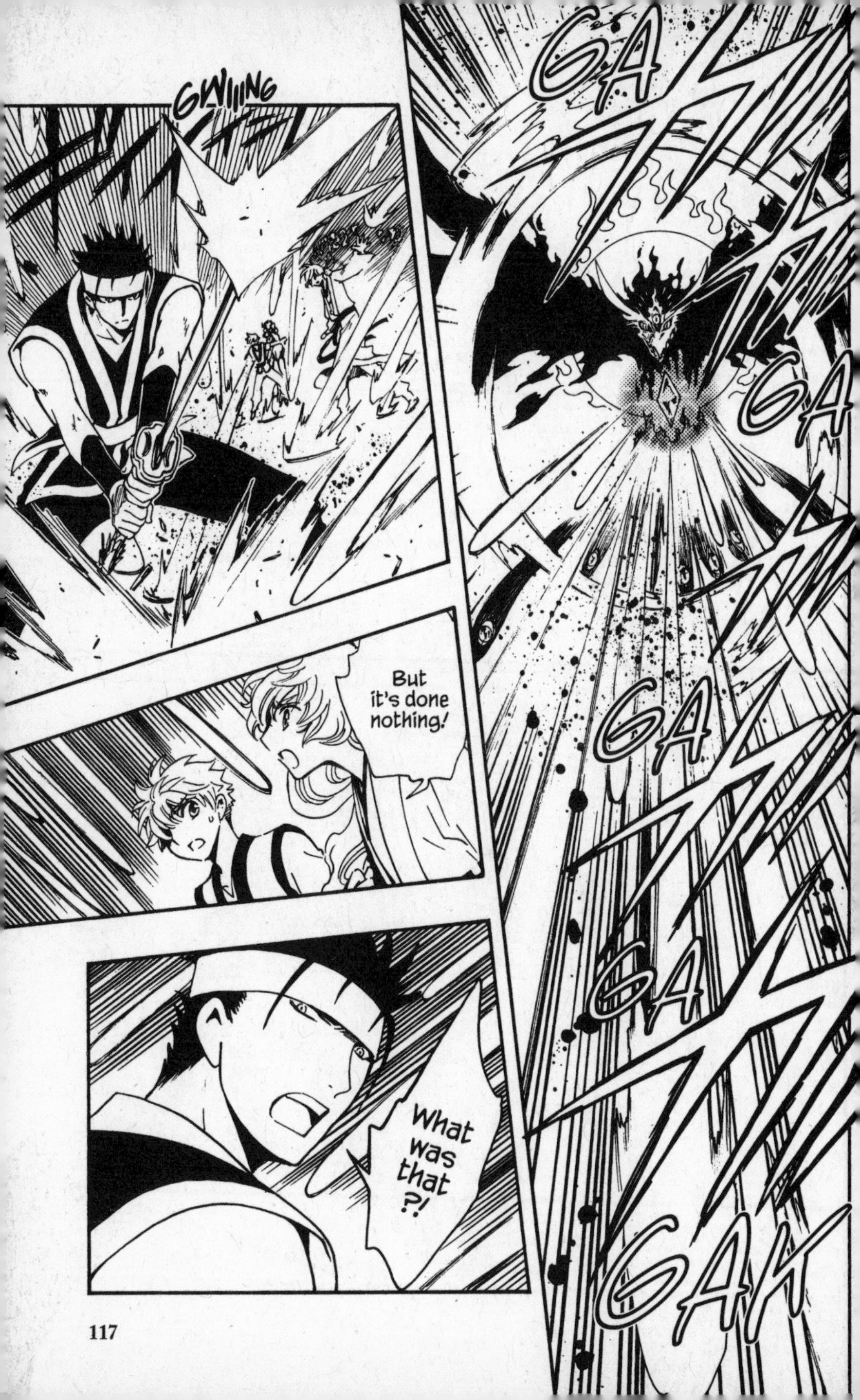
GA
GA
GA
GA
GAH
GWIIING
But it's done nothing!
What was that?!

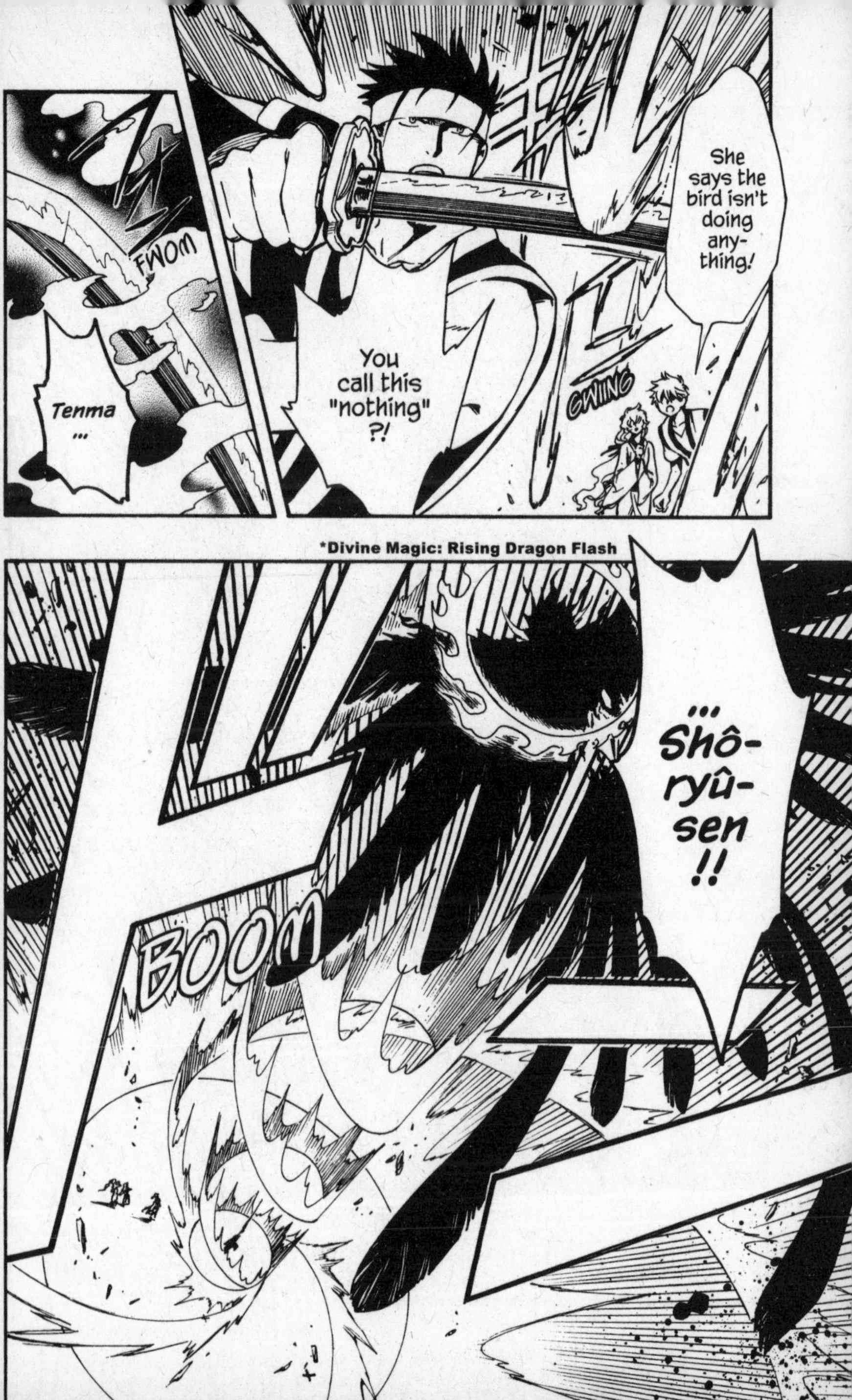
She says the bird isn't doing anything!
GWING
You call this "nothing"?!
FWOM
Tenma ...
*Divine Magic: Rising Dragon Flash
... Shô-ryû-sen!!
BOOM

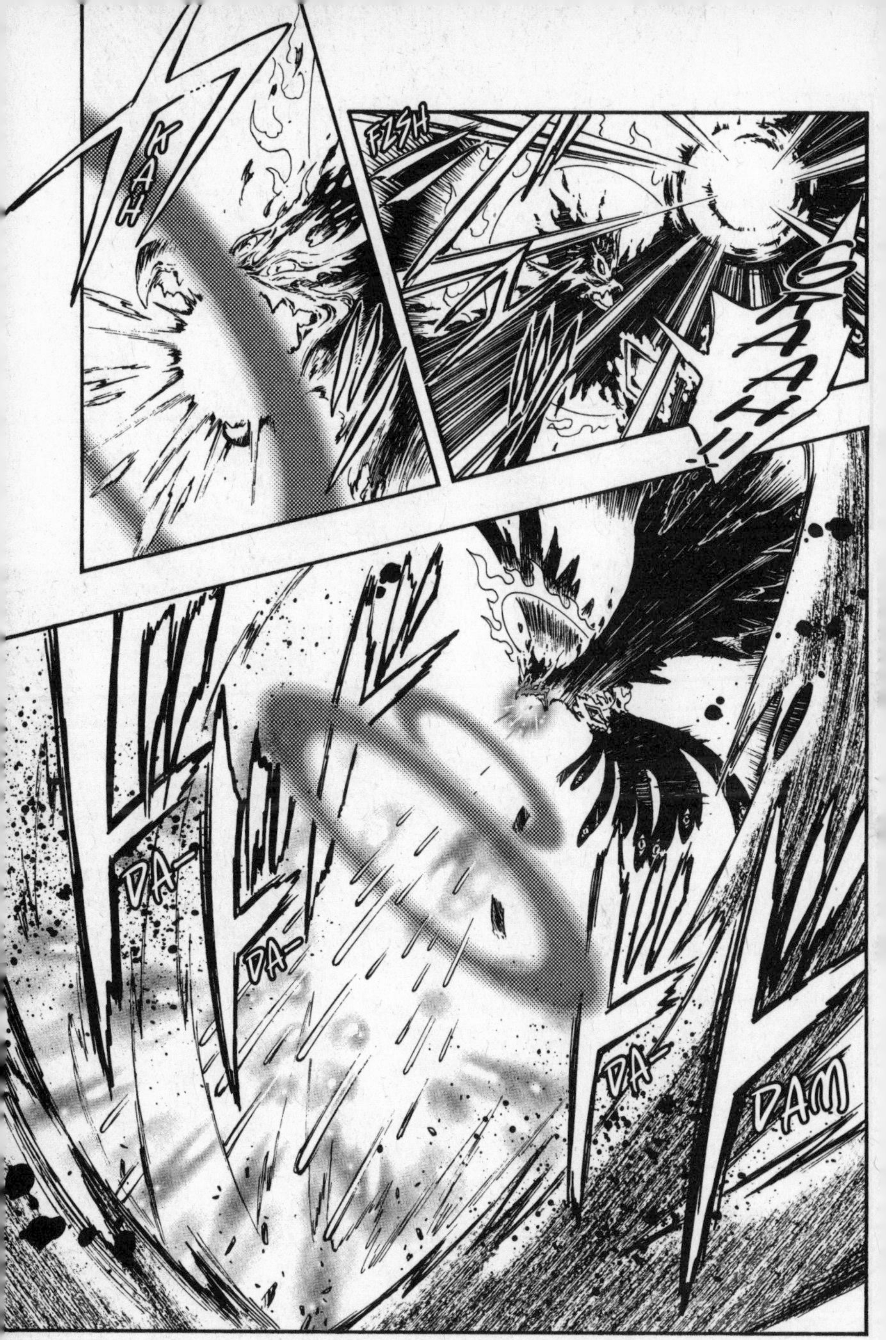
FZSH
GYAAH!!
KAAH
DA-
DA-
DA-
DAM

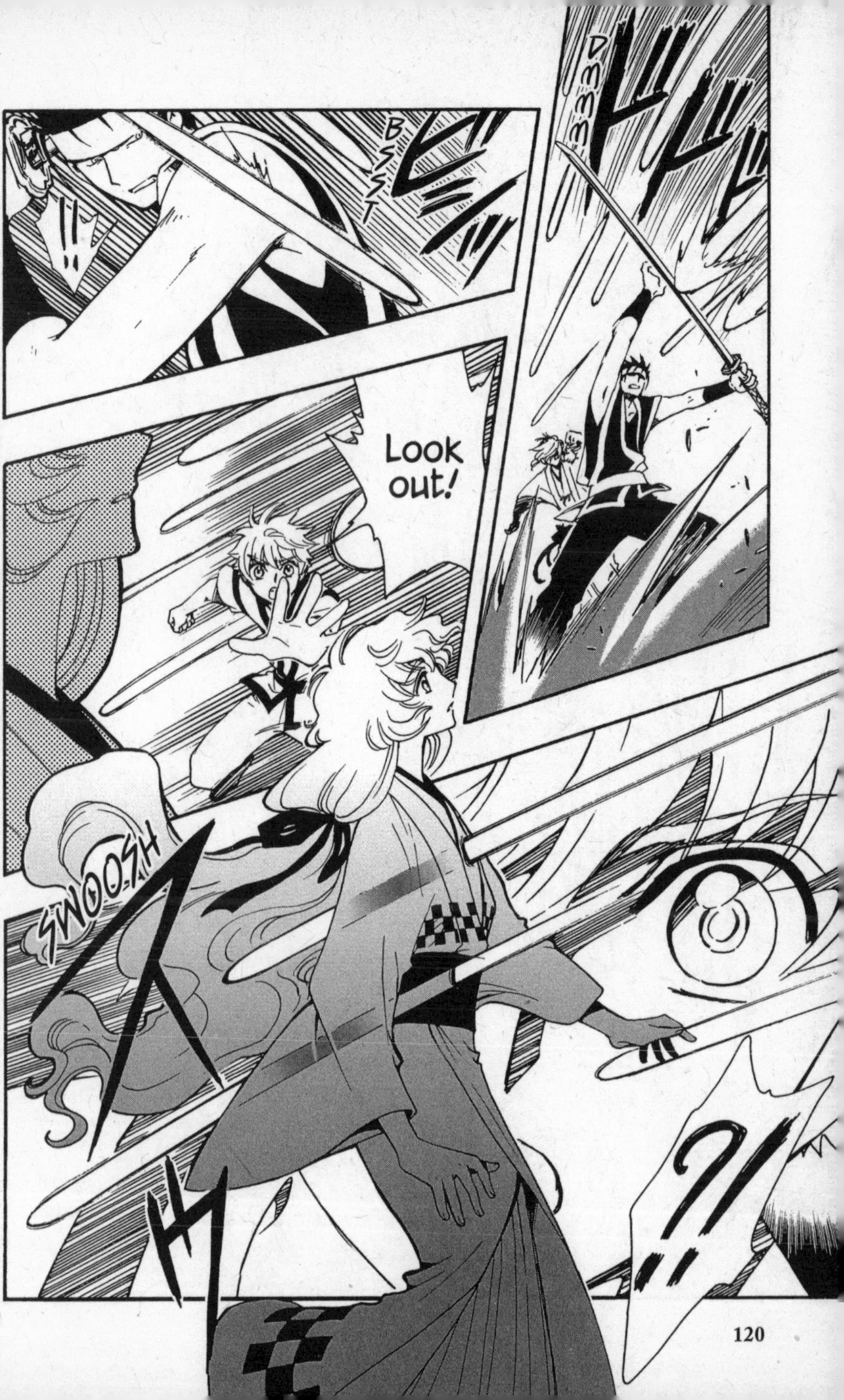
DMMM
BSST
!!
Look out!
SWOOSH
?!

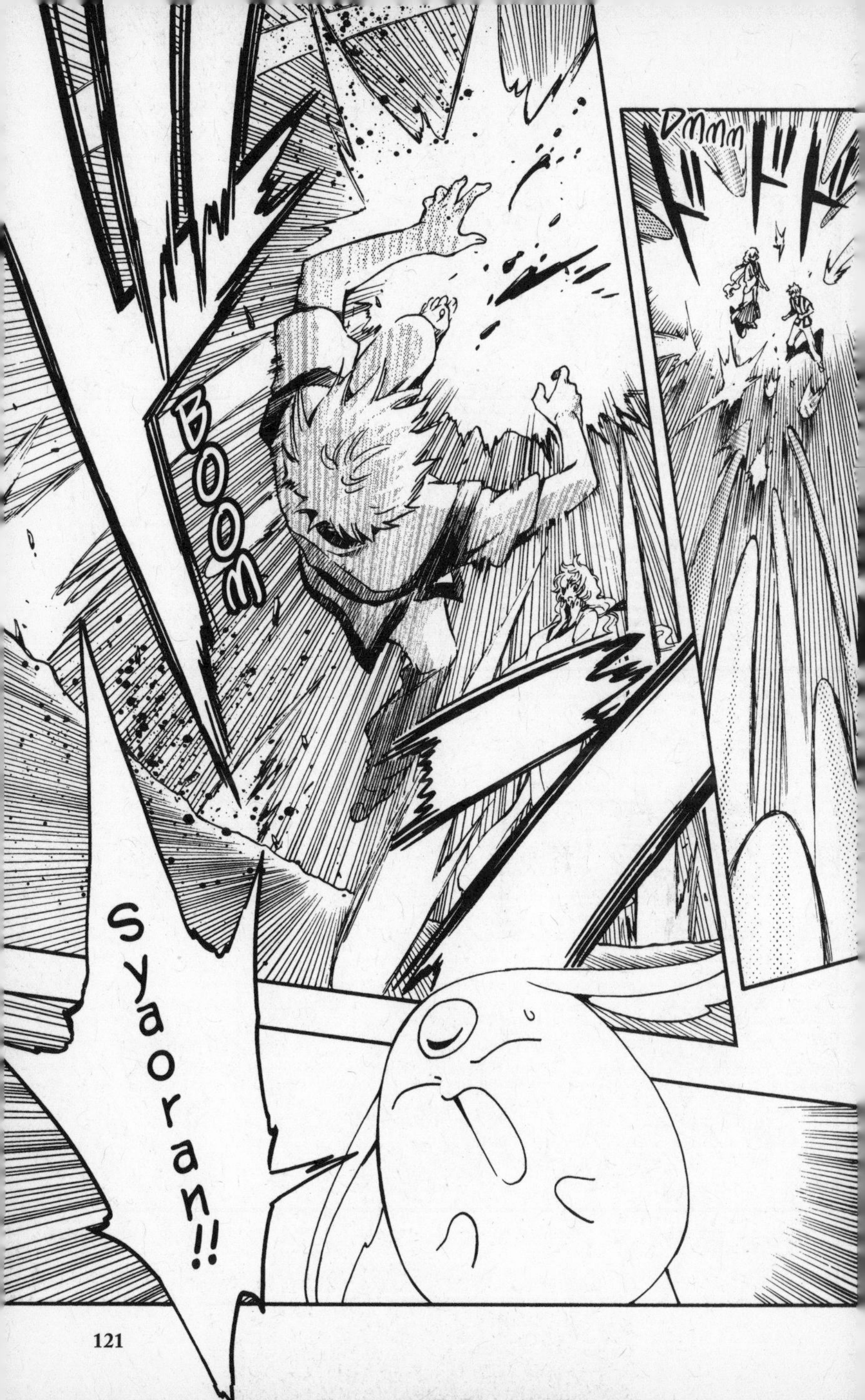
DMMM
BOOM
Syaoran!!

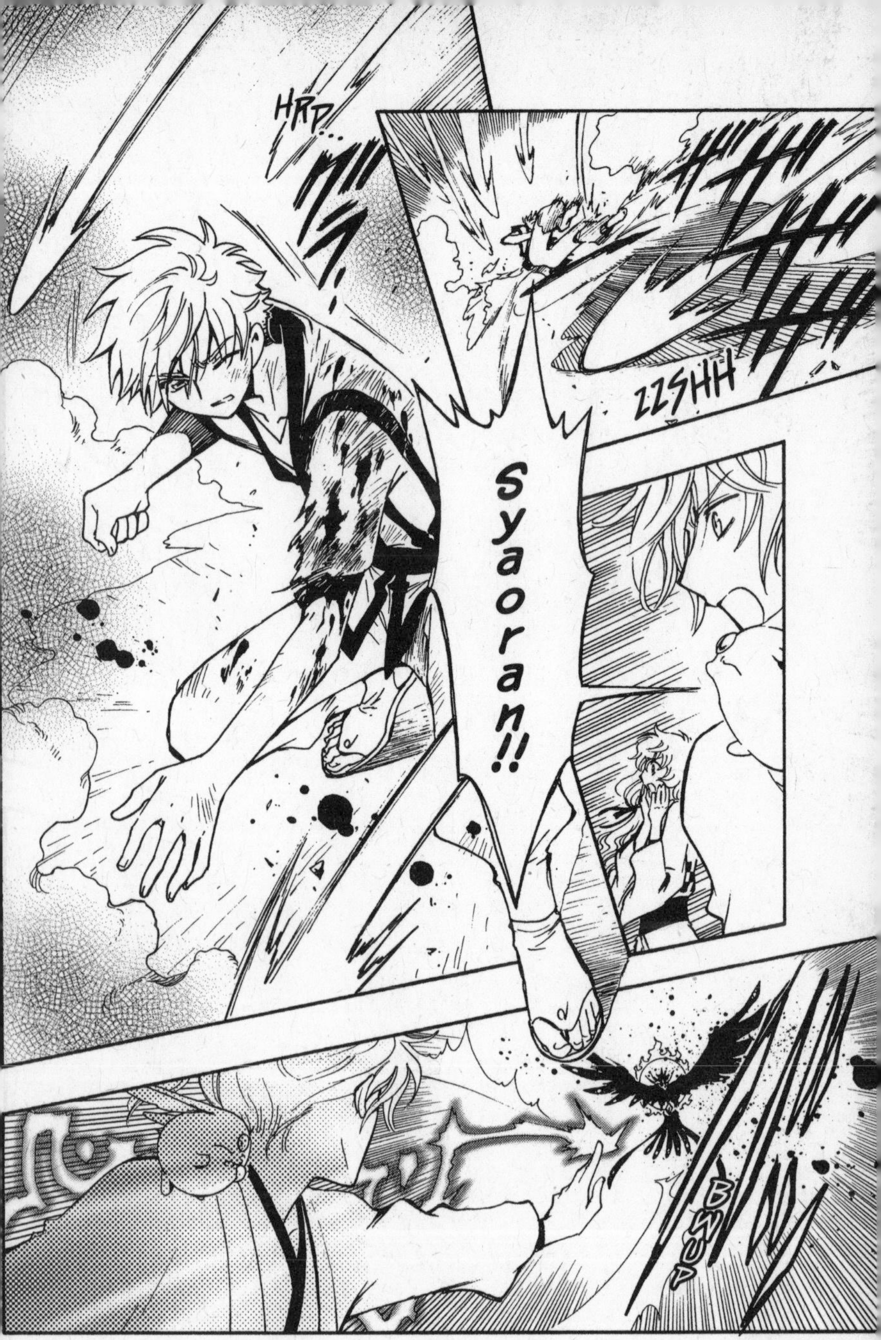
ZZSHH
Syaoran!!
HRP...
BWUP

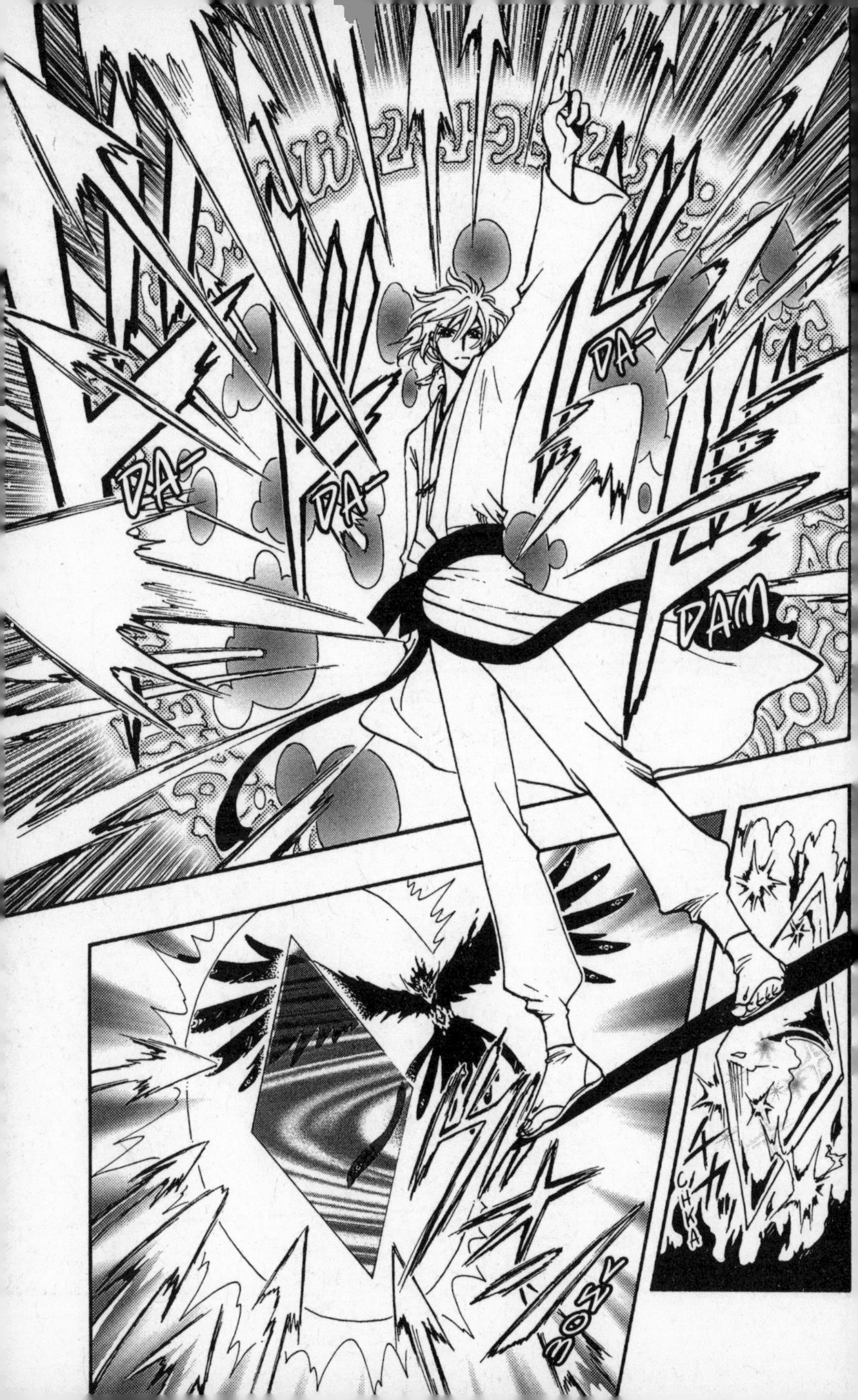
DA-
DAM
DA-
DA-
CHKA
VWOM

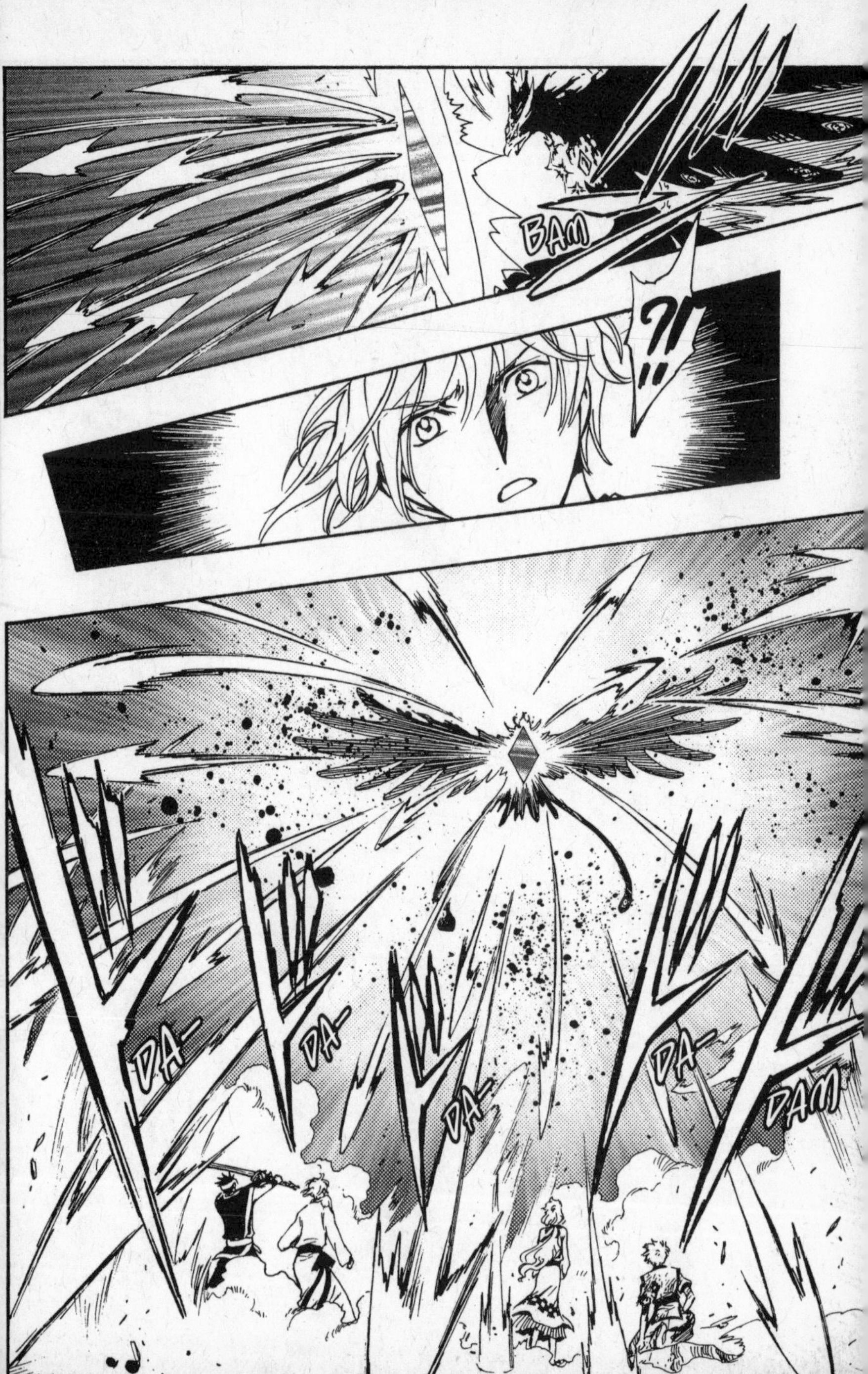
BAM
?!!
DAM
DA-
DA-
DA-
DA-

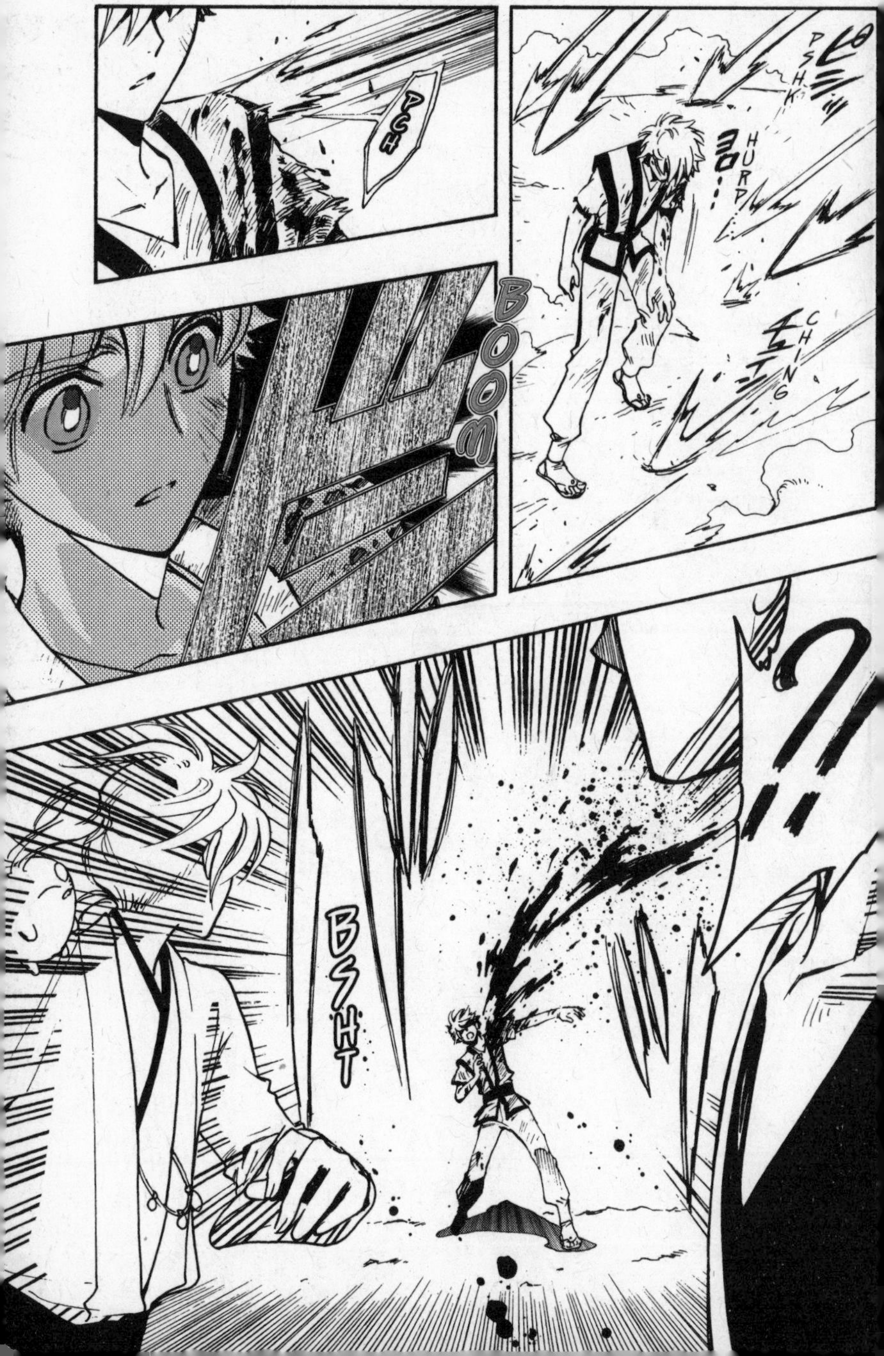
PSHK
HURP
CHING
PCH
BOOM
BSHT

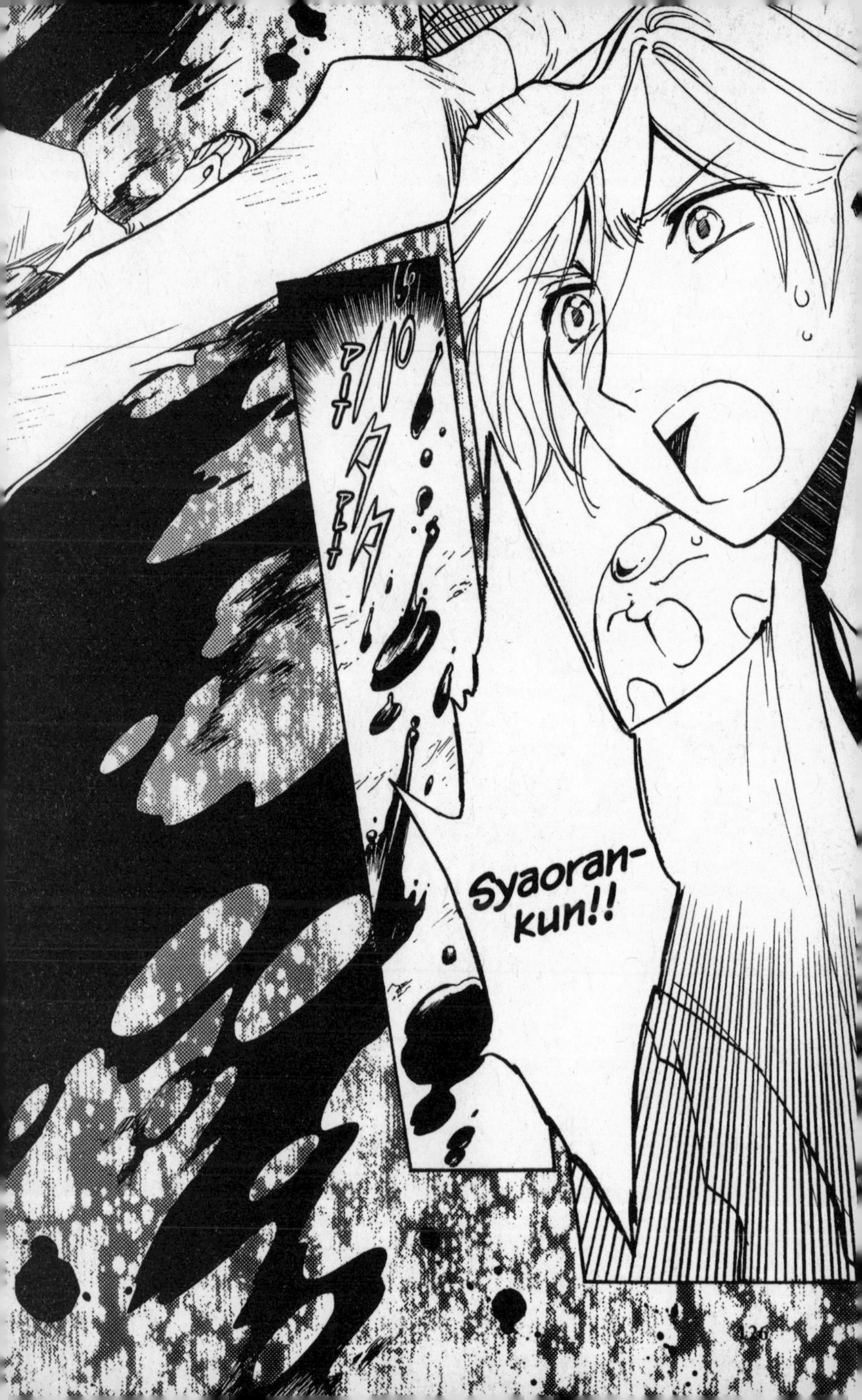
PIT PLIT
Syaoran-kun!!

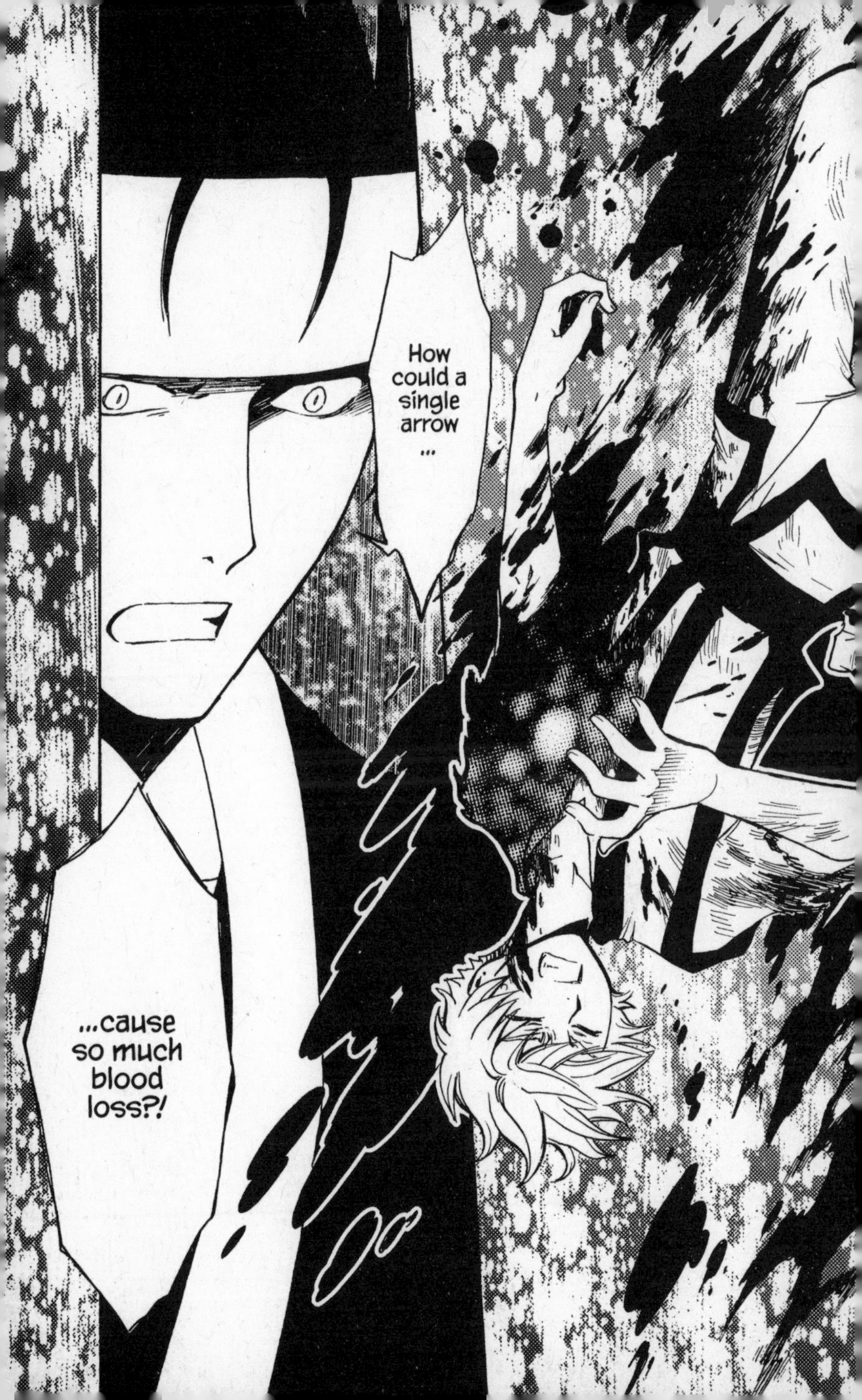
How could a single arrow ...
...cause so much blood loss?!

TSUBASA

WoRLD CHRoNiCLE: NIRAIKANAI

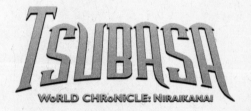

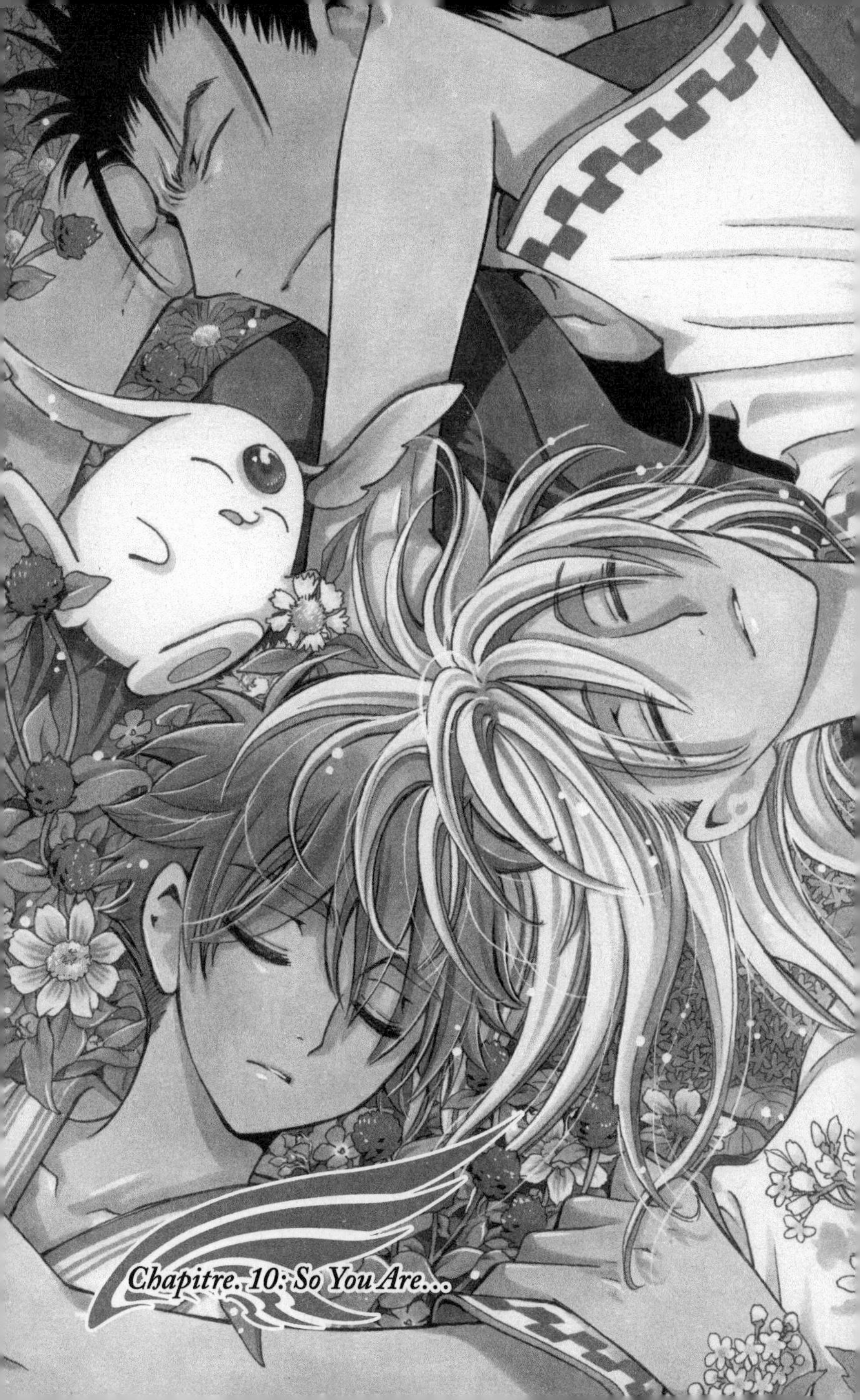
Chapitre. 10: So You Are...

TSUBASA

WoRLD CHRoNiCLE: NIRAIKANAI

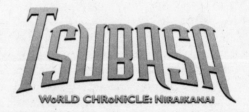

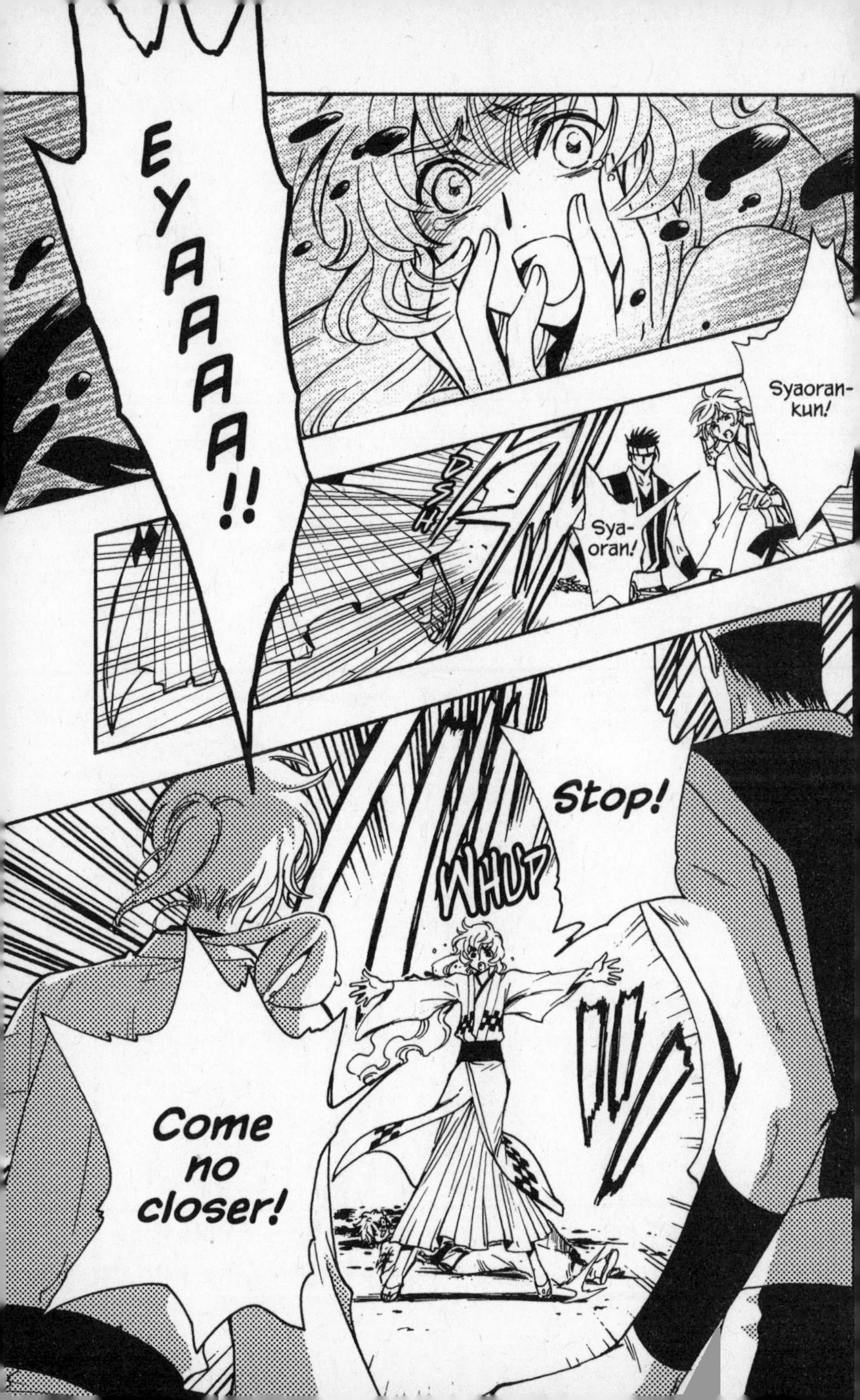
EYAAAAA!!
Syaoran-kun!
Sya-oran!
DSH
Stop!
WHUP
Come no closer!

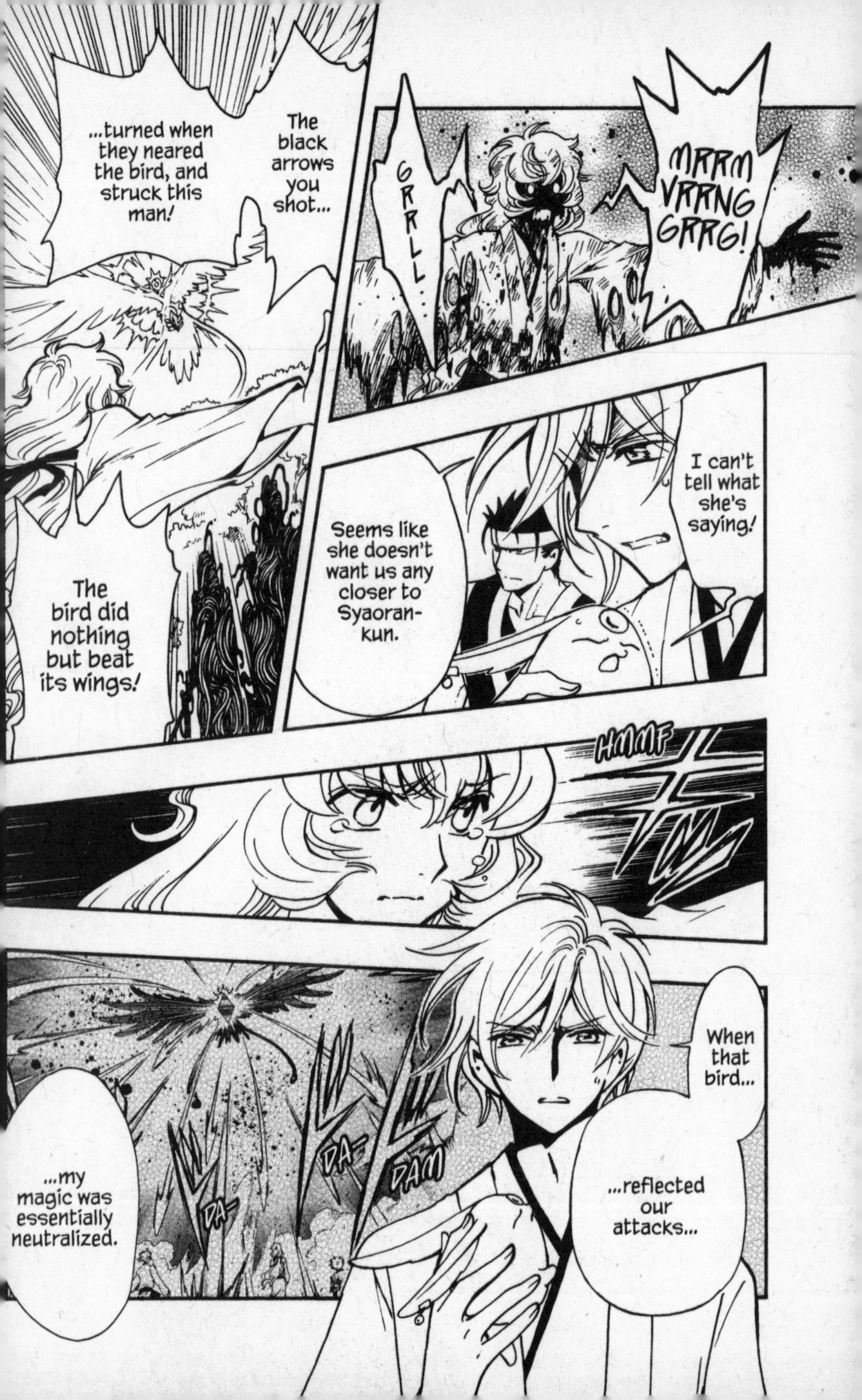
MRRM VRRNG GRRG!
GRRLL...
I can't tell what she's saying!
Seems like she doesn't want us any closer to Syaoran-kun.
The black arrows you shot...
...turned when they neared the bird, and struck this man!
The bird did nothing but beat its wings!
HMMF
When that bird...
...reflected our attacks...
DAM
DA
DA-
...my magic was essentially neutralized.

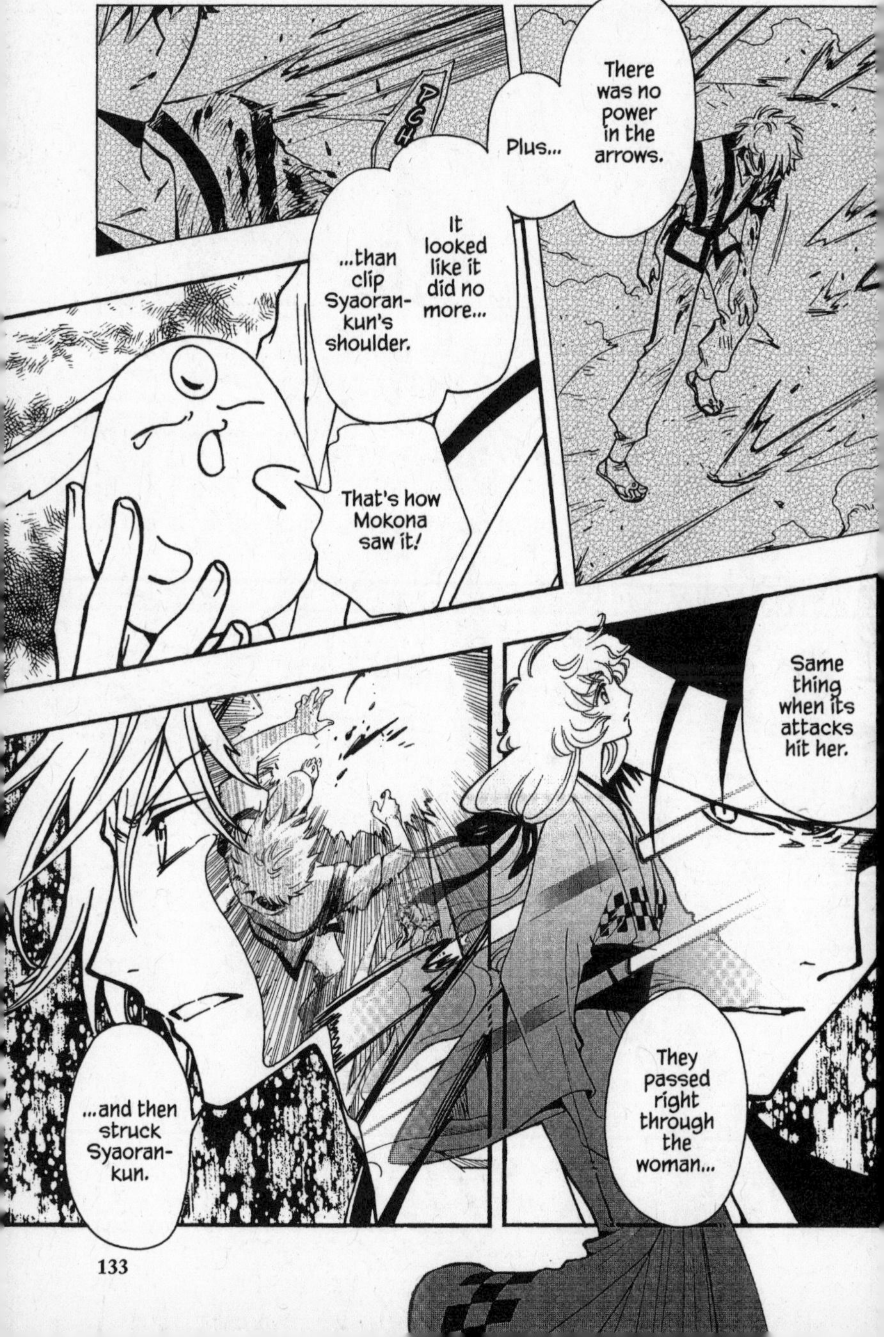
There was no power in the arrows.
Plus...
PCH
It looked like it did no more...
...than clip Syaoran-kun's shoulder.
That's how Mokona saw it!
Same thing when its attacks hit her.
They passed right through the woman...
...and then struck Syaoran-kun.

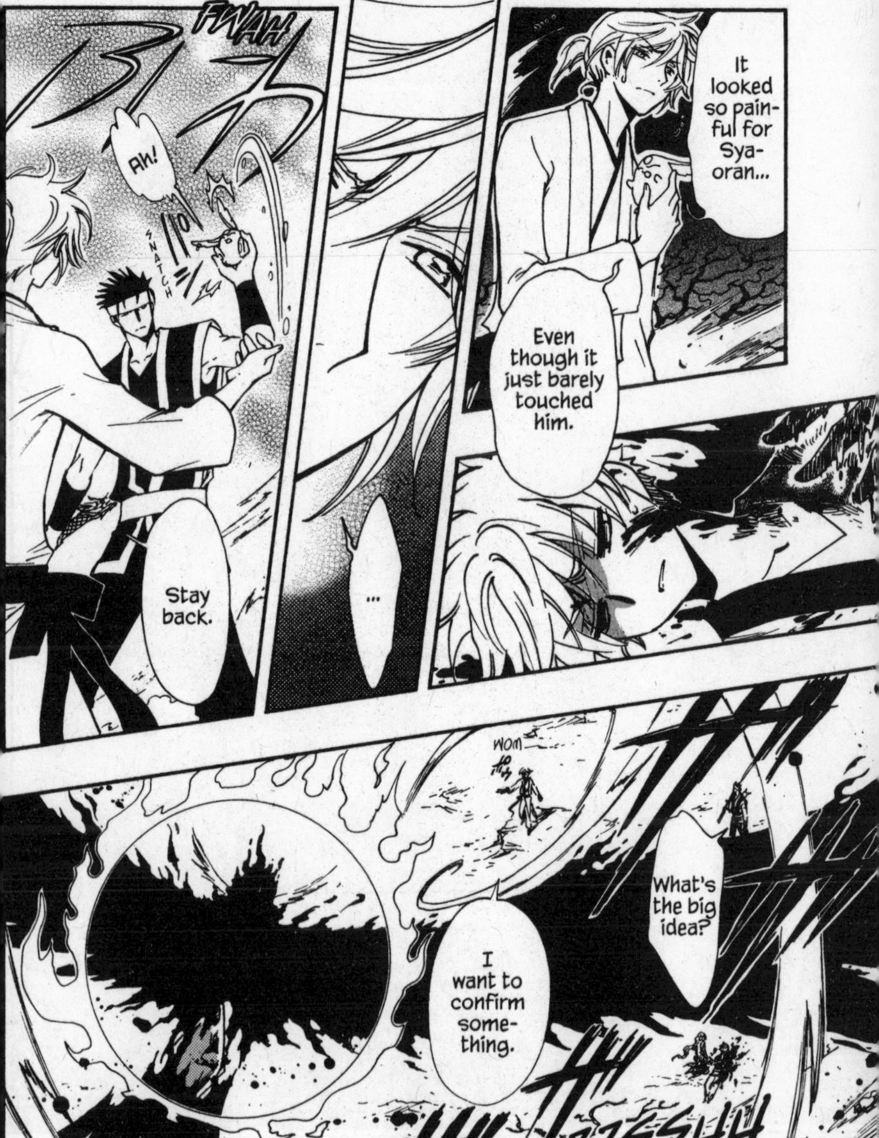
It looked so painful for Syaoran...
Even though it just barely touched him.
...
FWAH
Ah!
SNATCH
Stay back.
WOM
What's the big idea?
I want to confirm something.
ZZZSSHH

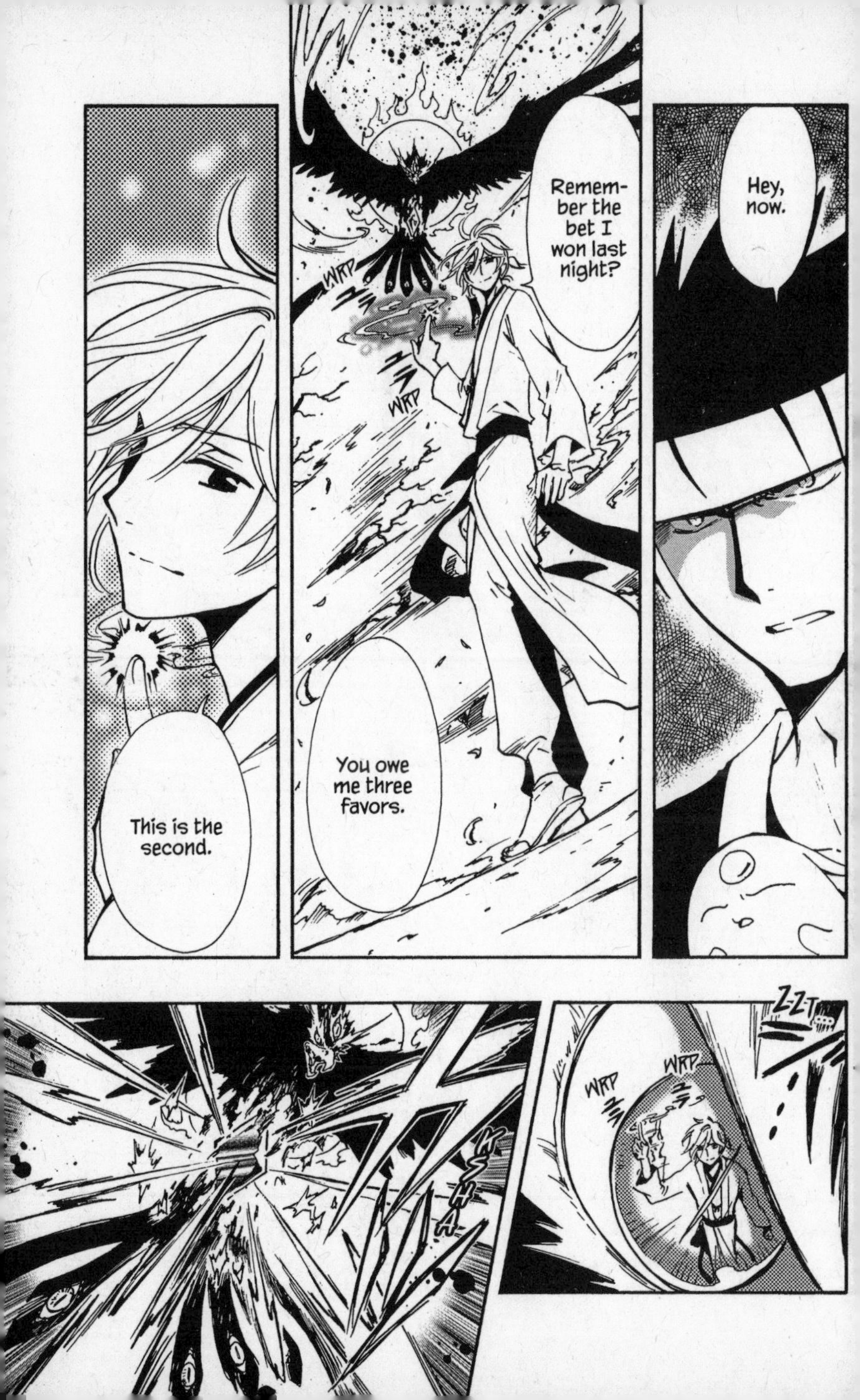
Hey, now.
Remember the bet I won last night?
WRP
WRP
You owe me three favors.
This is the second.
Z-Z-T...
WRP
WRP
KSHA

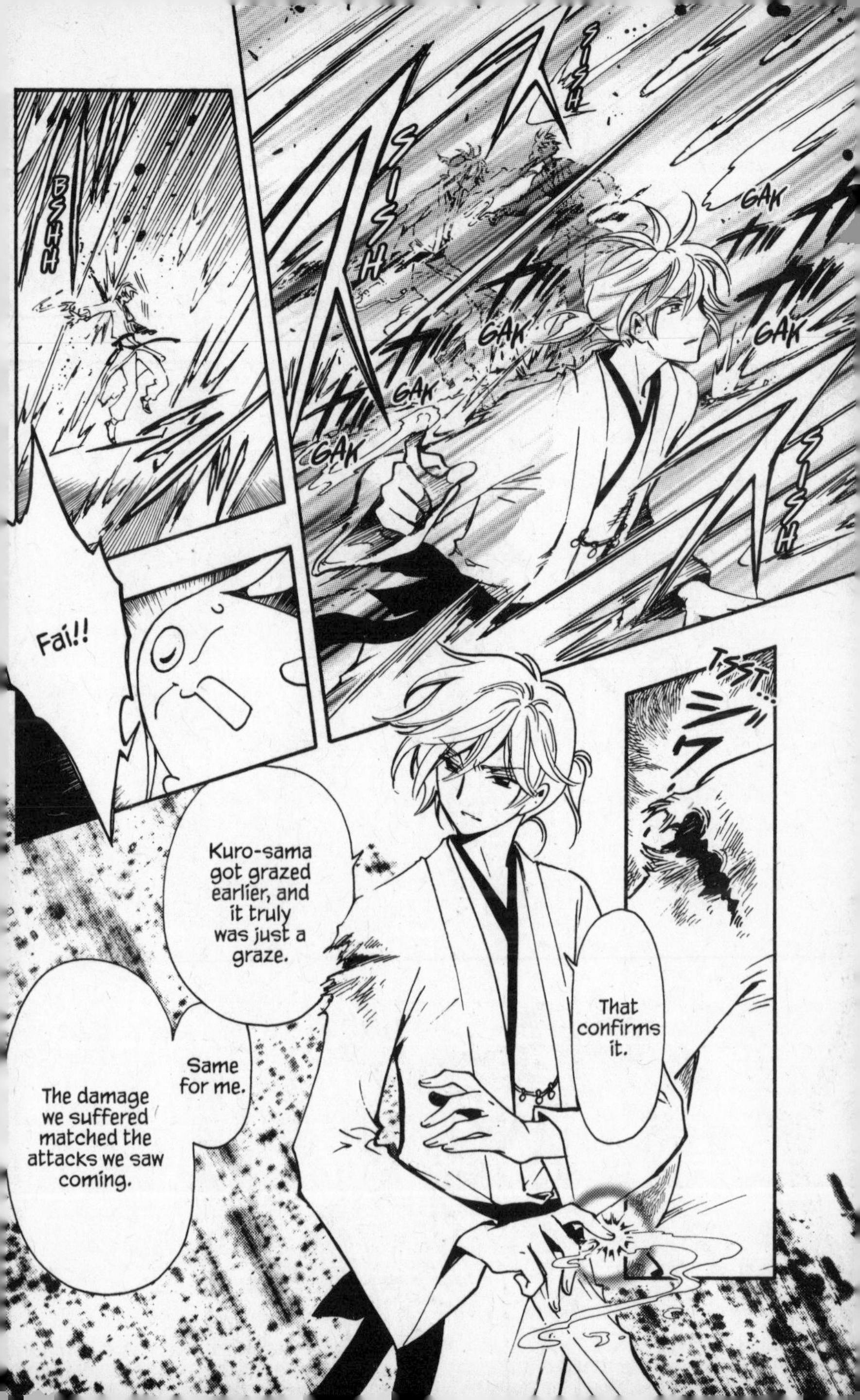
SHISH
SHISH
GAK
GAK
GAK
GAK
GAK
SHISH
BSHHH
Fai!!
TSST...
That confirms it.
Kuro-sama got grazed earlier, and it truly was just a graze.
Same for me.
The damage we suffered matched the attacks we saw coming.

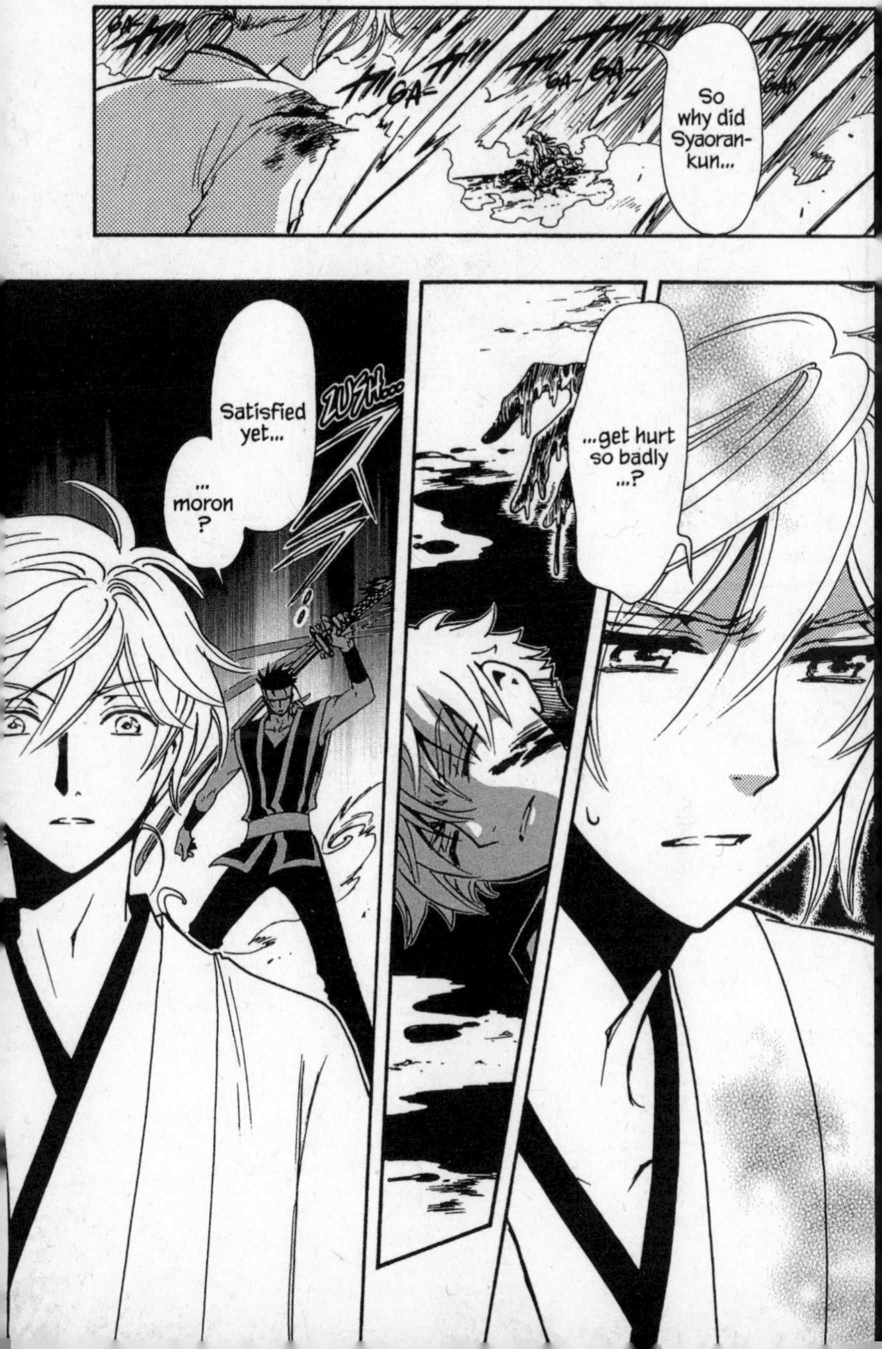
So why did Syaoran-kun...
...get hurt so badly ...?
ZUSHHooo
Satisfied yet...
... moron ?

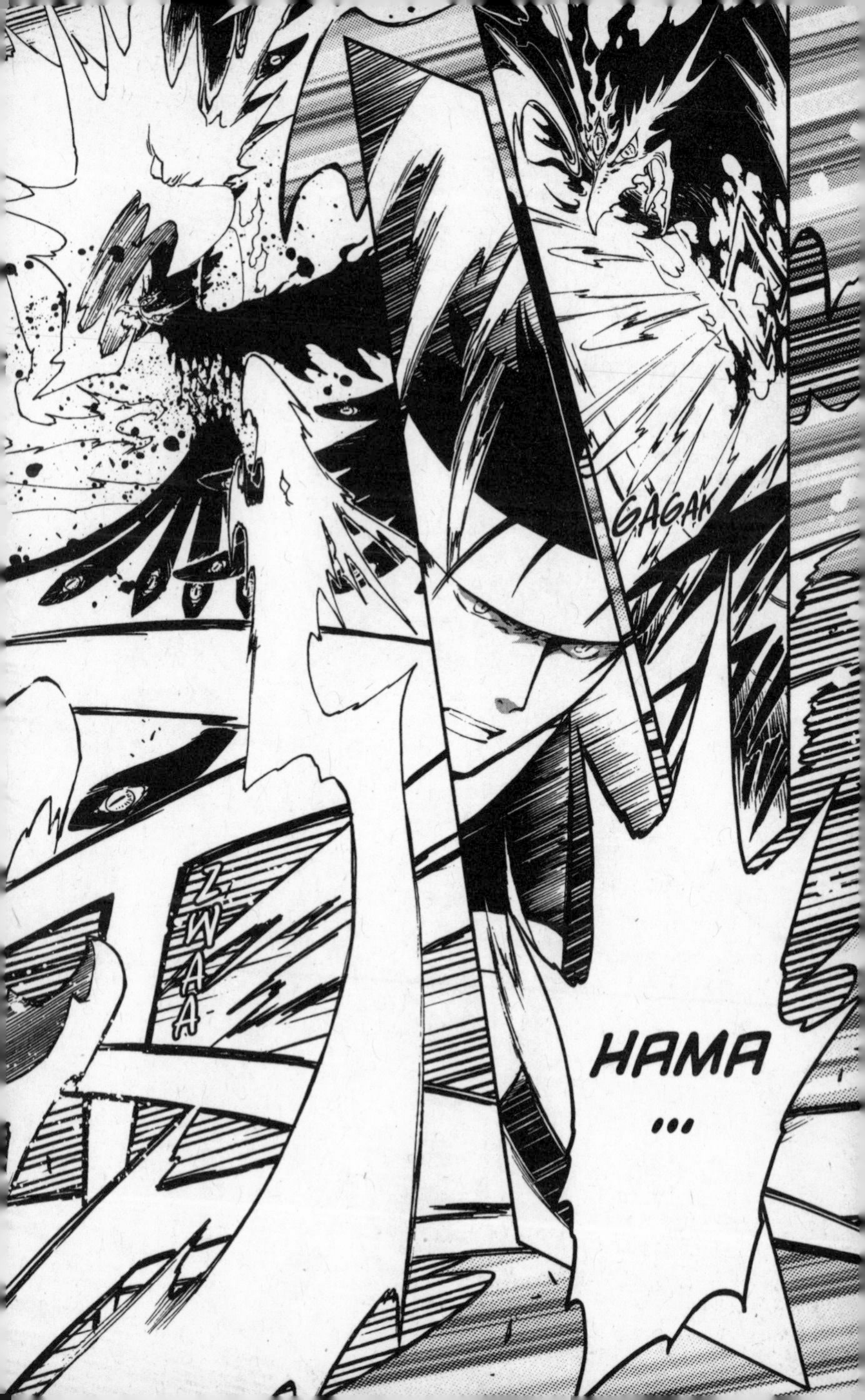
GAGAK
ZWAAA
HAMA
...

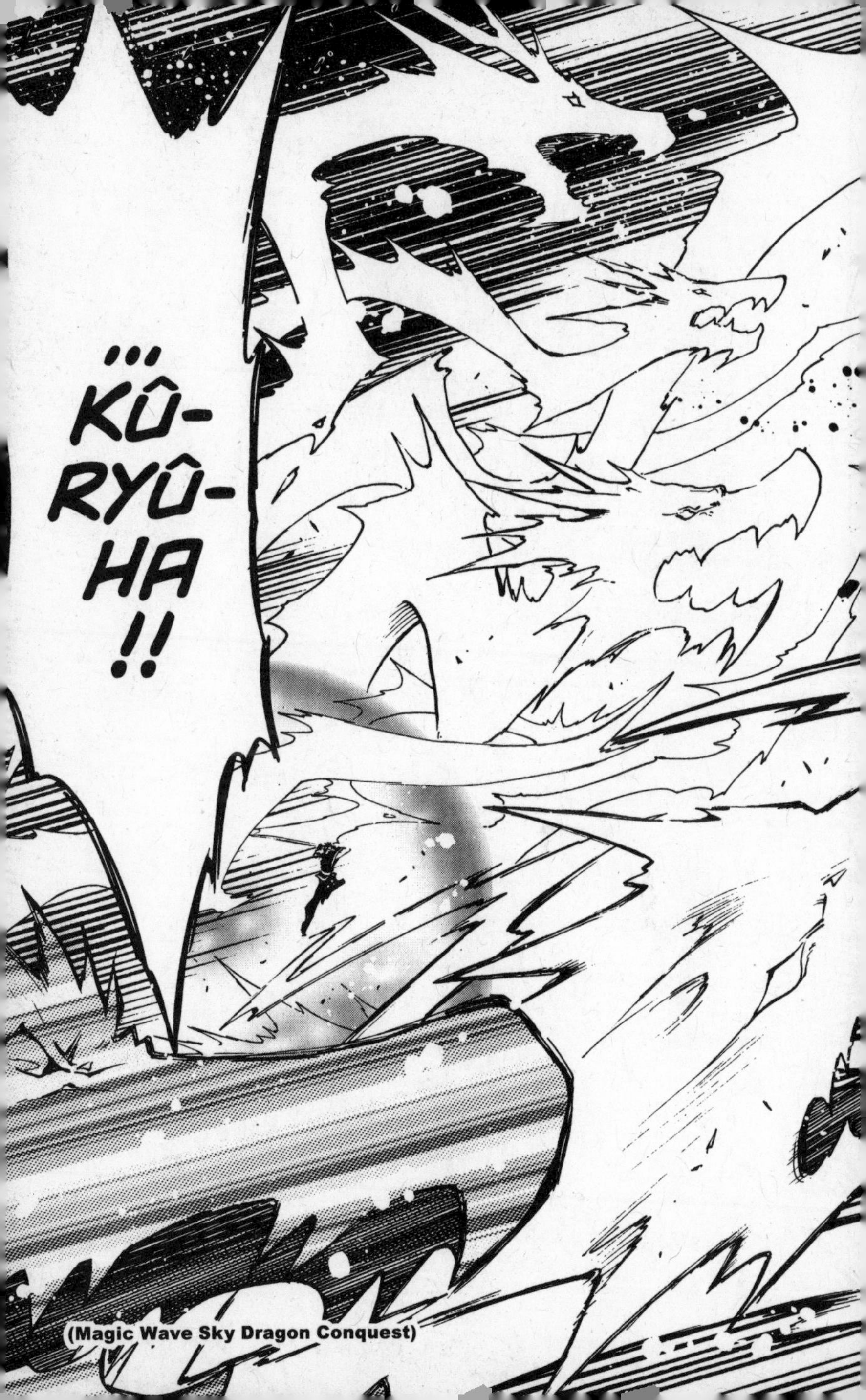
...KÛ-
RYÛ-
HA
!!
(Magic Wave Sky Dragon Conquest)

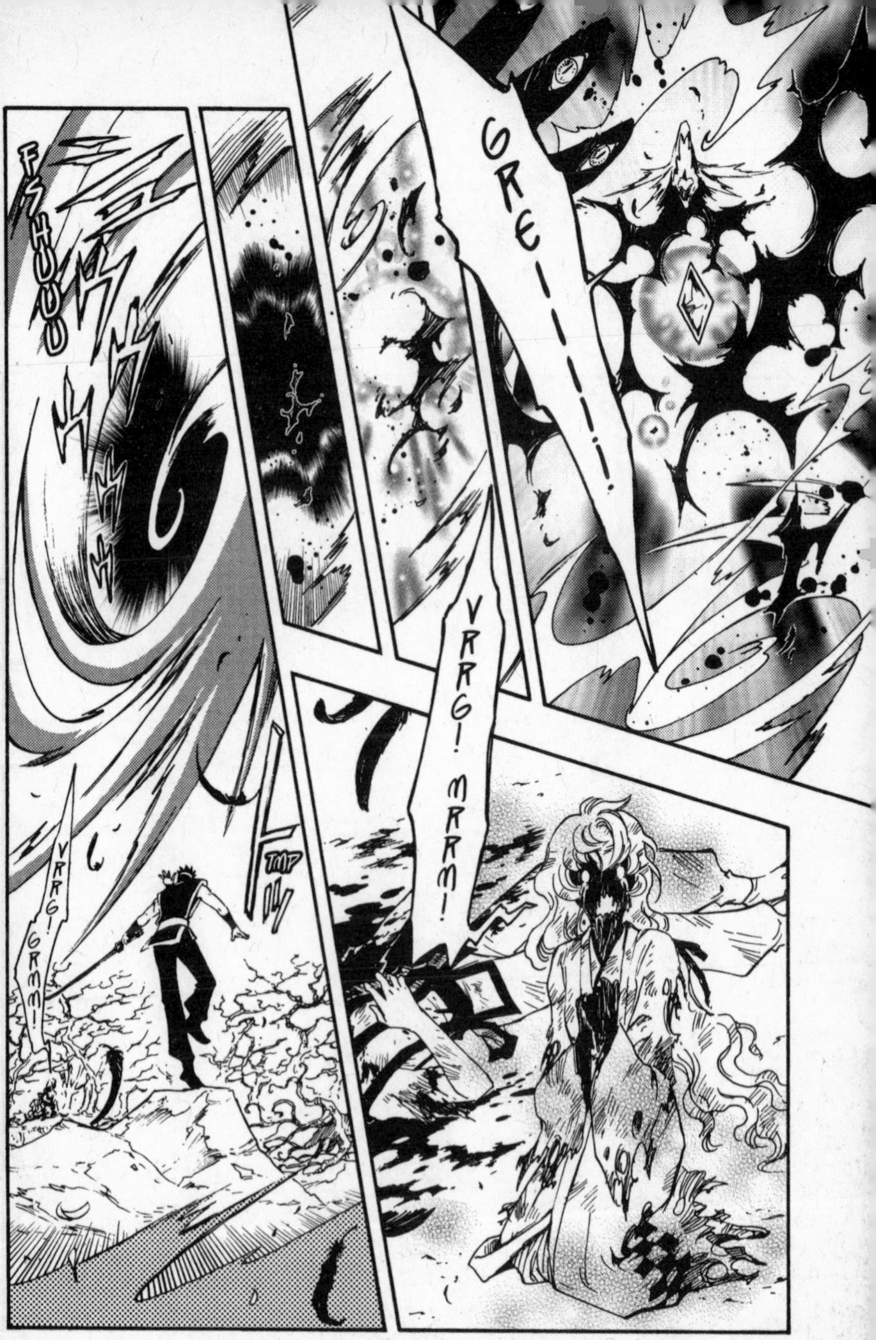
GRE---!!
VRRG! MRRRM!
FSHUUU
TMP
VRRG! GRMM!

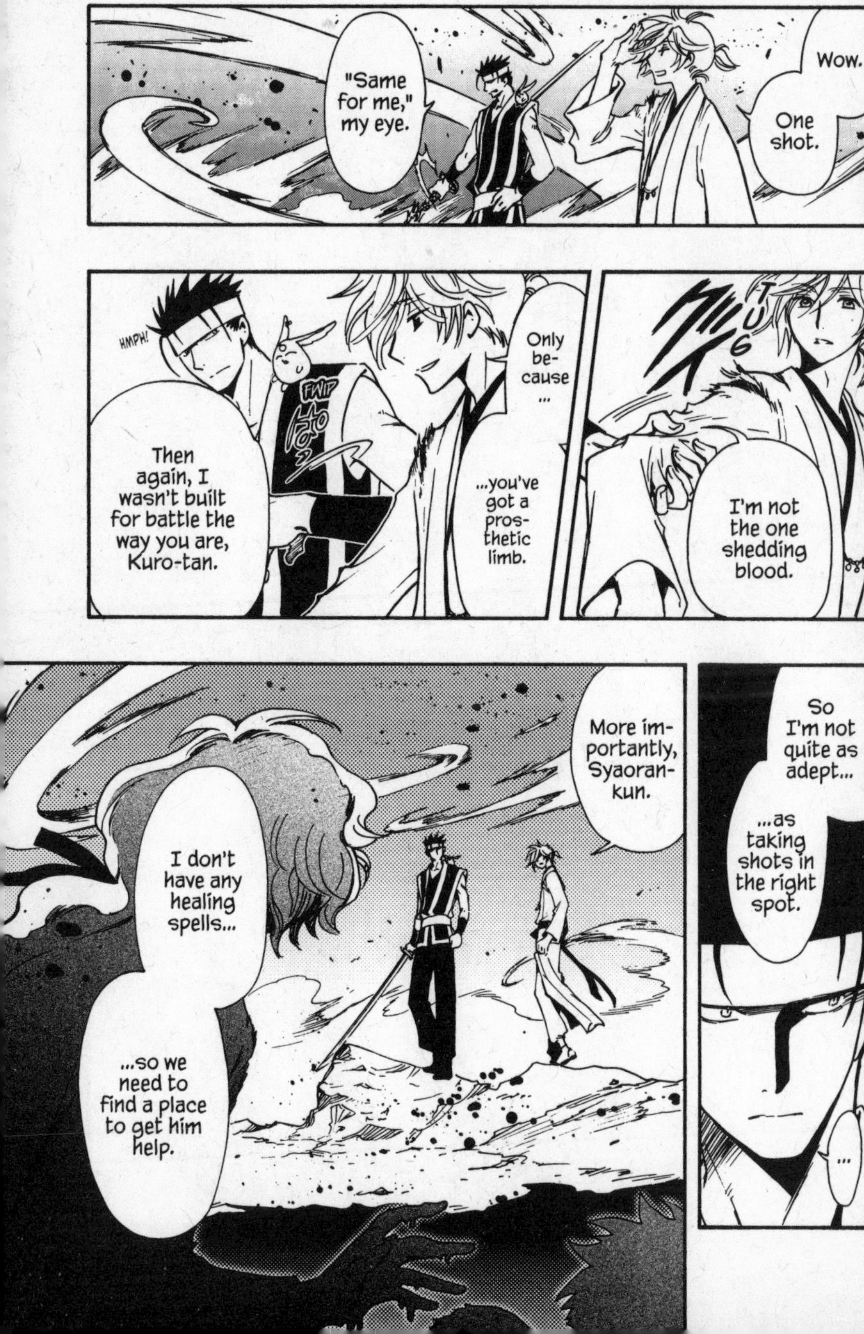

Wow.
One shot.
"Same for me," my eye.
TUG
I'm not the one shedding blood.
Only because...
...you've got a prosthetic limb.
HMPH!
FWIP
Then again, I wasn't built for battle the way you are, Kuro-tan.
So I'm not quite as adept...
...as taking shots in the right spot.
...
More importantly, Syaoran-kun.
I don't have any healing spells...
...so we need to find a place to get him help.

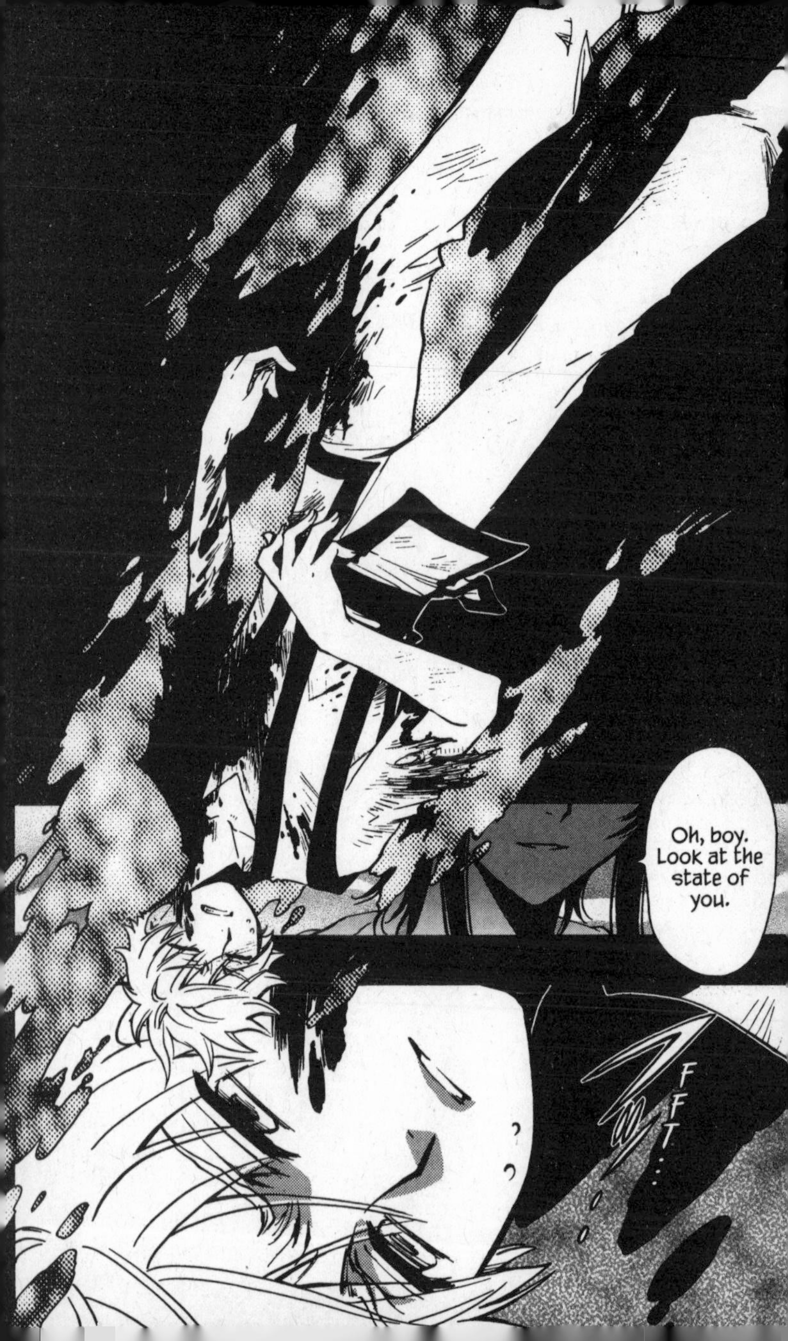
Oh, boy. Look at the state of you.
FFT...

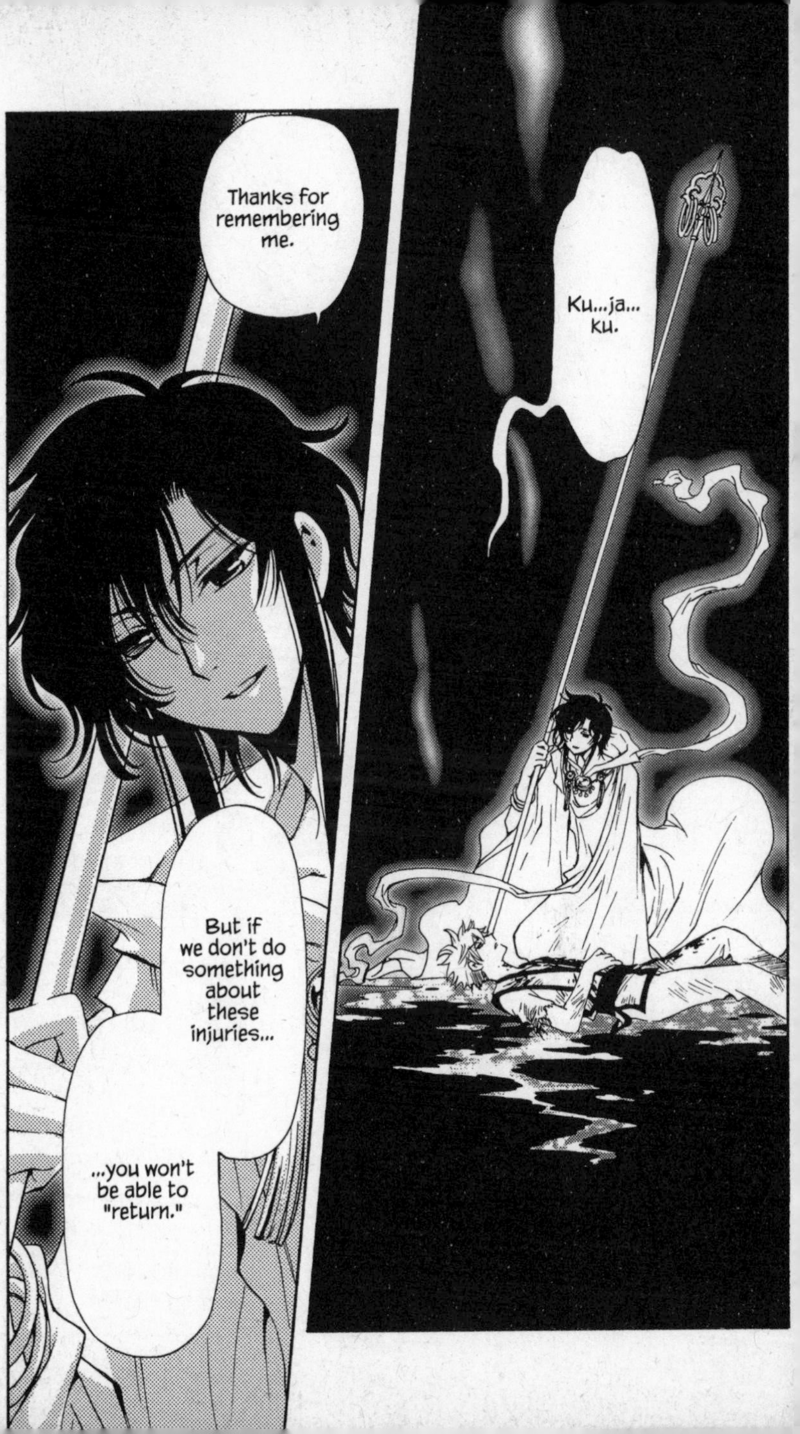
Ku...ja... ku.
Thanks for remembering me.
But if we don't do something about these injuries...
...you won't be able to "return."

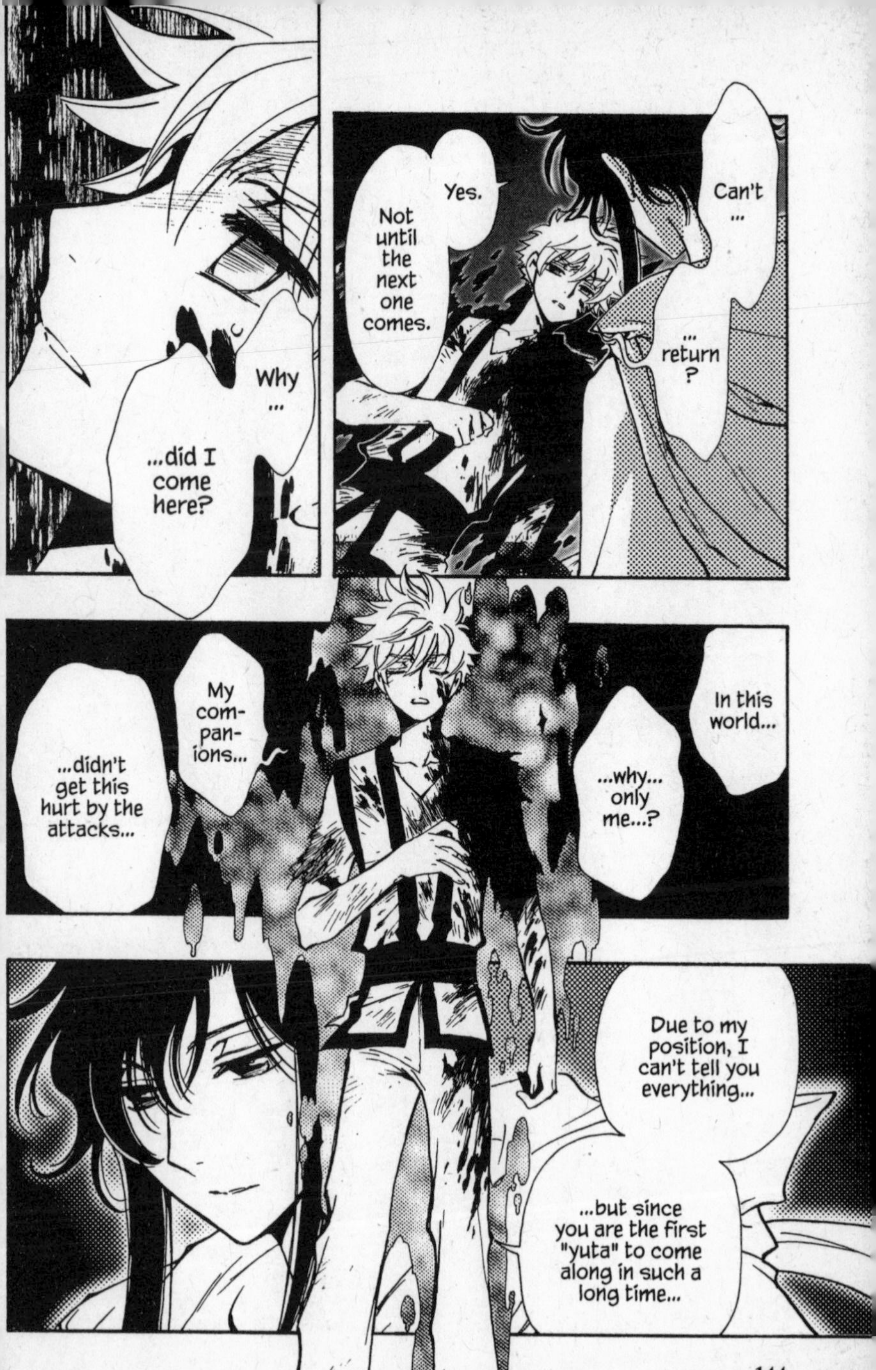
Can't ... ... return?
Yes.
Not until the next one comes.
Why ...
...did I come here?
In this world...
...why... only me...?
My companions...
...didn't get this hurt by the attacks...
Due to my position, I can't tell you everything...
...but since you are the first "yuta" to come along in such a long time...

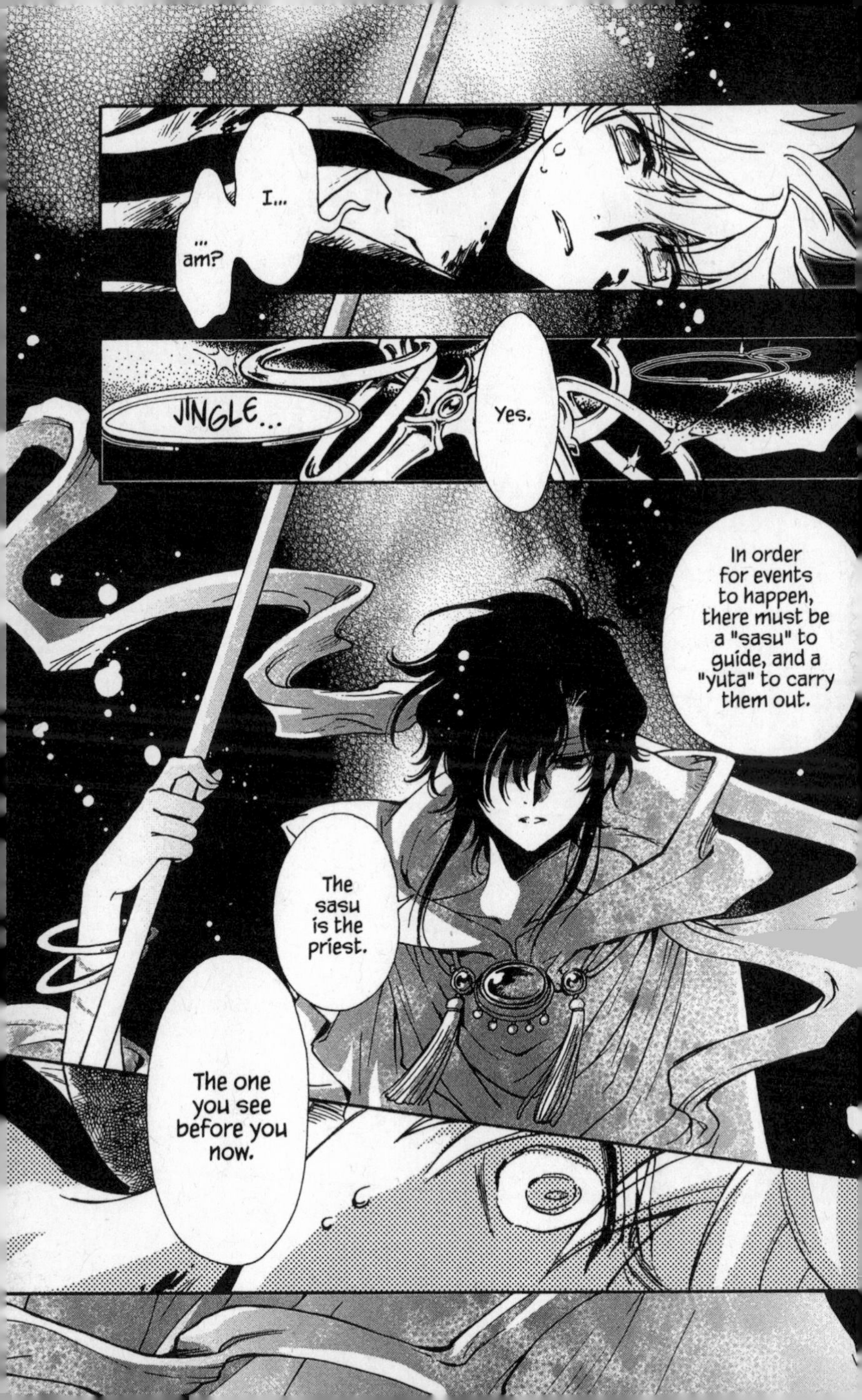
I...
... am?
Yes.
JINGLE...
In order for events to happen, there must be a "sasu" to guide, and a "yuta" to carry them out.
The sasu is the priest.
The one you see before you now.

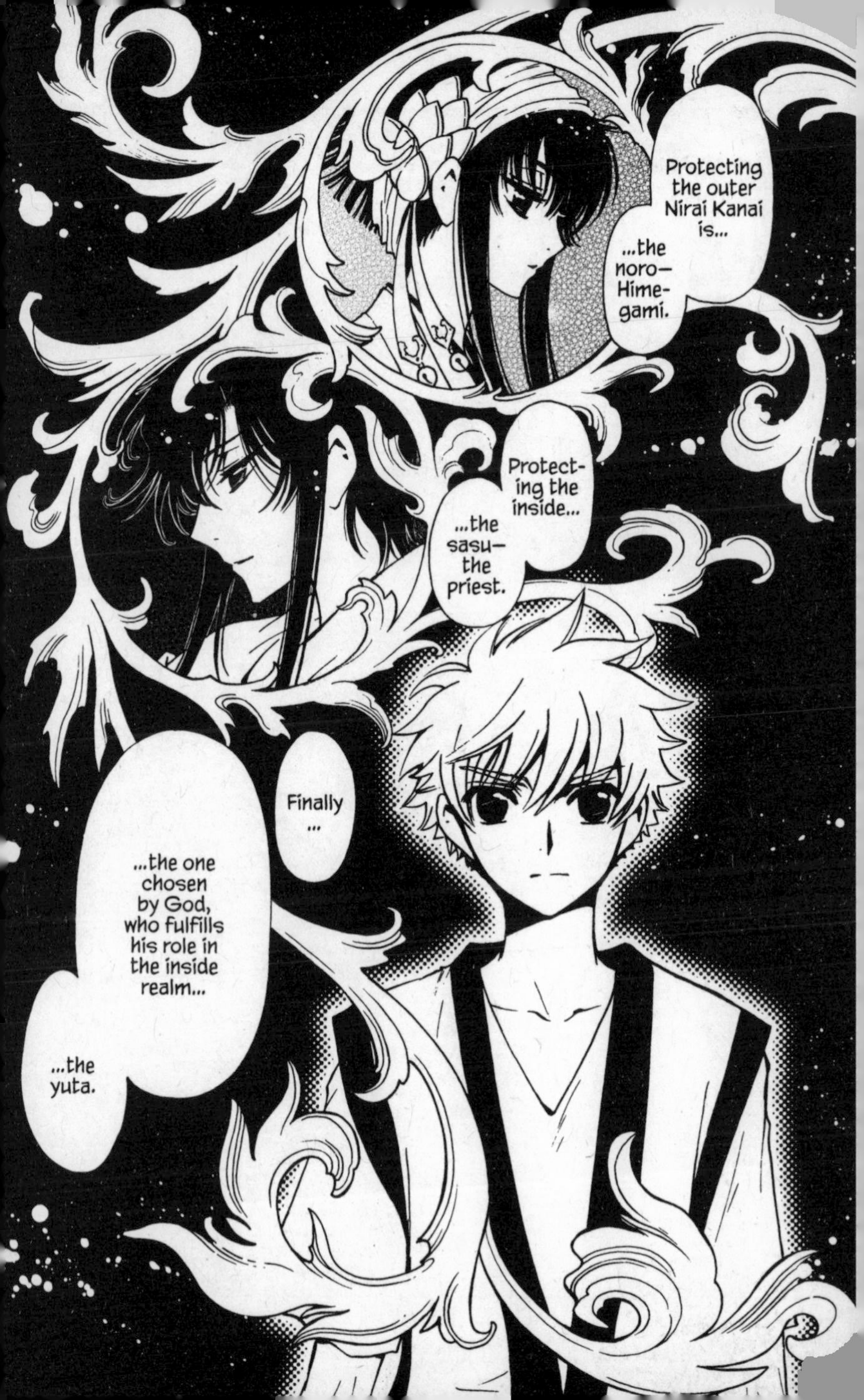
Protecting the outer Nirai Kanai is...
...the noro—Himegami.
Protecting the inside...
...the sasu—the priest.
Finally...
...the one chosen by God, who fulfills his role in the inside realm...
...the yuta.

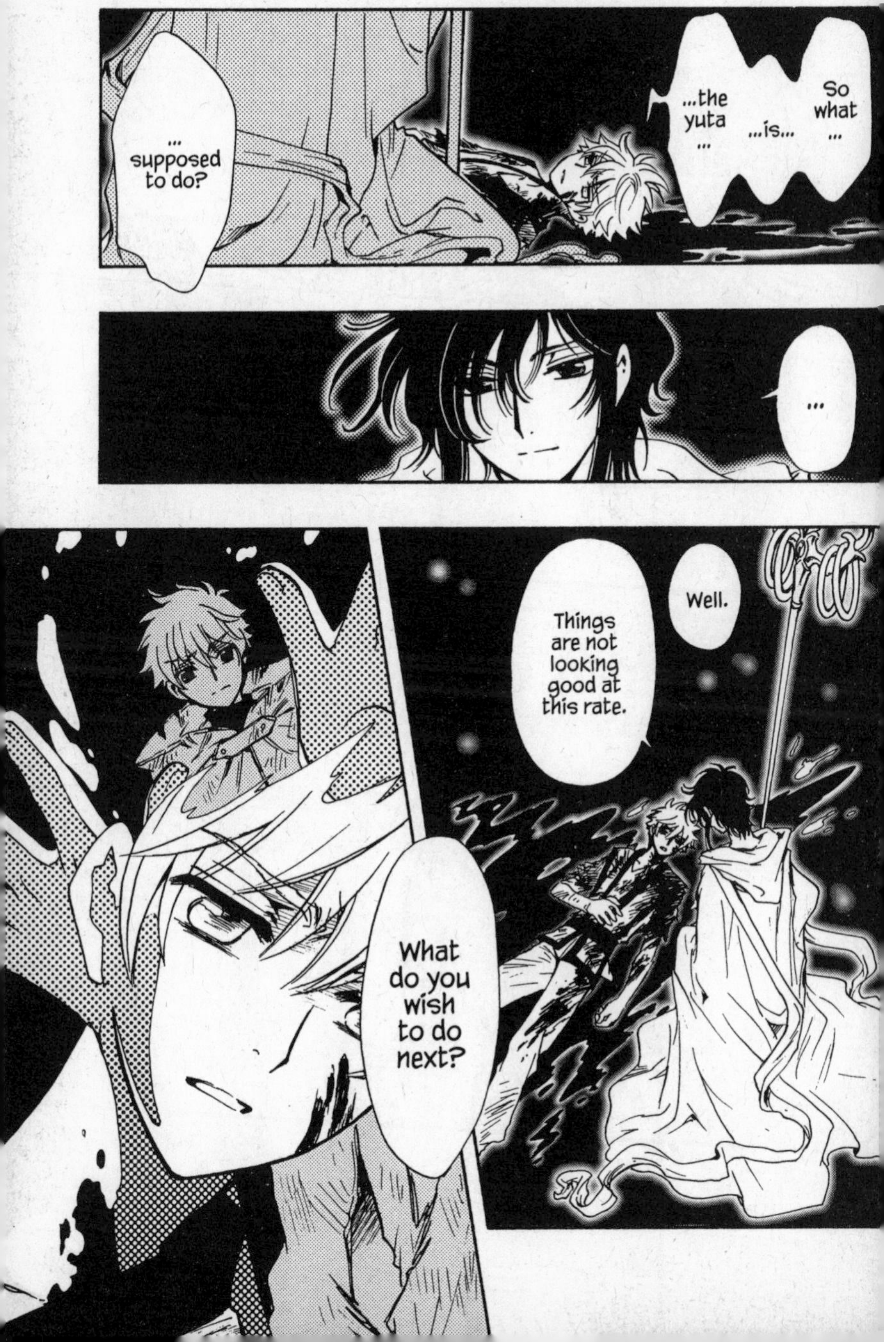
So what ...
...is...
...the yuta ...
... supposed to do?
...
Well.
Things are not looking good at this rate.
What do you wish to do next?

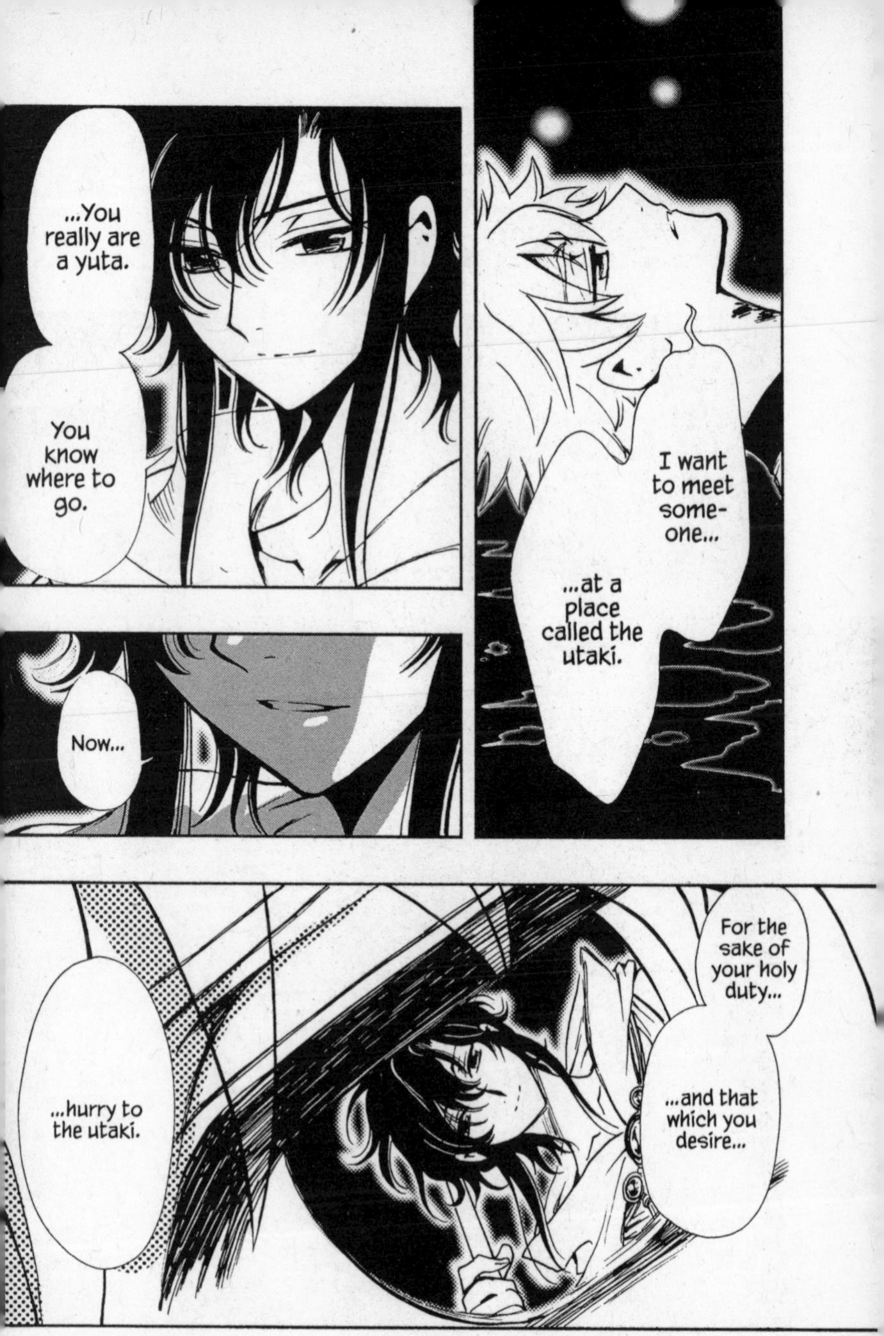
I want to meet some-one...
...at a place called the utaki.
...You really are a yuta.
You know where to go.
Now...
For the sake of your holy duty...
...and that which you desire...
...hurry to the utaki.

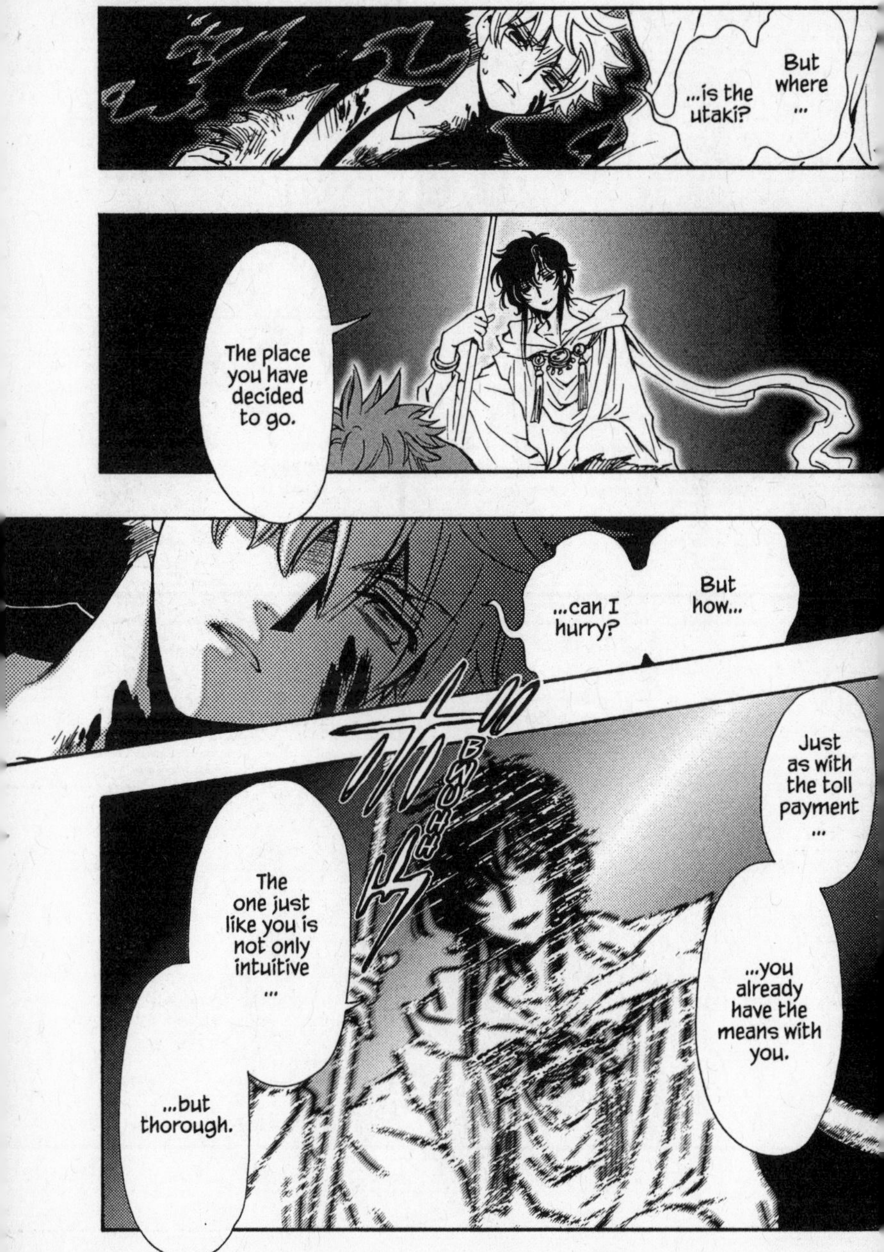
But where...
...is the utaki?
The place you have decided to go.
But how...
...can I hurry?
Just as with the toll payment...
...you already have the means with you.
BWUHHH
The one just like you is not only intuitive...
...but thorough.

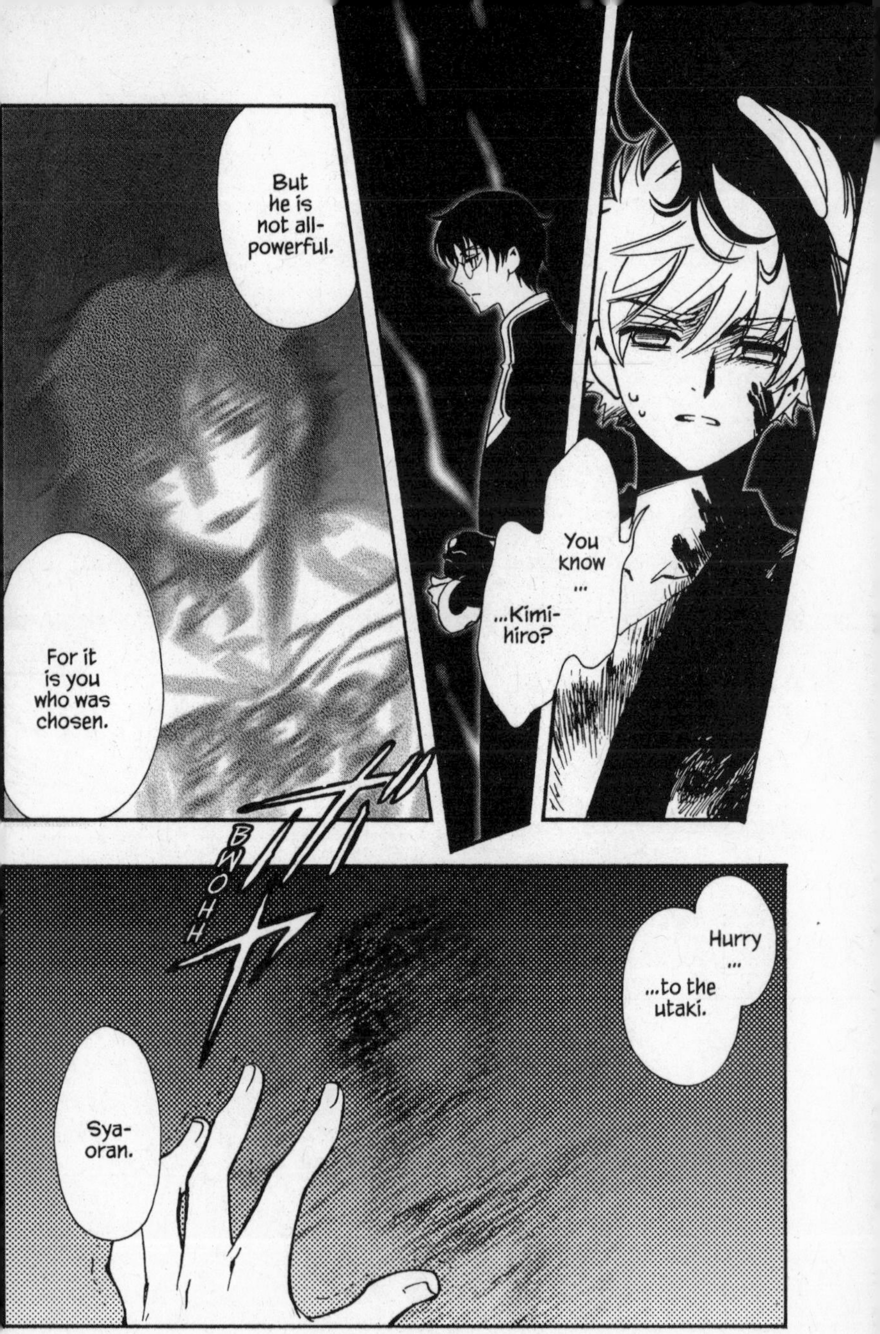
You know ...
...Kimihiro?
But he is not all-powerful.
For it is you who was chosen.
Hurry ...
...to the utaki.
BWOHH
Syaoran.

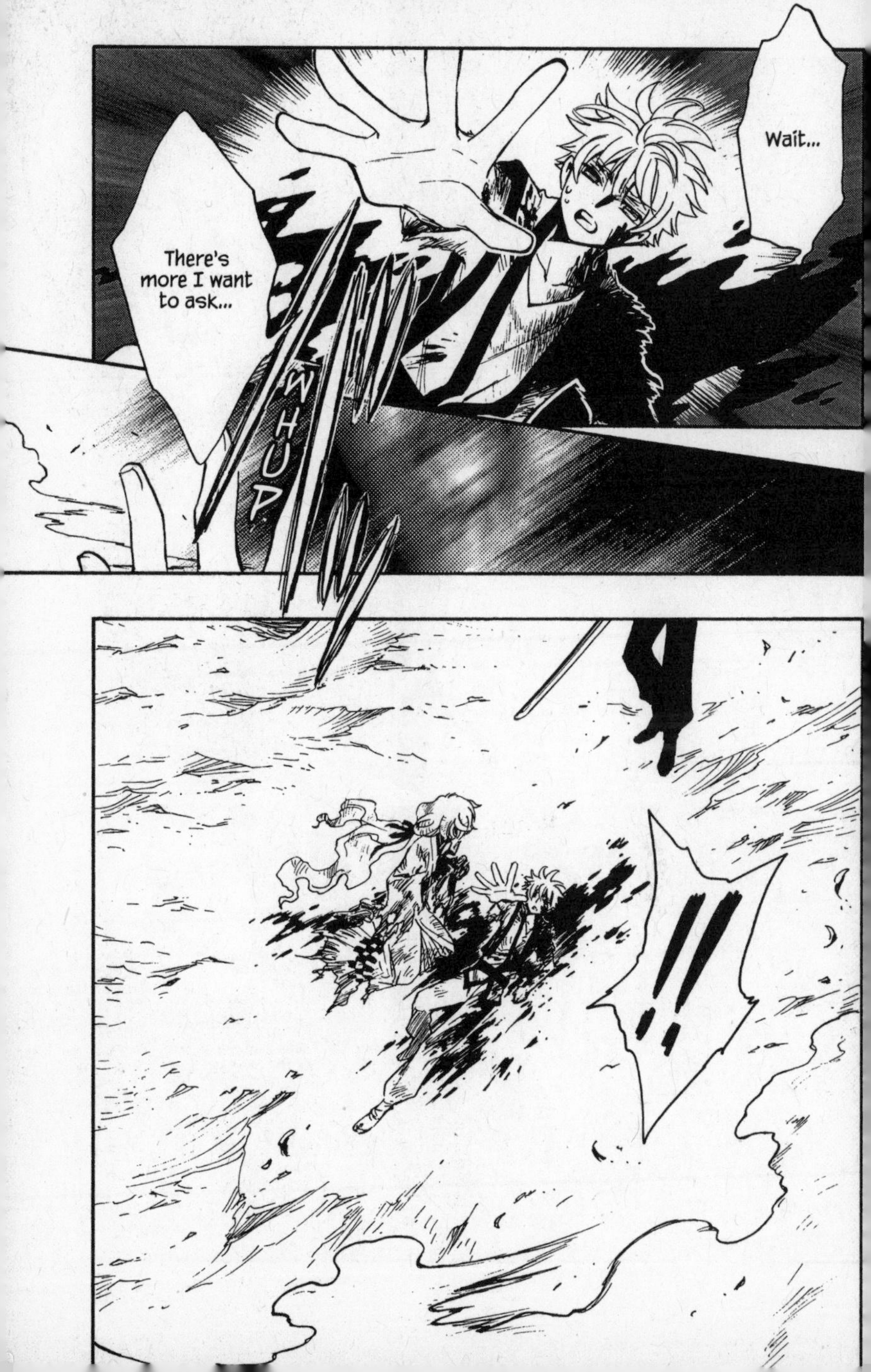
Wait...
There's more I want to ask...
WHUP
!!

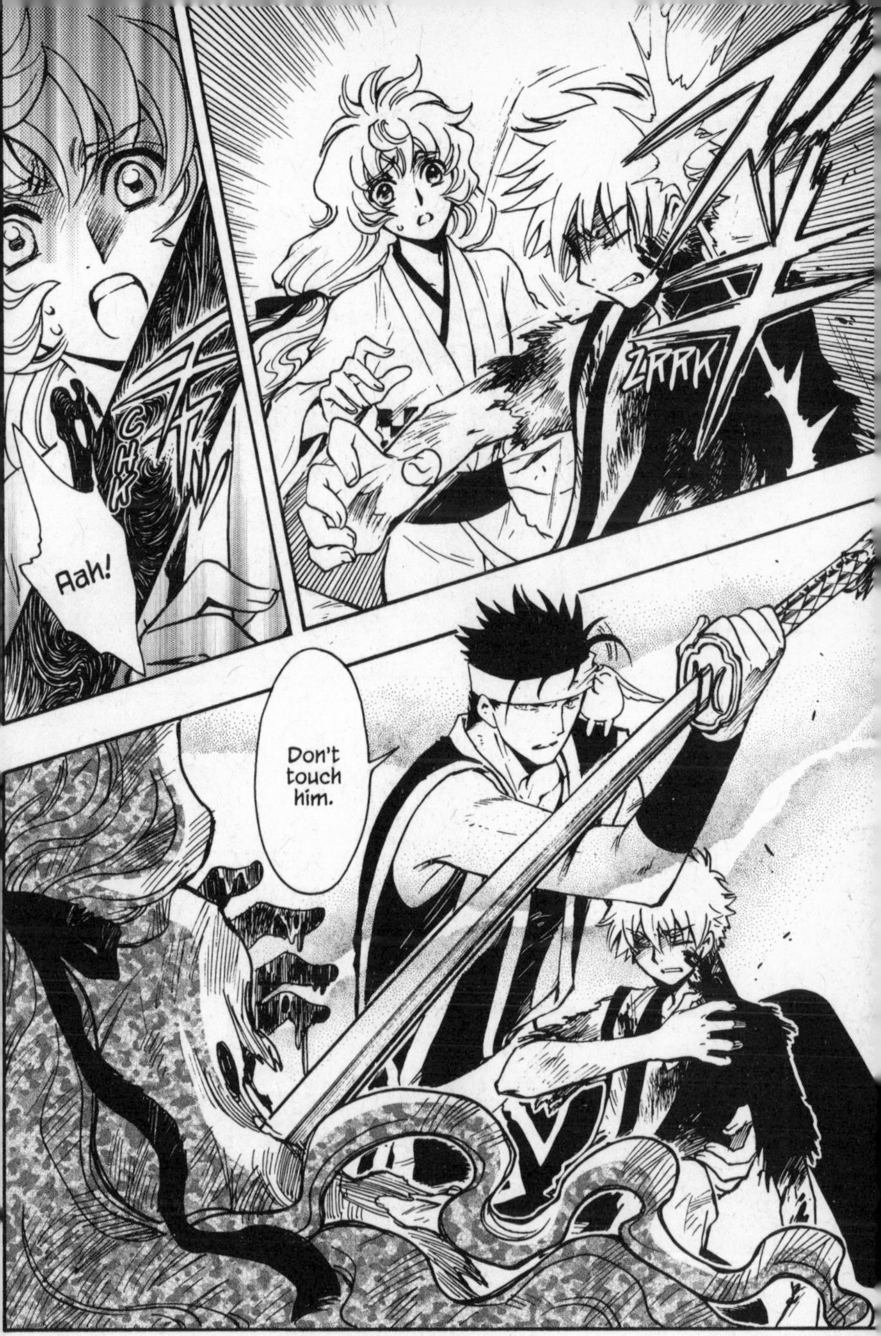
ZRRK
CHK
Aah!
Don't touch him.

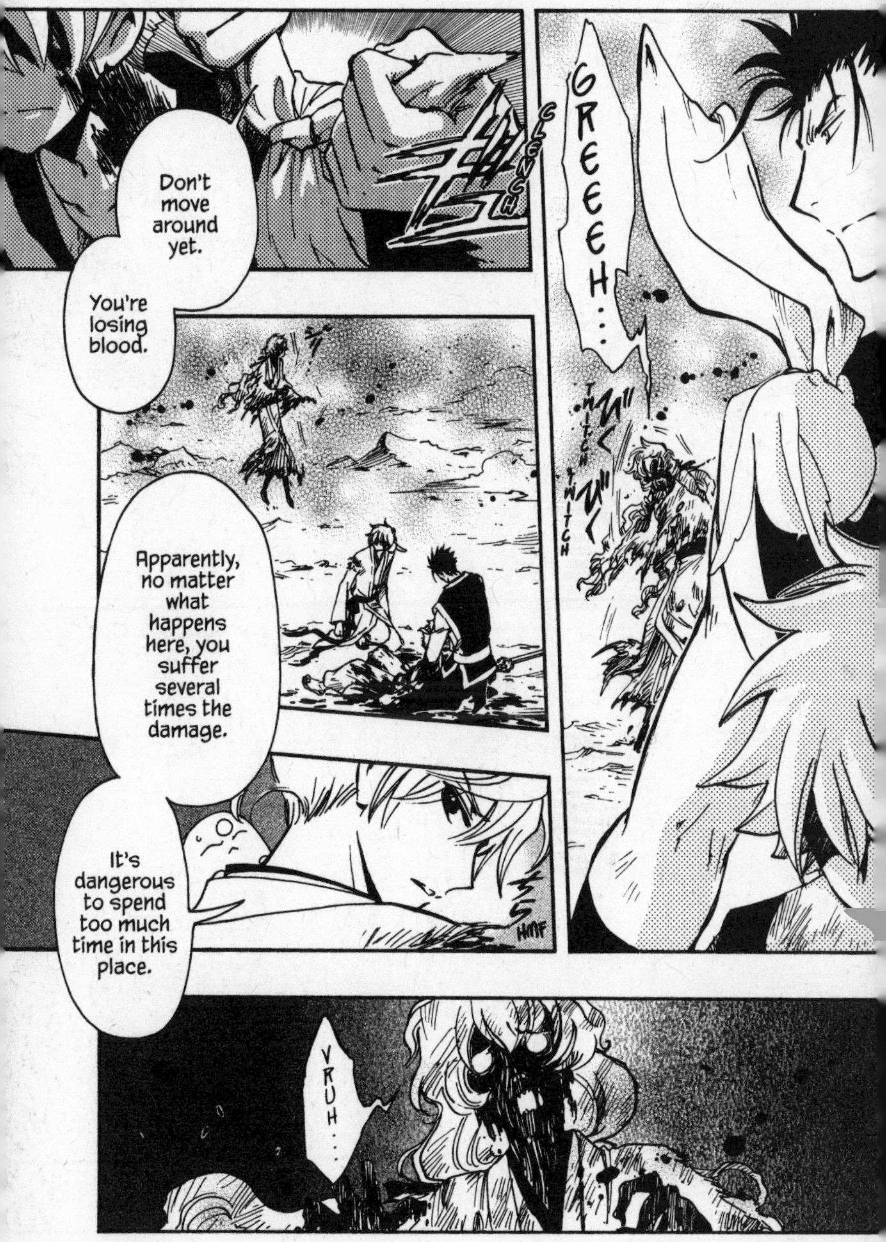
GREEEH...
TWITCH TWITCH
CLENCH
Don't move around yet.
You're losing blood.
Apparently, no matter what happens here, you suffer several times the damage.
HMF
It's dangerous to spend too much time in this place.
VRUH...

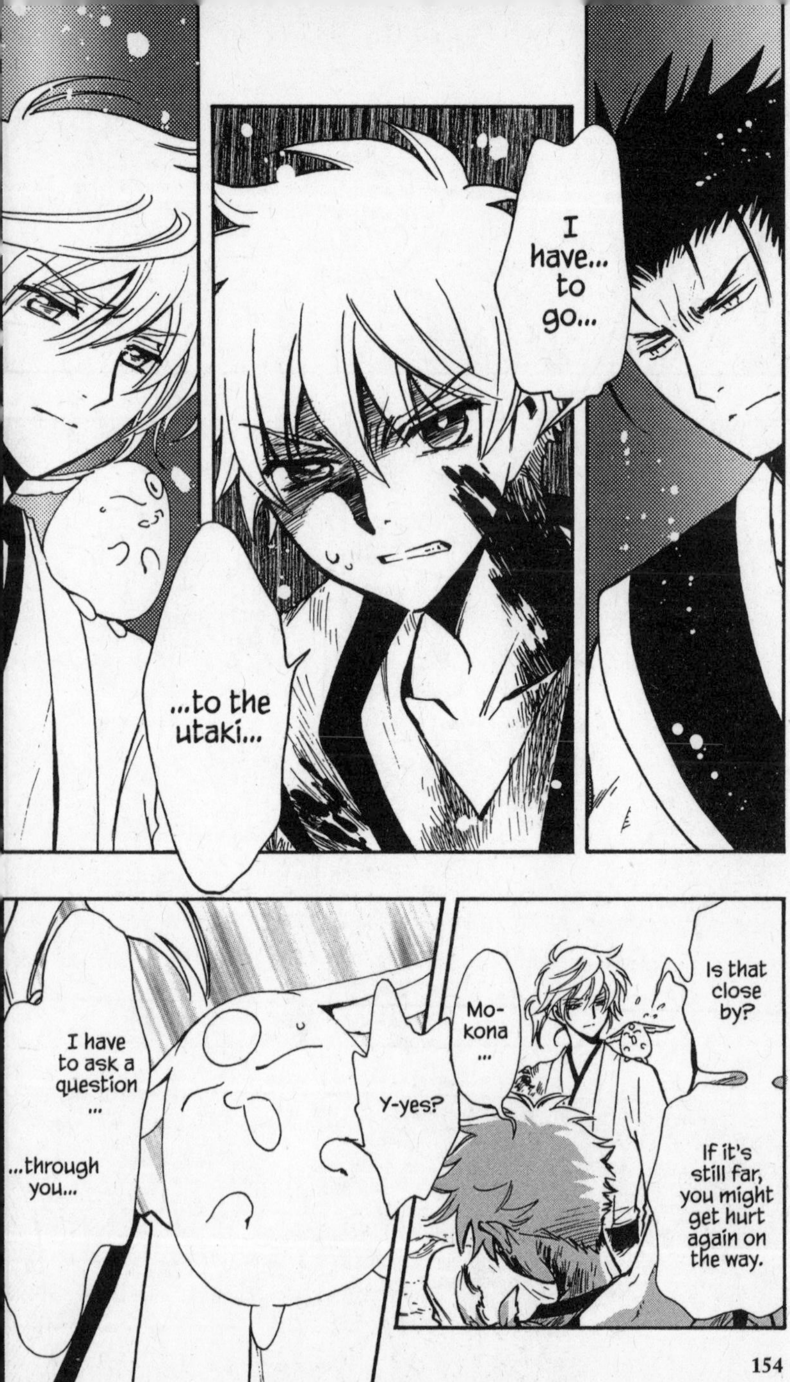
I have... to go...
...to the utaki...
Is that close by?
If it's still far, you might get hurt again on the way.
Mo-kona ...
Y-yes?
I have to ask a question ...
...through you...

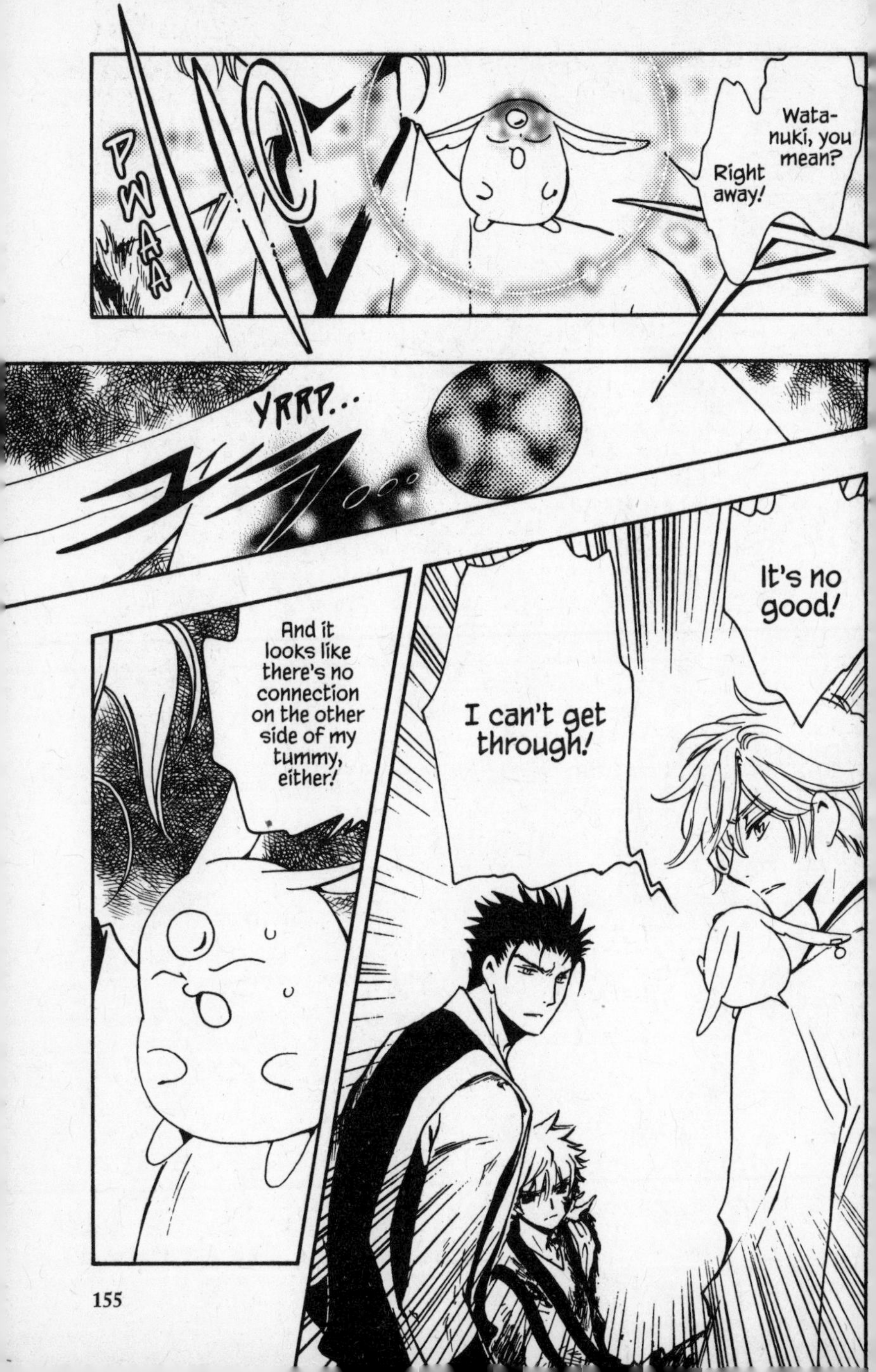
Wata-nuki, you mean?
Right away!
PWAAA
YRRP...
It's no good!
I can't get through!
And it looks like there's no connection on the other side of my tummy, either!

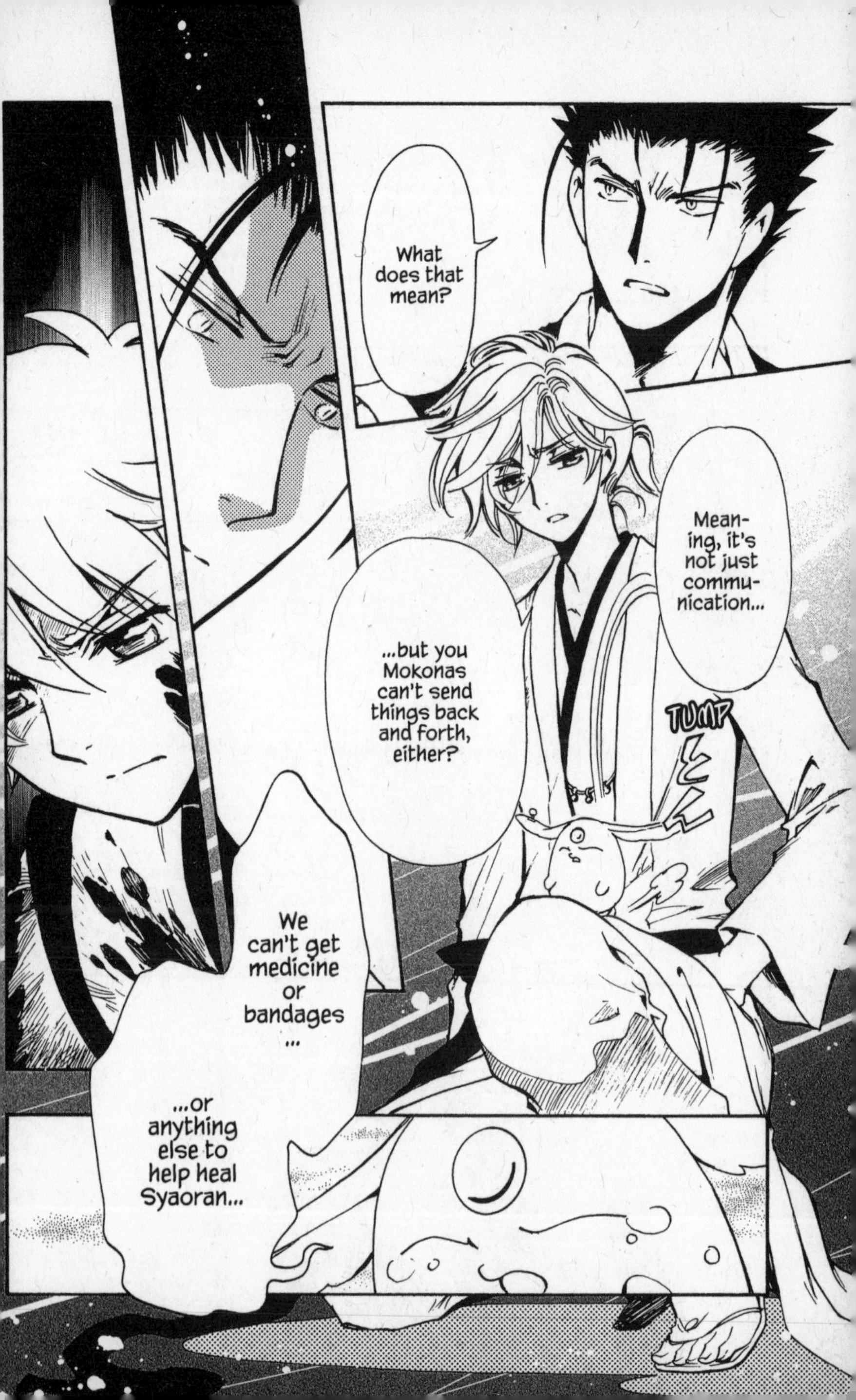
What does that mean?
Meaning, it's not just communication...
...but you Mokonas can't send things back and forth, either?
TUMP
We can't get medicine or bandages...
...or anything else to help heal Syaoran...

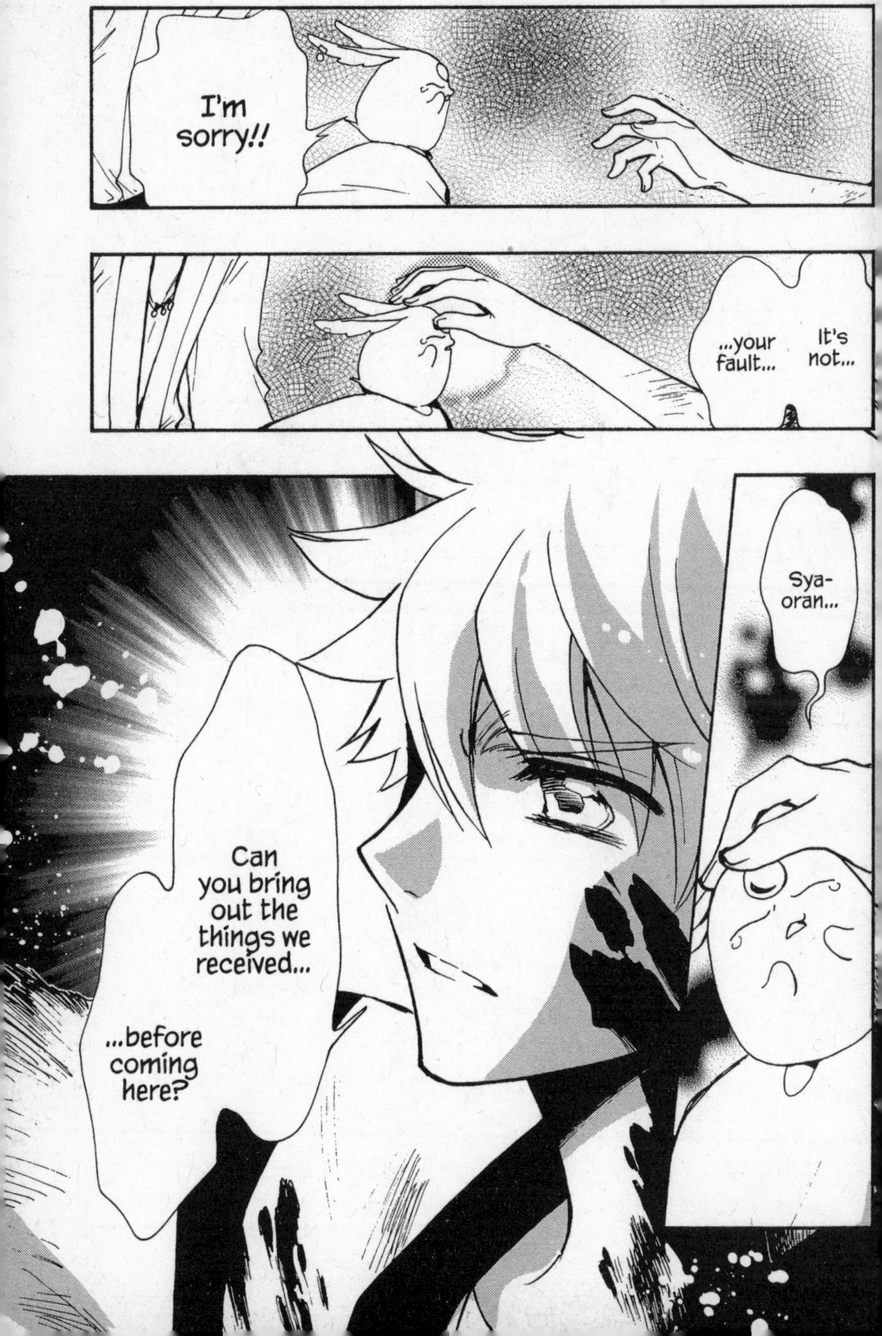
I'm sorry!!
It's not...
...your fault...
Sya-oran...
Can you bring out the things we received...
...before coming here?

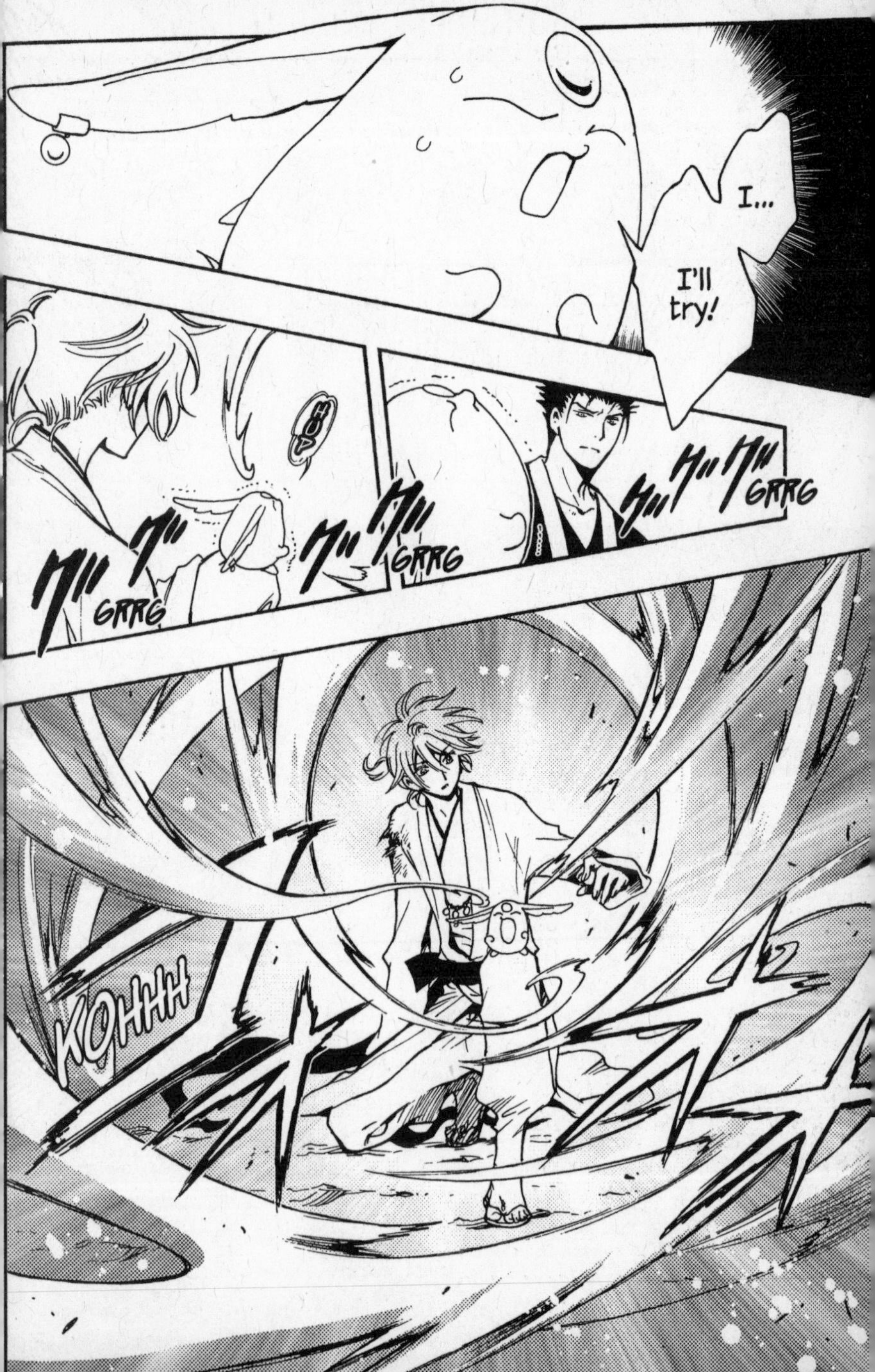
I...
I'll try!
GRRG
HOP
GRRG
GRRG
KOHHH

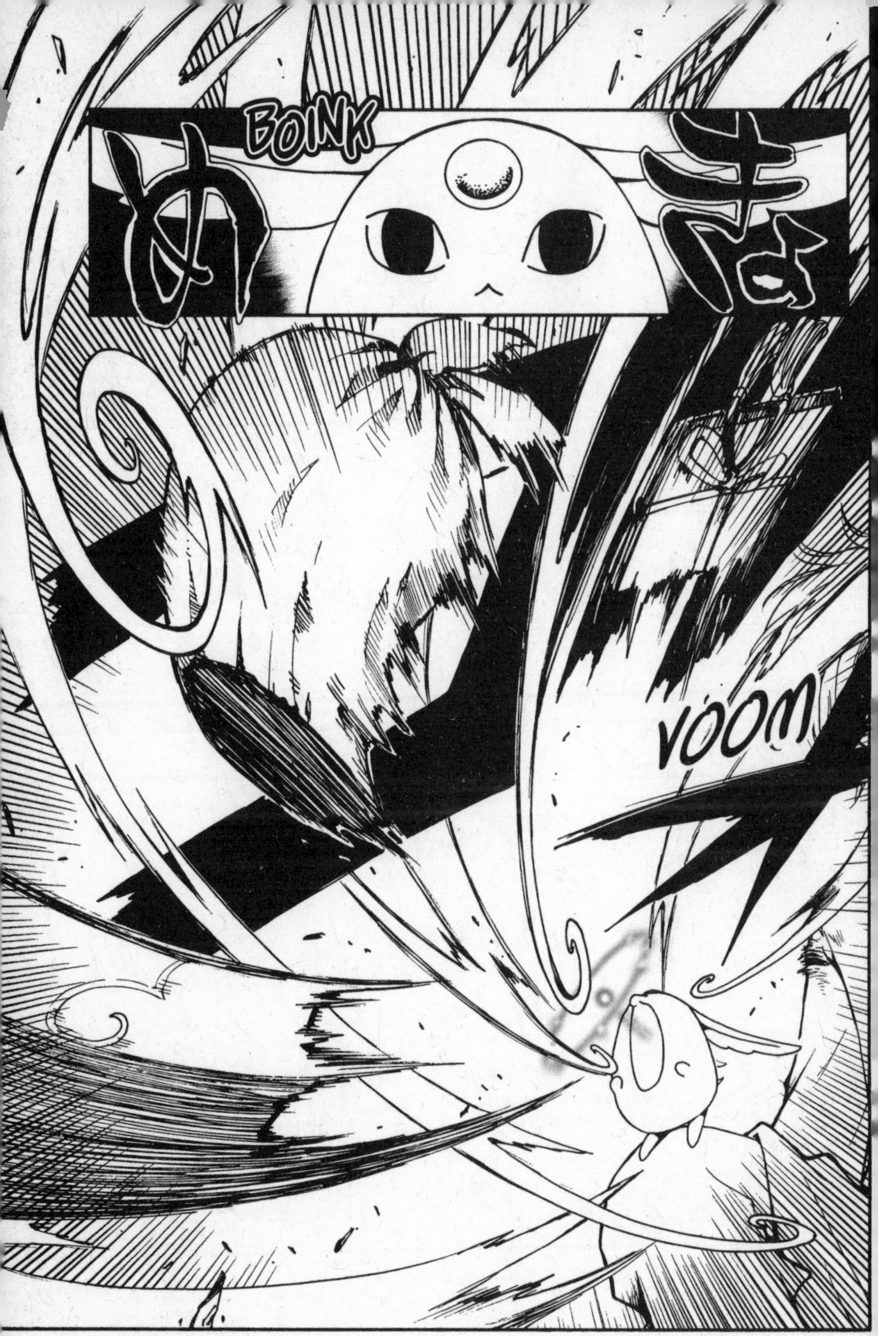
BOINK
めきょ
VOOM

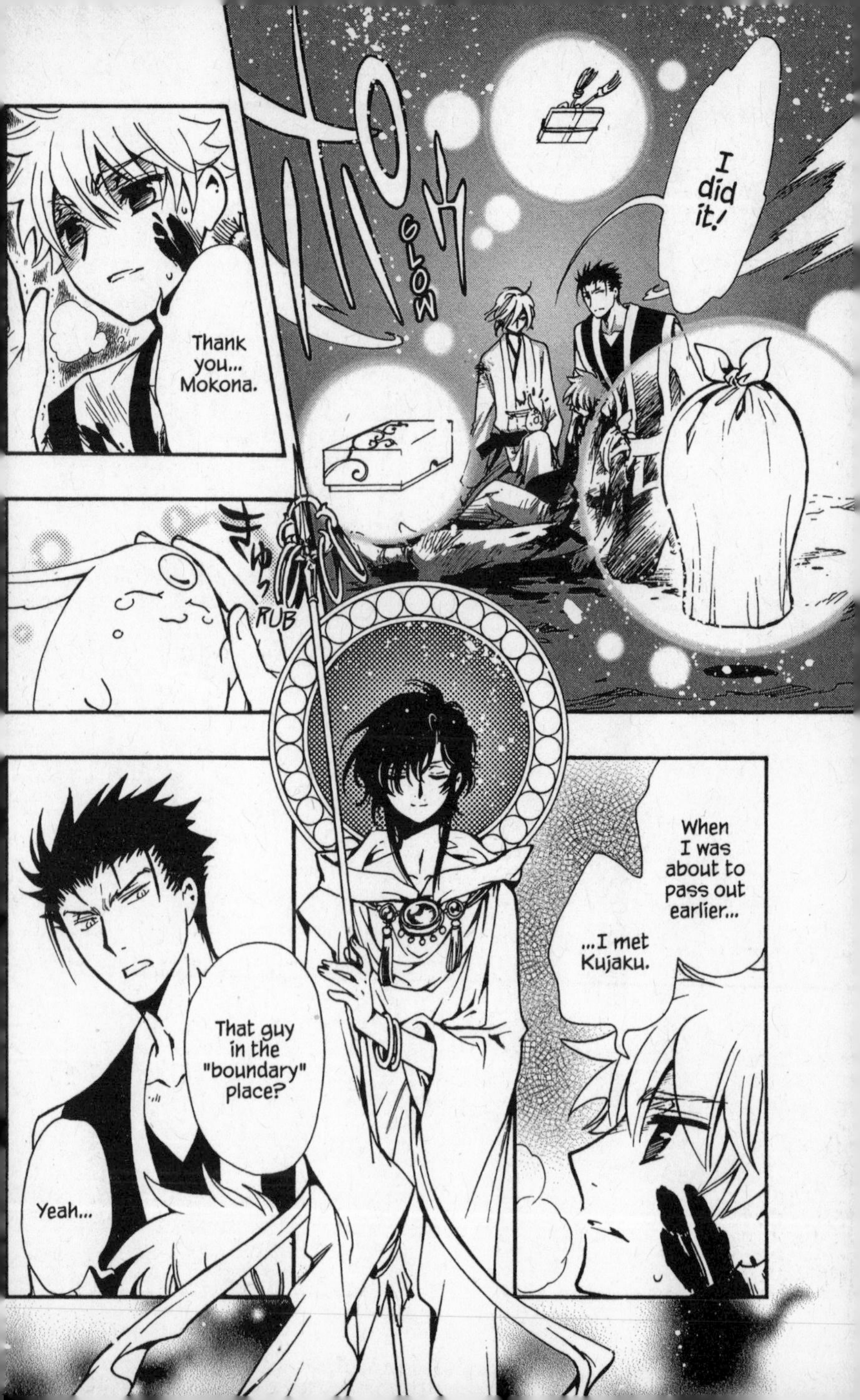
GLOW
I did it!
Thank you... Mokona.
RUB
When I was about to pass out earlier...
...I met Kujaku.
That guy in the "boundary" place?
Yeah...

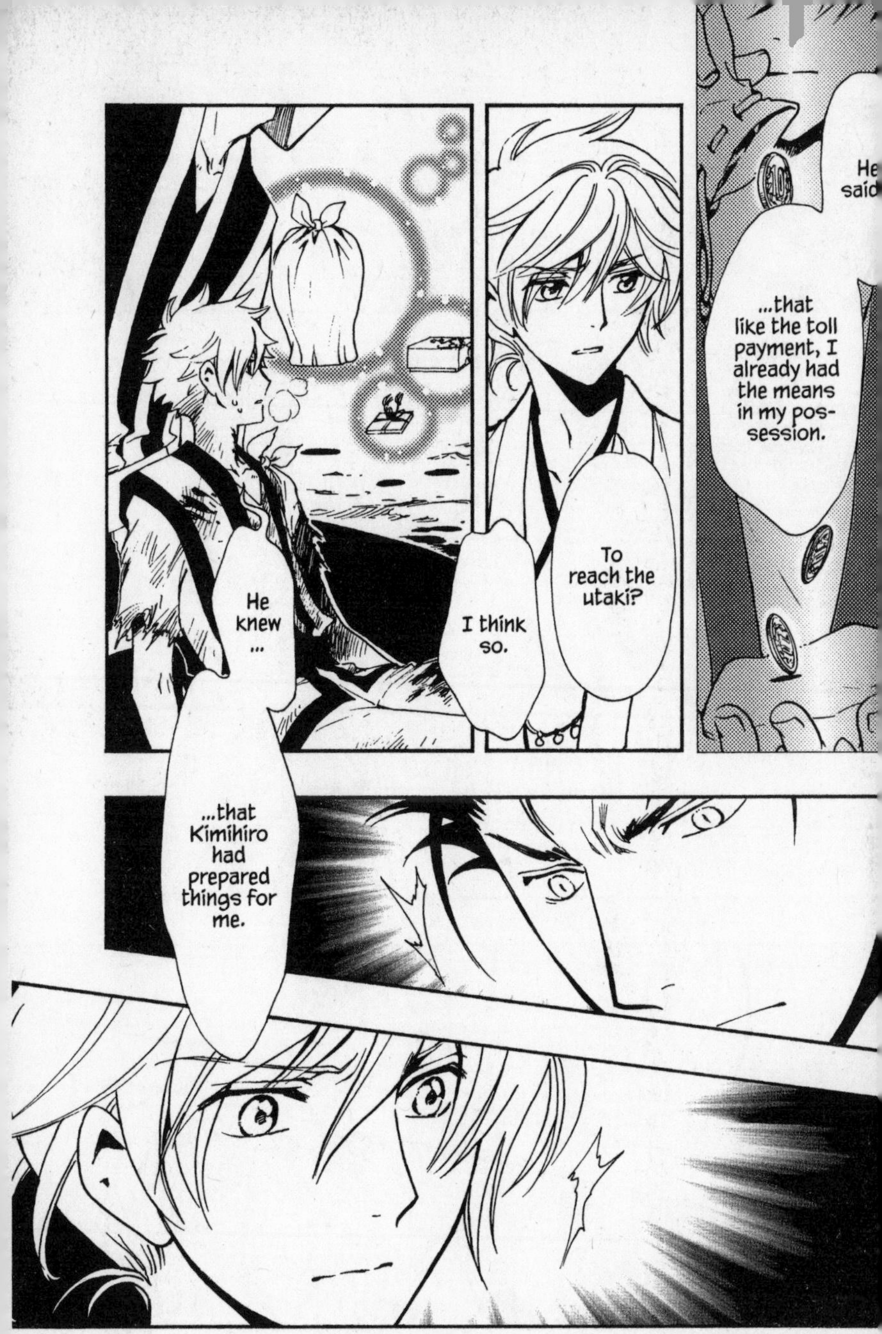
He said
...that like the toll payment, I already had the means in my possession.
To reach the utaki?
I think so.
He knew ...
...that Kimihiro had prepared things for me.

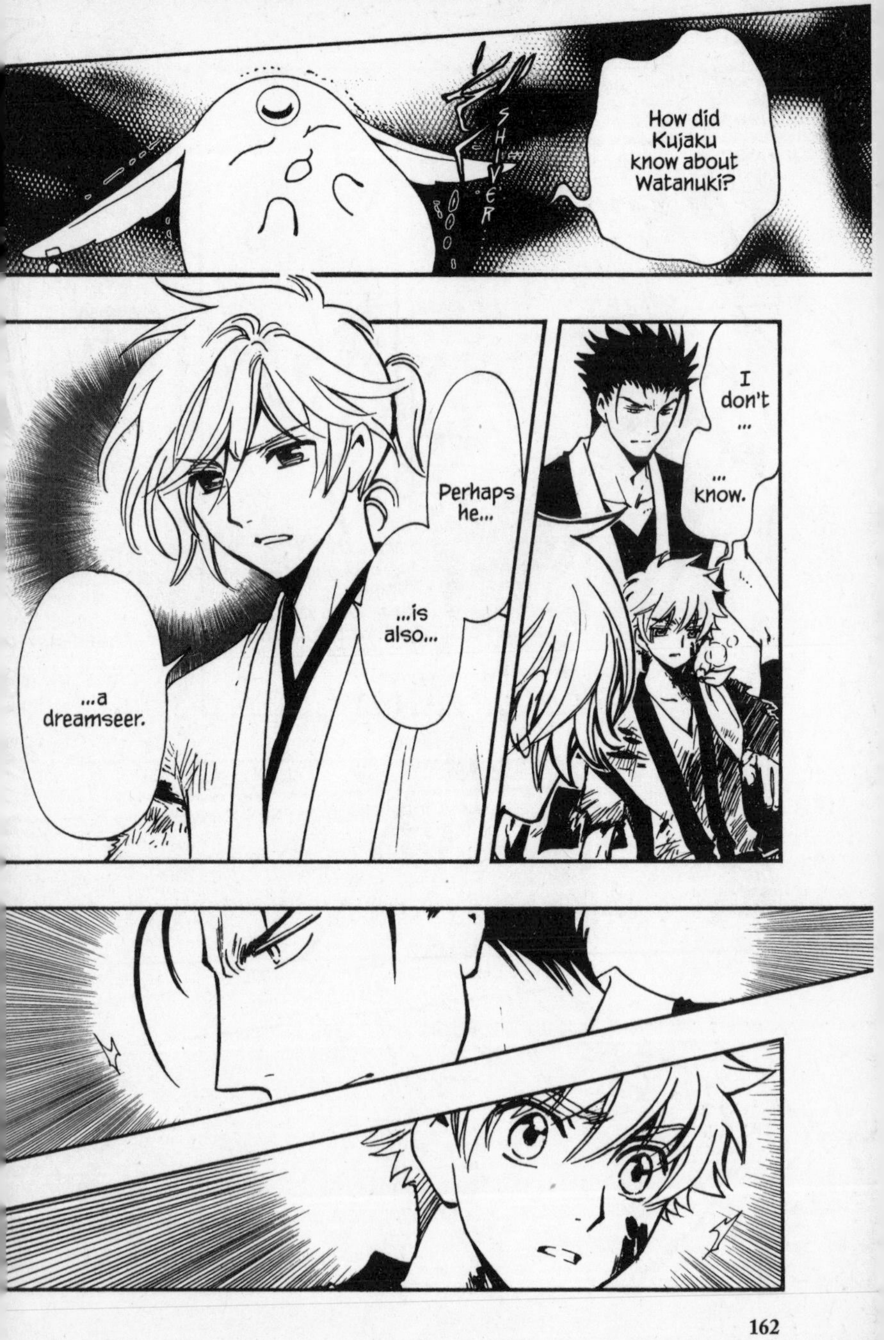
How did Kujaku know about Watanuki?
SHIVER
I don't ...
... know.
Perhaps he...
...is also...
...a dreamseer.

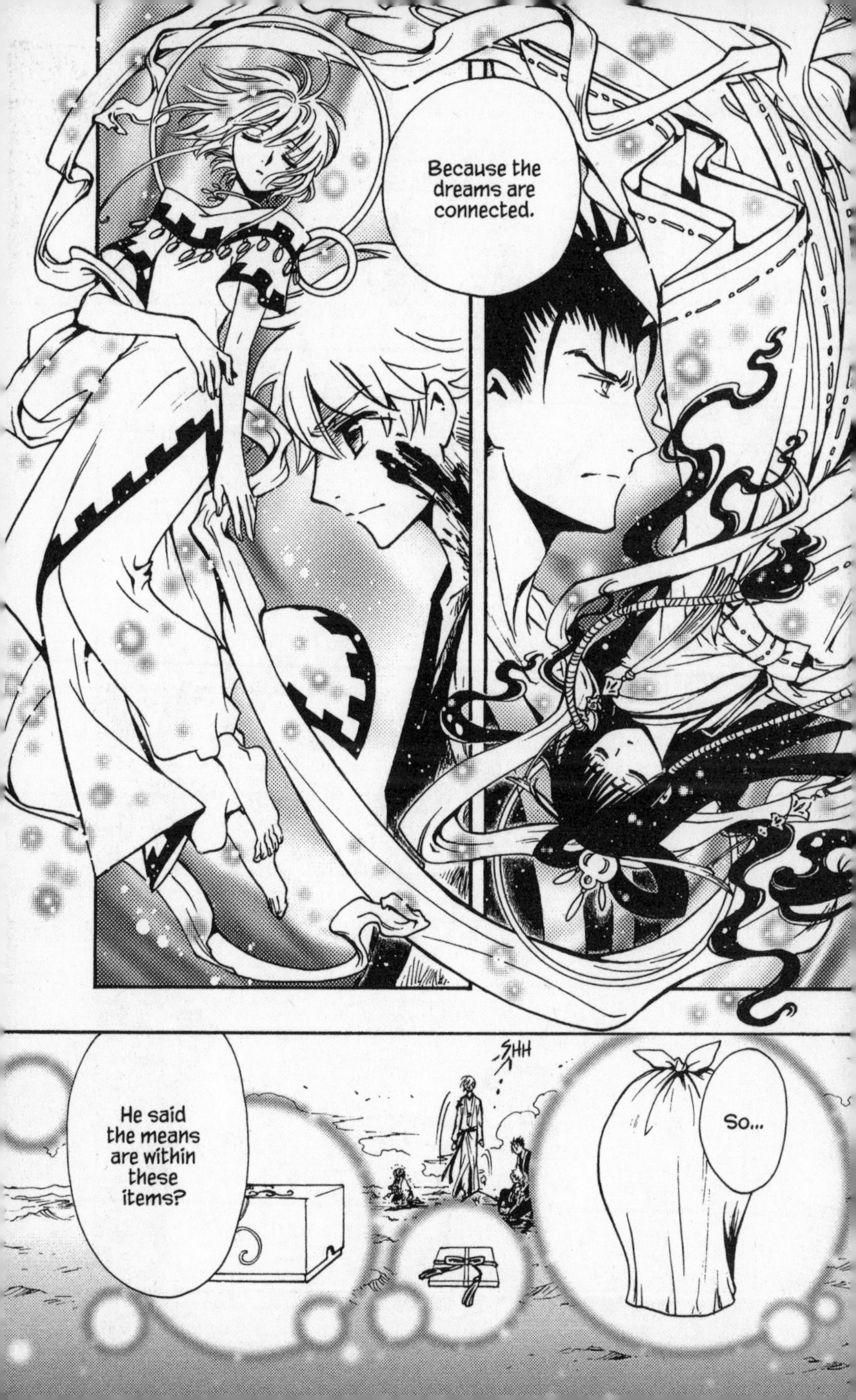
Because the dreams are connected.
So...
SHH
He said the means are within these items?

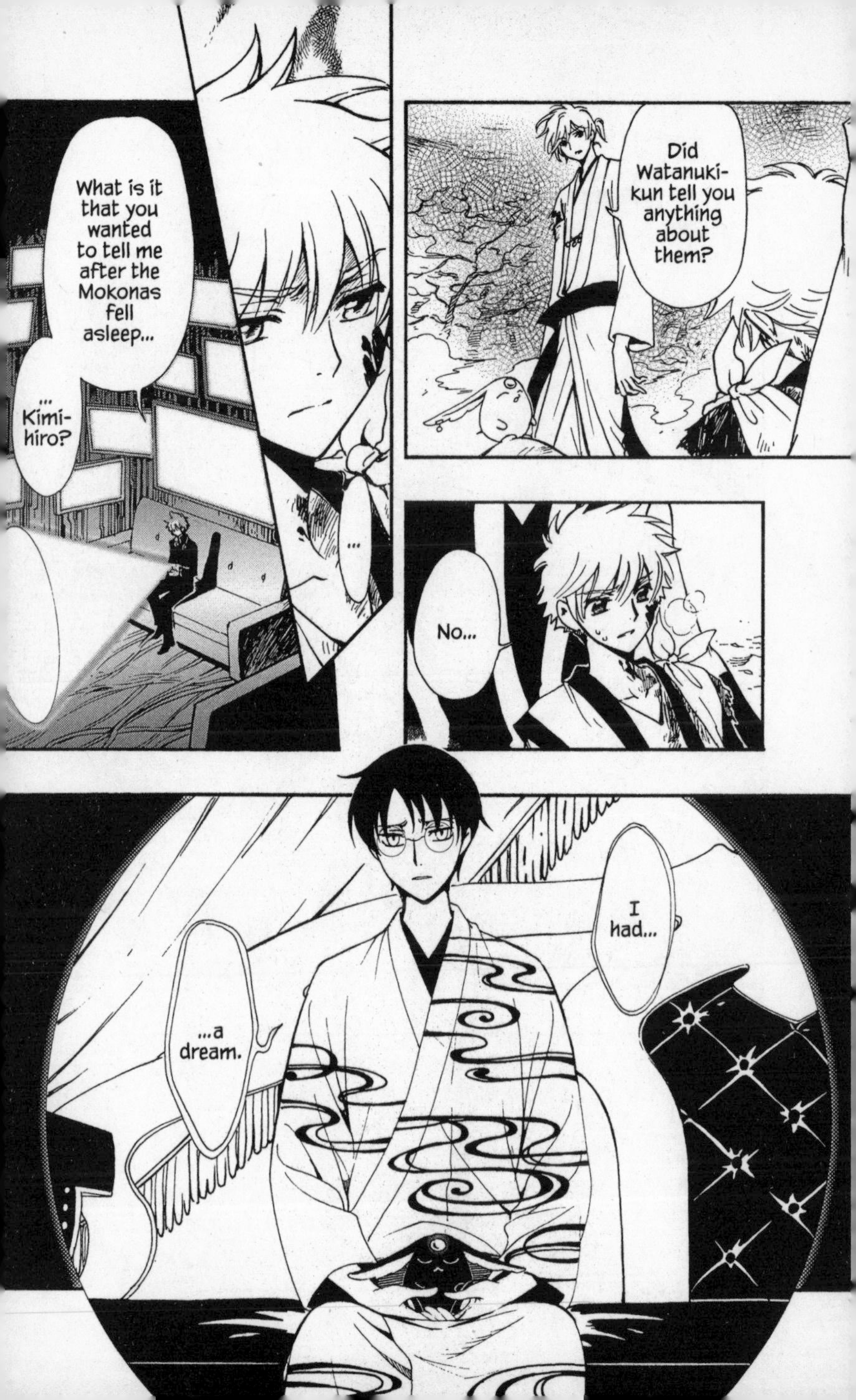
Did Watanuki-kun tell you anything about them?
No...
...
What is it that you wanted to tell me after the Mokonas fell asleep...
... Kimihiro?
I had...
...a dream.

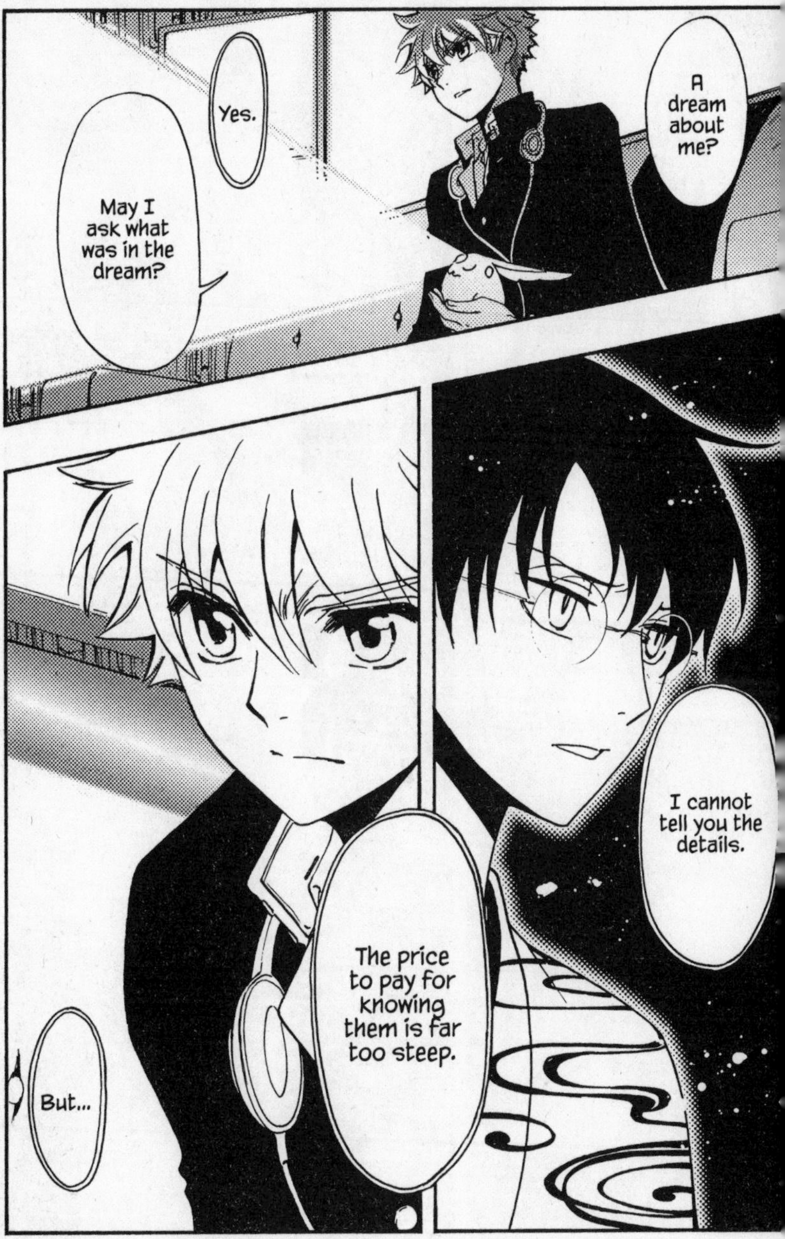
A dream about me?
Yes.
May I ask what was in the dream?
I cannot tell you the details.
The price to pay for knowing them is far too steep.
But...

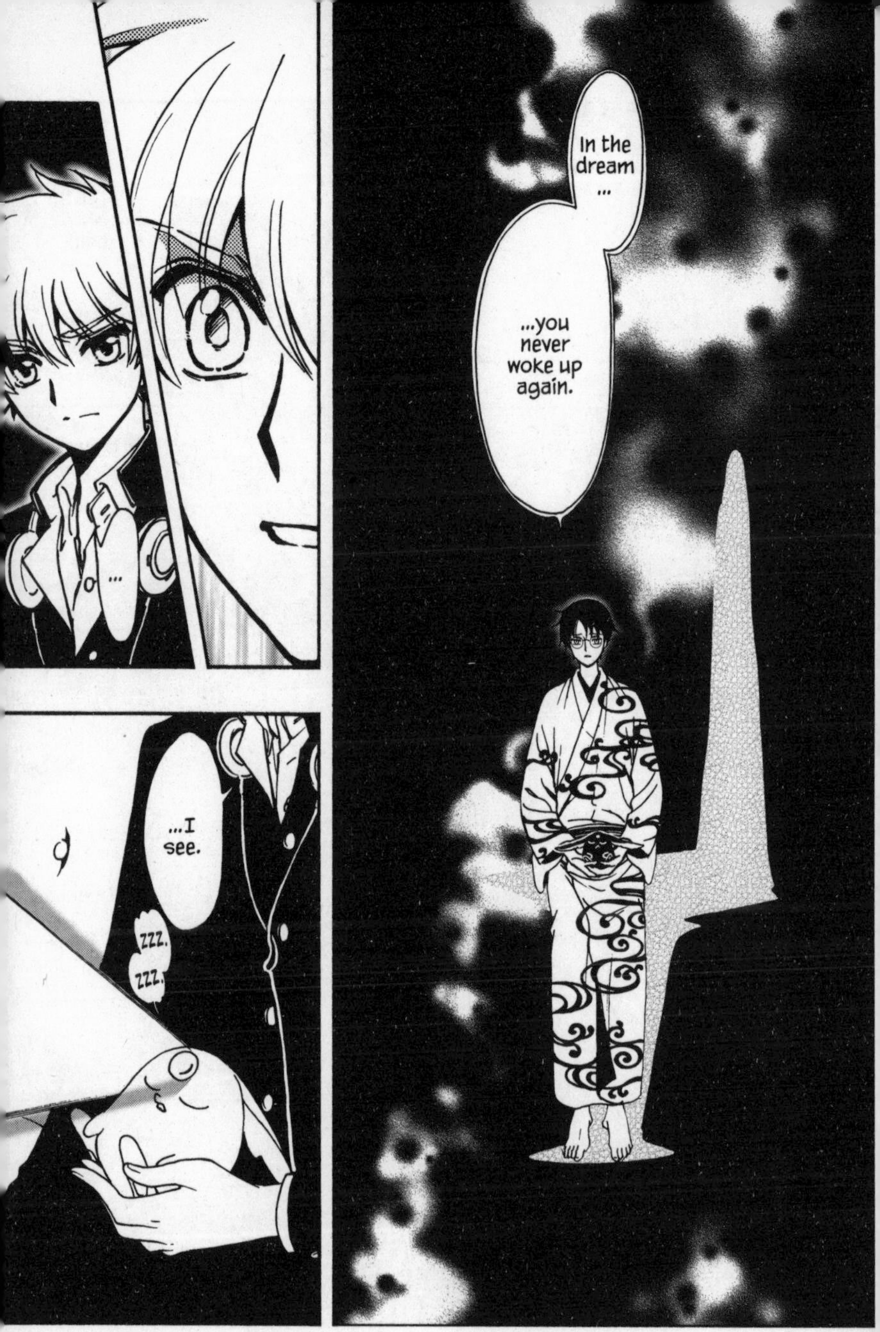
In the dream ...
...you never woke up again.
...
...I see.
ZZZ.
ZZZ.

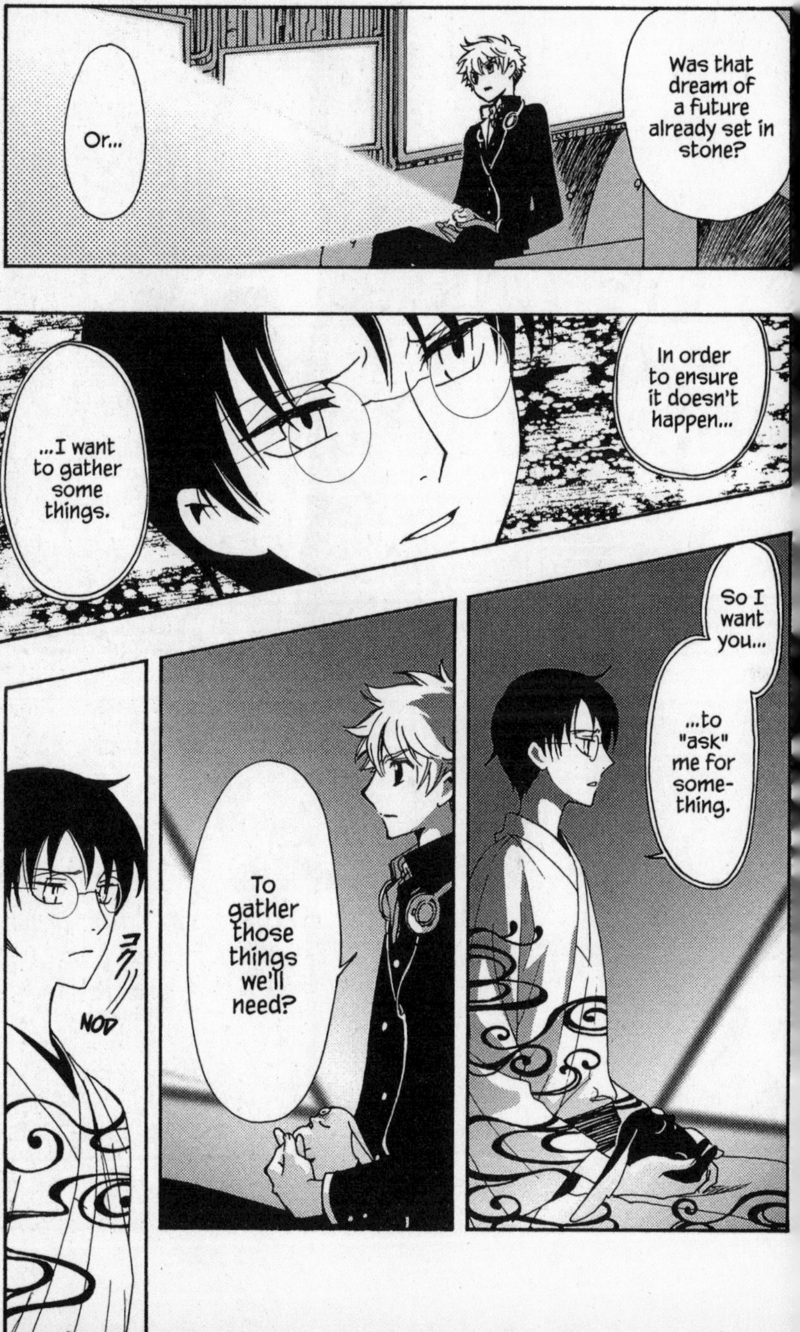
Was that dream of a future already set in stone?
Or...
In order to ensure it doesn't happen...
...I want to gather some things.
So I want you...
...to "ask" me for some-thing.
To gather those things we'll need?
NOD

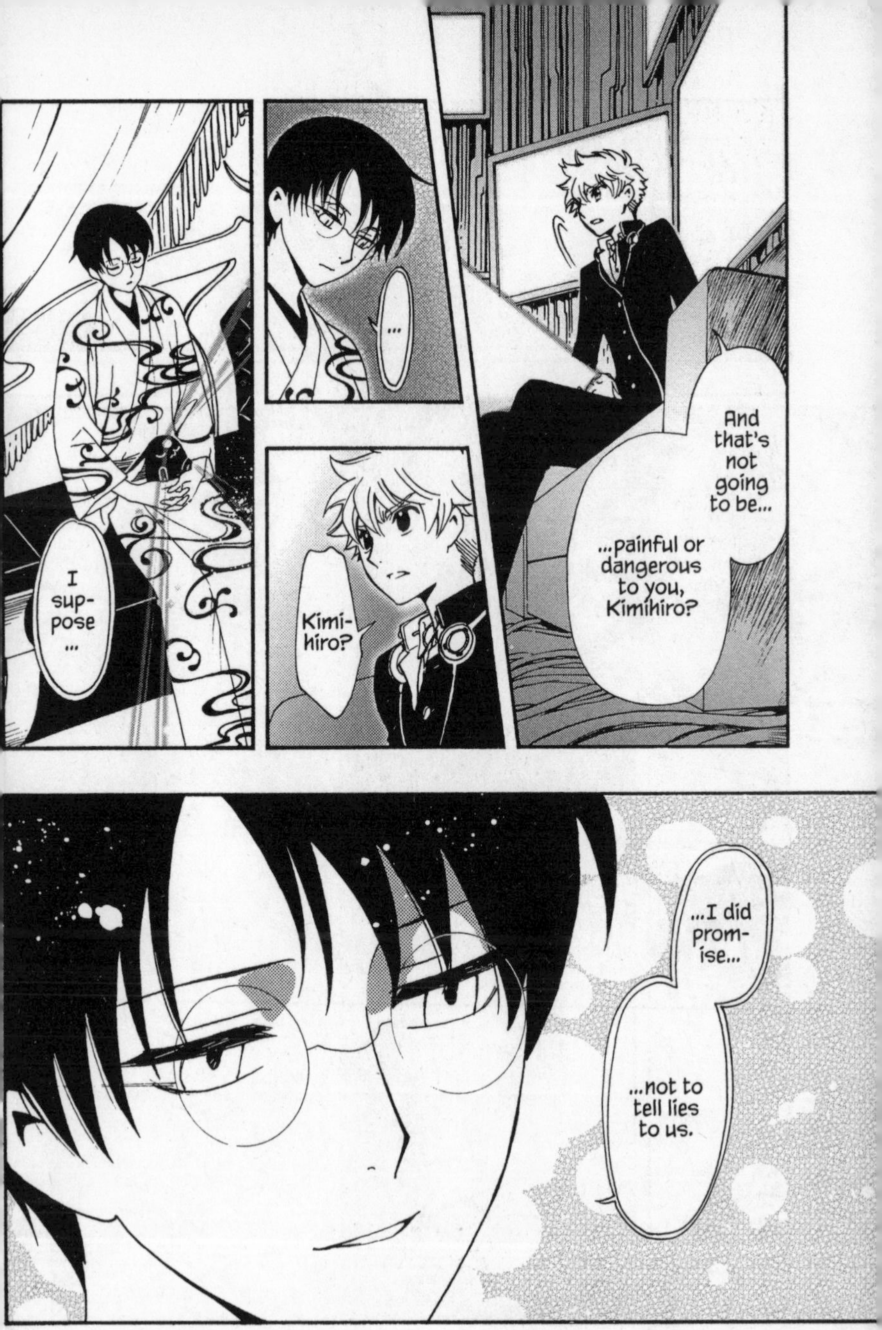
And that's not going to be...
...painful or dangerous to you, Kimihiro?
...
Kimi-hiro?
I sup-pose ...
...I did prom-ise...
...not to tell lies to us.

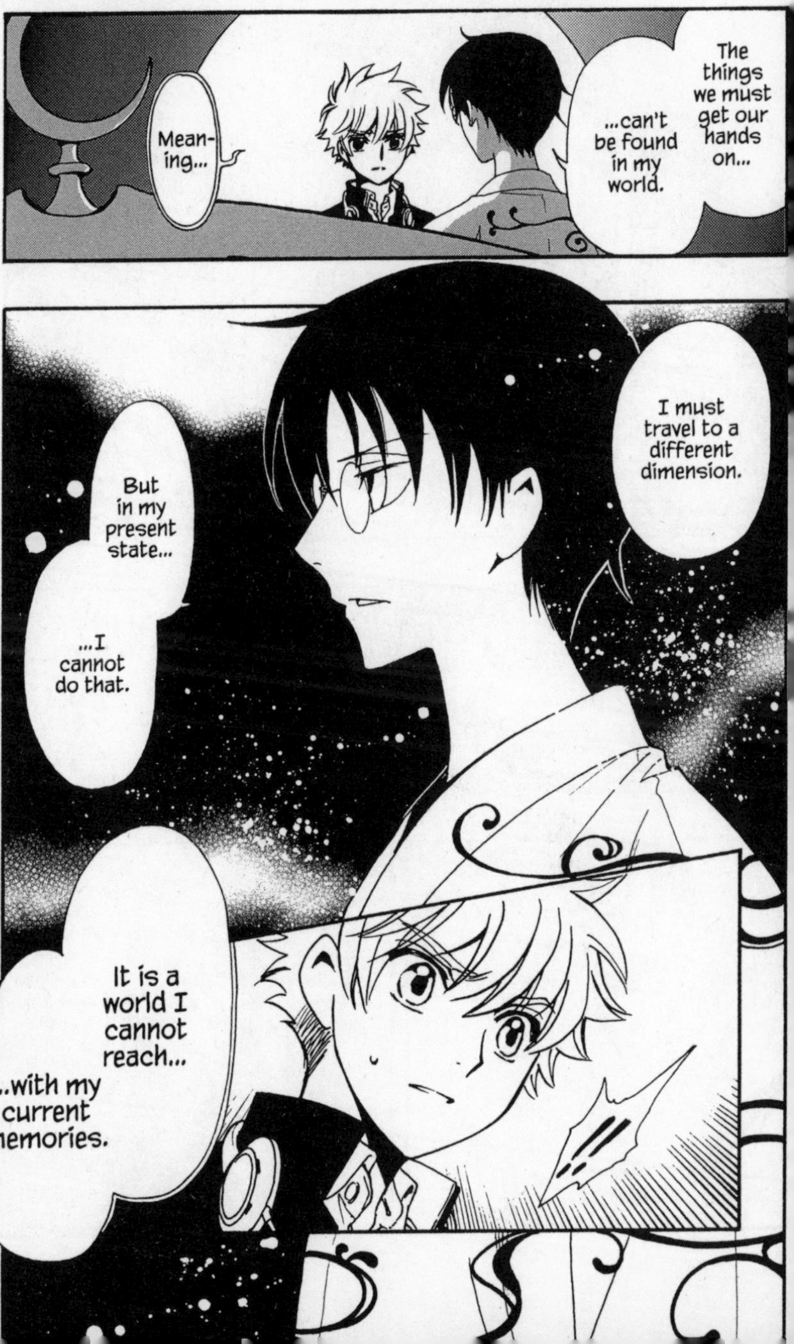
The things we must get our hands on...
...can't be found in my world.
Meaning...
I must travel to a different dimension.
But in my present state...
...I cannot do that.
It is a world I cannot reach...
...with my current memories.
!!

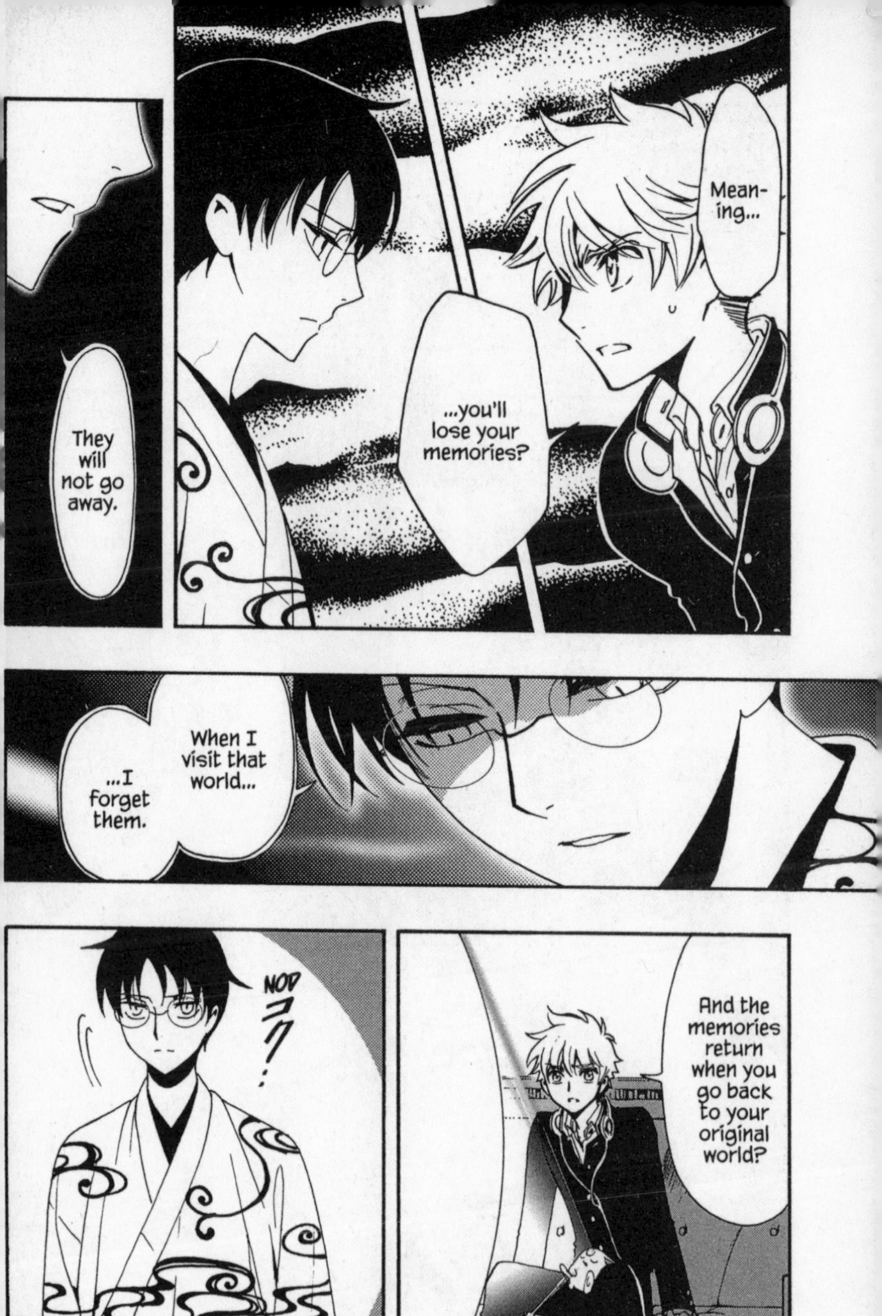
Meaning...
...you'll lose your memories?
They will not go away.
When I visit that world...
...I forget them.
And the memories return when you go back to your original world?
NOD

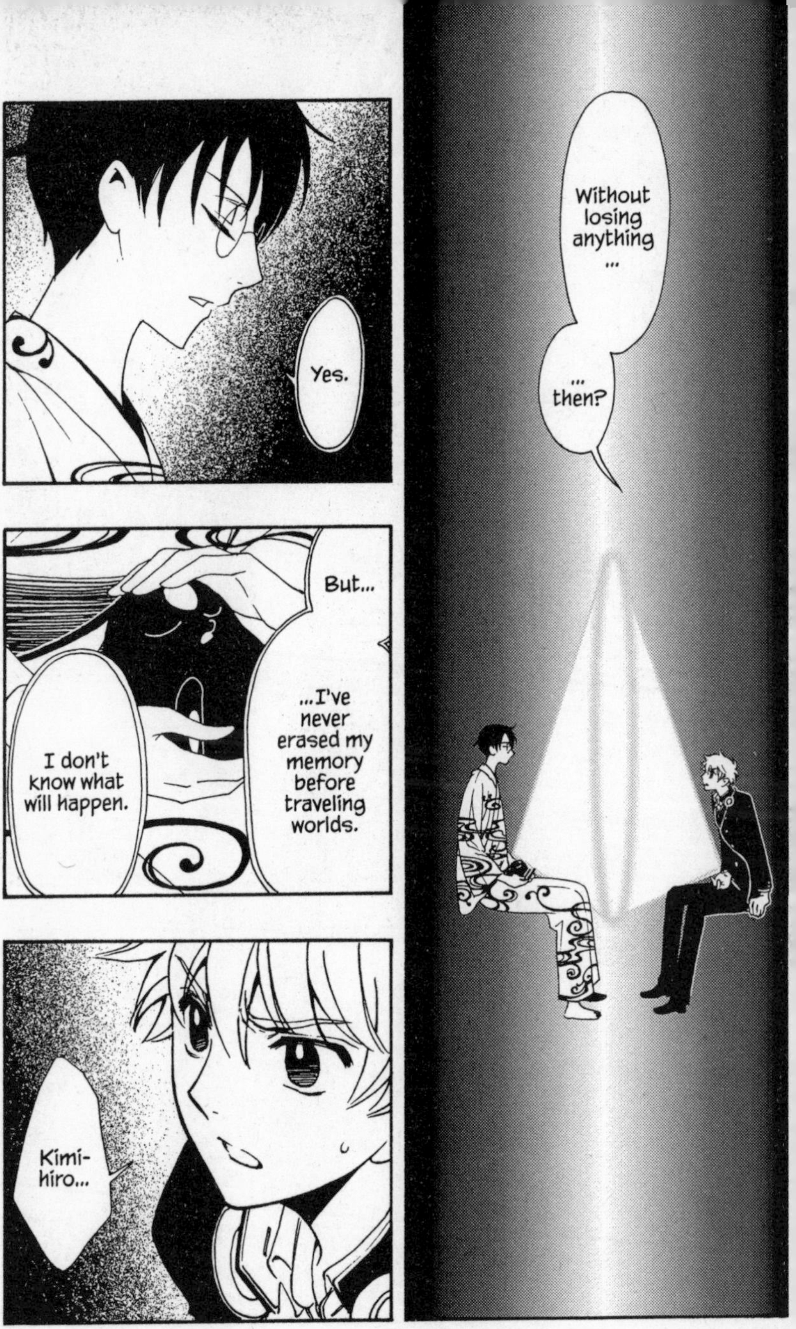
Without losing anything ...
... then?
Yes.
But...
...I've never erased my memory before traveling worlds.
I don't know what will happen.
Kimihiro...

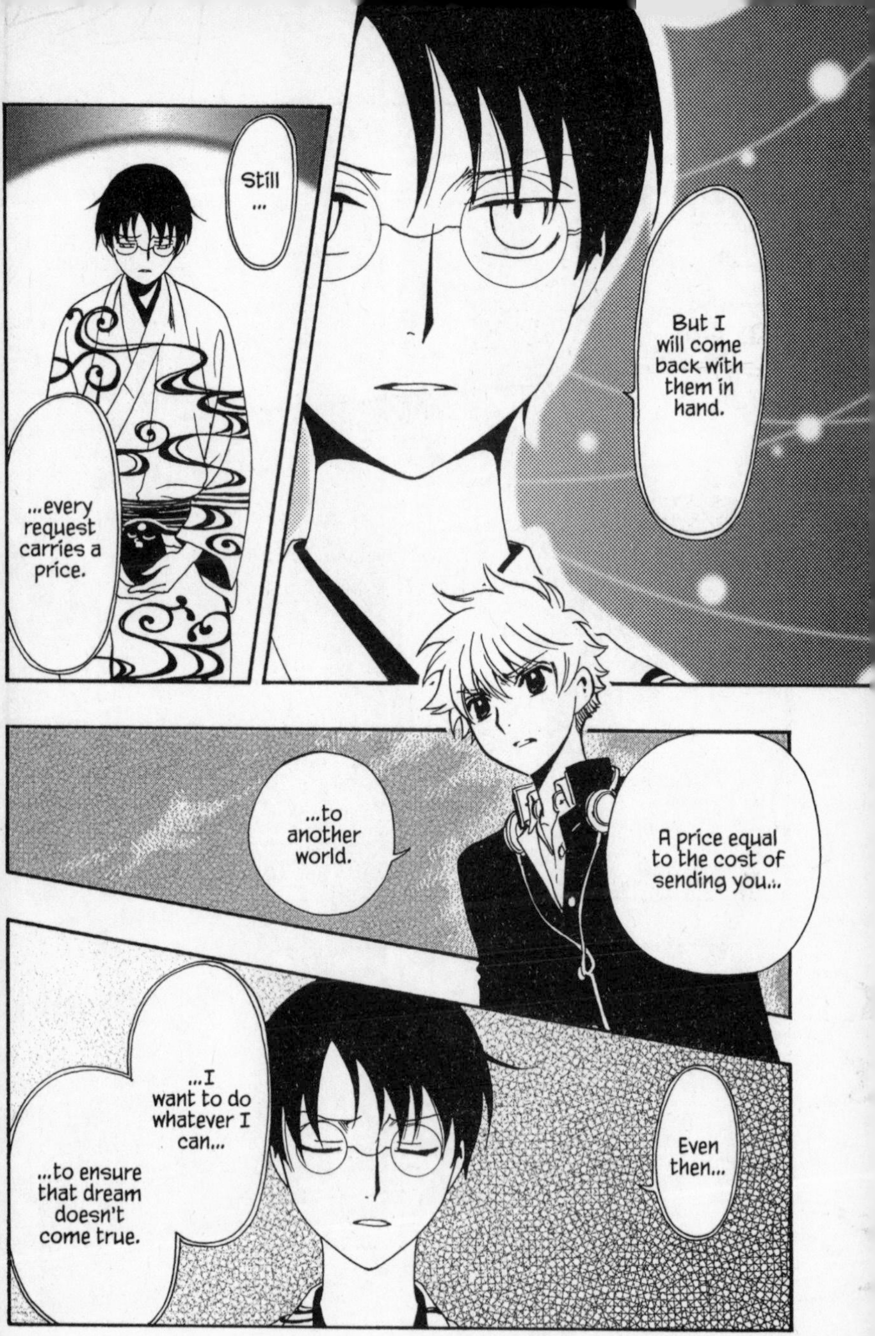
But I will come back with them in hand.
Still...
...every request carries a price.
A price equal to the cost of sending you...
...to another world.
Even then...
...I want to do whatever I can...
...to ensure that dream doesn't come true.

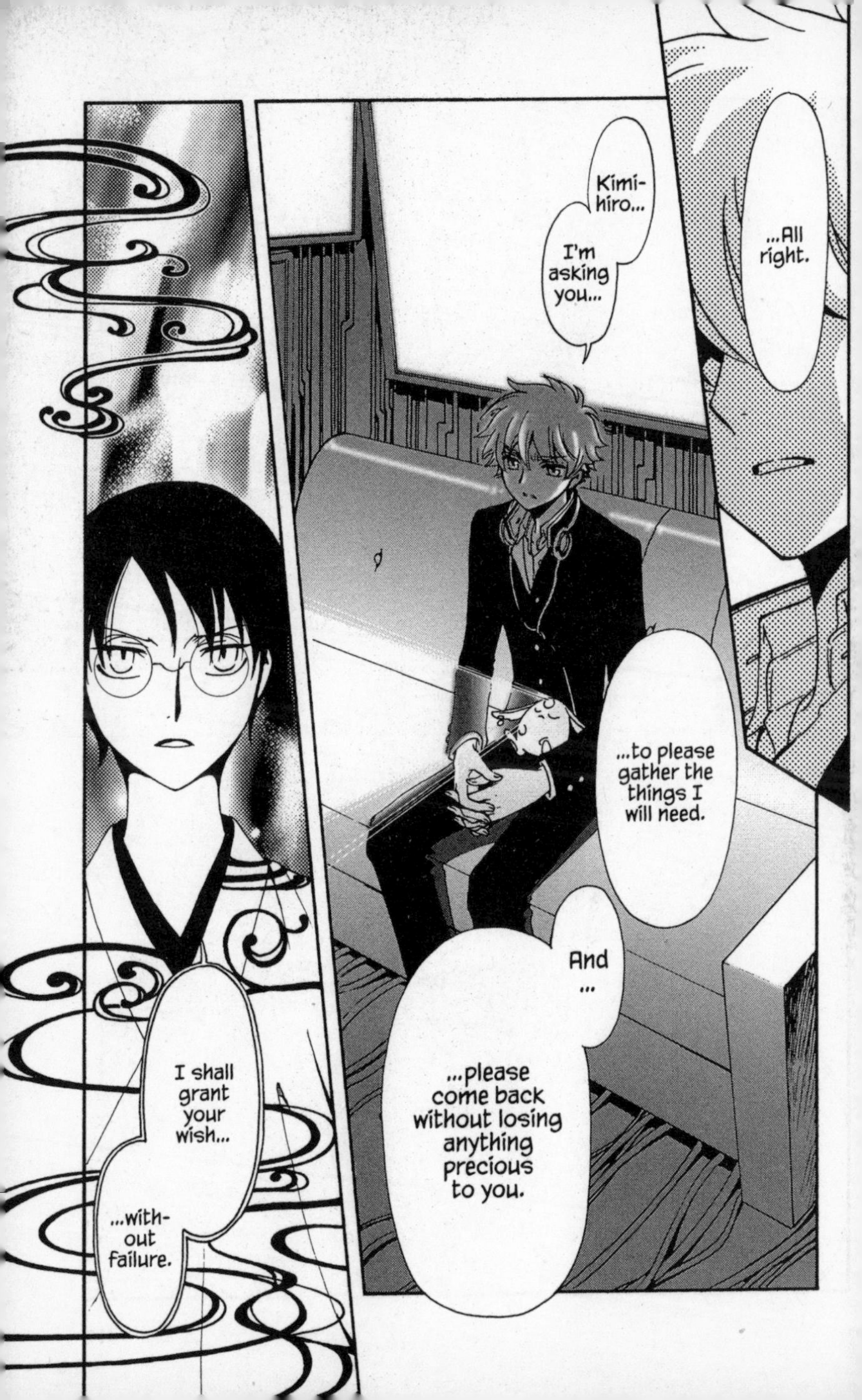
...All right.
Kimi-hiro...
I'm asking you...
...to please gather the things I will need.
And ...
...please come back without losing anything precious to you.
I shall grant your wish...
...with-out failure.

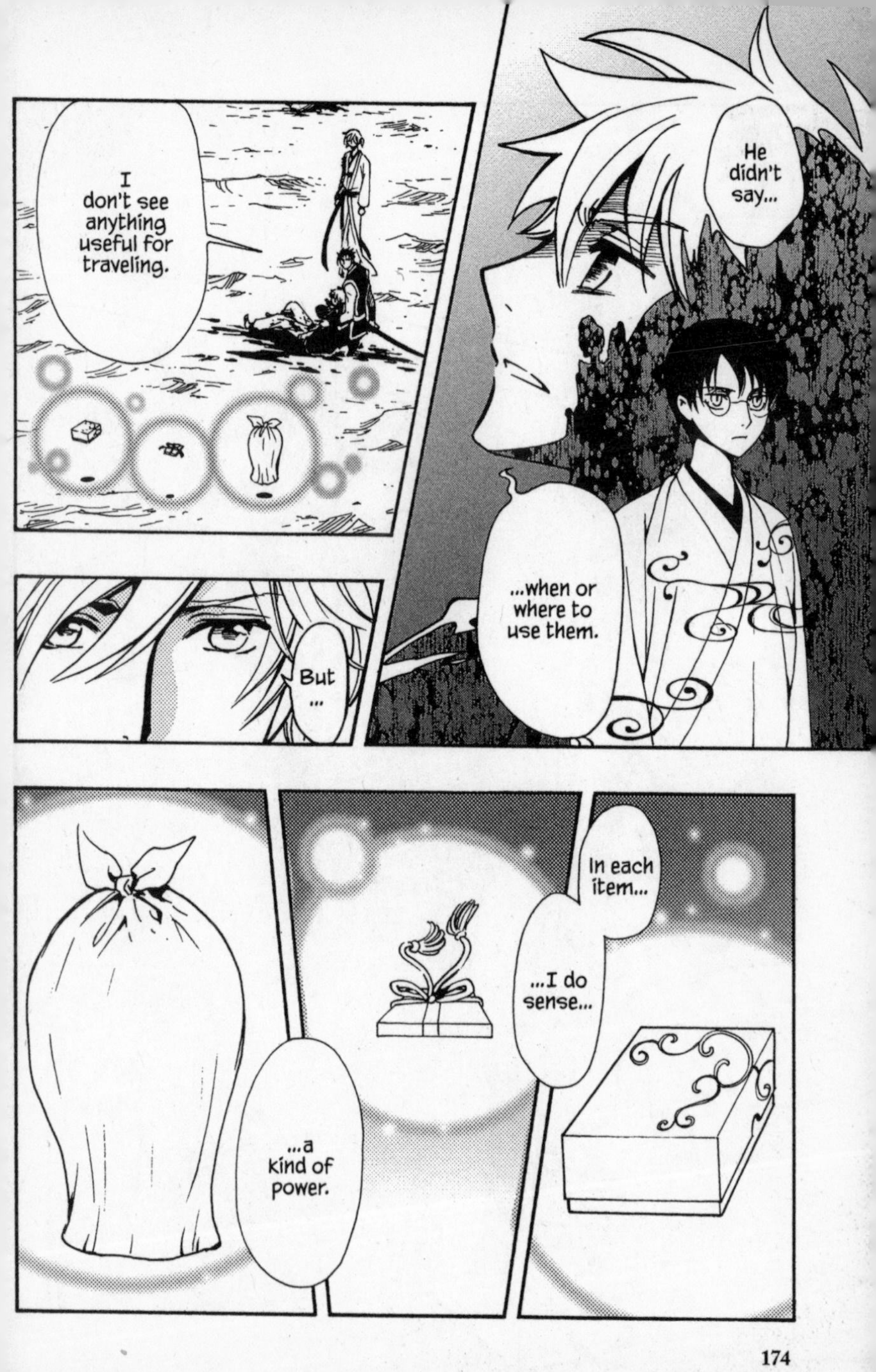
He didn't say...
...when or where to use them.
I don't see anything useful for traveling.
But ...
In each item...
...I do sense...
...a kind of power.

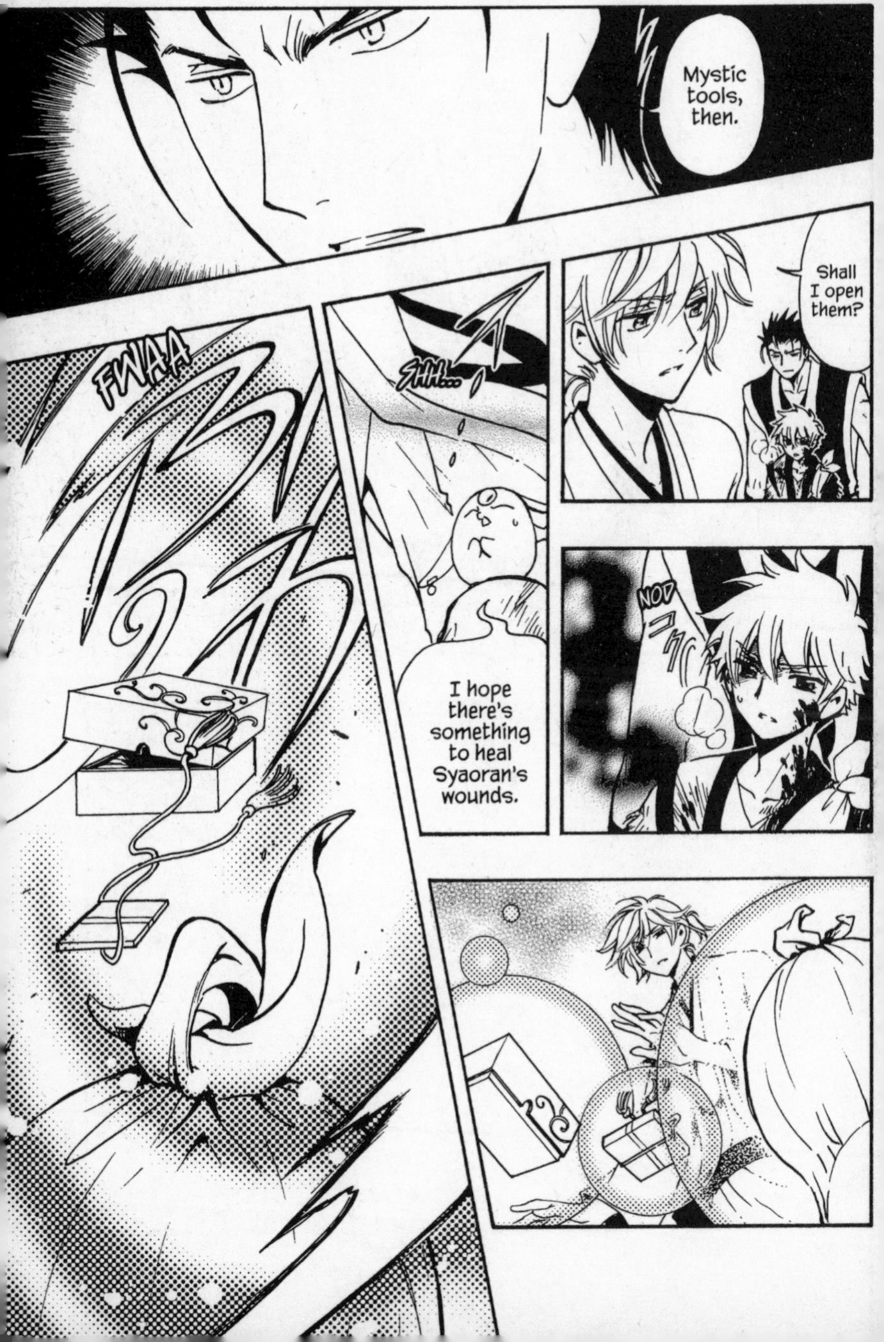
Mystic tools, then.
Shall I open them?
SHH...
FWAA
NOD
I hope there's something to heal Syaoran's wounds.

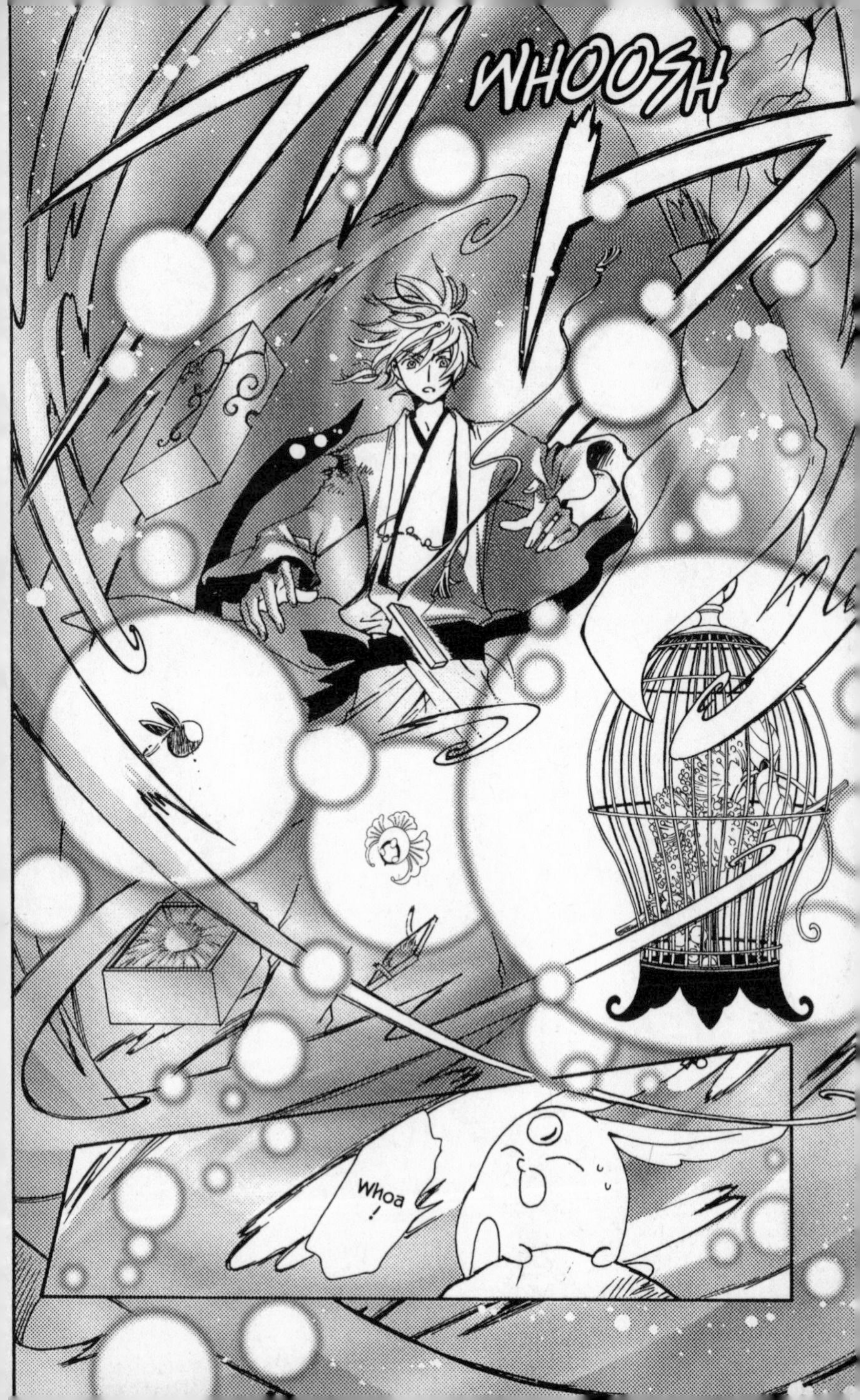
WHOOSH
Whoa!

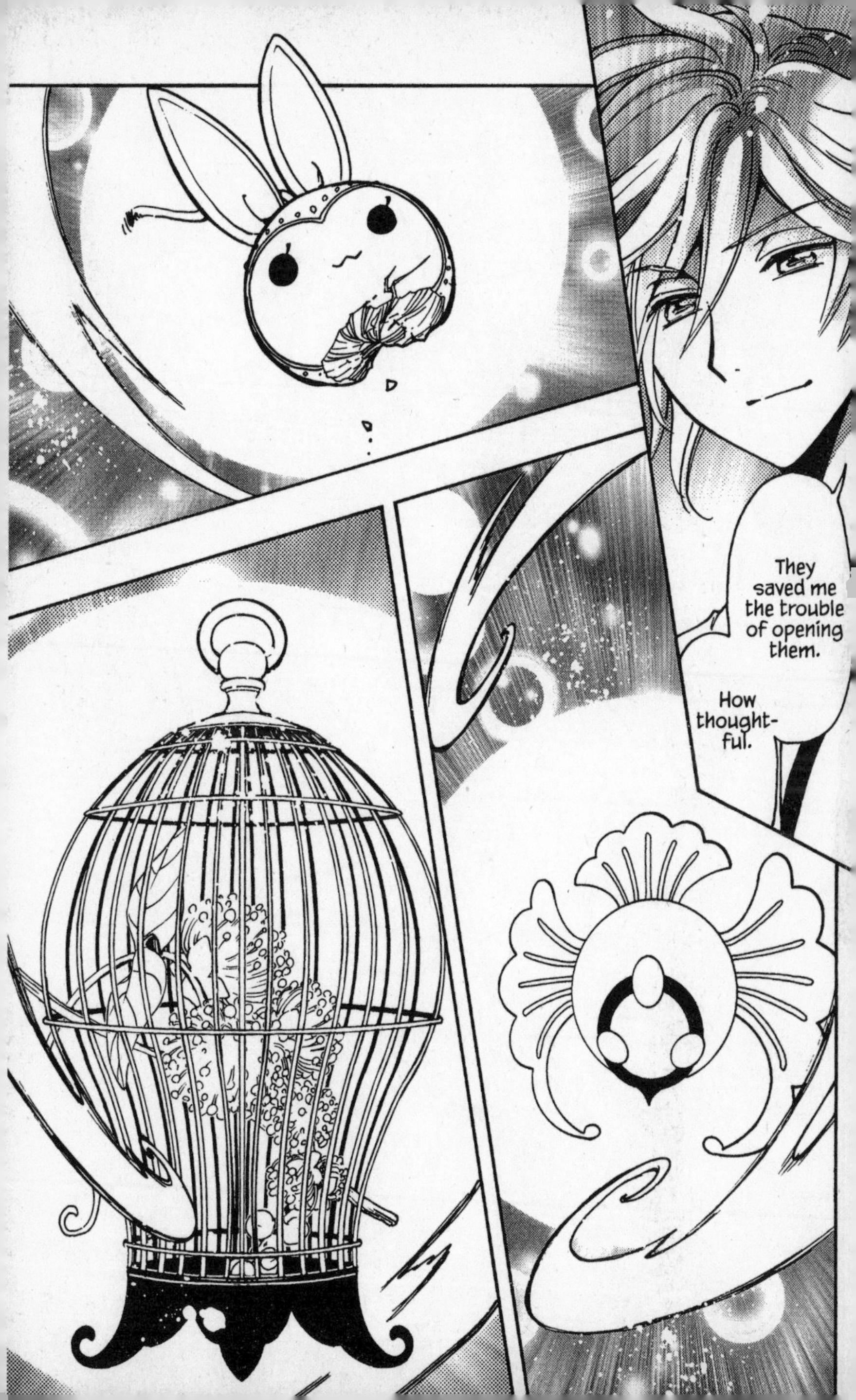
They saved me the trouble of opening them.
How thoughtful.

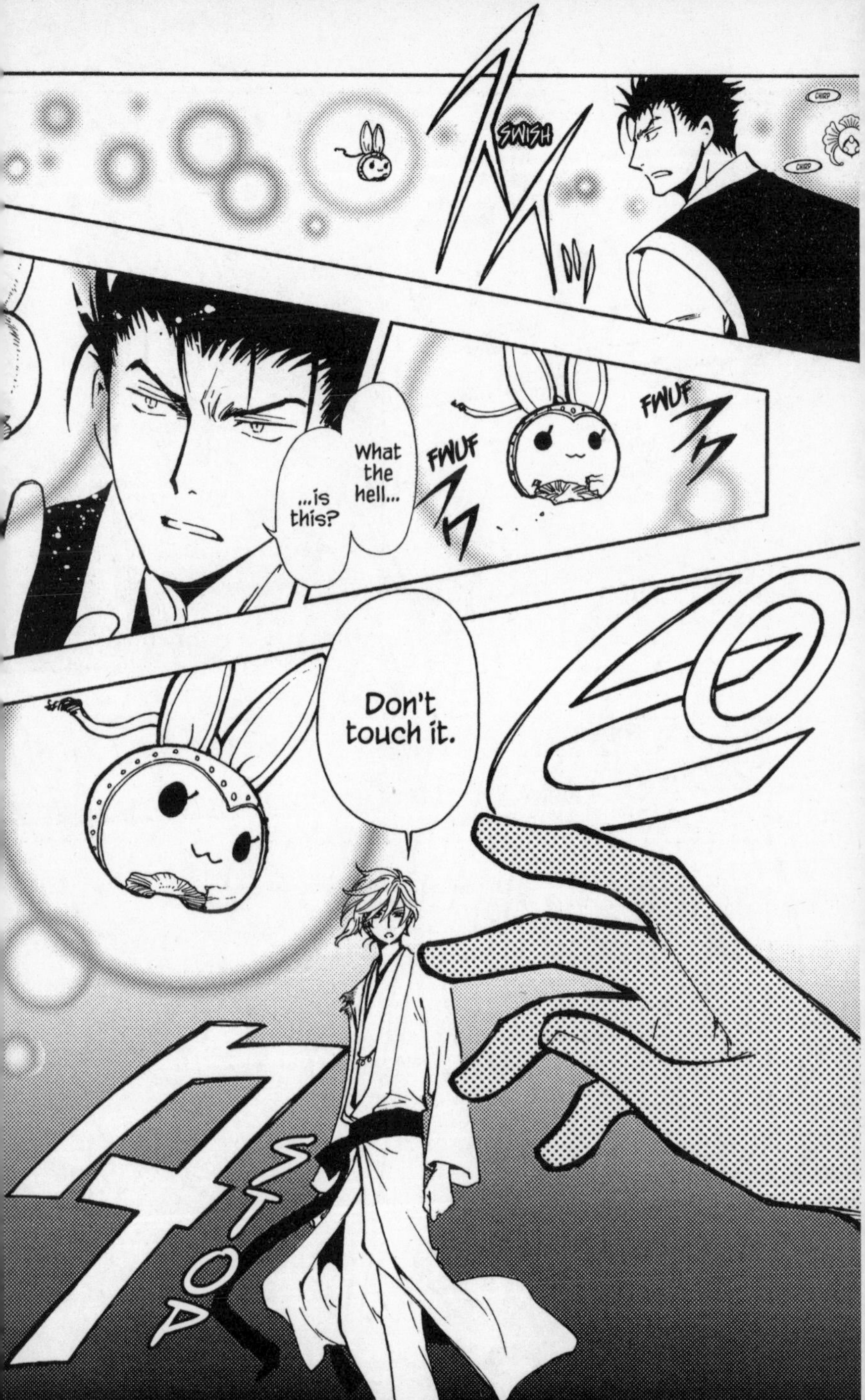
CHIRP
CHIRP
SWISH
FWUF
FWUF
What the hell...
...is this?
Don't touch it.
STOP

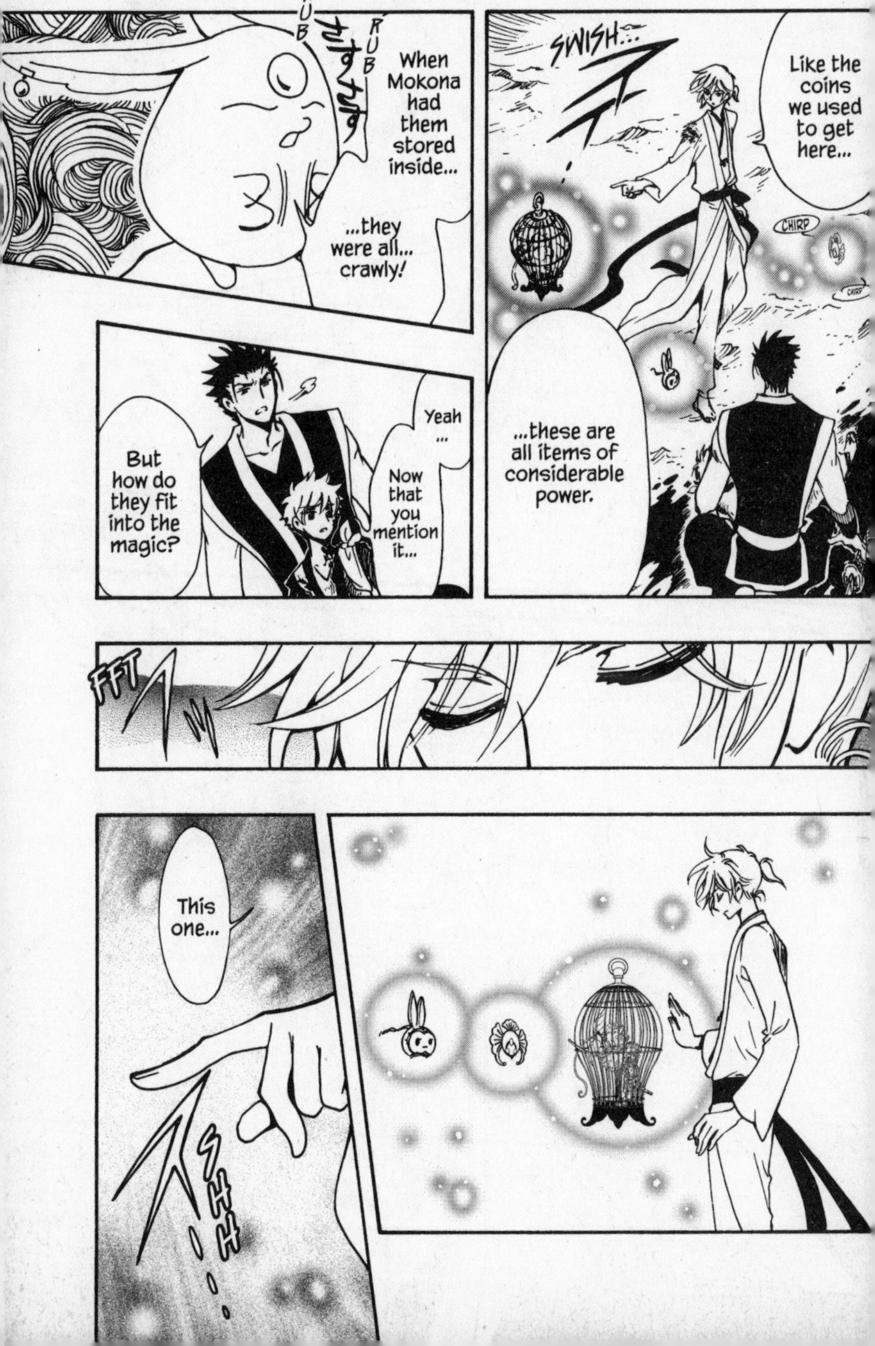
SWISH...
Like the coins we used to get here...
CHIRP
CHIRP
...these are all items of considerable power.
RUB RUB
さすさす
When Mokona had them stored inside...
...they were all... crawly!
Yeah... Now that you mention it...
But how do they fit into the magic?
FFT
This one...
SHH...

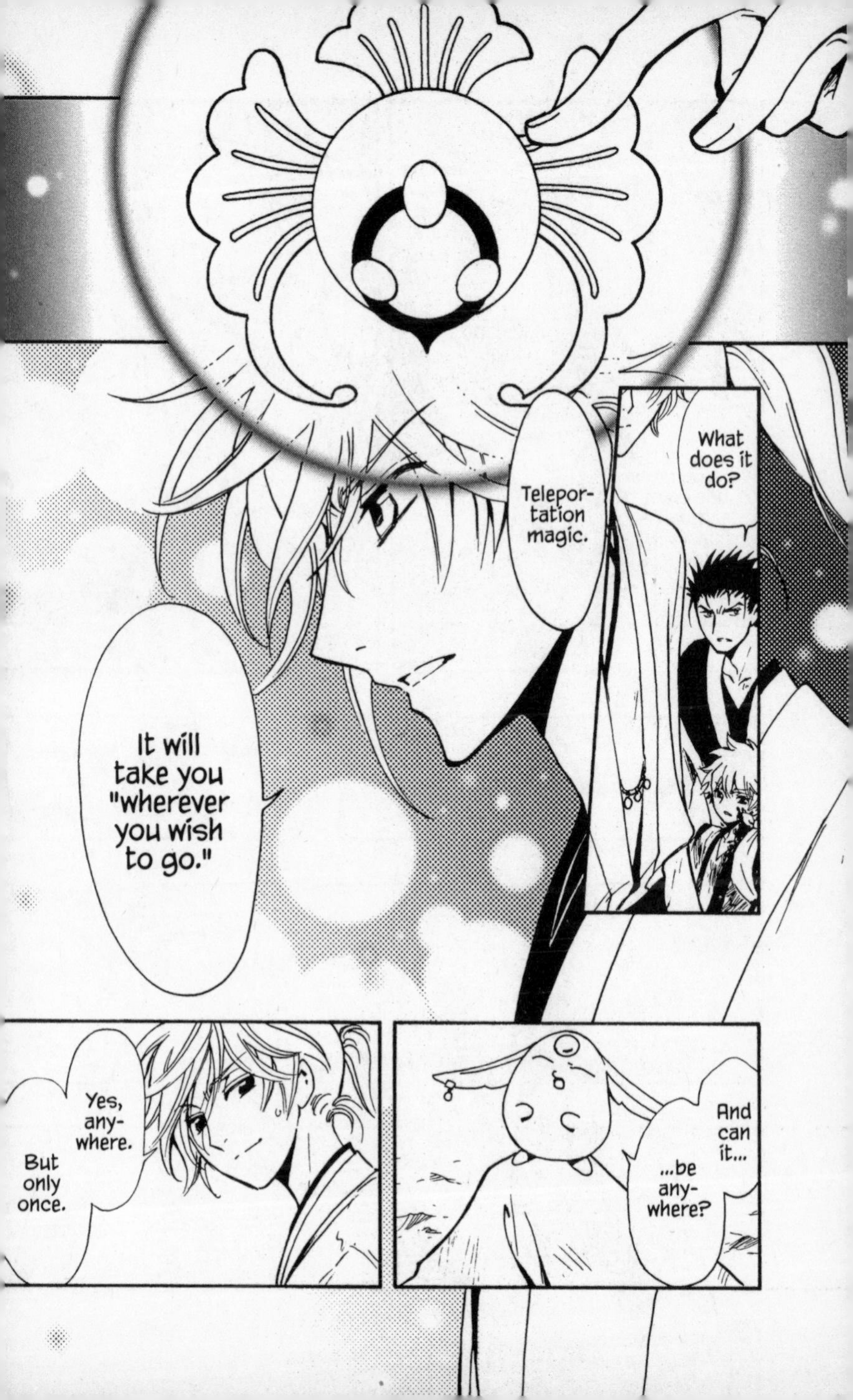
What does it do?
Teleportation magic.
It will take you "wherever you wish to go."
And can it...
...be anywhere?
Yes, anywhere.
But only once.

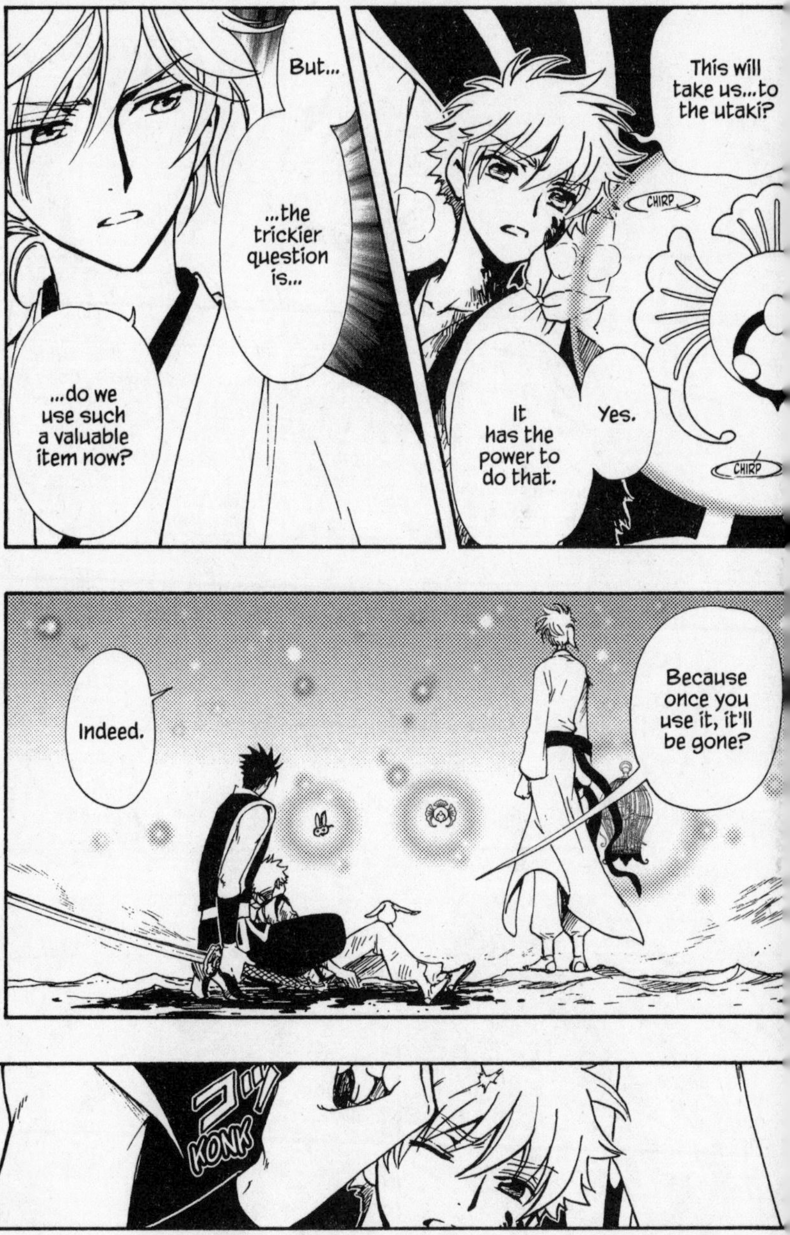
This will take us...to the utaki?
CHIRP
Yes.
It has the power to do that.
CHIRP
But...
...the trickier question is...
...do we use such a valuable item now?
Because once you use it, it'll be gone?
Indeed.
KONK

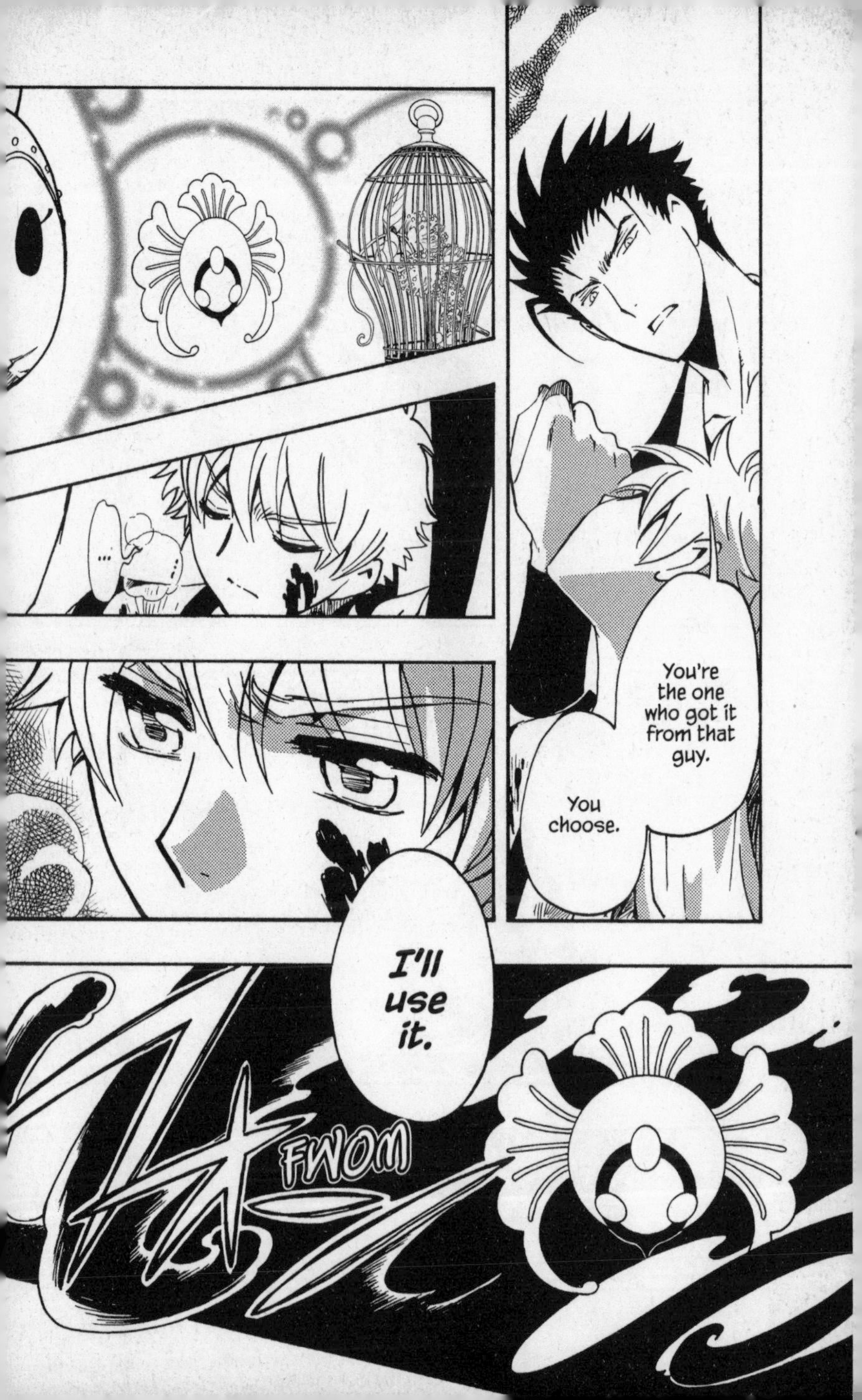
...
You're the one who got it from that guy.
You choose.
I'll use it.
FWOM

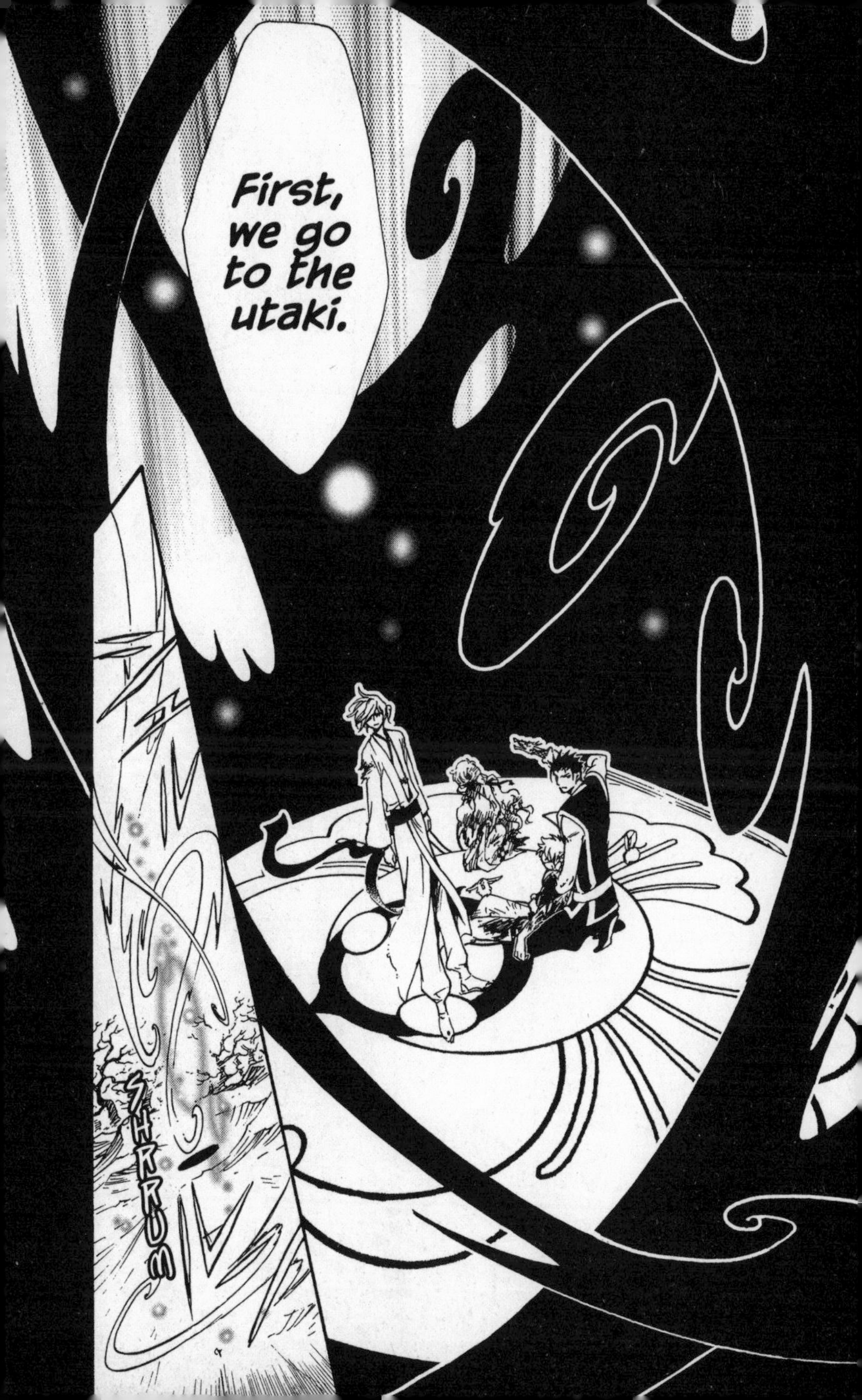
First, we go to the utaki.
SHRRUM

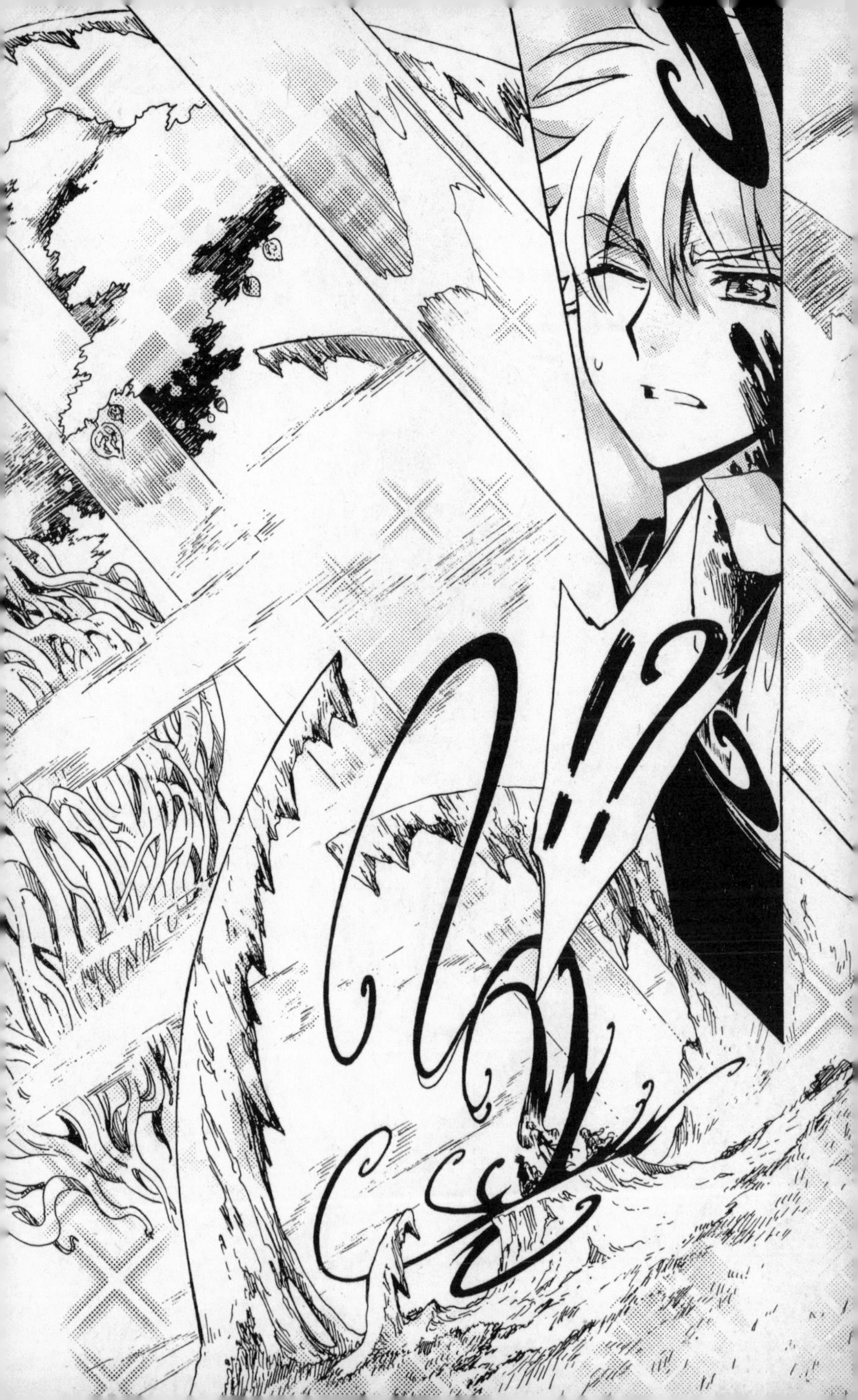
?!

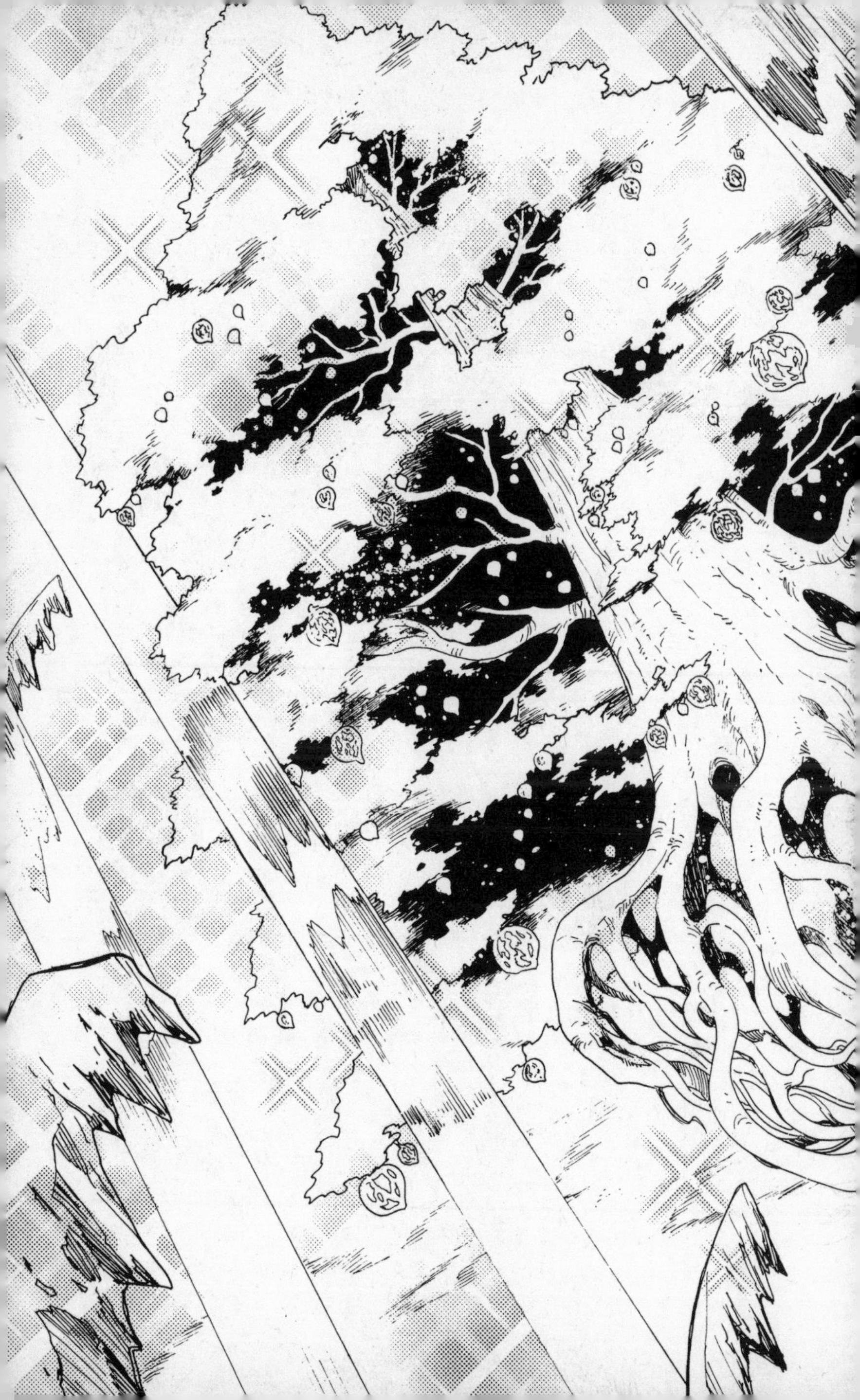

Originally published in Shonen Magazine Special,
No. 2 - No. 5, No. 7, No. 8, 2015

To Be Continued

TRANSLATION NOTES

Japanese is a tricky language for most Westerners, and translation is often more art than science. For your edification and reading pleasure, here are notes on some of the places where we could have gone in a different direction in our translation of the work, or where a Japanese cultural reference is used.

Seji, page 92
A spiritual power in Okinawan religion. A seji is that which infuses objects to make them holy or godly, and when they contact or reside within people, are responsible for acts of superhuman ability.

Don't you have a seji?! A godly power?!

Utaki, page 97
A holy place in Okinawan culture; every town or village has a holy grove, cave, or other natural area known as an utaki which is the home to the god that protects the village and its inhabitants.

Noro, Sasu, Yuta, page 146
These three terms belong to various holy occupations in Okinawan religion. The noro is a priestess who oversees the entire community, and in the past they assumed a matriarchal leadership role. The sasu, as described in the story, is a priest-like holy worker, but not on the same level of importance as a noro. The yuta is more like a working shaman, someone who deals with individuals or families in solving spiritual problems or providing specific blessings, and so on. The yuta were spiritual mediums who could summon or channel spirits to do their business.

It should be repeated that while these are rough descriptions of the roles of the real-life Okinawan occupations, it does not mean that CLAMP intends to match the exact details in their story, or if they intend to provide their own original spin to the fictional world of Nirai Kanai.

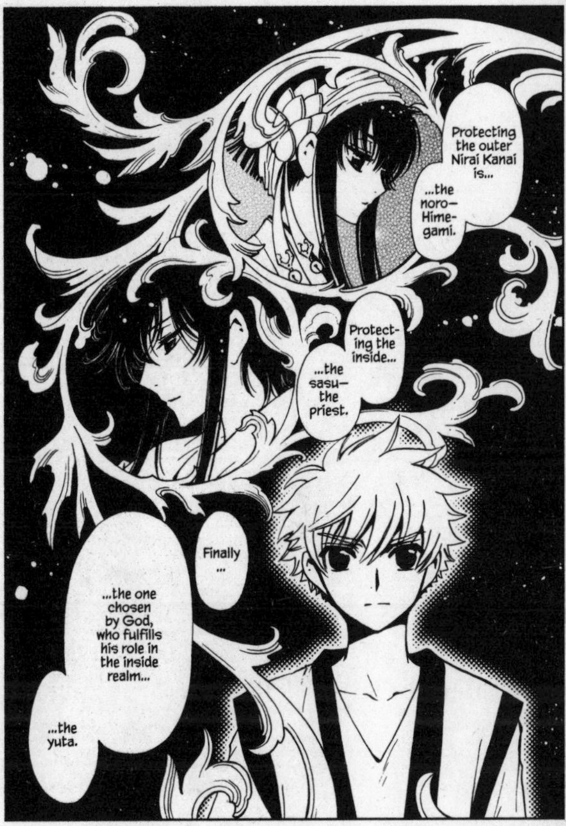
Protecting the outer Nirai Kanai is...
...the noro—Hime-gami.
Protect-ing the inside...
...the sasu—the priest.
Finally ...
...the one chosen by God, who fulfills his role in the inside realm...
...the yuta.

KC
KODANSHA
COMICS

THE HEROIC LEGEND OF
ARSLAN

READ THE NEW SERIES FROM THE CREATOR OF
FULLMETAL ALCHEMIST, HIROMU ARAKAWA!
NOW A HIT TV SERIES!

"Arakawa proves to be
more than up to the task
of adapting Tanaka's
fantasy novels and fans of
historical or epic fantasy
will be quite pleased with
the resulting book."
-Anime News Network

ECBATANA IS BURNING!

rslan is the young and curious prince of Pars who, despite his best efforts doesn't seem
have what it takes to be a proper king like his father. At the age of 14, Arslan goes to
s first battle and loses everything as the blood-soaked mist of war gives way to scorching
ames, bringing him to face the demise of his once glorious kingdom. However, it is Arslan's
estiny to be a ruler, and despite the trials that face him, he must now embark on a journey
reclaim his fallen kingdom.

vailable now in print and digitally!

© Hiromu Arakawa/Yoshiki Tanaka/Kodansha Ltd. All rights reserved.

SAVE THE DATE!

Celebrating **15** Years

FREE COMIC BOOK ·DAY·

1st SATURDAY IN MAY!

May 7, 2016
www.freecomicbookday.com

FREE COMICS FOR EVERYONE!

Details @ www.freecomicbookday.com

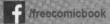 /freecomicbook

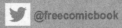 @freecomicbook

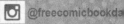 @freecomicbookda

Tsubasa WoRLD CHRoNiCLE: Niraikanai volume 2 is a work of fiction. Names, characters, places, and incidents are the products of the author's imagination or are used fictitiously. Any resemblance to actual events, locales, or persons, living or dead, is entirely coincidental.

A Kodansha Comics Trade Paperback Original.

Tsubasa WoRLD CHRoNiCLE: Niraikanai volume 2 copyright © 2015 CLAMP · ShigatsuTsuitachi CO., LTD./Kodansha
English translation copyright © 2016 CLAMP · ShigatsuTsuitachi CO., LTD./Kodansha

All rights reserved.

Published in the United States by Kodansha Comics, an imprint of Kodansha USA Publishing, LLC, New York.

Publication rights for this English edition arranged through Kodansha Ltd., Tokyo.

First published in Japan in 2015 by Kodansha Ltd., Tokyo, as *Tsubasa WoRLD CHRoNiCLE: Niraikanaihen* volume 2.

ISBN 978-1-63236-170-7

Printed in the United States of America.

www.kodanshacomics.com

9 8 7 6 5 4 3 2 1

Translation: Stephen Paul
Lettering: AndWorld Design
Editing: Lauren Scanlan
Kodansha Comics edition cover design: Phil Balsman